# JESUS
## BEGINNING MIDDLE AND END OF TIME?

*Eschatology in Gospels & Acts Research*

*Edited by Peter G. Bolt*

**SCD Press**
**2023**

CGAR SERIES, NO 4

*Jesus: Beginning, Middle, and End of Time?*
*Eschatology in Gospels & Acts Research*
*CGAR Series, No 4*
Edited by Peter G. Bolt

© SCD Press and contributors 2023

SCD Press
PO Box 6110
Norwest NSW 2153
Australia
scdpress@scd.edu.au

ISBN-13: 978-1-925730-37-1 (Paperback)
ISBN-13: 978-1-925730-38-8 (E-book)

Cover design and typesetting by Lankshear Design.

# JESUS
## BEGINNING MIDDLE AND END OF TIME?

*Eschatology in Gospels & Acts Research*

Edited by Peter G. Bolt

**SCD Press**
**2023**

CGAR SERIES, NO 4

**CGAR Series:**

1. Peter G. Bolt & James R. Harrison (eds.), *The Impact of Jesus of Nazareth: Historical, Theological, and Pastoral Perspectives.* Vol. 1: *Historical and Theological Studies* (Macquarie Park, NSW: SCD Press, 2020).

2. Peter G. Bolt & James R. Harrison (eds.), *The Impact of Jesus of Nazareth: Historical, Theological, and Pastoral Perspectives.* Vol. 2: *Social and Pastoral Studies* (Macquarie Park, NSW: SCD Press, 2021).

3. Peter G. Bolt (ed), *The Future of Gospels and Acts Research* (Macquarie Park, NSW: SCD Press, 2021).

4. Peter G. Bolt (ed), *Jesus: Beginning, Middle and End of Time? Eschatology in Gospels & Acts Research* (Norwest, NSW: SCD Press, 2023).

CONTRIBUTORS

**Peter G. Bolt** is the Director of Academic Strategy at Sydney College of Divinity, the Director of the Centre for Gospels and Acts Research, and the editor of the *Journal of Gospel and Acts Research*. His publications on the Gospels include *Jesus' Defeat of Death. Persuading Mark's Early Readers* (2003), *The Cross from a Distance. Atonement in Mark's Gospel* (2004), *Matthew: A Great Light Dawns* (2014), *The Narrative Integrity of Mark 13:24–27* (2021), and the *Concise Bible Commentary on Luke* (2022 online).

**Timothy P. Bradford** is the Senior Pastor of Petersham Baptist Church and a PhD student at Sydney College of Divinity researching the Gospel of Matthew and theological anthropology. On a similar theme to his present essay, he has previously published 'Born Eunuch: Recovering an Ancient Metaphor', in *The Future of Gospels and Acts Research* (2021).

Sr **Michele A. Connolly** rsj is a Sister of St Joseph of Lochinvar in the Hunter Valley. She is an Associate Professor of Biblical Studies and Biblical Studies Discipline Coordinator at the Sydney College of Divinity and lectures in Biblical Studies at Catholic Institute of Sydney, a pontifical institute of theology. After teaching in secondary schools for about ten years, she studied theology, starting at Yarra Theological Union, Melbourne, and then at the Catholic Theological Union, Chicago. Michele graduated in 2008 with the PhD from Graduate Theological Union, Berkeley, CA. Michele's principal area of interest is the Gospel of Mark. In 2018 her doctoral thesis was published by T&T Clark, under the title, *Disorderly Women and the Order of God: An Australian Feminist Reading of the Gospel of Mark*. Michele speaks regularly around Australia at conferences on the Scriptures.

Rev. Dr. **John D. Griffiths** is a Lecturer in the New Testament at Alphacrucis University College, Adelaide. His most recent publication is *The Spirit as Gift in Acts* (2022) with the JPTSSup in Brill. His research interests include the Holy Spirit in Luke-Acts, Pentecostal Ecotheology, and Pneumatology.

**Craig A. Evans** (Ph.D., Claremont; D.Habil., Budapest) is the John Bisagno Distinguished Professor of Christian Origins at Houston Christian University in Texas. He is the author of several books, including *Jesus and His Contemporaries* (1995), *Matthew* (2012), *Jesus and the Remains of His Day* (2015), and *Jesus and the Manuscripts* (2020). He has also appeared in many television documentaries and news programs.

**James R. Harrison** studied Ancient History at Macquarie University and graduated from the doctoral program in 1997. Professor Harrison, FAHA, is the Research Director at the Sydney College of Divinity. His recent monographs include *Paul and the Imperial Authorities at Thessalonica and Rome* (Mohr Siebeck, 2011), *Paul and the Ancient Celebrity Circuit* (Mohr Siebeck, 2019), and *Reading Romans with Roman Eyes* (Lexington/Fortress, 2020). He is also the chief editor of *New Documents Illustrating the History of Early Christianity Vols. 11–16* (forthcoming), co-editor with L. L. Welborn of *The First Urban Churches Vols. 1–7* (SBL, 2015–2022; Vols. 8–9 forthcoming 2023–2024), and is editor of the Cascade collection of E. A. Judge, *The Conflict of Cultures: The Legacy of Paul's Thought Today* (Cascade, 2019). Other edited collections on the papyri and the inscriptions (Zondervan, with Randolph Richards) and the ancient village and the rise of early Christianity (T&T Clark, with Alan Cadwallader, et al.) will appear in 2023. He has recently received the Festschrift, *God's Grace Inscribed on the Human Heart. Essays in Honour of James R. Harrison* (SCD Press, 2022).

Rev. **Daniel W. McManigal** (PhD Christ College, Sydney) is adjunct professor of Biblical and Theological Studies at Belhaven University and lecturer in New Testament at the Center for Theology and Mission (Seattle, Washington). He is the author of *Encountering Christ in the Covenants: An Introduction to Covenant Theology*, and *A Baptism of Judgment in the Fire of the Holy Spirit: John's Eschatological Proclamation in Matthew 3*.

Dr **Mary J. Marshall** MPS, PhC, BA [W.Aust], BA (Theology Hons) [Murdoch], PhD [Murdoch], is an Honorary Research Fellow, Murdoch University, Western Australia. Since completing her doctorate in 2002, Mary has widened her field of research, and her current interests include: Historical Jesus; Gospels and Acts; Last Supper; James, the brother of Jesus; Essenic influence; Christian origins; Parting of the Ways; and Jewish–Christian relations. She is passionately committed to fostering interfaith relations, working especially through her membership of the Council of Christians and Jews, at local, national, and international levels.

**Michael Modini** teaches Italian and Religious Education at a Catholic high school in Melbourne's east. His research interests range from systems of language to fifteenth century conciliar ecclesiology. His Master's thesis was on the participation of the Patriarchs at the Ecumenical Councils.

**David J. Neville** is Associate Professor of Theology and lecturer in New Testament studies at St Mark's National Theological Centre, the Canberra campus of Charles Sturt University's School of Theology. He is the author of two books on the synoptic problem and, more recently, *The Vehement Jesus: Grappling with Troubling Gospel Texts* (Cascade Books, 2017).

**Francis I. Otobo** obtained his PhD from the University of Divinity, Melbourne in 2019. He currently teaches New Testament at Yarra Theological Union, a member college of the University of Divinity. His research focus is the Synoptic Gospels, with particular interest in mission, the Holy Spirit, and life in the community of the early followers of Jesus.

**Anthony R. Petterson** is a Lecturer in Old Testament and Hebrew at Morling College (Australian College of Theology) in Macquarie Park, Sydney, Australia. He is author of *Haggai, Zechariah & Malachi* (Apollos, 2015) and *Behold Your King: The Hope for the House of David in the Book of Zechariah* (LHBOTS; T&T Clark, 2009).

**Denise Powell** completed her PhD in Religious Studies through University of Queensland in 2018. She has taught at Malyon Theological College, Trinity College Queensland and the Australian College of Ministries. Her publications include *Who Are the Righteous? The Narrative Function of the Δίκαιοι in the Gospel of Luke* (2021).

**Charles Bruce Riding** BSc, BSc(Hons), BD, Grad Dip Ed, MEd, PhD was born and raised in Brisbane. After teaching high school mathematics and science, he answered God's call into the ministry and served in six parishes of the Presbyterian Church of Australia in four states. His doctorate was on the origin of the Day of the LORD in the Old Testament prophets. From his retirement in Melbourne, he continues ministering regularly in several country parishes and writing, especially on the relationship between Christianity and the empirical sciences. Happily married for forty-six years, he has four children and five grand-children.

Having successfully completed an honours Baccalaureate in Arts and Theology (1996) at the Pontifical University, St. Patrick's College, Maynooth, **Debra Snoddy** continued post-graduate studies in Theology and Biblical Studies at the Catholic University of Louvain, Belgium (KULeuven) and was awarded a Master's Degree in Theology and an STL in Sacred Scripture in 1999. In 2000, she successfully completed a Master of Science degree in Family and Sexuality Studies in the Faculty of Medicine of KULeuven. Her doctoral thesis on the Gospel of John was awarded a PhD and an STD from KULeuven, Belgium (2014). Previously lecturing in Biblical Studies at All Hallows College Dublin, Ireland and in Theology and Biblical Studies for Carlow College, Carlow, Ireland, and serving as a diocesen worker for the Archdiocese of Armagh, Ireland, she currently lectures in Biblical studies at the Catholic Institute of Sydney. She is a founding member of the SCD Centre for Gospels and Acts Research, as well as holding memberships with the Research Group for the Study of the Johannine and Pauline Literature at the Faculty of Theology of KULeuven, Belgium, the Australian Catholic Biblical Society, the European Biblical Association, and the Association of Practical Theology in Oceania (executive member). She is a contributor to national and international publications in Biblical Studies and Pastoral Theology.

**Jonathan Thambyrajah** lectures in Biblical Studies and Hebrew at Broken Bay Institute: The Australian Institute of Theological Education, and the University of Sydney. His research focuses on Biblical languages, translations, and literature (particularly Esther and Matthew) in the cross-cultural context of the Second Temple period and its aftermath.

CONTENTS

Peter G. Bolt, *Introduction: It's About Time* .......................... xi

1. Craig A. Evans, *Kingdoms in Conflict I:*
   *The Four-Kingdoms Schema In The East And The West*............ 1
2. Craig A. Evans, *Kingdoms in Conflict II:*
   *The Jesus Movement And The Roman Empire*..................... 35
3. David J. Neville, *Ethics and Eschatology in the Synoptic*
   *Tradition: A Theological-Moral Response to*
   *N. T. Wright's Gifford Lectures*................................. 67
4. Mary J. Marshall, *The 'New Covenant' Debate Revisited* ............. 91
5. Jonathan Thambyrajah, *Wicked Wizards of the East:*
   *The μάγοι in Historical Context and Ambiguity as*
   *Narrative Technique in Matthew 2* ............................. 113
6. Daniel W. McManigal, *The Function of John's Baptism*
   *in Matthew's Gospel: A Dramatised Declaration*
   *of the Coming Judgement*....................................... 131
7. Timothy P. Bradford, *'Like the angels'?: Embodiment*
   *and Eschatology in Matthew's Gospel* .......................... 149
8. Michael Modini, *The Markan Alphabet Theory:*
   *Eschatological Origins of Mark's Gospel*........................ 165
9. Peter G. Bolt, *The Eschatological Coherence*
   *of Mark 11:20–25*.............................................. 173

10. Anthony Petterson, *The Apocalyptic Attack of Jerusalem by Non-Israelite Nations In Zechariah 9–14 and the Death of Jesus In Mark 13* .................................... 211

11. Michele A. Connolly, *Mark 13: Literary Impetus to the Passion Narrative and Christian Faith for All Generations* ............ 235

12. Denise Powell, *The View from the Ditch: Reading the Good Samaritan Parable as Wisdom not Virtue* ....................... 257

13. James R. Harrison, *From Petitionary Rhetoric to Eschatological Vindication: Comparing the Widow Aurelia Artemis from Theadelphia with Jesus' Persistent Widow (Luke 18:1–8)* ............. 271

14. Debra Snoddy, *Realising the Now and the Not Yet of the Realised Eschatology in the Gospel of John: John's Focus and Purpose and Why it Still Matters to All Christians* ................. 293

15. John D. Griffiths, *In The Last Days: Alteration, Eschatology, and the Spirit* ...................................................... 317

16. Francis Otobo, *'In the last days...' (Acts 2:17): Eschatology, Cultural Diversity, and the Challenge of Inclusivity in Acts* ........... 331

17. C. Bruce Riding, *Contrary to Popular Tradition, Saul/Paul was not Converted to Christianity on the Road to Damascus* .......... 355

INTRODUCTION

# It's About Time

### Peter G. Bolt

The best thing about Conzelmann's 1954 landmark work of redaction criticism was its title. Not its English title—for has there ever been a greater move towards the bland, than exalting his subtitle to headline as *The Theology of Luke*? But when set over against so many cyclical views of time, in which the world keeps spinning 'turn turn turn' with a season for everything in the futile perspective of those who must live 'under heaven' (Eccles 3:1–8), the German title dramatically announces that something has finally broken through: *Die Mitte der Zeit*. Even the God-given regularity of night following day and season following season (Gen. 1:14; 8:22; Jer. 31:35; 33:20,25) as befits an orderly creation fit for human habitation receives a radically linear jolt with Jesus' momentous claim that time itself is fulfilled (Mark 1:15). There was a before, but from then on there will ever be an after. On such a reckoning, Conzelmann's title proclaims the brilliant truth that Jesus of Nazareth came in *The Middle of Time*.

Time is so significant to human life, marking both our progress and decline, that it is surprising that Gospels scholarship has often sat rather uncomfortably with the eschatological (or, perish the thought, apocalyptic) claims of Jesus of Nazareth and his biographers. Even

Conzelmann wanted to smooth out human history to allow for a lengthy period after Jesus' momentous announcement, and he found that Luke apparently started that project. Undisturbed by any urgency of an imminent End, the Church Age would gradually unfold and Jesus' followers would settle down for business as usual across the long haul. Once said, Ethics must inevitably replace Eschatology. Perhaps, after all, he got the English title that he asked for.

Perhaps the Church did also, as pulpiteer and pew-sitter alike fell in step with their scholarly guides. The panicky urgency of the rush towards the precipice of an imminent End is replaced by a leisurely stroll down a gentle slope only to find the path proceeds with another slight rise and then over a series of similarly untaxing ups and downs through a rather picturesque landscape. Apocalypse gives way to application, as Jesus' teaching for the needs of yesterday is sifted by the myopic criterion of its relevance to meet the needs of today—a criterion always operating on terms native to the contemporary world, rather than those of a man locked into the ancient. Once the mid-point became a memory of a distant more primitive age, and the positive progress towards a humanly constructed utopia much more attractive to the Enlightenment mind, Lessing's wide, ugly, and uncrossable ditch between our 'now' and Jesus' 'then' simply became *de jour*. If Jesus was going to survive, he must be adapted to suit the ever-evolving fads and fancies of the divide and conquer human ideology that turned the picturesque landscape of the eighteenth century into the battlefields of the twentieth and the cancel-culture of the twenty-first. Even before there was so much blood on the floor of both study and lecture-hall, chancel and nave, the many purported attempts to describe the face of Jesus by gazing down Albert Schweitzer's way-too-deep well was only yielding the murky reflection of those who were gazing through such dank darkness. If such murky mirroring was accidental damage in Schweitzer's day, collateral to Lessing's horizontal ditch taking on a more vertical turn, now—as Jesus disappears from public interest, befogged by the smoke and mirrors of contemporary battlefields—it has almost become a necessity.

More easily moulded to suit the impatient requirements of self-absorbed humanity, perhaps the Messiah must remain timeless if he ever wants to occasionally escape the censors and enter public discourse—if only to be mocked a little more, or perhaps even crucified. After all, the apocalyptic announcement that time was fulfilled and the Kingdom of God had drawn near—with its underlying notions of great distress for the world, final battles with Belial, and redemption through atonement and resurrection—only seemed to get the preacher from Nazareth into further trouble. Yes, as narrative critics have shown us, the Gospels *use* time, but they also seem to be *about* time. And back behind those who narrate his story, Jesus not only happened *in* time, he also thought he was happening *to* time. But his world being as it wanted to be, it didn't appreciate being told about the world as he thought it was going to be. Begging to differ over such interfering eschatology, a man who confronted the guest preacher in the Capernaum synagogue became the screeching mouthpiece for so many at the time and ever since: what have you got to do with us, Jesus of Nazareth? Have you come to destroy us?

Perhaps foolishly, this volume is launched into a world battling to achieve its own versions of the future through whatever means of conflict requisite to its multifarious goals. *Jesus: Beginning, Middle, and End of Time?* offers seventeen essays, each addressing in their own way, *Eschatology in Gospels and Acts Research*.

The volume opens with three broader inquiries into Jesus of Nazareth and his proclamation about the future. Leading the charge, **Craig A. Evans**, firstly explores how Jesus' proclamation of the Kingdom of God might have struck against the views of others. He moves carefully through the evidence showing the hopes for future redemption expressed in the symbolism of 'four kingdoms', ubiquitous in the writings of both the ancient Near East, and also Greece and Rome. This widespread eschatology expressed a view that, despite having experienced a period of decline from a position much closer to the gods, human life will once again return to its previous glory in the future. Evans' second essay turns to how the proclamation of Jesus and his movement would have resonated with the Roman world, especially in relation to the 'good news' offered by Augustus and his successors, noting, however, its critique of, and clash with, both Jew and Roman alike.

Views of the future are announced in the present to be evaluated, at least in part, by the ethical stance of the hearers. **David J. Neville** probes the tension between ethics and eschatology that is presented by N.T. Wright's Gifford Lectures. If Jesus' future-oriented Son of Man and Kingdom of God sayings pertain to the destruction of Jerusalem in A.D. 70 taken as an act of divine judgement, this violent eschatology appears to clash with the peaceable mode of Jesus' historic mission as portrayed in the Gospels. Neville poses the question starkly, 'if Jesus' life and death were life-liberating, though nonviolent on Jesus' part, whence violently retributive eschatology?' He then identifies two theological-moral incongruities in Wright's reading of these sayings, seeking a greater congruity between Jesus' eschatological expectations and his messianic mission.

Although Jeremiah's view of the future included the expectation of a 'New Covenant' (Jer 31:31–34), the nature of its newness has been the subject of debate. Entering this discussion, **Mary J. Marshall** considers the interpretation of the relevant term in the Dead Sea Scrolls and the New Testament, building on her previous research into the dating of the Last Supper and its setting within an Essene household associated with Jesus' brother James. Approaching the question through the epistles of Paul and Hebrews, she finds Jesus' words over the cup to be in continuity with the Mosaic Law and his own teaching on love. In their historical setting, they speak of a covenant re-newed.

As the volume progresses to essays on each of the Gospels and Acts, the first of three essays on Matthew's Gospel asks after the impact of Matthew's portrayal of the 'wise men' arriving to visit the infant Jesus. **Jonathan Thambyrajah** sifts the ancient evidence to reveal conflicting views as to whether the μάγοι were positively or negatively regarded. Were they to be associated with the dubious reputation of Balaam (Numbers 24), or with the foreign kings worshipping the Lord in the latter days (Isaiah 60)? Through a clever use of ambiguity, Matthew's narrative seeks to have it both ways, starting with the dubious reputation of the wise men but ultimately showing them to be exemplars in relation to responding to the arrival of this infant king.

**Daniel W. McManigal** turns to another famous figure in Matthew who prepared the way for Jesus. Famous for his ritual action with water, what did John the Baptist seek to symbolise by it? With obvious associations between water and purification, when read against Old Testament prophetic actions, John's rite was also infused with the symbolism of eschatological judgement.

When Jesus spoke about the eschatological resurrection using the expression 'like the angels' (Matt. 22:30, Mark 12:25), what was he seeking to convey? Interacting with views that such an angelic comparison concerns the future erasure of sexual differentiation, **Timothy P. Bradford** considers afresh the depiction of angelic bodies in the Old Testament and Second Temple Judaism, and the tradition of comparing humans to angels or their characteristics. Tracing such ideas through Jesus' promise of the vindication of the righteous (Matt. 13:43) and his own transfiguration (Matt. 17:2) leads to the conclusion that the angelic comparison is less about the transformation of human bodies, than it is about the assurance of human resurrection and glorification.

After three essays on Matthew, another four focus on Mark. Behind Mark lie the events surrounding Jesus Christ, which were epoch-defining, bringing in the last days. Against this background, **Michael Modini** examines 'the Markan Alphabet theory', which proposes that three alphabet sequences provide the foundations of Mark's Gospel. Noting an eschatological component to the synthesis of these sequences, the essay explores some areas where alphabet and eschatology converge.

Although Mark's series of sayings on faith, prayer, and forgiveness (11:22–25[26]) following a sequence of dramatic events after Jesus enters Jerusalem are usually treated as rather random, **Peter G. Bolt** argues that they are disconnected neither from each other, nor from Mark's carefully structured narrative. After analysing these sayings in their own right, this essay reads them in the context of the narrative-movement towards Jesus' end, and against apocalyptic expectation of the movement of the world towards the Kingdom of God. These sayings have a profound eschatological coherence focused upon the End.

In his two-part essay, **Anthony R. Petterson** firstly reviews Paul T. Sloan's explanation of Mark 13 against the eschatological framework of Zechariah 13:7, before critiquing his view that the Gospel utilises Zechariah to sequence Jesus' death, the Fall of Jerusalem, and the parousia. Instead, Mark picks up the apocalyptic language describing the attack of Jerusalem by non-Israelite nations in Zechariah 9—14, to speak symbolically of Jesus' death alone.

Also focusing upon Mark 13, **Michele A. Connolly** reads Jesus' 'apocalyptic discourse' against the evangelist's task of ensuring that the faith of later generations was as grounded in reality as that of the first generation who believed in Jesus. Primarily adopting a literary method, paying special attention to prediction and fulfilment, the vocabulary of *chronos* and *kairos*, verbs of perception, and the 'fourth wall' technique, the essay examines how Mark 13 uses time to carry the audience into the Passion Narrative and into the time beyond the resurrection. Instituting a circular process, Mark is constructed so that to encounter its end is to be directed to return to its beginning. On the imaginative journey evoked by the encounter with this narrative, having persevered through the trauma of both the suffering and death of Jesus as well as the astonishing announcement of his resurrection, every disciple who was not with Jesus in the flesh is nevertheless provided with a means of encountering the full Jesus story.

Constituting the volume's contribution to Lukan studies, **Denise Powell** and **James R. Harrison** each provide a discussion of one of Luke's parables. Whereas the Good Samaritan is often understood as promoting altruistic behaviour towards our neighbour—selfless concern for the welfare of others, no matter who they are—**Powell** argues that it encourages pragmatic wisdom rather than virtue. Responding to a neighbour with compassion and mercy is ultimately in our best interests. As an experiment in intertextuality, she illustrates with the current real-world scenario of 'vaccine diplomacy'.

Reaching into the real world closer to New Testament times, **James R. Harrison** examines the Parable of the Unjust Judge with its widow persistently presenting her petition for justice, against the backdrop of the papyrus petitions of antiquity. Touching briefly on the 'widow' petitions in the papyri, the essay then compares the rhetorical strategies of Aurelia Artemis of Theadelphia in her three petitions to the Roman governor of Egypt, with the petitions of the widow of Luke 18:1–8. A consideration of the respective audiences of Aurelia Artemis, and of the Lukan parable illuminates its meaning in both its original Palestinian context and in its Lukan retelling three generations later.

As the volume's sole contribution on the Gospel of John, **Debra Snoddy** argues that, in the unique tension of the Gospel's 'realised eschatology', Jesus' coming as the light makes a difference for the Johannine community's understanding of past, present, and future. Just as eternal life is a current reality, so is human death, and this presents an opportunity for insight, even though some remain in their blindness. This is a dissonance in search of resolution. But what is it that enables moving forward towards resolving the dissonance into harmony, both within the Johannine Gospel and for Christians today? Tracing several instances from John, the essay shows how and why the eschatological dissonance is resolved into a unique Johannine harmony, which is of even more relevance to the communities of faith today, than it was to John's original community.

The volume concludes with three essays on Acts—two of them on the second chapter. Observing the editorial addition of 'in the last days' to the quotation of Joel 3:1–5, **John D. Griffiths** inquires after its impact on Luke's account both of Peter's Pentecost sermon and of the Pentecost event itself. With nuances imported by its quotation of Isa 2:2, the addition implies that Pentecost is likewise a temple inauguration, which is reinforced by further temple imagery in Acts 2.

**Francis Innocent Otobo** also takes Peter's Pentecost sermon as a point of departure, especially its suggestion that in the eschaton God's salvific activities will transcend Israel (homogeneous culture) to include everyone (cultural heterogeneity). As the narrative of Acts unfolds, it highlights the fulfilment of this eschatological expectation in the communities of the early followers of Jesus. While this cultural diversity fulfils eschatological hope, it also brings real-life challenges in the communities (Acts 6:1–7; 11:1–18; 13:44–45; 15:1–35), as the emerging cultural heterogeneity is experienced within them. These challenging accounts have a significant role in Luke's narrative about the expansion of the church from Jerusalem to the ends of the earth.

Focusing upon the man who became so integral to that movement, **Charles Bruce Riding** argues that the arch-enemy of earliest Christianity was not converted on the road to Damascus, for he was still an unbeliever before his conversation with Ananias. The conversion of Paul is narrated three times in detail by the narrative of Acts, indicating its great importance. When and where Paul was converted has implications for other important theological topics such as Baptismal Regeneration and whether the Baptism with the Holy Spirit is a Second Blessing or not.

According to the New Testament portrayal, Jesus of Nazareth came in the middle of the world's chronological time, at the end of Israel's long time of interacting with the God of their ancestors, and as the beginning of time shaped by the imminent expectation of the Kingdom of God. Whatever else Jesus achieved, this reconfiguring of time, once grasped, not only transforms the days in which we live and move and have our being, but also changes the manner in which we live in them. Each of these essays are offered as a contribution towards this eschatological life transformation.

Peter G. Bolt
February 2023

CHAPTER 1

# Kingdoms in Conflict: The Four-Kingdoms Schema in the East and the West

## Craig A. Evans

Thirty-five years ago the great British New Testament scholar George Beasley-Murray published an impressive study, *Jesus and the Kingdom of God*. In my opinion one of the strengths of his book was its treatment of the Old Testament background and context for Jesus' proclamation of the kingdom. Under the heading of 'The Coming of God in the Old Testament' Beasley-Murray discusses such important topics as 'theophany', 'the Day of the Lord', 'the Kingdom of God', and 'the coming of God in Daniel 7'.[1] Beasley-Murray also pursues these important themes in inter-testamental writings, much of it focused on apocalyptic literature.[2]

What is missing in Beasley-Murray's fine treatment is discussion of the wider cultural and religious context of the Old Testament literature and its ancient antecedents, as well as the later inter-testamental literature. Apart from his mention that the author of the book of

---

1   Beasley-Murray, *Jesus and the Kingdom of God*, 3–35.
2   Beasley-Murray, *Jesus and the Kingdom of God*, 39–68.

Daniel redacted 'the ancient myth' of the human figure who comes with the clouds (Daniel 7),[3] Beasley-Murray does not discuss the ancient Near Eastern antecedents of the four kingdoms and the hope of redemption. Neither is anything said of the hopes of the Greeks and Romans in the classical period. For the kingdom proclamation of Jesus to be fully understood, the eschatology of the ancient world must be taken into account.[4]

Talk of a coming rule of God presupposes ancient ideas of human history and destiny. The idea that in their beginning humans were closer to divinity in physical, moral, and spiritual properties, then after judgement at the hands of the gods (often described as a great flood) humans began to degenerate, and after a period of decline and degeneration humanity would experience a return to its previous glories was in various forms widespread in the ancient Near East and in the west in the classical period. The cultures of the ancient Near East and classical west appropriated and applied this idea in different ways, but that it was a common idea, however differently expressed, seems clear. It was believed that during the period of degeneration and decline the human lifespan became shorter, health became poorer, and morality, knowledge, and wisdom declined. During this decline kingdoms became increasingly incompetent and oppressive, and the rule of kings became shorter and less just. So far as we know, all cultures of antiquity articulated a history and an eschatology of this nature. They believed that humanity, though suffering decline, would someday see better days.

There is an enormous amount of material from the ancient Near East and the Mediterranean world of the classical period that is relevant for the present inquiry. The present essay can only review some of it and will do so in two parts: (1) the relevant texts and traditions from ancient Near Eastern sources and (2) the relevant texts and traditions from classical sources.

---

3  Beasley-Murray, *Jesus and the Kingdom of God*, 58.
4  Most scholarly studies focus only on the Jewish context of the kingdom of God. Rudolf Otto's treatment of the subject is in this regard exceptional. In *The Kingdom of God and the Son of Man*, 20–33, Otto provides a brief discussion of Persian beliefs regarding the 'Kingdom of Asura'. He is correct to say that 'the eschatology of late Jewish apocalyptic ... goes far beyond the Messianism of ancient Israel', but Otto exaggerates the extent of Persian influence on Jewish eschatology.

# 1. Ancient Near Eastern and Classical Western Eschatological Ideas

## Part 1: The ancient Near East

Under this heading I shall look at the traditions that speak of the longevity of human life, the length of rule of kings and kingdoms, and the decline of rule.

### *The Longevity of Life and Rule*

In the book of Genesis we read that Adam and Eve, the first human beings, were created 'in the image of God' (Gen. 1:26–27; 5:1). They were told that they could eat from any of the trees of the garden in which they found themselves with the exception of the tree of knowledge of good and evil. If they eat from this tree they will die (2:16–17). Of course, they did eat from this tree and they did die, but not until they reached a very great age (3:19; 5:5).

The great ages of the patriarchs are given in Genesis 5 and 11.[5] In the former we are told that Adam lived to nine hundred and thirty years. Adam's son Seth died at the age of nine hundred and twelve years (5:8). Seth's son Enosh died at nine hundred and five (5:11). Enosh's son Kenan lived to be nine hundred and ten (5:14). Kenan's son Mahalalel lived to be eight hundred and ninety-five (5:17). Mahalalel's son Jared lived to be nine hundred and sixty-two (5:20). Jared's son Enoch lived three hundred and sixty-five years and apparently did not die but was taken up by God (5:24).[6] Enoch's son Methuselah lived the longest of all, dying at the age of nine hundred and sixty-nine years (5:27).[7]

After the death of Methuselah the lifespan of humans became shorter, though Noah is an exception. Methuselah's son Lamech died at the age of seven hundred and seventy-seven years (5:31). Lamech's

---

5   The problematic nature of the great longevity of the biblical patriarchs has been much discussed. It should be noted that the numbers vary in the Masoretic Text, the Samaritan Pentateuch, and the LXX. For a helpful overview, see Etz, 'The Numbers of Genesis V 3–31'. See also Wenham, *Genesis 1–15*, 123–25.
6   Josephus: ἀνεχώρησε πρὸς τὸ θεῖον, 'He returned to the divinity' (*Ant.* 1.85). Perhaps an adumbration of humanity's return to its better, more divine-like origins.
7   In Genesis 5 the formula is 'and thus all the days of' (כָּל־יְמֵי וַיְהִי) so-and-so.

son Noah broke the downward trend, dying at the age of nine hundred and fifty years.

In Genesis 11 we have the following:

> Shem, son of Noah, lived six hundred years (11:10–11).
> Arpachshad, son of Shem, lived four hundred and thirty-eight years (11:12–13).
> Shelah, son of Arpachshad, lived four hundred and thirty-three years (11:14–15).
> Shelah's son Eber lived four hundred and sixty-four years (11:16–17).
> Eber's son Peleg lived two hundred and thirty-nine years (11:18–19).
> Peleg's son Reu lived two hundred and thirty-nine years (11:20–21).
> Reu's son Serug lived two hundred and thirty years (11:22–23).
> Serug's son Nahor lived one hundred and forty-eight years (11:24–25).
> Nahor's son Terah lived two hundred and five years (11:32).[8]

Elsewhere in Genesis we are told:

> Nahor's son Abram/Abraham lived one hundred and seventy-five years (25:7).
> Sarai/Sarah, wife of Abraham, lived one hundred and twenty-seven years (23:1).
> Abraham's son Ishmael lived one hundred and thirty-seven years (25:17).
> Abraham's son Isaac lived one hundred and eighty years (35:28).
> Isaac's son Jacob lived one hundred and forty-seven years (47:28).
> Jacob's son Joseph lived one hundred and ten years (50:22,26).

---

8  In Genesis 11 the formula is simply so-and-so 'lived' (וַיְחִי). Josephus usually says the patriarchs βιώσαντα/ζήσας, 'lived' (*Ant.* 1.83–85), but in the case of some of the patriarchs he says they ἀρχήν/ἄρξας/ ἦρξε, 'ruled' (*Ant.* 1.86–87).

In Exodus we are told:

> Jacob's son Levi lived one hundred and thirty-seven years (6:16).
> Levi's son Kohath lived one hundred and thirty-three years (6:18).
> Kohath's son Amram lived one hundred and thirty-seven years (6:20).

In Numbers and Deuteronomy we are told:

> Amram's son Aaron lived one hundred and twenty-three years (Num. 33:39).
> Amram's son Moses lived one hundred and twenty years (Deut. 34:7).

And finally we learn in Joshua and Judges that Joshua the son of Nun lived one hundred and ten years (Josh. 24:29; Judg. 2:8).

Earlier in Genesis we are told that Yahweh said, 'My spirit [רוּחִי / τὸ πνεῦμά μου] shall not abide in man for ever, for he is flesh, but his days shall be a hundred and twenty years' (Gen. 6:3). Given the number of men who live well beyond one hundred and twenty years, this statement seems out of place. However, commentators think the verse is placed here in the context of the sin of the 'sons of God' and in anticipation of the subsequent reduction in the human lifespan.[9] The specific number 'one hundred and twenty' may reflect the age of Moses. It is interesting to note, too, that in Psalm 90 we are told that 'the years of our life are seventy'.[10] The Psalter here may well have been inspired by the tradition that David lived to be seventy years of age (2 Sam. 5:4).

Commentators on Genesis point to the correlation between long ages of the patriarchs in Genesis 5 and 11 and the lengthy reigns of

---

9 According to Targum Onqelos, God allowed humans to live to the age of 120, that they might have the opportunity to repent. The other major targums (Neof., Ps.-J., and Frag.) add that despite the granting of this opportunity 'they did not repent'. Much of rabbinic interpretation interprets Gen. 6:3 this way. Josephus says the ancient patriarchs lived a long time because 'they were beloved of God and the creatures of God himself' (*J.W.* 1.105–104). Presumably later generations lost this divine favour and so no longer enjoyed great longevity.

10 'The years of our life are seventy, or even by reason of strength eighty; yet their span is but toil and trouble; they are soon gone, and we fly away' (Ps. 90:10).

kings in the Sumerian King List.¹¹ Hermann Gunkel sees a close parallel between the ten patriarchs and the ten primordial Babylonian kings (*den zehn Urkönigen Babyloniens*).¹² Although the parallels are not as close as is sometimes asserted,¹³ there is, nevertheless, a general similarity that reflects a widely held understanding of human history and eschatology. Ongoing discoveries and publications have shown that apart from the general schema of long-lived kings and rule, with gradual decline, the specifics and numbers varied. In short, there was no 'canonical form'. There is a general parallel in which people lived longer or kings ruled longer (and more capably) before the flood and people lived shorter and kings ruled shorter (and less capably) after the flood.

It is also important to note that the statement that God's 'spirit shall not abide in man for ever, for he is flesh' (Gen. 6:3) implies a reduction of the human status, if not quality as well. The reduction or complete loss of God's spirit (רוח)¹⁴ implies at least in some sense degeneration. Recall that according to Genesis 2:7 human beings gained life through the breath (or spirit) of God.¹⁵ To lose God's spirit implies a loss of life.¹⁶ Indeed, the withdrawal of God's life-giving spirit readies humanity for the deluge, in which 'all flesh died ... everything on the dry land in whose nostrils was the breath of life' (Gen. 7:21–22). God's breath gave life; the deluge will snuff it out. The description of humankind as 'flesh' (בָּשָׂר/σάρξ) underscores, moreover, the non-divine, even unspiritual nature of fallen humanity. Thus, human life has been reduced in measure, in that its lifespan has been shortened, and it has been reduced in quality, in that the human being is less spiritual and less god-like than the first generation.

---

11  Jacobsen, *The Sumerian King List*. See also Finkelstein, 'The Antediluvian Kings'.
12  Gunkel, *Genesis*, 121 n.2. In a lengthy note Gunkel (pp. 122–23 n.3) defends the correspondence and the likelihood that Genesis is dependent on the Babylonian tradition. See also the older work by Budde, *Die biblische Urgeschichte*, 89–116, to which Gunkel also refers.
13  See Hasel, 'The Genealogies of Gen 5 and 11', citing Zimmern, *Urkönige und Uroffenbarung*, 530–43, here 539, as an example. Zimmern claims that 'it can hardly be doubted' (*kann kaum bezweifelt werden*) that Gen. 5 is 'basically identical' (*im Grunde identisch*) to the Babylonian tradition about the ten pre-flood kings.
14  And what precisely Gen. 6:3 is saying is open to interpretation. For review of the major interpretations, see Driver, *The Book of Genesis*, 83–84.
15  The Lord 'breathed [וַיִּפַּח/καὶ ἐνεφύσησεν] into his nostrils the breath of life [נִשְׁמַת חַיִּים/πνοὴν ζωῆς]; and man became a living being [נֶפֶשׁ חַיָּה/ψυχὴν ζῶσαν]'.
16  Wenham, *Genesis 1–15*, 141.

## The Decline of Just Rule

Another way of expressing the general decline of human life and civilisation was the use of symbolic imagery, usually in terms of different metals, beginning with gold and ending with iron or lead.[17] In the Judaeo-Christian world the best-known example of this is found in the book of Daniel, in which we find the tradition of the succession of kingdoms, or empires.[18] There are three visions, but best known is the dream of Nebuchadnezzar, the Babylonian king. Of all the king's wise men only Daniel, the Jewish captive, can interpret the dream. When God revealed to Daniel, 'in a vision in the night', the meaning of the mysterious dream, Daniel gave thanks to God:

> Blessed be the name of God forever and ever, to whom belong wisdom and might. [21] He changes times and seasons; he removes kings and sets up kings; he gives wisdom to the wise and knowledge to those who have understanding; [22] he reveals deep and mysterious things; he knows what is in the darkness, and the light dwells with him. [23] To thee, O God of my fathers, I give thanks and praise, for thou hast given me wisdom and strength, and hast now made known to me what we asked of thee, for thou hast made known to us the king's matter. (Dan. 2:20–23, RSV)

The prayer is important, for it presupposes the belief that the succession of empires, which is assumed in the explanation of the dream to follow, is divinely ordained and that understanding it is a matter of divine revelation. This point is emphasised when Daniel is brought before the king. The king asks Daniel, 'Are you able to make known to me the dream that I have seen and its interpretation?' Daniel replies: 'No wise men, enchanters, magicians, or astrologers can show to the king the mystery which the king has asked, [28] but there is a God in heaven who reveals mysteries, and he has made known to King Nebuchadnezzar

---

17  My research in this important area has been greatly aided by the recent appearance of Perrin and Stuckenbruck (eds.), *Four Kingdom Motifs*.
18  Modern scholarship dates the canonical book of Daniel to the second century BC, though it is acknowledged that many of its traditions date to much earlier periods. See Collins, *The Apocalyptic Vision of the Book of Daniel*; Collins, *Daniel*.

what will be in the latter days' (Dan. 2:26–28).

Daniel then describes to Nebuchadnezzar his dream (with the various metals presented in bold type face):

> You saw, O king, and behold, a great image. This image, mighty and of exceeding brightness, stood before you, and its appearance was frightening. ³² The head of this image was of fine **gold**, its breast and arms of **silver**, its belly and thighs of **bronze**, ³³ its legs of **iron**, its feet partly of iron and partly of clay. ³⁴ As you looked, a stone was cut out by no human hand, and it smote the image on its feet of iron and clay, and broke them in pieces; ³⁵ then the **iron**, the clay, the **bronze**, the **silver**, and the **gold**, all together were broken in pieces, and became like the chaff of the summer threshing floors; and the wind carried them away, so that not a trace of them could be found. But the stone that struck the image became a great mountain and filled the whole earth. (Dan. 2:31–35)

Daniel then explains the meaning of the dream:

> This was the dream; now we will tell the king its interpretation. ³⁷ You, O king, the king of kings, to whom the God of heaven has given the kingdom, the power, and the might, and the glory, ³⁸ and into whose hand he has given, wherever they dwell, the sons of men, the beasts of the field, and the birds of the air, making you rule over them all—you are the head of **gold**. ³⁹ After you shall arise another kingdom inferior to you, and yet a third kingdom of **bronze**, which shall rule over all the earth. ⁴⁰ And there shall be a fourth kingdom, strong as **iron**, because iron breaks to pieces and shatters all things; and like iron which crushes, it shall break and crush all these. ⁴¹ And as you saw the feet and toes partly of potter's clay and partly of iron, it shall be a divided kingdom; but some of the firmness of iron shall be in it, just as you saw iron mixed with the miry clay. ⁴² And as the toes of the feet were partly iron and partly clay, so the kingdom shall be partly strong and partly brittle. ⁴³ As you saw the iron mixed with miry

clay, so they will mix with one another in marriage, but they will not hold together, just as iron does not mix with clay. ⁴⁴ And in the days of those kings the God of heaven will set up a kingdom which shall never be destroyed, nor shall its sovereignty be left to another people. It shall break in pieces all these kingdoms and bring them to an end, and it shall stand forever; ⁴⁵ just as you saw that a stone was cut from a mountain by no human hand, and that it broke in pieces the **iron**, the **bronze**, the **clay**, the **silver**, and the **gold**. A great God has made known to the king what shall be hereafter. The dream is certain, and its interpretation sure. (Dan 2:26–45, RSV)

In response, the king falls before Daniel, orders sacrifice and incense be offered to him, and confesses, 'Truly, your God is God of gods and Lord of kings, and a revealer of mysteries, for you have been able to reveal this mystery' (Dan. 2:46–47). Nebuchadnezzar had confidence in Daniel's interpretation because Daniel accurately described the dream itself, which the king's wise men could not do (cf. Dan. 2:1–11).

The vision of the image is understood as eschatological in a universal sense, not just predictive of Nebuchadnezzar's fate, as is made clear when the vision is described as 'what will be in the latter days [בְּאַחֲרִית יוֹמַיָּא]' (Dan. 2:28). The eschatological understanding of the history of the four kingdoms is not surprising. Following ancient presentations of the four-kingdom schema we should understand the gold kingdom in reference to the Babylonians, the silver in reference to the Medes, the bronze (or brass) in reference to the Persians, and the iron in reference to Macedonian/Greeks.

Daniel's adaptation of the schema is unique in assigning the gold head to the Babylonians (instead of the Assyrians) and the two legs of iron to the Seleucid/Antiochid Empire of Syria to the north and northeast and to the Ptolemaic Empire of Egypt to the south and southwest. The image in Daniel is further modified by introducing clay (or ceramic) mixed with the iron of the feet, thus alluding to the intermarriage between the Macedonian/Greeks and the Syrian and Egyptian locals and implying weakness. The stone carved 'by no human hand', another innovation, is the anticipated eschatological kingdom (and perhaps the Messiah), which will demolish the image, thus bringing gentile dominance to an end.[19] The end of these gentile kingdoms is so complete, we are told, that they 'became like the chaff of the summer threshing floors; and the wind carried them away, so that not a trace of them could be found' (Dan. 2:35).

The succession of empires is depicted in two more visions. In Daniel 7, Daniel himself has a vision or dream. He describes it thus (with key elements in bold type face):

> I saw in my vision by night, and behold, the four winds of heaven were stirring up the great sea. ³ And **four great beasts** came up out of the sea, different from one another. ⁴ The **first** was **like a lion** and had eagles' wings. Then as I looked its wings were plucked off, and it was lifted up from the ground and made to stand upon two feet like a man; and the mind of a man was given to it. ⁵ And behold, another beast, a **second** one, **like a bear**. It was raised up on one side; it had three ribs in its mouth between its teeth; and it was told, 'Arise, devour much flesh.' ⁶ After this I looked, and lo, **another, like a leopard**, with four wings of a bird on its back; and the beast had four heads; and dominion was given to it. ⁷ After this I saw in the night visions, and behold, a **fourth** beast, **terrible and dreadful** and exceedingly strong; and it had great **iron** teeth; it devoured and broke in pieces, and stamped the residue with its feet. It was different from all the beasts that were before it; and it had **ten horns**. ⁸ I considered the horns, and behold, there came up among them another horn, a little one, before which three of the first horns were plucked up by the roots; and behold, in this horn were eyes like the eyes of a man, and a mouth speaking great things. (Dan. 7:2–8, RSV)

In this vision we again have the four empires. The fourth beast, which again refers to the Greeks' iron kingdom, which in the present vision

---

19 The stone of Daniel's vision probably has its origin in Ps. 118:22 ('The stone which the builders rejected has become the head of the corner') and Isa. 28:16 ('Behold, I am laying in Zion for a foundation a stone, a tested stone, a precious cornerstone, of a sure foundation: "He who believes will not be in haste"').

has 'great iron teeth', is said to have 'ten horns'. Although it is debated, these horns probably represent the Seleucid/Antiochid kings. The horn with the big mouth that plucks up three other horns is probably Antiochus IV, the adversary against whom the Jewish people struggle in the 160s BC. This enemy is doomed, for Daniel's dream continues:

> As I looked, thrones were placed and one that was ancient of days took his seat; his raiment was white as snow, and the hair of his head like pure wool; his throne was fiery flames, its wheels were burning fire. [10] A stream of fire issued and came forth from before him; a thousand thousands served him, and ten thousand times ten thousand stood before him; the court sat in judgment, and the books were opened. (Dan. 7:9–10, RSV)

The fourth kingdom with iron teeth and a bragging, blasphemous horn faces certain doom, for God has convened the heavenly court. The books are opened and the truth now is presented before the 'ancient of days'. In the final part of the vision the beast is slain, his body is burned (v.11), the other beasts lose their kingdoms (v.12), and 'one like a son of man' (v.13) is presented to God, seated on his throne. This mysterious human-like personage (in contrast to the beasts) is given 'dominion and glory and kingdom, that all peoples, nations, and languages should serve him; his dominion is an everlasting dominion, which shall not pass away, and his kingdom one that shall not be destroyed' (v.14).

When Daniel asks for the interpretation of the dream, he is told: 'These four great beasts are four kings who shall arise out of the earth' (v.17). He is assured that 'the saints of the Most High shall receive the kingdom, and possess the kingdom for ever, for ever and ever' (v.18). The four kings match the four kingdoms in Nebuchadnezzar's dream in Daniel 2.

The third vision in Daniel is found in Chapter 8 (vv.2–14). We are told of a ram with two horns (vv.3–4) and a he-goat with a horn between his eyes (v.5). The latter defeats the former (vv.6–8). 'Out of one of them' arose a little horn that 'magnified itself' (vv.9–11). The 'little horn' represents the blasphemous Antiochus IV and his desecration of the Jewish temple (vv.12–14).

Daniel's visions represent reworked materials that reach back centuries, if not millennia. We have two versions in Zoroastrian texts of uncertain age that approximate the tradition we find in Daniel 2 and in Graeco-Roman literature. The first version reads as follows (with the various metals in bold type face):

> 1. As is manifest from the Stûtgar: Zaratûhst asked for immortality from Aûhrmazd. 2. Then, Aûhrmazd showed the wisdom of all-knowledge to Zaratûhst. 3. Through it, he saw the trunk of a tree, on which there were four branches: one of **gold**, one of **silver**, one of **steel**, and one of **mixed iron**. 4. Thereupon he considered that he saw this in a dream. 5. When he arose from sleep, he, Zaratûhst, spoke: 'Lord of the spiritual and material existences! It seems that I saw the trunk of a tree, on which there were four branches'. 6. He, Aûhrmazd, spoke to Spitûmûn Zaratûhst: 'The trunk of a tree, which you saw, is the material existence, which I, Aûhrmazd, created. 7. The four branches are the four periods which will come. 8. That of **gold** is that when I and you will hold a conference of religion, king Vistâsp shall accept the religion ... 9. That of **silver** is the reign of Artakhsîr the Kaê. 10. And that of **steel** is the reign of Khasrûy son of Kavât, of immortal soul. 11. And that of **mixed iron** is the evil sovereignty of the dîvs, having disheveled hair,[20] of the seed of Aêsam, when your tenth century will be at an end, O Spitûmûn Zaratûhst!'[21] (*Zand-i Vahuman Yasn* 1.1–11)

Ohrmazd, creator of the material world, put wisdom into the water of the world. Zardusht (i.e. Zarathustra) drank of this water. Orhmazd then speaks to him (with the various metals presented in bold type face):

> Ohrmazd said to Spitaman Zardusht: 'What have you beheld?' Zardusht said to him: '... I beheld a tree on which there were seven branches: one of **gold**, one of **silver**, one of **copper**, one

---

20  Some interpreters think the ruler with 'disheveled hair' is Alexander the Great.
21  Translation based on Anklesaria, *Zand-i Vahuman Yasn*, 101–2; cf. Boyce, *Textual Sources*, 91–92. The *Zand* versions are later forms of the tradition.

of **brass**, one of **lead**, one of **steel**, and one of **blended iron**'. Ohrmazd said: 'Spitaman Zardusht! This is what I declare. The trunk of the tree which you beheld is the worldly existence which I, Ohrmazd, created. The seven branches which you beheld are the seven times which are to come. That of gold is the reign of King Vishtasp ... That of silver is the reign of Kay Ardashir[22] ... that of copper is the reign of Valakhsh the Arsacid ... that of brass is the reign of Ardashir[23] ... that of lead is the reign of King Vahram Gor ... that of steel is the reign of King Khusrow ... that of blended iron is the evil rule of devs with disheveled hair, the seed of Eshm, at the end of your millennium, O Spitaman Zardusht!' (*Zand-i Vahman Yasht* 3.15–29).[24]

It is believed that the oldest of the traditions preserved in the Yashts could reach back to about the second millennium BC. What has been cited above perhaps reaches back in its earliest form to the end of the First Temple period, though the oldest extant manuscripts date no earlier than the ninth and tenth centuries AD.[25] Although it has been asserted that Daniel's visions of the four kingdoms depend directly on the Persian tradition,[26] it is more likely that they are independent compositions.[27] I will say more about this at the end of the present chapter.

## Part 2: The Classical West

The ancient Near Eastern legends of long life and glorious but declining reigns were known to the Greeks and Romans. I begin with Hesiod's *Works and Days*. The English translations do not reflect the word-

---

22  Boyce, *Textual Sources*, 91–92, notes that Kay Ardashir is the Achaemenian Artaxerxes II.
23  Boyce, *Textual Sources*, 92, notes that Ardashir is the Sasanian Arcashir I.
24  Translation based on Boyce, *Textual Sources*, 91–92.
25  Hultgård, 'Bahman Yasht', 133.
26  E.g. see Newsom, *Daniel*, 76.
27  E.g. see Lucas, 'The Origin of Daniel's Four Empire Scheme Re-Examined'. Related is the question of the Four Empires theme in the fourth oracle in the *Sibylline Oracles*. David Flusser and John Collins have argued that *Sib. Or.* 4 contains an old oracle that reaches back to the time of Alexander the Great, which later has been updated to reflect the rise of Rome. See Collins, 'The Place of the Fourth Sibyl'; Flusser, 'The Four Empires in the Fourth Sibyl'.

order and they hardly capture the poetic art (with key terms in bold type face):[28]

> **χρύσεον** μὲν **πρώτιστα** γένος μερόπων ἀνθρώπων
> ἀθάνατοι ποίησαν Ὀλύμπια δώματ' ἔχοντες.
> οἳ μὲν ἐπὶ Κρόνου ἦσαν, ὅτ' οὐρανῷ ἐμβασίλευεν:
> ὥστε θεοὶ δ' ἔζωον ἀκηδέα θυμὸν ἔχοντες
> νόσφιν ἄτερ τε πόνων καὶ ὀϊζύος .... (1.109–113)

> **First** of all the deathless gods who dwell on Olympus made a **golden** race of mortal men who lived in the time of Cronos when he was reigning in heaven. And they lived like gods without sorrow of heart, remote and free from toil and grief .... (1.109–113)

> **δεύτερον** αὖτε γένος πολὺ χειρότερον μετόπισθεν
> **ἀργύρεον** ποίησαν Ὀλύμπια δώματ' ἔχοντες,
> χρυσέῳ οὔτε φυὴν ἐναλίγκιον οὔτε νόημα. (1.127–129)

> ... then they who dwell on Olympus made a **second** generation which was of **silver** and less noble by far. It was like the golden race neither in body nor in thought .... (1.127–129)

> Ζεὺς δὲ πατὴρ **τρίτον** ἄλλο γένος μερόπων ἀνθρώπων
> **χάλκειον** ποίησ', οὐκ ἀργυρέῳ οὐδὲν ὁμοῖον,
> ἐκ μελιᾶν, δεινόν τε καὶ ὄβριμον: οἷσιν Ἄρηος
> ἔργ' ἔμελεν στονόεντα καὶ ὕβριες .... (1.143–146)

> ... Zeus the Father made a **third** generation of mortal, a **bronze** race, sprung from ash trees; and it was in no way equal to the silver age, but was terrible and strong. They loved the lamentable works of Ares and deeds of violence .... (1.143–146)

> αὖτις ἔτ' ἄλλο **τέταρτον** ἐπὶ χθονὶ πουλυβοτείρῃ
> Ζεὺς Κρονίδης ποίησε, δικαιότερον καὶ ἄρειον,

---

28  For Greek text and English translation, see Evelyn-White, *Hesiod*, 10–17.

ἀνδρῶν ἡρώων θεῖον γένος, οἳ καλέονται
ἡμίθεοι, προτέρη γενεὴ κατ' ἀπείρονα γαῖαν. (1.157–160)

... Zeus the son of Cronos made yet another (generation), the **fourth**, upon the fruitful earth, which was nobler and more righteous, a god-like race of men who are called demi-gods, the race before our own, throughout the boundless earth. (1.157–160)

**Πέμπτον** δ' αὖτις ἔτ' ἄλλο γένος θῆκ' εὐρύοπα Ζεὺς
ἀνδρῶν, οἳ γεγάασιν ἐπὶ χθονὶ πουλυβοτείρῃ.
... νῦν γὰρ δὴ γένος ἐστὶ **σιδήρεον** ...
... Ζεὺς δ' ὀλέσει καὶ τοῦτο γένος μερόπων ἀνθρώπων ....
(1.169a–169b, 176, 179)

And again the far-seeing Zeus made yet another generation, the **fifth**, of men who are upon the bounteous earth ... truly a race of **iron** ... Zeus will destroy this race of mortal men ....
(1.169a–169b, 176, 179)

Hesiod goes on to describe the fifth generation as wicked and disrespectful, 'delighting in evil'. Historians date Hesiod's *Works and Days* to c. 700 BC.[29] The four-kingdoms schema is altered by the appearance of the 'race called demi-gods' between the bronze (third) and iron (fifth) races. It is suspected that it is a secondary insertion, though whether by Hesiod himself or the tradition on which he drew is unclear.[30]

The idea that the downward spiral of humanity would someday be reversed is expressed in Plato. In the dialogue between Socrates and 'the stranger', the series of kingdoms, starting with Cronos, seems presupposed, even though the discussion itself is highly philosophical and speculative:

> During a certain period God himself goes with the universe as a guide in its revolving course, but another epoch, when the cycles have at length reached the measure of his allotted time,

---

29  *OCD*³ 700. For argument for an earlier date, see Evelyn-White, *Hesiod*, xxv–xxvi.
30  Momigliano, 'Origins', 535.

he lets it go, and of its own accord it turns backward in the opposite direction ....[31] (*Politicus* 13 = 269cd).

Socrates asks the stranger for the reason that the universe turns back. The stranger explains that 'absolute and perpetual immutability is a property of only the most divine things'. The stranger goes on to explain:

> Therefore at that moment God, who made the order of the universe, perceived that it was in dire trouble, and fearing that it might founder in the tempest of confusion and sink in the boundless sea of diversity, he took again his place as its helmsman, reversed whatever had become unsound and unsettled in the previous period when the world was left to itself, set the world in order, restored it and made it immortal and ageless [ἀθάνατον αὐτὸν καὶ ἀγήρων].[32] (*Politicus* 13 = 273e).

Although there is no reference to specific kingdoms, the schema of deterioration followed by restoration is clear.

Polybius, who accompanied Cornelius Scipio Aemilianus and witnessed the destruction of Carthage in 146 BC, later reports (with key elements in bold type face):

> Scipio, when he looked upon the city as it was utterly perishing and in the last throes of its complete destruction, is said to have shed tears and wept openly for his enemies. After being wrapped in thought for long, and realizing that all cities, nations, and authorities must, like men, meet their doom; that this happened to Ilium, once a prosperous city, to the empires of **Assyria**, **Media**, and **Persia**, the greatest of their time, and to **Macedonia** itself, the brilliance of which was so recent, either deliberately or the verses escaping him, he said:
>
> > 'A day will come when sacred Troy shall perish,
> > And when Priam and his people shall be slain'.

---

31 For Greek text and translation, see Lamb, *Plato VIII*, 50–51.
32 Lamb, *Plato VIII*, 64–55.

> And when Polybius speaking with freedom to him, for he was his teacher, asked him what he meant by the words, they say that without any attempt at concealment he named his own country, for which he feared when he reflected on the fate of all things human. Polybius actually heard him and recalls it in his history.[33] (*Historiae* 38.22.1–3, *apud* Appian, *Punica* 19.132)

The empires of Assyria, Media, Persia, and Macedonia reflect the four-kingdoms understanding of history. But Scipio adds Rome (i.e. 'his own country') to the sequence. He does this by quoting two lines from the *Iliad* (6.448–449), which in this context find new application in the old prophetic utterance. Scipio's grim realisation 'that all cities, nations, and authorities must, like men, meet their doom' coheres with his famous dream recounted in Cicero, *De re publica* 6.9–26, and perhaps also explains Scipio's foreboding thoughts in the fragment preserved in Appian. That the fate of Troy anticipated the fate of Rome is confirmed by Scipio himself thus lending credibility to the prophecy.[34]

In his *Bibliotheca* Diodorus reviews great antiquity (with key elements in bold type face):

> The remaining kings followed his example, son succeeding father upon the throne, and reigned for thirty generations down to Sardanapallus; for it was under this ruler that the empire of the **Assyrians** fell to the **Medes**, after it had lasted more than thirteen hundred years, as Ctesias of Cnidus says in his Second Book.[35] (*Bibliotheca* 2.21.8)

Diodorus describes the debauchery and defeat of Sardanapallus, the last ruler of Assyria (*Bibliotheca* 2.23–27), then he adds:

---

33 Translation based on Paton, *Polybius*, 441.
34 See Miltsios, *The Shaping of Narrative in Polybius*, 82. Recall, too, that in antiquity (and in biblical literature!) it was believed that dreams could be prophetic. For comments on Scipio's dream, see Lewis, *The Interpretation of Dreams*, 20–22. Lewis sees the dream as oracular, prophetic, and enigmatic. It is important, too, to note that in this fragmentary part of *Historiae* 38, which has been reconstructed from various later sources, we may not know exactly how Polybius himself understood Rome's relation to the four-kingdoms schema. The caveat is expressed in Momigliano, 'Origins', 544.
35 Translation based on Oldfather, *Diodorus Siculus* I, 420–23.

> So the empire of the **Assyrians**, which had endured from the time of Ninus through **thirty generations**, for more than one **thousand three hundred years**, was destroyed by the **Medes** in the manner described above.[36] (*Bibliotheca* 2.28.8)

He continues:

> Now, as the Chaldaeans say, the world is by its nature eternal, and neither had a first beginning nor will at a later time suffer destruction; furthermore, both the disposition and the orderly arrangement of the universe have come about by virtue of a divine providence, and today whatever takes place in the heavens is in every instance brought to pass, not at haphazard nor by virtue of any spontaneous action, but by some **fixed and firmly determined divine decision**.[37] (*Bibliotheca* 2.30.1)

Diodorus goes on to describe Chaldean belief about the stars and planets foretelling the future. He continues his historical survey appealing to Herodotus and describing the rise and fall of the Medes and the Persians (*Bibliotheca* 2.32.2–3).

Virgil, won over to Octavian, the new emperor now known as Augustus,[38] wrote epic poetry as part of the propaganda whose purpose was to promote the idea that with the advent of Augustus the Golden Age, foretold and hinted at in many ancient prophecies, had at last appeared. In his *Fourth Eclogue* the poet writes (with key elements in bold type face):

> Now is come the **last age** [*ultima ... aetas*] of the song of Cumae;
> the great line of the centuries begins anew.
> Now the Virgin returns, the reign of Saturn returns;
> now a new generation descends from heaven on high.
> Only do you, pure Lucina, smile on the birth of the child,
> under whom the **iron brood** [*ferrea*] shall first cease,
> and a **gold race** [*gens aurea*] spring up throughout the world!

---

36 Oldfather, *Diodorus Siculus* I, 444–45.
37 Oldfather, *Diodorus Siculus* I, 448–49.
38 Starr, 'Virgil's Acceptance of Octavian'.

Your own Apollo now reigns!³⁹ (*Eclogue* 4.4–10)

Reference to the 'last age' (*ultima ... aetas*) is not to be missed. The last age, of course is the 'gold race', that is, the Golden Age. The 'song of Cumae' refers, of course, to the prophecy of the ancient Sibyl who lived in Cumae (northwest of Naples) and foretold the coming restoration. Thus it can be said that 'the great line of the centuries begins anew'.⁴⁰ Indeed, the 'Virgin' has returned,⁴¹ the 'reign of Saturn' has begun, the birth of a special child has brought to an end the 'iron brood' and in its place a 'gold race' has sprung up throughout the world. 'Iron' refers to the last of the four kingdoms, while 'gold' recalls the first generation of humanity, which was more god-like. Thanks to Augustus, the gold race has finally sprung up and Rome now has its own Apollo for her king. The much-discussed birthday calendar inscription, well preserved at Priene, refers, as we would expect, to the birth of Augustus. The part of Virgil's *Fourth Eclogue* that I have quoted puts in poetic form what the calendar inscription declares in prosaic form. Part of the inscription reads:

> Providence ... has given us Augustus, whom she filled with virtue that he might benefit humankind, sending him as a savior [σωτῆρα], both for us and our descendants, that he might end war and arrange all things, and ... by his appearance, surpassing all benefactors [εὐεργέτας] ... and since the birth of the god [ἡ γενέθλιος τοῦ θεοῦ] Augustus was on account of him the beginning of the good news for the world [ἦρξεν δὲ τῶι κόσμωι τῶν δι' αὐτὸν εὐαγγελίων] .... (*OGIS* 458, 9 BCE)⁴²

Virgil has more to say about Augustus and the new age. For example, the poet bids farmers to pray to Caesar for rain (*Georg.* 1.100). He urges

---

39 Latin text and English translation are based on Fairclough, *Virgil: Ecologues*.
40 Note the appearance of *nova* ('new') and especially *iam* ('now' or 'already'), which occurs three times in these lines.
41 That is Astraea, who abandoned a corrupt and unjust earth and ascended into heaven as the star Virgo, one of the signs of the Zodiac. Thanks to the advent of Augustus and the justice he brings, Astraea will now return to earth.
42 The inscription is composite, made up mostly of the fragments from Priene. For Greek text, see Dittenberger, *Orientis Graeci Inscriptiones Selectae: Supplementum Sylloges Inscriptionum Graecarum*, 2:51–52 (no. 458). For bibliography, translation, and notes, see Danker, *Benefactor*, 215–22. At the beginning of the first column the inscription references 'the birthday of most divine Caesar' (ἡ τοῦ θειοτάτου Καίσαρος γενέθλιος ἡμέρα).

sailors to pray for favourable weather and safe passage (*Georg*. 1.42).

Under Virgil's influence Horace also supported Augustus, at least for a time.[43] Some of his *Odes* allude to the idea that in the advent of Augustus the Golden Age has appeared:[44]

> Descendant of the kindly gods [*divis orte bonis*],[45]
> best guardian of Romulus' folk, you have already been away
>     too long.
> You promised an early return to the august assembly of the
>     fathers; so return.[46]
> Bring back the light, dear leader, to your country;
> for when your face shines like spring upon the citizens,
> the day passes more happily and the sun's radiance is brighter.
>     (IV.5.1–8)[47]

> Each man spends all day until sunset in his own hills,
> wedding the vine to the unmarried trees;
> then he returns happily to his wine and at the second course[48]
>     requests your divine [*deum*] presence.
> He honours you with many a prayer, pouring libations from
>     the dish,
> and combines your worship with that of the household gods,
> as Greece does when remembering Castor and mighty
>     Hercules.[49] (IV.5.29–36)

> Senate and people are anxious to immortalise your virtues for
>     all time
> with full honours through inscriptions and public records.[50]
>     (IV.14. 1–2)

---

43  Starr, 'Horace and Augustus'.
44  Latin text and English translation based on Rudd, *Horace*. For commentary and notes, see Moore, *Horace*; Wickham, *Horace. I*.
45  It was claimed that Augustus descended from Aneneas, son of Venus.
46  I.e. awaiting the return of Augustus in 13 BC (cf. *Odes* IV.2).
47  Rudd, *Horace*, 232–33; Moore, *Horace*, 350–54.
48  During the second course of the meal libations were poured to the gods before the drinking began.
49  Rudd, *Horace*, 234–35.
50  Rudd, *Horace*, 256–57.

> Your age, Caesar, has brought back rich harvests to the fields,
> and restored to our Jove the standards torn down from the
>     proud doorposts of the Parthian;[51]
> it has closed the temple of Janus Quirinus, now empty of war;
> it has put a bridle on licence which was straying beyond the
>     proper limits,[52]
> removed sin, and revived the ancient arts by which the name
>     of Latium, the power of Italy,
> and the prestige and majesty of the Empire were extended
>     from the sun's western bed to his rising.[53] (IV.15.4–16)

> As for ourselves, on working days and holidays,
> surrounded by the merry God of Freedom's[54] gifts,
> along with our wives and children, we shall first offer due
>     prayers to the gods;
> then in song accompanied by Lydian pipes we shall sing in
>     our fathers' fashion of leaders
> who lived their lives like true men, of Troy and Anchises and
>     the offspring of kindly Venus.[55] (IV.15.25–32)

In his *Carmen Saeculare*, 'Hymn for a (New) Age',[56] Horace writes:

> ... chosen girls and boys of good character should sing a hymn to the gods who look with favour on the Seven Hills.[57] ... may you never behold anything greater than the city of Rome![58] (*Carm. Saec.* 7–9, 11–12)

---

51  Through diplomatic pressure the standards lost in 53 BC were returned to Rome in 20 BC.
52  A reference to the moral legislation passed in 18 BC.
53  Rudd, *Horace*, 258–59.
54  The reference is to Bacchus (or Dionysios), the god of wine.
55  Rudd, *Horace*, 260–61. Once again the reference is to Augustus, descendant of Aeneas, son of Venus.
56  The *Carmen Saeculare* was produced in 17 BC, ten years after the title Augustus was conferred on Octavian and the empire had enjoyed stability. See Moore, *Horace*, 388–91. The hymn was presented in song before the Temple of Apollo and was accompanied by dance. See Frank, 'The *Carmen Saeculare* of Horace'. For points of connection between the hymn and *Odes* IV.5 and IV.15, see Bitto, '*Regina Odarum*?'.
57  The 'Seven Hills' (*septem ... colles*) refers, of course, to the city of Rome.
58  Rudd, *Horace*, 262–63.

> If Rome is indeed your creation, if the squadrons that settled
>     the Etruscan shore came from Troy—
> a remnant bidden to change their home and city in a voyage
>     that brought salvation,
> for whom the righteous Aeneas, a Trojan survivor,
> built unscathed through the blazing city a road to freedom,
> destined, as he was, to give them more than they had left
>     behind[59]—
> then, o ye gods, give sound character to a young generation
>     enabling them to learn;
> give rest to the old ensuring their contentment;
> and to the people of Romulus as a whole give wealth and
>     children and every blessing.
> What the glorious descendant of Anchises and Venus[60] asks
>     of you with white oxen,
> may he obtain; may he be victorious in battle over his foes yet
>     merciful once they are down.[61] (*Carm. Saec.* 37–52)

Horace gives expression to the belief or hope that the new age will be an eternal one and that Rome will prosper. This will happen because of the advent of Augustus. Writing a few years later Dionysius of Halicarnassus reviews world history, noting, as many have, the succession of the Assyrians, the Medes, the Persians, the Macedonians, and the Romans (*Antiquitates romanae* 1.3.1–5). The last empire is the greatest, he believes, for it has conquered much more than the previous empires (1.2.2–4). In contrast to them, says Dionysius,

> Rome rules every country that is not inaccessible or uninhabited, and she is mistress of every sea, not only of that which lies inside the Pillars of Hercules but also of the Ocean, except that part of it which is not navigable; she is the first and only State recorded in all time that ever made the risings and the settings of the sun the boundaries of her dominion. Nor has her

---

59  These lines allude to the *Aeneid*, which had only recently been published.
60  This reference is again to Augustus, said to be a descendent of Aeneas, son of the goddess Venus.
61  Rudd, *Horace*, 264–65.

supremacy been of short duration but more lasting than that of any other common wealth or kingdom. For from the very beginning, immediately after her founding, she began to draw to herself the neighbouring nations, which were both numerous and warlike, and continually advanced, subjugating every rival. And it is now seven hundred and forty-five years from her foundation down to the consulship of Claudius Nero,[62] consul for the second time, and of Calpurnius Piso, who were chosen in the one hundred and ninety-third Olympiad. From the time that she mastered the whole of Italy she was emboldened to aspire to govern all mankind, and after driving from off the sea the Carthaginians, whose maritime strength was superior to that of all others, and subduing Macedonia, which until then was reputed to be the most powerful nation on land, she no longer had as rival any nation either barbarian or Greek; and it is now in my day already the seventh generation that she has continued to hold sway over every region of the world, and there is no nation, as I may say, that disputes her universal dominion [τῆς κοινῆς ἡγεμονίας] or protests against being ruled by her.[63] (*Antiquitates romanae* 1.3.1–5)

Proof of Rome's great power was her subjugation of Macedonia, the great empire founded by Alexander the Great. After that, says Dionysius, Rome 'no longer had as rival any nation'. That Roman dominance has lasted seven generations is compelling evidence that Rome's greatness is not a fleeting thing.

In his *Metamorphoses* Ovid brings together all of our elements, the quality of the metals and the kingdoms with which they correspond. After speaking of creation, Ovid says, 'A living creature of finer stuff than these, more capable of lofty thought, one who could have dominion over all the rest, was lacking yet. Then man was born, whether he (God) made this one made with divine seed [*natus homo est, sive hunc*

---

62 Claudius Nero is not to be confused with the later emperor. Claudius Nero and Calpurnius Piso were consuls in 7 BC.
63 Greek text and translation are based on Cary, *Dionysius of Halicarnassus: Roman Antiquities I*, 10–13.

*divino semine fecit*]' (*Metam.* 1.76–78). This man, we are told, was made from a mixture of earth and water 'and moulded into the form of the all-controlling gods' (1.82–83).[64]

Next come the four kingdoms. The poet says (with key elements in bold type face):

> **Aurea prima** *sata est aetas, quae vindice nullo,*
> *Sponte sua, sine lege fidem rectumque colebat.*[65] (*Metam.* 1.89–90)

> **Golden** was the **first** age, which, with no one to compel,
> of its own will, without a law kept faith and did right.
>     (*Metam.* 1.89–90)

> *Postquam Saturno tenebrosa in Tartara misso*
> *sub Iove mundus erat, subiit* **argentea** *proles,*
> *auro deterior, fulvo pretiosior aere.*
> *Iuppiter antiqui contraxit tempora veris.* (*Metam.* 1.113–116)

> After Saturn had been banished to the dark land of death,
> And the world was under the sway of Jove, the **silver** race came in,
> lower in the scale than gold, but of greater worth than yellow brass.
> Jove now shortened the bounds of the old-time spring.
>     (*Metam.* 1.113–116)

> **Tertia** *post illam successit* **aenea** *proles,*
> *saevior ingeniis et ad horrida promptior arma,*
> *non scelerata tamen; du duro* **ultima ferro**.
> *protinus inrupit venae peioris in aevum omne nefas*
> *fugitque pudoe verumque fidesque.* (*Metam.* 1.125–129)

> Next after this and **third** in order came the **bronze** race,
> of sterner disposition, and more ready to fly to arms savage,

---

64 One must wonder if the creation story in Genesis is echoed in these lines. In Gen. 1:26, humanity is made in God's image and is given dominion over all creatures. In Gen. 2:7, Adam is made from the dust of the earth. See Riley, *The Metamorphoses of Ovid*, 8–9.
65 Latin text and translation based on Miller, *Ovid* III. *Metamorphoses* I, 8–11.

but not yet impious; the age of hard **iron** came **last**.
Straightway all evil burst forth into this age of baser vein;
modesty and truth and faith fled the earth .... (*Metam.*
1.125–129)

Ovid's description of the Golden Age in 1.89–105, in which humans were faithful and law-abiding, living without the need of law enforcement, is reminiscent of Adam and Eve in the Garden of Eden (Gen. 2:15–25).[66] The decline of humanity begins with the silver race. God shortens the spring season for this generation. For them work is hard in the face of harsher weather (1.117–124). We again have rough correspondence with Genesis, which speaks of a more difficult life for Adam and Eve after the fall (Gen. 3:16–19). The bronze race, the third age of humanity, was quick to violence and war, while evil and all that is base characterised the fourth age of humanity, the iron race. The bronze and iron races seem to reflect some of the characteristics of the antediluvian generation described in Genesis (cf. Gen. 4:3–6; 6:1–5). Ovid's poetic recasting of the four-kingdoms schema reflects elements in Hesiod, as well as elements in the ancient Near East, perhaps including the book of Genesis.

Velleius Paterculus is perhaps the most enthusiastic supporter of the otherwise not well-liked Tiberius, successor to his stepfather Augustus.[67] In his *Historiae Romanae* he expresses his conviction that the glories of the Golden Age continue under the leadership of the new emperor (1.6.6). He begins with a review of human history (with key elements in bold type face):

> In the following age—about eight hundred and seventy years ago—the sovereignty [*imperium*] of Asia passed to the **Medes** from the **Assyrians**, who had held it for ten hundred and seventy years. Indeed, it was their king Sardanapalus, a man enervated by luxurious living, whose excesses of fortune was his undoing. Thirty-third,[68] in direct succession of

---

66 Riley, *The Metamorphoses of Ovid*, 10.
67 Recent scholarship has addressed the bias and motives in Paterculus. See Connal, 'Velleius Paterculus'. See also Sumner, 'The Truth about Velleius Paterculus'.
68 On the chronological difficulties, see Shipley, *Velleius Paterculus*, 12–15 notes.

father and son, from Ninus and Semiramis, who had founded **Babylon**, he was deprived alike of his empire and his life by Arbaaces the Mede.... In this period, sixty-five years before the founding of Rome, Carthage was established by the Tyrian Elissa, by some authors called Dido. About this time also Caranus, a man of royal race, eleventh in descent from Hercules, set out from Argos and seized the kingship of **Macedonia**. From him Alexander the Great was descended in the seventeenth generation, and could boast that, on his mother's side, he was descended from Achilles, and, on his father's side, from Hercules. [Aemilius Sura says in his book on the chronology of Rome: 'The Assyrians were the first of all races to hold world power, then the Medes, and after them the Persians, and then the Macedonians. Then through the defeat of Kings Philip and Antiochus, of Macedonian origin, following closely upon the overthrow of Carthage, **the world power passed to the Roman people**. Between this time and the beginning of the reign of Ninus the king of the Assyrians, who was the first to hold world power, lies an interval of nineteen hundred and ninety-five years.'][69] (1.6.1–2, 4–6)

The bracketed material is a gloss from a lost work by Aemilius Sura, who wrote in the second century BC.[70] It is the earliest example in Roman literature of the four-kingdoms schema.[71] Of course, in Sura the schema is updated by adding the comment that after the overthrow of Carthage, 'the world power passed to the Roman people'. Evidently, Sura believed that Rome was the last of the great empires.[72]

Paterculus expresses his firm confidence that the power that had passed to the Roman people will continue with Tiberius (with key elements in bold type face):

---

69 Latin text and translation are based on Shipley, *Velleius Paterculus*, 12–15.
70 Alonso-Núñez, 'Aemilius Sura'. Alonso-Núñez argues that the fragment dates to the 170s or 180s BC.
71 Alonso-Núñez, 'Aemilius Sura', 113–14. 'Sura's formulation became simply a Roman adaptation of' the four-kingdoms schema. The omission of reference to Carthage points to the eastern origin of the schema.
72 Alonso-Núñez, 'Aemilius Sura', 114.

But fortune, which had removed the **hope** of the great name of Caesar, had already **restored** to the state her real protector; for the return of Tiberius Nero from Rhodes in the consulship of Publius Vincius, your father, and before the death of either of these youths, had filled his country with joy. Caesar Augustus did not long hesitate, for he had no need to search for one to choose as his successor but merely to choose the one who towered above the others. Accordingly, what he had wished to do after the death of Lucius but while Gaius was still living, and had been prevented from doing by the strong opposition of Nero himself, he now insisted upon carrying out after the death of both young men, namely, to make Nero his associate in the tribunician power, in spite of his continued objection both in private and in the senate; and in the consulship of Aelius Catus and Gaius Sentius, on the twenty-seventh of June, he adopted him, seven hundred and fifty-four years after the founding of the city, and twenty-seven years ago. The rejoicing of that day, the concourse of the citizens, their vows as they stretched their hands almost to the very heavens, and the **hopes** which they entertained for **the perpetual security** and **the eternal existence of the Roman empire**, I shall hardly be able to describe to the full even in my comprehensive work, much less try to do it justice here. I shall simply content myself with stating what a day of good omen it was for all. On that day there sprang up once more in parents **the assurance of safety** for their children, in husbands for the sanctity of marriage, in owners for the safety of their property, and in all men the assurance of **safety**, order, **peace**, and tranquillity; indeed, **it would have been hard to entertain larger hopes, or to have them more happily fulfilled**.[73] (2.103.1–5)

In his *Prefatio* to his Roman history Appian reviews the history of empires (with key elements in bold type face):

---

73 Latin text and translation are based on Shipley, *Velleius Paterculus*, 262–65.

The mastery of Asia is not to be compared, as to labor and bravery, with that of the smallest of the countries of Europe, on account of the effeminacy and cowardice of the Asiatic peoples, as will be shown in the progress of this history. Such of the Asiatic nations as the Romans hold, they subdued in a few battles, though even the Macedonians joined in the defence, while the conquest of Africa and of Europe was in many cases very exhausting. Again, **the duration of the Assyrians, Medes, and Persians taken together (the three greatest empires before Alexander)**, does not amount to nine hundred years, **which that of Rome has already reached**, and **the size of their empire I think was not half that of the Romans, whose boundaries extend from the setting of the sun and the Western ocean to Mount Caucasus and the river Euphrates**, and through Egypt to Ethiopia and through Arabia as far as the Eastern ocean, so that **their boundary is the ocean both where the sun-god rises and where he sinks**, while they control the entire Mediterranean, and all its islands as well as Britain in the ocean. The greatest sea-power of the Medes and Persians included either the gulf of Pamphylia and the single island of Cyprus or perhaps some other small islets belonging to Ionia in the Mediterranean. They controlled the Persian gulf also, but how much of a sea is that?[74] (*Praefatio* 9)

From these comments it seems clear that with the long and successful rule of Augustus Graeco-Roman writers believed that the Golden Age had in fact arrived, that the ancient prophecies of the four kingdoms had finally been fulfilled. But Rome's greatness, if not destiny, was perceived long before the appearance of Octavian. Alonso-Núñez assembles several texts that show that by the middle of the second century BC Rome was widely seen as the new superpower without rival.[75] Besides the fragment of Aemilius Sura, we have significant comments in Pompeius Trogus (as preserved in the *Epitoma* of Justinus) and in several of the writers quoted above.

---

74 Translation based on White, *Appian's Roman History*, 12–15.
75 Alonso-Núñez, 'Aemilius Sura', 115–19.

Alonso-Núñez notes, too, that the great earthquake in 197 BC that caused the island Hiera to appear between the islands of Thera and Therasia was interpreted as a sign that rule of the world had transitioned from the Greeks and Macedonians to the Romans.[76] According to Pompeius Trogus the soothsayers said in response to the earthquake: *Oriens Romanorum imperium vetus Graecorum ac Macedonum voratur*, 'The eastern empire of the Romans devours the ancient Greeks and Macedonians' (*apud* Justinus, *Epitoma* 30.4.4). The significance of the Roman victory over the Seleucid/Antiochid Empire is underscored when it is remembered what was declared with respect to Antiochus I Soter (ruled 280–262 BC). An inscription engraved (in cuneiform!) on a stone arch reads: 'I am Antiochus [*An-ti-'u-ku-us*], the great king, the legitimate king, the king of the world, king of Babylon, king of all countries'.[77]

## Conclusion

The origin of the four-kingdoms schema may be debated,[78] but its antiquity and ubiquity are not. In his introduction to the collection of studies concerned with the four-kingdoms schema Andrew Perrin rightly remarks:

> The four kingdoms schema has enabled writers of various cultures, times, and locations, to periodize all of history as the staged succession of empires barreling towards the consummation of history and arrival of a utopian age. ... regardless

---

76 Alonso-Núñez, 'Aemilius Sura', 116.
77 Translation from Pritchard, *Ancient Near Eastern Texts*, 317. For transliteration of the original text, see Weissbach, *Die Keilinschriften der Achämeniden*, 132–35. For image of the cuneiform text, see Rawlinson, *The Cuneiform Inscriptions*, plate 66. The epithet, 'king of all countries', appears in Mesopotamian texts. See Wilson, 'Titles of the Persian kings'.
78 Momigliano, 'Origins', 534, argues for a Greek origin. Most scholars are persuaded that the four-kingdoms schema originated in the ancient Near East. The Balaam inscription from Tell Deir 'Allā, whose original text could date to the tenth century BC and which finds a remarkable parallel in Genesis 24 and may be related in some way to the 'ambiguous oracle' mentioned by Josephus (*J.W.* 6.312–313), could be related to the four-kingdoms schema. If so, then we have additional evidence that points to an origin in the ancient Near East.

of its beginnings, the four kingdoms motif has acquired a remarkably broad reach and diverse reception.[79]

What is important to recognise is that Rome's belief that in the advent of Augustus a new Golden Age has dawned and that Christianity's belief that in the advent of Jesus of Nazareth the kingdom of God has dawned we do not have unrelated ideas. They are very much related and they are very competitive. These competing ideas occupy the same social, ideological, eschatological, and theological space. They are diametrically opposed, of course, but they offer the Roman world what most humans craved: assurance of a new era, an era in which poverty, violence, and sickness will recede. In short, the Roman world craved peace and safety. How the message of Jesus addressed this hope will be treated in the chapter that follows.

Craig A. Evans
Houston Christian University

---

79 Perrin, 'Introduction', 1–2. This important book (see n.18 above) appeared after I gave my lectures at the conference sponsored by Sydney College of Divinity. I was relieved to find that the contributors arrived at similar conclusions.

# Bibliography

Alonso-Núñez, J. M.   'Aemilius Sura', *Latomus* 48 (1989), 110–19.

Anklesaria, B. T.   *Zand-i Vahuman Yasn and Two Pahlevi Fragments* (Bombay: K. L. Bhargava, 1957).

Beasley-Murray, G. R.   *Jesus and the Kingdom of God* (Grand Rapids, MI: Eerdmans, 1986).

Bitto, Gregor   '*Regina Odarum*? Zur Publikation des *Carmen Saeculare*', *Rheinisches Museum für Philologie* n.f. 155 (2012), 166–84.

Boyce, M.   *Textual Sources for the Study of Zoroastrianism* (Chicago, IL: The University of Chicago Press, 1984).

Budde, Karl   *Die biblische Urgeschichte* (Berlin: de Gruyter, 1883).

Cary, E.   *Dionysius of Halicarnassus: Roman Antiquities I Books I–II* (LCL 319; London: Heinemann; Cambridge, MA: Harvard University Press, 1937).

Collins, J. J.   *Daniel: A Commentary on the Book of Daniel* (Hermeneia; Minneapolis, MN: Fortress, 1993).

Collins, J. J.   *The Apocalyptic Vision of the Book of Daniel* (HSM 16; Missoula, MT: Scholars, 1977).

Collins, J. J.   'The Place of the Fourth Sibyl in the Development of Jewish Sibyllina', *JJS* 25 (1974), 365–80.

Connal, R. T.   'Velleius Paterculus: The Soldier and the Senator', *The Classical World* 107 (2013), 49–62.

Danker, F. W.   *Benefactor: Epigraphic Study of a Graeco-Roman and New Testament Semantic Field* (St. Louis, MO: Clayton, 1982).

Dittenberger, W. (ed.)   *Orientis Graeci Inscriptiones Selectae: Supplementum Sylloges Inscriptionum Graecarum* (2 vols., Leipzig: S. Hirzel, 1903–5).

Driver, S. R.   *The Book of Genesis, with Introduction and Notes* (Westminster Commentaries; 6th edn; London: Methuen, 1907).

Etz, D. V.   'The Numbers of Genesis V 3–31: A Suggested Conversion and Its Implications', *VT* 43 (1993), 171–89.

Evelyn-White, H. G.   *Hesiod: The Homeric Hymns and Homerica* (LCL 57; Cambridge, MA: Harvard University Press, 1936).

Fairclough, H. R.     *Virgil: Ecologues, Georgics, Aeneid 1–6* (LCL 63; London: Heinemann; Cambridge, MA: Harvard University Press, 1978).

Finkelstein, J. J.     'The Antediluvian Kings: A University of California Tablet', *Journal of Cuneiform Studies* 17 (1963), 39–51.

Flusser, D.     'The Four Empires in the Fourth Sibyl and in the Book of Daniel', *IOS* 2 (1972), 148–75.

Frank, Tenney     'The *Carmen Saeculare* of Horace', *The American Journal of Philology* 42 (1921), 324–29.

Gunkel, H.     *Genesis* (Göttingen: Vandenhoeck & Ruprecht, 1901).

Hasel, G. F.     'The Genealogies of Gen 5 and 11 and Their Alleged Babylonian Background', *AUSS* 16 (1978), 361–74.

Hultgård, A.     '*Bahman Yasht*: A Persian Apocalypse', in J. J. Collins and J. H. Charlesworth (eds.), *Mysteries and Revelations: Apocalyptic Studies since the Uppsala Colloquium* (JSPSup 9; Sheffield: JSOT Press, 1991), 114–34.

Jacobsen, T.     *The Sumerian King List* (Assyriological Studies 11; Chicago, IL: University of Chicago Press, 1939).

Lucas, E. C.     'The Origin of Daniel's Four Empire Scheme Re-Examined', *TynBul* 40 (1989), 185–202.

Lamb, W. R. M.     *Plato VIII* (LCL 164; Cambridge, MA: Harvard University Press, 1925).

Lewis, N.     *The Interpretation of Dreams and Portents* (Aspects of Antiquity; Toronto: Hakkert, 1976).

Miller, F. J.     *Ovid* III. *Metamorphoses* I. Books I–VIII (LCL 42; 2nd edn, Cambridge, MA: Harvard University Press, 1921).

Miltsios, N.     *The Shaping of Narrative in Polybius* (Trends in Classics 23; Berlin: de Gruyter, 2013).

Momigliano, A.     'The Origins of Universal History', *Annali della Scuola Normale Superiore di Pisa* serie III 12 (1982), 533–60.

Moore, C. H.     *Horace: The Odes, Epodes and Carmen Saeculare* (New York, NY: American Book Company, 1902).

Newsom, C. A.     *Daniel: A Commentary* (NTL; Louisville, KY: Westminster John Knox, 2014).

Oldfather, C. H.    *Diodorus Siculus* I. Books I–II.34 (LCL 279; Cambridge, MA: Harvard University Press, 1933).

Otto, R.    *The Kingdom of God and the Son of Man: A Study in the History of Religion* (London: Lutterworth, 1938). Original: *Reichgottes und Menschensohn: Ein religionsgeschichtlicher Versuch* (Munich: Beck, 1934).

Paton, W. R.    *Polybius: The Histories VI* (LCL 161; Cambridge, MA: Harvard University Press, 1927).

Perrin, A. B., and L. T. Stuckenbruck (eds.)    *Four Kingdom Motifs before and beyond the Book of Daniel* (Themes in Biblical Narrative 28; Leiden: Brill, 2021).

Perrin, A. B.    'Introduction to the Four Kingdoms as a Time Bound, Timeless, and Timely Historiographical Mechanism and Literary Motif', in Perrin and Stuckenbruck (eds.), *Four Kingdom Motits*, 1–12.

Pritchard, J. B.    *Ancient Near Eastern Texts Relating to the Old Testament* (Princeton: Princeton University Press, 1969).

Rawlinson, H. C.    *The Cuneiform Inscriptions of Western Asia* (Vol. V; London: Trustees of the British Museum, 1909).

Riley, H. T.    *The Metamorphoses of Ovid* (London: George Bell & Sons, 1889).

Rudd, N.    *Horace: Odes and Epodes* (LCL 33; Cambridge, MA: Harvard University Press, 2012).

Shipley, F. W.    *Velleius Paterculus: Compendium of Roman History* (LCL 152; Cambridge, MA: Harvard University Press, 1924).

Starr, C. G.    'Horace and Augustus', *American Journal of Philology* 90 (1969), 58–64.

Starr, C. G.    'Virgil's Acceptance of Octavian', *American Journal of Philology* 76 (1955), 34–46.

Sumner, G. V.    'The Truth about Velleius Paterculus: Prolegomena', *Harvard Studies in Classical Philology* 74 (1970), 257–97.

Weissbach, F. H.    *Die Keilinschriften der Achämeniden* (Leipzig: J. C. Hinrichs, 1911).

Wenham, G. J.    *Genesis 1–15* (WBC 1; Dallas, TX: Word, 1987).

| | |
|---|---|
| White, Horace | *Appian's Roman History* (LCL 2; London: Heinemann, 1912). |
| Wickham, E. C. | *Horace. Vol. I: The Odes, Carmen Saeculare and Epodes, with Commentary* (Oxford: Clarendon, 1904). |
| Wilson, R. D. | 'Titles of the Persian kings', in G. Weil (ed.), *Festschrift Eduard Sachau zum siebzigsten Geburtstage* (Berlin: Georg Reimer, 1915), 179–207. |
| Zimmern, H. | *Urkönige und Uroffenbarung* (Gottingen: Vandenhoeck und Ruprecht, 1902). |

CHAPTER 2

# Kingdoms in Conflict: The Jesus Movement and the Roman Empire

Craig A. Evans

The present chapter resumes where the preceding chapter ended. The preceding chapter reviewed a number of texts from the ancient Near East and from the western classical period. It was observed that these texts interpreted human history as a series of declining periods, often speaking of 'races' of people characterised by various metals, beginning with gold and descending in value to iron or lead. However, this schematised interpretation of history was not simply historical; it was also eschatological, for it was hoped that the gold race, or 'Golden Age', would return. It would be an era of peace, safety, health, and tranquility. It would be an era when humans would treat each other with justice and be in harmony with the will of the gods.

For Jews and Christians this longed-for Golden Age was far more theocentric. It will be a time when God's rule will be fully operative on earth, even as it is in heaven. The God of Israel will be recognised as King of the earth and his anointed one will serve as his vice-regent. It will be a time of virtue and righteousness. It will be a time when God's people, the Israelites, descendants of Abraham, will be lifted up, no longer trodden down by the pagans.

It is against this backdrop that Jesus' proclamation of the kingdom of God should be understood. He proclaimed the good news foretold in Isaiah, but it was a 'good news' that resonated with the Roman world, a world that had in recent years heard much about the good news offered by Augustus and his successors. The proclamation of Jesus was deeply rooted in the Scriptures of Israel—of that there can be no doubt—but his proclamation both challenged and summoned an audience well beyond the physical descendants of Abraham.

I turn now to the second part of my study, which focuses on Christian eschatology and the proclamation of the kingdom of God.

## 2. Christian Eschatology and Proclamation of the Kingdom of God

The Christian proclamation of its faith in the risen Messiah encountered significant resistance from Jews and non-Jews alike because (1) it apparently did not measure up to Jewish expectations and (2) its claim of a new era brought about by its Messiah ran up against the belief in the Roman world that Augustus had ushered in the Golden Age. Jews were unpersuaded because many who longed for the appearance of a messiah (and not all Jews longed for a messiah) objected that the ministry, death, and alleged resurrection of Jesus changed nothing for the Jewish people at home or in the diaspora. After all, a resurrected rabbi or prophet would be interesting, but how does it really make a difference? Romans, of course, believed that in Augustus they had found their saviour and son of god, so what does the crucified Jewish healer have to offer? Through Caesar life is better—healthier, more prosperous, and more secure. In case of serious illness or injury, there was always Asclepius and his healing centres.

For Christianity's early theologians the answer to Jewish objections was that in both his suffering as well as his glorious resurrection Jesus had fulfilled Israel's ancient prophecies. Indeed, according to Paul, the crucifixion of Jesus was necessary if humankind was to be saved from its sin. Jesus suffered the penalty of sin in humanity's place. He took the curse of the cross upon himself. In his resurrection, say Christian theologians to Roman skeptics, Jesus offers humanity what no emperor can: peace with God and eternal life.

There was also much about the Roman cult of the divine emperor that could be criticised. When Jesus was crucified and his following proclaimed his resurrection, the unpopular and unloved Tiberius was emperor (ruled AD 14–37). When he passed out and his family thought him dead and then he suddenly revived, he was smothered beneath a pile of bedclothes.[1] The senate refused to confer on Tiberius post-mortem divine honours. Veleius Paterculus may have gushed over his appointment as successor to Augustus, but not too many people shared his love and loyalty for the man.

Caligula (ruled AD 37–41) was a disaster. His vanity and vindictive disposition toward the Jewish people that prompted him to have his image placed in the Jewish temple almost led to open rebellion.[2] After his assassination in early 41, no one recommended his divinisation. Caligula was succeeded by the stuttering, limping, slobbering, hunched Claudius (AD 41–54).[3] After his assassination by poisoning and an utterly insincere ceremony in which his divinity was recognised (though later neglected, then finally rescinded),[4] Nero became emperor (AD 54–68). In his first years as emperor Nero was celebrated. Some expressed the belief that his rule would inaugurate a new Golden Age.[5] But in a few years Nero's pathological nature came to expression in full force. In AD 66 war broke out in Israel, for which Rome was unprepared. Condemned by the senate as an enemy of state, Nero committed suicide.[6] His death was followed by three failed would-be successors: Galba, Otho, and Vitellius (AD 68–69). When Vespasian,

---

1   Tacitus, *Annales* 6.50.
2   Josephus, *Ant.* 18.261–309.
3   Suetonius, *Claudius* 30.
4   Suetonius, *Claudius* 44–45.
5   Writing at the beginning of Nero's rule, and often echoing the poetry of Virgil who sang the praises of Augustus, Calpurnius Siculus in his *Eclogues* writes, 'The Golden Age returns once more with undisturbed peace [*Aurea secura cum pace renascitur aeta*]' (*Ecl.* 1.42). Here 'peace' alludes to the *pax Augusta*, the 'Augustan peace'. Nero is referenced as 'this youth' (e.g. 4.137: *hunc iuvenem*). The new emperor is called a 'god' (*deus*) several times (e.g. 1.46, 73; 4.142–144). Nero is said to stand beside Jupiter (4.93–94) and to have the benefit of Apollo as his companion (4.87–88). Coins were struck in Alexandria that described Nero as the 'new Augustus'. See Martin, 'Calpurnius Siculus' "New" *aurea aetas*'.
6   Suetonius, *Nero* 49.

who had been directing the war against the Jewish people, was proclaimed emperor, no one knew if his reign would last any longer than those of his three predecessors.

Since the death of Augustus in AD 14 more than a half century had passed. Seven emperors had ruled, some quite briefly. Only one had been divinised, only to be later rescinded. An eighth emperor, Vespasian, now ruled but how successfully only time will tell. The most patriotic Roman could be forgiven for thinking that the Golden Age had lost its lustre. Perhaps the new era that Augustus had inaugurated and Nero supposedly had rejuvenated wasn't so eternal after all.

It is important also to note that in Jewish interpretation the fourth kingdom of Daniel had come to be understood in reference to Rome, not to the Greeks (as was likely the original meaning in Daniel 2 and the visions in Chapters 7 and 8). Identifying the fourth kingdom with Rome was Jewish and pagan, as attested in Josephus (*Ant.* 15.384–387) and other sources. However, the implications of this identification, from a Jewish point of view, embarrassed Josephus and he refused to comment on it (*Ant.* 10.208–210: 'But if anyone, anxious for precision ... wishing to learn about the unexplained—what is to happen—let him make the effort to read the book of Daniel. He will find this among the sacred writings').

Criticisms of the Roman adoption and adaptation of the ancient understanding of human history and eschatology are found throughout the teaching and activities of Jesus, at least as they are presented in the New Testament Gospels. Key criticisms are also found in many of the other writings that make up the New Testament canon and many writings after the New Testament era. I begin with Jesus and the Gospels.

## Part 1: Jesus and the Gospels

### Jesus

Although Jesus most likely understood his mission in terms of the prophecies and great traditions of Israel's ancient and sacred Scriptures, there can be little doubt that he also saw his ministry, at least in part, as a challenge to and critique of Roman imperial power. From beginning to end we observe actions or hear teaching that outperforms, rivals, or contradicts Roman doctrine.

*Descent of the dove at baptism.* All four New Testament Gospels say that a dove descended on Jesus when he was baptised. Greeks and Romans attached great significance to birds as omens and signs. The appearance of a bird or birds required interpretation and sometimes led to fateful decisions. One of the signs of the approaching death of Augustus was a bird that flew overhead.[7] Of course, the meaning of the flying bird was not understood until after the emperor died. Shortly before Tiberius was recalled to Rome an eagle, 'a bird never before seen in Rhodes, perched upon the roof of his house'.[8] Other omens were observed and recalled. Again, it was only after Augustus died and Tiberius succeeded his stepfather as the new emperor that the appearance of an eagle was understood to mean something significant.

The descent of the dove on Jesus was not mysterious and required no interpretation, for a voice from heaven spoke: 'You are my beloved Son; with you I am well pleased' (Mark 1:11; cf. Matt. 3:17; Luke 3:22; John 1:32–33). Even the wording of the voice conveys clarifying meaning. The declaration, 'You are my Son', alludes to Psalm 2:7, widely interpreted in reference to the royal descendant of David, even the awaited Messiah. The clause, 'with you I am well pleased', probably alludes to Isaiah 42:1, which is in reference to the Lord's Servant. Jesus is recognised as God's Son and Servant, not after puzzling over the appearance of a bird, which may or may not convey significant meaning, but because God has spoken and has identified Jesus as his Son.

*Stilling of the storm.* In his praise of Augustus, Virgil urges sailors to pray to Caesar for safe passage on the sea.[9] According to the Gospels Jesus does what no Caesar ever did: He commanded the storm to be still: 'Peace! Be still!' The disciples, only terrified a moment earlier, are astounded and ask, 'Who then is this, that even wind and sea obey him?' (Mark 4:41). Jewish readers and auditors, familiar with Israel's ancient and sacred Scripture, would know that it is Yahweh himself who 'stills the roaring of the seas, the roaring of the waves' (Ps. 65:7) and saves men who cry out to him when overwhelmed by the sea (Ps.

---

7   Suetonius, *Augustus* 97.1.
8   Suetonius, *Tiberius* 14.3–4.
9   Virgil, *Georg.* 1.42; cf. Calpurnius Siculus, *Eclogue* 4.97–100: Caesar 'has driven the east winds hence'.

107:27–29: 'he made the storm be still, and the waves of the sea were hushed').

*The destruction of a legion of evil spirits.* One of eeriest events in the Gospel narratives is the casting out of a legion of evil spirits into a nearby herd of swine, which then stampede over a cliff into the Sea of Galilee and drown. As most commentators recognise, when the possessed man says his name is 'Legion, for we are many', most readers in antiquity would have thought of the Roman legions. The Greek and Latin words for legion were used as loan words in Hebrew and Aramaic texts. Commentators will also note that Legion X Fretensis was stationed north of Galilee in Syria. This legion was the first to enter Galilee when the Jewish rebellion erupted in AD 66. Several artifacts have been found in and around Jerusalem that testify to the presence of Legion X Fretensis during and after the rebellion. That fact that the legion's mascot was a boar's head makes comparison with the story of the demonised man on the east side of the Sea of Galilee almost irresistible.

But was Legion X Fretensis and its boar's head mascot known to the people of Galilee? Because the legion was stationed in Syria, some commentators think the story of the demonised man was either created after AD 70 or was edited after AD 70. But what has been overlooked is that a Greek inscription has been found in Israel (Ascalon/Ashkelon), which was inscribed some years prior to the outbreak of the rebellion.[10] In this inscription an officer in Legion X Fretensis is thanked for his goodwill toward the city. I suspect, too, that commentators are unaware that attachments, or cohorts, of legions were sometimes sent on errands, as it were, and so marched through neighbouring territories. In any case, why should we assume that Galileans, living a few miles south of Syria, would be unaware of the presence of a Roman legion, whose mascot happens to be a boar's head?

The single-handed destruction of a legion of evil spirits—surely

---

10  *CIIP* 3:272–72 (no. 2335). The inscription reads: 'The council and the people honor Aulus Instuleius Tenax, centurion of the tenth legion Fretensis, for his goodwill'. Ascalon is 30 miles south of Tel Aviv.

more dangerous than a legion of mortal men[11]—would have greatly impressed hearers of this story. Many would likely think, 'Caesar may command legions, but Jesus can destroy them!'

*Healing the woman with the haemorrhage.* The evangelist's comment that the woman 'had suffered much under many physicians, and had spent all that she had, and was no better but rather grew worse' (Mark 5:26) is similar to the attitude some, including the emperors themselves, had of physicians.[12] But the idea that Jesus could heal someone, almost without knowing it, is remarkable. Arrian tells us that people would run up to Alexander the Great and touched his hands, or knees, or his clothes,[13] but nothing is said of healing. A woman approaches first-century BC Roman Sulla from behind and pulls a fragment of wool from his garment, hoping to receive 'some of his good fortune'.[14]

*Feeding the hungry.* In Mark 6 and 8 (and parallels in the other three Gospels) Jesus feeds the hungry multitude. One of the emperor's responsibilities is to provide the 'grain dole' for the poor and hungry and to send shipments of grain to regions in the empire stricken by drought and famine.[15] By feeding thousands from a few loaves and fish Jesus demonstrates that his power to feed the hungry far outpaces the power of Caesar (Isa. 25:6).

*The healing of the blind and lame.* Jesus' healing of the blind and lame has been compared to the similar healings said to have been performed by Vespasian in Egypt, shortly after he was proclaimed emperor.[16] Vespasian spat in the eyes of a blind man who regained his sight; he touched the leg of a lame man and the man was once again able to walk. The purpose of these miracles was to show that the newly

---

11  The demons were probably understood as the spirits of the dead, perhaps inhabiting the very necropolis inhabited by the demonised man. See Bolt, 'Jesus, the Daimons, and the Dead', esp. 56–57. For further treatment of Mark 5:1–20, see Bolt, *Jesus' Defeat of Death*, 143–54.
12  Pliny tells us that one Archagathus, a physician, acquired the nickname 'executioner' and that 'his profession, with all physicians, became objects of loathing in general' (*Nat. hist.* 29.13). Elsewhere Pliny complains of their avarice (29.21). Sometimes a physician was called *carnifex*, 'one who slays'. In one of his letters Cicero says of his physician: 'I am far from satisfied with his treatment' (*Fam.* 16.4.1).
13  Arrian, *Anabasis of Alexander* 6.13.3.
14  Plutarch, *Life of Sulla* 35.
15  Rowland, 'The "Very Poor" and the Grain Dole'.
16  Suetonius, *Vespasian* 7.2–3; Tacitus, *Historiae* 4.81; Cassius Dio, *Historia romana* 65.8.

proclaimed emperor did indeed enjoy the blessing of the gods (and the presence of the priest of Serapis lent gravitas to the occasion, as well as theological insight).[17] These were the only miraculous healings that Vespasian performed.

In the case of Jesus, however, he healed many, not only the blind and lame, but lepers, paralysed, those suffering various ailments, and on occasion even raised the dead. Healing was not exceptional with Jesus; it was commonplace.

*Healing of the Centurion's servant.* Matthew and Luke preserve the story of the healing of the centurion's servant (Matt. 8:5–13; Luke 7:1–10). A number of inferences may be drawn from this story. First, the centurion has had no success in finding someone who can heal his servant. In desperation he turns to Jesus (not to Caesar or the cult of Asclepius or a cult or priest who recommends directing prayer to Caesar). Second, the centurion has so much respect for Jesus (and the Jewish people and their religious traditions) that he confesses that he is 'not worthy' to have Jesus even enter his house. Jesus need 'only say the word and [the] servant will be healed' (Matt. 8:8). Jesus is impressed by the centurion's faith, which he says exceeds the faith of many in Israel. Jesus is cast in the role of one who discerns and judges between Jew and Gentile. Jesus is willing to say the word, and the servant is healed 'at that very moment' (v.13). The idea that Jesus need only speak and a work of power takes place exceeds the authority of Caesar himself.

*Peter's confession and Jesus' prophecy.* When Peter confesses Jesus to be the Messiah, Son of God, Jesus replies, 'I tell you, you are Peter, and on this rock I will build my church, and the powers of death shall not prevail against it' (Matt. 16:18). Jesus' affirmation that he will build his church on rock (*petra*), which is an obvious play on the name given to Simon Peter (*petros*), may have been intended as a challenge to tetrarch Philip's recent announcement that the village of Bethsaida, the home town of Simon Peter, Andrew, and the apostle Philip, was to be upgraded to city status and renamed Julias in honour of Julia Livia, the late widow and adopted daughter of the late emperor Augustus. Julia (née Livia) had died in AD 29 and, we believe, the following year

---

17  Eve, 'Spit in Your Eye'.

tetrarch Philip made his announcement. Had Philip, the most hellenised and romanised of Herod the Great's surviving sons, lived longer (he died in AD 34), he might well have built a temple dedicated to Julia atop the rocky precipice at the north shore of the Sea of Galilee.[18]

Peter's confession and Jesus' pronouncement may have been uttered in either AD 29 or 30. If this is not a mere coincidence, then Jesus may have ironically declared that his lead disciple, Simon Peter, who happens to be a native of Bethsaida, will build something much greater than what a sycophantic supporter of the Roman cult intends to build, something that the very gates of Hades cannot stop. It is important to note that support for the divinisation of Julia Livia was a very important part of confirming and prolonging the cult of the divine Caesar that Augustus had worked so hard to establish. Whether or not Tiberius, son of Livia, believed in this cult (and he had no personal interest in divinising his late mother) is difficult to say.

*Passion predictions.* Prior to entry into Jerusalem, where Jesus will be seized and crucified, he made three formal predictions of his passion. Unlike Roman emperors who are warned of approaching danger through dreams or omens, which are very much open to interpretation, Jesus predicts his passion without ambiguity. In the case of Alexander the Great a voice in India spoke from a tree. Reluctant translators explain that the voice has foretold the fate of the conqueror, informing him that he will not return to his mother but will die in Babylon.[19] In the third prediction, Jesus tells his frightened disciples, 'Behold, we are going up to Jerusalem; and the Son of man will be delivered to the chief priests and the scribes, and they will condemn him to death, and deliver him to the Gentiles; and they will mock him, and spit upon him, and scourge him, and kill him; and after three days he will rise' (Mark 10:33–34). No one needs to explain an omen to Jesus, or to warn him; Jesus knows what is coming and is prepared for it. The same is seen in his prayer in Gethsemane, when he prays, 'Abba,

---

18 There is no evidence yet of a temple at Bethsaida built in honour of Julia Livia, though archaeologist Rami Arav has identified an older building that may have been used as a temple for this purpose. In this building an incense shovel and an image of Livia with her distinctive hair arrangement were recovered. See Strickert, 'The Renaming of Bethsaida'; McNamer, 'Philip, Julia, and the Imperial Cult'.
19 Ps.-Callisthenes, *The Life and Deeds of Alexander* 3.17.7–11.

Father, all things are possible for you; remove this cup from me; yet not what I will, but what you will' (Mark 14:36).

*Transfiguration.* Romans believed that following death heroic men were sometimes transformed into gods. This was called *apotheōsis*. There are also stories about the sudden and unexpected transfiguration of gods or goddesses. In one of these stories the goddess Demeter disguised herself as an old woman and served as a nurse for a royal family. She later gave up her disguise and 'changed her stature and her looks ... beauty spread round about her and a lovely fragrance was wafted from her sweet-smelling robes, and from the divine body of the goddess a light shone ... so that the strong house was filled with brightness as of lightning'.[20]

Jesus is transformed, or experiences a form of *apotheōsis*, prior to his death.[21] The description we find in the Gospels is similar to what was said of the goddess Demeter: Jesus 'was transfigured before them, and his garments became glistening, intensely white, as no fuller on earth could bleach them' (Mark 9:2–3); 'he was transfigured before them, and his face shone like the sun, and his garments became white as light' (Matt. 17:2); 'the appearance of his countenance was altered, and his raiment became dazzling white' (Luke 9:29).

*To serve or be served?* When his disciples complain of the requests made by James and John, Jesus calls together his disciples and tells them:

> You know that those who are supposed to rule over the Gentiles lord it over them, and their great men exercise authority over them. But it shall not be so among you; but whoever would be great among you must be your servant, and whoever would be first among you must be slave of all. For the Son of man also came not to be served but to serve, and to give his life as a ransom for many (Mark 10:42–45).

---

20 *Homeric Hymn* 2 to Demeter. Cf. Callimachus, *Hymn* 6 to Demeter: 'Demeter ... put on her goddess shape. Her steps touched the earth, but her head reached to Olympus. And they [the men felling the trees of her sacred grove], half-dead when they beheld the lady goddess, rushed suddenly away ...'. Cf. the second-century *Gospel of Peter*, where we are told that the head of Jesus surpassed the clouds when he emerged from the tomb (*Gos. Pet.* 10.40).
21 Recently it has been suggested that the transfiguration of Jesus was understood as a 'preview' of his Easter *apotheōsis*. See Burkett, 'The Transfiguration of Jesus (Mark 9:2–8)'.

In the parallel passage in Luke, Jesus says:

> The kings of the Gentiles exercise lordship over them; and those in authority over them are called benefactors. But not so with you; rather let the greatest among you become as the youngest, and the leader as one who serves. For which is the greater, one who sits at table, or one who serves? Is it not the one who sits at table? But I am among you as one who serves (Luke 22:25–27).

In the Markan passage, Jesus has subverted Daniel 7:13–14, in which the figure 'like a son of man' appears before God: 'And to him was given dominion and glory and kingdom, that all peoples, nations, and languages should serve him; his dominion is an everlasting dominion, which shall not pass away, and his kingdom one that shall not be destroyed' (v.14). No free person wished to be a slave.[22] All Roman emperors claim in one sense or another to serve the people or serve the state. A popular way of expressing this is to claim to be a 'benefactor' (εὐεργέτης). The version in Luke speaks directly to this when Jesus begins his teaching by saying, 'The kings of the Gentiles exercise lordship over them; and those in authority over them are called benefactors [εὐεργέται]. But not so with you ...'. Unlike Caesar, who lusts for power, Jesus is a true benefactor who saves humans.

*Jesus' entrance into Jerusalem.* Known as the Triumphal Entry, Jesus' entrance into Jerusalem, which began what became known as Passion Week, parallels a number of entrances of prominent persons into Jerusalem or other cities. Years ago David Catchpole cited twelve examples of celebrated entries, six from 1 and 2 Maccabees, and six from Josephus, of a 'more or less fixed pattern of entry'.[23] Entries involving major figures include Alexander who enters Jerusalem, is greeted with ceremony, and is escorted into the city where he participates in cultic activity (*Ant.* 11.325–339); Apollonius who enters Jerusalem accompanied by torches and shouts (2 Macc. 4:21–22);

---

22  Aristotle, *Nic. Eth.* 10.6 (1177a); Philo, *Prob.* 60; Epictetus, *Diatr.* 4.1.33: 'the slave wishes to be set free'.
23  Catchpole, 'Entry'.

Judas Maccabeus who returns home from a military victory and is greeted with hymns and 'praising God' (1 Macc. 4:19–25; Josephus, *Ant.* 12.312); Judas Maccabeus, again, who returns from battle and enters Jerusalem amidst singing and merrymaking, followed by sacrifice (1 Macc. 5:45–54; *Ant.* 348–349); Jonathan brother of Judas, who is greeted by the men of Askalon 'with great pomp' (1 Macc. 10:86); Simon brother of Judas, who enters Gaza, expels idolatrous inhabitants, cleanses idolatrous houses, and enters the city 'with hymns and praise' (1 Macc. 13:43–48); Simon brother of Judas, again, who enters Jerusalem and is met by crowds 'with praise and palm branches, and with harps and cymbals and stringed instruments and with hymns and songs' (1 Macc. 13:49–51); Antigonus who with pomp enters Jerusalem, then the Temple precincts, but with so much pomp and self-importance he is criticised by some for imagining that he himself was 'king' (*J.W.* 1.73–74; *Ant.* 13.304–306); Marcus Agrippa who enters Jerusalem, is met by Herod, and is welcomed by the people with acclamations (*Ant.* 16.12–15); and Archelaus who, hoping to confirm his kingship, journeys to and enters Jerusalem amidst acclamation of his procession (*Ant.* 17.194–239).

The elements that make up this pattern include: (a) 'A victory already achieved and a status already recognised for the central person'. (b) 'A formal and ceremonial entry'. (c) 'Greetings and/or acclamations together with invocations of God'. (d) 'Entry to the city climaxed by entry to the Temple, if the city in question has one'. (e) 'Cultic activity, either positive (e.g. offering of sacrifice), or negative (e.g. expulsion of objectionable persons and the cleansing away of uncleanness)'. Catchpole remarks:

> Mark 11 contains all of these major and recurrent features. It also contains minor agreements with occasional features of some of the other stories, for example, the reference to the royal animal ... Mark's story thus conforms to a familiar pattern in respect of both its determinative shape and some of its incidental details.[24]

---

24  Catchpole, 'Entry', 321.

We might add one more to Catchpole's list. Roman hearers of the honour extended to Jesus might think of Cato. In Plutarch we read:

> When the time of Cato's military service came to an end, he was sent on his way, not with blessings, as is common, nor yet with praise, but with tears and insatiable embraces, the soldiers casting their mantles down for him to walk upon, kissing his hands, things which the Romans of that day rarely did, and only to a few of their imperators.[25]

*Cursing the fruitless fig tree.* On his way to the temple precincts Jesus sees a fig tree in full leaf. He approaches the tree hoping to find something to eat but is disappointed. 'May no one ever eat fruit from you again!' says Jesus (Mark 11:14). The tree withers (either immediately, as in Matthew; or the next day, as is implied in Mark's version of the story) ἐκ ῥιζῶν, 'from its roots'. We are reminded of the death of the laurel trees that over the years the Julio-Claudian family had planted. The 'whole grove died', says Suetonius, 'from the root up [*silva omnis exaruit radicitus*]'.[26] Some readers of Mark's story of the cursed and withered fig tree probably thought of the report of the death of the imperial grove. Those who did would have been struck by the contrast. For the death of the imperial grove signified the end of the imperial line—in power for a full century. But in the case of Jesus it was Jesus himself who caused the tree to die, a tree that represented the temple establishment that sought his death.

*Taxes.* Jesus is asked about paying taxes to Caesar. His response, 'Render to Caesar the things that are Caesar's, and to God the things that are God's' (Mark 12:17), clearly implies a dichotomy between Caesar and God. To render what belongs to one is not to render to the other. In the Roman mind Caesar is a representative of God (or the gods). Indeed, he is high priest. Loyalty to Caesar, which includes faithfully paying his taxes, is loyalty to God. Jesus' reply undermines that assumption.[27]

---

25  Plutarch, *Parallel Lives*, 'Life of Cato the Younger', 12.
26  Suetonius, *Galba* 1.
27  Carter, 'Paying the Tax to Rome'.

*'What is the sign of your coming?'* The question raised by the disciples in Matthew 24:3 will make most readers think of the idea of the emperor's παρουσία or *adventus* (e.g. Polybius, *Hist.* 18.48.4). Nero issued *adventus* coins, probably as part of the Golden Age renewed.

*The abomination that makes desolate.* Jesus warns of a coming 'abomination' that makes the temple, presumably, desolate or no longer fit for sacred function (Matt. 24:15; Mark 13:14). The language comes from Daniel and the Hasmonean struggle. But Caligula's attempt to place his image in the temple may also be in view. More will be said about this below. Jesus warns his disciples, 'For as the lightning comes from the east and shines as far as the west, so will be the coming of the Son of Man' (Matt. 24:27), and then adds cryptically, 'Wherever the body is, there the eagles will be gathered together' (Matt. 24:28; cf. Luke 17:37). Commentators think the 'eagles' could allude to the Roman standards.[28] If so, Jesus has cast Rome into the role of a power that will come into play in the day of judgement. It has also been suggested that in the analogy of the lightning that 'comes from the east and shine as far as the west' Jesus may have hinted that Rome, the power in the west, will be overtaken by a greater power from the east.[29] Lightning was regarded in Roman superstition as a very significant omen, often indicating regime change.[30]

*You see the Son of Man coming with the clouds of heaven.* Jesus' appeal to Daniel 7:13 in his response to the high priest's question, 'Are you the Messiah, the Son of the Blessed?' (Mark 14:61–62), suggests that Jesus understood himself as the human figure described in Daniel's vision. If so, then Jesus envisions himself as the one who will execute God's judgement on the fourth kingdom, now understood as Rome not Macedonia or Greece. It has already been noted that Josephus in the first century believed that the fourth and final evil human kingdom, that will be destroyed by the messianic stone, is Rome, not

---

28  Josephus, *J.W.* 3.123: The ensign with an image of an eagle 'precedes every legion … an omen of victory'.
29  Carter, *Matthew and the Margins*, 476.
30  A German soothsayer tells Domitian that recent lightning portends the emperor's death (Suetonius, *Domitian* 16.1). This is ironic, for Domitian had lightning depicted on some of the coins he issued. Regime change has taken place in heaven, for elsewhere Jesus says, 'I saw Satan fall from heaven like lightning' (Luke 10:18).

Greece. Jesus' reply to Caiaphas not only implies that he will come at God's right hand on his chariot throne (Daniel 7 + Ps. 110) in judgement on Caiaphas and his corrupt colleagues, it also implies that he will bring an end to the era of Gentile domination, which means an end to Roman dominion.

*The Passion as subversion of the Roman triumph.* It has been suggested that the Passion narrative is told as an ironic subversion of the Roman triumph.[31] The climax of the crucifixion scene is found in the centurion's confession, 'Truly this man was son of God [υἱὸς θεοῦ]' (Mark 15:39). The centurion's confession recalls the imperial cult, in which Caesar is hailed as 'son of god'. The centurion ascribes to Jesus what he had earlier ascribed to Caesar: Caesar is not υἱὸς θεοῦ or *divi filius* ('son of God', alluding to the title of the great emperor Augustus), Jesus is.[32]

*The resurrection and ascension of Jesus.* The discovery of the empty tomb and the appearance of the risen Jesus to several of his followers would have impressed Romans as an extraordinary example of the *apotheōsis* of a divine or righteous man. One will recall the rumour that arose that Julius Caesar ascended into the heavens as a comet.[33]

## *The Evangelists*

The evangelists themselves frame their respective stories of Jesus in ways that sharpen the parallels and contrasts with the Roman imperial cult. I shall limit my discussion to Mark's incipit and the Matthean and Lukan infancy narratives.

*Mark 1:1.* Mark begins his Gospel with the well-known incipit: ἀρχὴ τοῦ εὐαγγελίου Ἰησοῦ Χριστοῦ υἱοῦ θεοῦ, 'The beginning of the gospel of Jesus Christ, the Son of God'. (Without argument here, I affirm the originality of the longer reading—all early manuscripts have it,

---

31 Schmidt, 'Mark 15.16–32: The Crucifixion Narrative and the Roman Triumphal Procession'.
32 Kim, 'The Anarthrous υἱὸς θεοῦ in Mark 15,39'; Winter, *Divine Honours for the Caesars*, 63–71. Both Kim and Winter rightly note the significance of the centurion's anarthrous υἱὸς θεοῦ, in contrast to the Christian habit of speaking of Jesus as ὁ υἱὸς θεοῦ, 'the Son of God'.
33 Suetonius, *Julius* 88.1. Plutarch says people reported that 'amazing signs and apparitions [σημεῖα θαυμαστὰ καὶ φάσματα] were seen', such as 'lights in the heavens, crashing sounds borne all about by night, and birds of omen [ὄρνιθας] coming down into the forum' (*Caesar* 63.1–2).

including Codex Sinaiticus, whose support for the shorter reading is often cited in a misleading manner.[34]) Many commentators have rightly noted the parallel with the imperial cult, especially as expressed in the birthday calendar of 9 BC in honour of Augustus. His birth was the beginning of the good news for the world; and he is a 'god' and 'son of god'.

Mark's incipit directly challenges the imperial cult in that the evangelist declares that the good news, or gospel, begins with Jesus the Messiah, the Son of God, not with Augustus, whose successors are no more divine than he was. At the beginning of this chapter it was noted that the successors of Augustus did not live up to the ideals that the emperor envisioned and that only one of his successors, at the time the Gospel of Mark was published, had been divinised and even then only half-heartedly and in time ignored altogether. The Markan evangelist's bold claim that Jesus was the (genuine) Son of God, in whom the good news truly does begin, was a bold challenge to the imperial cult and its attempt to appropriate the ancient eschatology that envisioned a return of a Golden Age, when the wickedness of humanity would finally be remedied and humanity would finally be restored. The evangelist Mark not only challenged the Roman idea by identifying Jesus as the true Son of God, he also defined the good news, or gospel, in the proclamation of Isaiah and the ancient Scriptures of Israel.

*Omens in the Gospel birth narratives.* The Roman imperial cult was also challenged in the Matthean and Lukan birth narratives.[35] I will provide a sample of potential parallels from the Gospel of Matthew.

There are relatively few omens, strictly speaking, in the birth narratives of the Gospels of Matthew and Luke, but there are several features that nevertheless would have been viewed by Jew and Gentile alike as presaging Jesus' greatness. Commentators rightly call attention to approximate parallels with stories told about the birth of Octavian, who later will become Emperor Augustus.[36] Suetonius, writing a few decades after the evangelists Matthew and Luke, remarks in reference

---

34 For compelling argument in favour of the longer reading, see Wasserman, 'The "Son of God"'.
35 I explore several examples in, 'Romulus, Roman Omens, and the Portents of the Birth and Passion of Jesus'.
36 Talbert, *Reading Luke*, 16–17. Talbert succinctly sums up the components in the respective infancy narratives of Octavian and Jesus.

to Octavian that 'it will not be out of place to add an account of the omens which occurred before he was born, on the very day of his birth, and afterwards, from which it was possible to anticipate and perceive his future greatness'.[37] The evangelists could have said the same in reference to Jesus of Nazareth. In fact, that is what Matthew and Luke have done; they have added an account of the strange and marvellous events that took place before the birth of Jesus, the day of his birth, and the time that followed.

In Matthew, Mary is found to be with child before the consummation of her marriage to Joseph (Matt. 1:18). An angel of the Lord appears to Joseph in a dream (ἄγγελος κυρίου κατ' ὄναρ ἐφάνη αὐτῷ), informing him that her pregnancy is of the Holy Spirit (1:20). Joseph is told that Mary will bear a son, who will be called Jesus, because (playing on the meaning of *Jesus*, or Yeshu'a, 'the Lord saves') 'he will save his people from their sins' (1:21). This dream is not called an omen or sign, but this is how it would have been understood by Jews, Greeks, and Romans in late antiquity. What Joseph is told fulfils an ancient prophecy (1:22–23; i.e. Isa. 7:14).

Mary's unexpected pregnancy is not called a miracle or omen as such, but that is how it would have been viewed, at least by those who took the story seriously. We think of Julius Caesar's dream, interpreted by some to the effect that he would one day rule the world.[38] Caesar also claimed that he descended from the goddess Venus on his father's side.[39] In the second century AD the adventurer and trickster Alexander of Abonoteichus claimed that his father was none other than Zeus.[40] For Matthew, of course, Mary's miraculous conception fulfils Jewish Scripture, not pagan mythology.

Magi come to Jerusalem seeking the one 'born king of the Jews', for they 'have seen his star' and so 'have come to worship him' (Matt. 2:1–2). Those familiar with Israel's ancient Scriptures would probably think of Balaam's mysterious oracle about the star that will go forth from Jacob (Num. 24:17), an oracle that in Jewish and Christian

---

37 *Divus Augustus* 94.1. Translation based on Rolfe, *Suetonius*, Volume I, 287.
38 Suetonius, *Julius* 7.2.
39 Suetonius, *Julius* 6.1; Marcus Velleius Paterculus, *Historiae* 2.41.1.
40 *Apud* Lucian, *Alexander pseudomantis* 7.

traditions alike was understood in messianic terms. Prophecies and omens about stars, signifying the fall and rise of kings and kingdoms, were not limited to Jewish tradition but reached back to the ancient Near East and by the time of Augustus and Jesus were widespread in the Roman world. For example, Suetonius says: 'There had spread all over the Orient an old and established belief that it was fated at that time for men coming from Judea to rule the world ...'.[41]

It is interesting, too, to note that the magi of Matthew do not utter prophecies or offer counsel (which often happens in the stories about the Roman emperors). No *haruspex*, 'dream interpreter', explains anything to Joseph or Mary. In seeing the star, the magi deduce (how, we are not sure[42]) that the 'king of the Jews' has been born (Matt. 2:2), but when they see the holy family we are only told that they rejoiced and offered gifts (2:10–11). The magi are then warned in a dream to return home by a different route (2:12).

Comets, or 'long-tailed stars', were usually interpreted as omens portending the death of various Roman emperors. In Matthew the star portends the birth of a new king of the Jews, to be sure, but from a Roman point of view the star portended the imminent death of the reigning king. Apparently that is how Herod the Great perceived it. We should assume that however knowledgeable of Jewish Scripture and interpretation Herod might have been, his understanding of the world, which would have included the meaning of omens, would have been very Roman. The birth of Jesus and the accompanying star constituted a serious threat from his point of view, for these events implied that Herod will soon die and that his dynasty will come to an end. Long-tailed stars or comets, says astrologer Claudius Ptolemy, means a king or a prince 'will die'.[43] Herod probably understood the star the same way, so it was no wonder that in Matthew's narrative world the ageing, fearful monarch desired to kill the infant Jesus in a desperate bid to cancel the omen and hopefully prolong his life. (The parents of

---

41 Suetonius, *Vespasianus* 4.5. See van Henten, 'The World Leader from the Land of the Jews'; Jacobus, 'Balaam's "Star Oracle" (Num 24:15–19)'; and Newman, 'Stars of the Messiah'.
42 In my view their deduction is dependent, at least in part, on the mysterious oracles of Numbers 24, mentioned above, as well as the ancient prophecy in Micah 5.
43 *Centiloquy* §100; cf. *Sib. Or.* 3:334–336.

Vitellius attempt to avert the omen regarding their son.[44] Nero has several prominent men murdered to annul an omen.[45])

Like the magi, Joseph is also warned in a dream to flee to Egypt (Matt. 2:13). After Herod dies, 'an angel of the Lord appeared in a dream to Joseph in Egypt', commanding him to return to the land of Israel (2:19–20). Joseph is again warned in a dream to relocate to Galilee, in the village of Nazareth (2:22–23). Six times in the Gospel of Matthew people are instructed or warned in dreams. Four times Joseph is warned. The magi were warned once and the wife of Pontius Pilate the governor will also be warned regarding Jesus (27:19). Dreams were commonplace in the stories of Rome's emperors.[46] In the Jewish world, of course, dreams involving men named Joseph are not unknown.[47]

Herod attempts to nullify the omen of the star and birth of the infant in Bethlehem by slaughtering all recently-born youths. Commentators rightly point out the potential parallel in the story of Octavian (Augustus), in which it was remembered that a 'portent' had been observed in Rome, which was interpreted as signifying that a woman was about to give birth to a man who would rule over Rome as a king. The senate decreed that 'no male child born that year should be raised'.[48] It is likely that many readers of the Gospel of Matthew would have been aware that Herod and Augustus had been friends and had been mutually supportive. The approximate parallel between the threatened infancy of Octavian and the threatened infancy of Jesus, at the hands of Herod, would have been appreciated by many. And as just mentioned above, Nero attempted to nullify omens (*ostenta*) portending his death by assassinating several distinguished men.[49] Examples such as these show how seriously omens were taken, even by the educated elite.

---

44  Suetonius, *Vitellius* 3.2.
45  Suetonius, *Nero* 36.2.
46  E.g. Julius Caesar's dream, in Suetonius, *Julius* 81.3; his wife's dream, in Plutarch, *Caesar* 63.5–6; the dream of Octavian's mother regarding his birth, in Suetonius, *Augustus* 94.4; et al.
47  E.g. Joseph in Genesis 40—41; cf. Josephus in *J.W.* 3.351–353. Josephus took great interest in the dream stories of Joseph, son of Jacob, recounting them at length (*Ant.* 2.11–86). See the major study of Josephus and dreams in Gnuse, *Dreams and Dream Reports in the Writings of Josephus*.
48  Suetonius, *Augustus* 94.3.
49  Suetonius, *Nero* 36.1–2.

The Passion narratives contain a number of omens that inhabitants of late antique Rome would have appreciated, especially in reference to great men. This belief is expressed in reference to an eclipse that occurred as Pelopidas prepared his army for battle: '[T]he sun was eclipsed and the city was dark [σκότος] in the daytime ... for it was supposed to be a great sign from heaven with regard to a conspicuous man'.[50] All three of the Synoptic Gospels speak of darkness while Jesus was on the cross: 'Now from the sixth hour there was darkness [σκότος] over all the land [ἐπὶ πᾶσαν τὴν γῆν] until the ninth hour' (Matt. 27:45; cf. Mark 15:33; Luke 23:44–45a).[51] Plutarch tells us that after the death of Julius Caesar, the sun's rays were dim. 'For during all that year its orb rose pale and without radiance, while the heat that came down from it was slight and ineffectual, so that the air in its circulation was dark and heavy owing to the feebleness of the warmth that penetrated it ...'.[52] Diogenes Laertius tells us that when the philosopher Carneades died, 'the moon is said to have been eclipsed ... the brightest luminary in heaven next to the sun thereby gave token of her sympathy'.[53]

Darkness over the land as an omen either in anticipation of death or after death has occurred was a belief that reached back to ancient times. Legend had it that 'there was a total eclipse of the sun and a general darkness [σκότος] as in the night covered the earth [τὴν γῆν]' when the mother of Romulus was violated and 'that at his death the same thing happened'.[54]

As already noted, the sun grew dark when Julius Caesar died.[55] Late

---

50  Plutarch, *Pelopidas* 31.2–3. Translation based on B. Perrin, *Plutarch, Lives: Agesilaus and Pompey, Pelopidas and Marcellus*, 421. As it turned out, the eclipse was not a positive omen, for Pelopidas was shortly thereafter killed in battle. Note, too, that this eclipse was called ἐξ οὐρανοῦ ... σημεῖον, 'a sign from heaven', as in Mark 8:11 (σημεῖον ἀπὸ τοῦ οὐρανοῦ).
51  Luke adds, apparently by way of explanation, 'while the sun's light failed'. The fourth Gospel says nothing about darkness. The Synoptic tradition of darkness is embellished in the second-century narratives found in the *Gospel of Peter* (5:15, 18) and *Acts of Pilate* (11:1–2).
52  Plutarch, *Caesar* 69.3–4. Translation from Perrin, *Plutarch Lives: Demosthenes and Cicero, Alexander and Caesar*, 607.
53  Diogenes Laertius, *Vita Philosophorum* 4.64. Hicks, *Diogenes Laertius I*, 441.
54  Dionysius of Halicarnassus, *Antiquitates romanae* 2.56.6. Translation based on Cary, *Dionysius of Halicarnassus: Roman Antiquities I*, 475. See also Cicero, *De re publica* 6.22; Ovid, *Fasti* 2.493; Plutarch, *Romulus* 27.6.
55  Virgil, *Georgica* 1.467–468.

antique Jewish ideas about darkness were similar. The ninth plague against Egypt was darkness. Exodus says that 'there was a thick darkness [σκότος γνόφος]⁵⁶ in all the land [ἐπὶ πᾶσαν γῆν] of Egypt three days', though the Israelites had light (Exod. 10:21–23).⁵⁷ Some of the language and ideas about darkness and solar eclipses are reflected in Philo's retelling of the ninth plague. He says that 'a plague arose greater than all that had gone before; for, in bright daylight, darkness was suddenly overspread [ἐξαπιναίως ἀναχεῖται σκότος], possibly because there was an eclipse of the sun more completely than the ordinary ...'⁵⁸

According to the Synoptic tradition, when Jesus died, the 'curtain of the temple was torn in two, from top to bottom' (Matt. 27:51a; cf. Mark 15:38; Luke 23:45). Matthew adds that 'the earth shook, and the rocks were split' (27:51b); so also on Sunday, the day of the resurrection, 'there was a great earthquake' (28:2). As already mentioned, damage to buildings, statues, and other structures is another omen or indicator of the presence of a deity. Similarly when Jesus dies, the curtain of the Jerusalem temple was torn. (Which curtain is in view and how it could be seen from Golgotha is debated.⁵⁹) In Jewish tradition the story of the tearing of the temple curtain seems to be unique.⁶⁰ The portents described in Josephus (*J.W.* 6.293–296), in the apocryphal

---

56  Lit. 'a dark darkness'.
57  Mark 15:33 reads ἐφ' ὅλην τὴν γῆν, 'upon the whole land' (followed in Luke 23:44), which in Matt. 27:45 reads, ἐπὶ πᾶσαν τὴν γῆν, 'upon all the land', perhaps as an intentional echo of OG Exod. 10:22.
58  Philo, *De vita Mosis* 1.123. Translation from Colson, *Philo VI*, 339. In Luke 23:45 the darkness is said to have been due to 'the sun's light having failed [ἐκλιπόντος]', that is, having been eclipsed. Both Philo and the evangelist Luke are attempting to explain the darkness.
59  It was probably the inner curtain (cf. LXX Exod. 27:16). It is described in Josephus, *J.W.* 5.207–212. I hardly think it is necessary to conclude that the evangelists thought Golgotha was located on the Mount of Olives; *pace* Jackson, 'The Death of Jesus in Mark', 24–25.
60  The apparent exceptions in *T. Levi* 10:3 and *Vita Prophetarum* 12:12a are probably Christian glosses. On the meaning of the *velum scissum*, the torn curtain, in the Synoptic Gospels, see Gurtner, *The Torn Veil*. Gurtner argues plausibly that the torn curtain is the inner curtain of the temple (not the outer curtain) and that its tearing signifies God's relocation from the sanctuary to his Son Jesus. For Matthew, this is the significance of the prophecy fulfilled in Jesus ('the Lord saves'): Immanuel, 'God with us' (Matt. 1:23).

life of Habakkuk and in Tacitus, say nothing about the curtain.[61] In later Christian tradition the temple building itself is damaged.[62]

Earthquakes, strikes of lightning, and damaged buildings were also seen as omens in the Graeco-Roman world.[63] Herodotus remarks that there had been such a long run of bad luck in Greece, 'it was no marvel that there should be an earthquake [κινηθῆναι] in Delos when there had been none before.'[64]

More importantly, earthquakes were often linked to theophanies. This is seen in Old Testament and ancient Near Eastern literatures (Exod. 19:18: When Yahweh descended on Sinai 'the whole mountain quaked greatly'; 1 Kgs 19:11–12; Job 9:6; Ps. 18:7; 77:18; 97:4; Isa. 6:4; 24:20; Joel 3:16; Hag. 2:6).[65] It is also seen in the classic tradition, as in the appearance of Apollo,[66] the appearance of Dionysus,[67] the appearance of Mars,[68] and the appearance of Asclepius.[69] It is in response to the darkness, the shout of Jesus, and the tearing of the temple curtain that the Roman centurion exclaims, ἀληθῶς οὗτος ὁ ἄνθρωπος υἱὸς θεοῦ ἦν, 'Truly this man was son of god' (Mark 15:39). The centurion's anarthrous υἱὸς θεοῦ, as noted above, is the equivalent of the Latin *filius dei* or (more usually) *divi filius*, in reference to the

---

61 *Vita Prophetarum* 12:12; Tacitus, *Historiae* 5.13. Josephus refers to the eastern gate found open morning after morning, which frightens the priests, while Tacitus speaks of 'gates'. *Vita Prophetarum* 12:12 says, 'the capitals of the two pillars will be taken away'. The omens against the temple, especially those in reference to the gate(s), appear in later rabbinic literature (e.g. *y. Sota* 6.3; *b. Yoma* 39b).
62 *Gospel of the Nazarenes, apud* Jerome, *Epistula* 120 [*ad Hedibian*]). Jerome writes: 'But in the Gospel that is written in Hebrew characters we read not that the curtain of the temple was torn, but that the lintel of the temple of wondrous size collapsed'. This tradition is repeated elsewhere in Jerome and in other Christian writings.
63 E.g. Plutarch, *Antonius* 60.2; Suetonius, *Tiberius* 74; *Galba* 18.2.
64 Herodotus, *Historiae* 6.98.3 Translation from Clarke, *Shaping the Geography of Empire*, 268. Herodotus literally says, 'a shaking' or 'a movement'. See also cf. Thucydides, *Historiae* 3.89.1–2, who reports that σεισμῶν δὲ γενομένων πολλῶν ... τῶν σεισμῶν κατεχόντων, 'many earthquakes occurring ... earthquakes kept happening'.
65 In a Sumerian hymn, King Shulgi declares, 'On that day, the storm howled, the tempest swirled, Northwind (and) Southwind roared eagerly, Lightning devoured in heaven alongside the seven winds, The deafening storm made the earth tremble' (*Hymn of Shulgi* 62–65). Translation from Pritchard, *Ancient Near Eastern Texts Relating to the Old Testament*, 586.
66 E.g. Callimachus, *Hymn* 1 to Apollinem: 'How the shrine shakes [ἐσείσατο]!'
67 E.g. Euripides, *Bacchae* 585–593: 'Shake [σεῖε] the world's floor, you spirit of earthquake ...!'
68 E.g. Publius Papinius Statius, *Thebais* 7.65: 'the earth quakes [*tremit*]' at the approach of the god.
69 E.g. Ovid, *Metamorphoses* 15.671–672: 'at his coming the statue, altars, doors, the marble pavement and gilded roof, all rocked'.

emperor.⁷⁰ The epiphanic qualities of the risen Jesus are exaggerated in second-century literature.⁷¹

The Matthean evangelist adds two conspicuous omens, one ordinary and the other extraordinary. The ordinary omen is the report of Pilate's wife's dream. She warns her husband: 'Have nothing to do with that righteous man, for I have suffered much over him today in a dream' (27:19). Pilate's wife sent word of her dream to her husband, when he had sat down on the judgement seat (ἐπὶ τοῦ βήματος). Many readers will be reminded of Julius Caesar's wife's dream⁷² and her urging her husband to seek divine guidance.⁷³ In the context of Matthew's Gospel, where God has previously warned Joseph and the magi through dreams, Pilate's wife's dream would be understood as a message from God and therefore a divine witness that Jesus was indeed 'righteous' and not deserving of condemnation. Alas, for Caesar and Pilate; neither heeded the warnings of their wives' dreams. For Caesar this meant assassination; for Pilate it meant an ignominious suicide.⁷⁴

Matthew also relates an extraordinary omen. Matthew, and Matthew alone, narrates the story of the saints who are raised up when Jesus dies:

> And behold, the curtain of the temple was torn in two, from top to bottom; and the earth shook, and the rocks were split; ⁵² the tombs also were opened, and many bodies of the saints who had fallen asleep were raised, ⁵³ and coming out of the tombs after his resurrection they went into the holy city and appeared to many. ⁵⁴ When the centurion and those who were with him, keeping watch over Jesus, saw the earthquake and what took place, they were filled with awe, and said, 'Truly this was the Son of God!' (27:51–54).

70 E.g, BGU 628; SB 401. See also n.32 above.
71 E.g. *Descensus Christi ad Inferos* 5:1.
72 Plutarch, *Caesar* 63.5–6; cf. Suetonius, *Julius* 81.3; Velleius Paterculus, *Historiae* 2.57.1–2.
73 Plutarch, *Caesar* 63.6.
74 Eusebius reports that not long after his removal from office Pilate committed suicide (*Hist. eccl.* 2.7.1). In Byzantine and Medieval apocrypha (e.g. *Cura sanitatis Tiberii*, *Mors Pilati*, and *Vindicta Salvatoris*) the suicide of Pilate is described in lurid and fantastic terms. According to *Mors Pilati*, demons haunt the corpse of Pilate and terrify people. One thinks of the hasty burial of the assassinated Caligula in the gardens of the Lamian family, after which they were haunted by ghosts and fearsome apparitions (Suetonius, *Caligula* 59). On the traditions of Pilate's suicide, see Grüll, 'The Legendary Fate of Pontius Pilate'.

Matthew has inserted vv.51b–53 into the material he finds in Mark (that is, between verses 38 and 39 in Mark 15). The earthquake explains the tearing of the curtain (which appears in Mark but without explanation). The earthquake also splits rocks and breaks open tombs, thus allowing 'many bodies' (πολλὰ σώματα) of dead 'holy ones' (ἁγίων), or saints, to arise and exit their tombs. This of course creates a theological problem, for the resurrection of Jesus constitutes the 'first fruits of those who have fallen asleep' (cf. 1 Cor. 15:20, 23; Col. 1:18 'firstborn from the dead'). Jesus dies on Friday and is raised on Sunday; but the dead saints are raised *on Friday*, thus in a sense making *them not Jesus* the first fruits of those who have fallen asleep. The evangelist or a later copyist tries to remedy the problem by adding at the beginning of Matthew 27:53 the qualifying phrase, μετὰ τὴν ἔγερσιν αὐτοῦ, 'after his resurrection'.[75] But this gloss really does not solve the problem, for saints were still raised up *before* Jesus, whenever they exit their tombs. The gloss, moreover, creates a new problem, for we are to imagine the raised saints loitering in their tombs from Friday afternoon until Sunday morning when they finally emerge.

Although it is debated, Matthew 27:52–53 as a whole may represent an early gloss that attempts to narrate the Harrowing of Hades, in which Jesus rescues the righteous dead.[76] This idea is probably expressed in 1 Peter: 'For Christ also died for sins ... that he might bring us to God, being put to death in the flesh but made alive in the spirit; [19] in which he went and preached to the spirits in prison' (3:18–19; cf. 4:6 'the gospel was preached even to the dead, that though judged in the flesh like men, they might live in the spirit like God').

---

75 E.g. Allen, *A Critical and Exegetical Commentary on the Gospel according to St. Matthew*, 296 (added by the evangelist); Klostermann, *Das Matthäusevangelium*, 225 (a later scribal gloss inspired by 1 Cor. 15:20; Col. 1:18). Several recent commentaries and studies have taken one or other of these positions.
76 For two competent studies that argue against seeing Matt. 27:53a as gloss or an interpolation, or the whole of 27:52–53 as an interpolation, see Quarles, 'Μετὰ τὴν ἔγερσιν αὐτοῦ'; Quarles, 'Matthew 27:51–53: Meaning, Genre Intertextuality, Theology, and Reception History'. In agreement with Quarles, I concede that there is virtually no early manuscript evidence in support of proposed glosses or interpolations. However, it should be noted that Matt. 27:51b–53 does not appear in the *Gospel of Peter* (mid-second century), which otherwise relies heavily on Matthean material in its distinctive Passion narrative.

Several early Christian texts appear to presuppose the tradition.[77]

## Part 2: Paul and the Epistles

In several places Paul implicitly criticises the Roman cult of the divine emperor. In 1 Thessalonians 4 he appropriates the Hellenistic tradition, which the Romans have appropriated, of the celebrated general or monarch who enters a city in victory. The people go out to meet the hero and accompany him on the remainder of his journey. In 1 Thessalonians 5 Paul warns the faithful of coming danger, when those in darkness speak of 'peace and safety', which the emperor supposedly guarantees. Not so, says Paul, destruction will come upon them suddenly.

In 2 Thessalonians 2 Paul corrects rumours and misinformation relating to the 'apostasy' and the 'man of lawlessness'. Paul says:

> Let no one deceive you in any way; for that day will not come, unless the rebellion comes first, and the man of lawlessness is revealed, the son of perdition, who opposes and exalts himself against every so-called god or object of worship, so that he takes his seat in the temple of God, proclaiming himself to be God (2 Thess. 2:3–4).

The apostle goes on to say of the 'son of perdition' that 'the Lord Jesus will slay him with the breath of his mouth and destroy him by his appearing and his coming' (1 Thess. 2:8). Paul speaks of παρουσία, 'coming' or 'presence', which in Latin is *adventus*. In exalted contexts

---

77 E.g. Eph. 4:8–10: 'In saying, "He ascended", what does it mean but that he had also descended into the lower parts of the earth?'; *Gos. Pet.* 10:41: 'Have you preached to them that sleep?'; *Mart. Asc. Isa.* 9:17: 'Many of the righteous will ascend with him'; *Odes of Solomon* 42:10–20, esp. v.11: 'Sheol saw me and was shattered, and Death ejected me and many with me'; *Acts of Thomas* 10: 'who went down even to Hades; who also, having opened the doors, brought out from there those who had been shut in for many ages in the treasuries of darkness, and showed them the way that leads up on high'; 32, where Satan says: 'I am he who inhabits and hold the abyss of Tartarus, but the Son of God has wronged me against my will and selected his own out of me'; 156: 'gathered all'. For literature that treats the Harrowing of Hades, see Brown, *The Death of the Messiah*, 2:1127–29; Trumbower, 'Jesus' Descent to the Underworld'; Allison, '"After His Resurrection" (Matt 27,53)'; Frank, 'Christ's Descent to the Underworld in Ancient Ritual and Legend'. For a recent study of the origin and development of the *descensus* tradition, see Charlesworth, 'Exploring the Origins of the *descensus ad inferos*'. The translation of *Odes of Solomon* 42 is from p.379. The translations of *Acts of Thomas* 10, 32 are from Elliott, *The Apocryphal New Testament*, 451, 460.

this is the language of the emperor. When Jesus comes, the wicked emperor will be destroyed.

I believe Paul consciously alludes to the cult of the divine emperor who brings on the Golden Age, when he says in Galatians:

> But when the time had fully come, God sent forth his Son, born of woman, born under the law, ⁵ to redeem those who were under the law, so that we might receive adoption as sons (Gal. 4:4–5).

We hear in this statement a number of points of agreement with the birthday inscription (as in *OGIS* 458), which celebrates the birth of Augustus, asserting that this birth was the will of Providence and that Augustus was in some sense divine.

Because of the limitations of space I can only discuss two more examples from Paul. In exhorting the Philippian Christians to be unified and at peace with one another, Paul says:

> Have this mind among yourselves, which is yours in Christ Jesus, ⁶ who, though he was in the form of God, did not count equality with God a thing to be grasped, ⁷ but emptied himself, taking the form of a servant, being born in the likeness of men. ⁸ And being found in human form he humbled himself and became obedient unto death, even death on a cross. ⁹ Therefore God has highly exalted him and bestowed on him the name which is above every name, ¹⁰ that at the name of Jesus every knee should bow, in heaven and on earth and under the earth, ¹¹ and every tongue confess that Jesus Christ is Lord, to the glory of God the Father (Phil. 2:5–11).

'Grasping' for 'equality with God' (ἴσα θεῷ) was what *apotheōsis* was all about. Every emperor longed to be divinised.[78] Jesus, rather, emptied

---

78 The Greek despots, too, long before the rise of the Roman emperors. An Egyptian inscription reads: 'to all who have honored the savior Ptolemy with honors accorded to gods [ἰσοθέοις]' (*SIG* 390.27 [281 BC]). Three centuries later Germanicus says in reference to his father Tiberius: 'Your acclamations, which for me are offensive and such as are accorded to gods [ἰσοθέους] ... they are appropriate only to him who is actually savior and benefactor of the whole human race, my father' (*Selected Papyri* no. 211 [19 AD]).

himself of power and privilege and did the will of his Father by becoming a slave and dying a slave's death, death on the cross. Crucifixion was, after all, called *servile supplicium*, 'slaves' punishment'. He does this, though he existed in ἐν μορφῇ θεοῦ, 'in the form of God'!

In fulfilling his mission, in serving humanity as a true benefactor, the divine identity of Jesus is recognised. For this reason Paul can rightly apply to Jesus Yahweh texts, as he does here in Philippians 2.[79] Yahweh declares,

> 'To me every knee shall bow, every tongue shall swear" (Isa. 45:23b).

The application of a 'Yahweh text' to Jesus puts his divinity well above the alleged divinity of the emperors.

In another of his Prison Letters Paul, drawing upon older confessional material, says of Jesus:

> He is the image of the invisible God, the first-born of all creation; [16] for in him all things were created, in heaven and on earth, visible and invisible, whether thrones or dominions or principalities or authorities—all things were created through him and for him. [17] He is before all things, and in him all things hold together. [18] He is the head of the body, the church; he is the beginning, the first-born from the dead, that in everything he might be pre-eminent. [19] For in him all the fulness of God was pleased to dwell, [20] and through him to reconcile to himself all things, whether on earth or in heaven, making peace by the blood of his cross (Col. 1:15–20).

Augustus could have only dreamed that such things would be said of him!

---

[79] On this important topic, see Capes, *Old Testament Yahweh Texts in Paul's Christology*; Dunn, *The Theology of Paul the Apostle*, 251–52: 'Most striking of all ... these words in Isaiah are spoken by God ... it was *God* who would be glorified in the confession of *Jesus*'.

## Conclusion

When Jesus was born, Augustus was Rome's emperor. The Golden Age had arrived. The downward cycle of human history had been reversed. The warring iron race had given way to the peace, security, and justice of the gold race. Heaven had given Rome a divine son, a new Aeneas, son of Venus. Humanity's fortunes were beginning to change for the better. The future looked promising. Or so it was hoped. When Jesus began his proclamation of the kingdom of God, Augustus was dead and his unpopular adopted son Tiberius was emperor. The contest between the competing visions of kingdom was now under way.

The mighty colossus that was Rome held the Christian communities in check for three centuries. Critics of the Church scoffed at the absurdity of the notion of a crucified Lord and Saviour. How can he save others when he could not save himself? The critics demanded, instead, allegiance to and faith in the imperator, the commander of legions, the *pontifex maximus* who interceded with the gods on behalf of humanity. But it was the Roman imperial doctrine that in time struck most as absurd, as one corrupt and violent emperor after another was deposed. In the fourth century an imperial family embraced the crucified Lord, and the old doctrine crumbled.

The messianic stone that Daniel envisioned had indeed smashed the dominion of the four pagan kingdoms. All alike—from gold to iron and clay—were shattered and, like chaff blown by the wind, vanished. The point of this study is not to advance Christian triumphalism, but to explore more fully the social and political context of the world—east and west—in which Jesus and the early Church made their appearance. The proclamation of the kingdom was deeply rooted in Israel's ancient Scriptures and prophetic hopes, but it was a proclamation that resonated with and challenged long-held ideas, even if expressed in divergent ways and in many settings. To be better understood, the proclamation of Jesus and the evangelism and apologetics of the early Church must be interpreted in this fuller context.

Craig A. Evans
Houston Christian University

## Bibliography

Allen, W. C. — *A Critical and Exegetical Commentary on the Gospel according to St. Matthew* (ICC; Edinburgh: T & T Clark, 1907).

Allison, D. C. — '"After His Resurrection" (Matt 27,53) and the *descens ad inferos*', in P. Lampe (ed.), *Neutestamentliche Exegese im Dialog: Hermeneutik – Wirkungsgeschichte – Matthäusevangelium. Festschrift für Ulrich Luz zum 70. Geburtstag* (Neukirchen-Vluyn: Neukirchener, 2008), 335–54.

Bolt, P. G. — 'Jesus, the Daimons, and the Dead', in C. A. Evans and A. Z. Wright (eds.), *Gods, Spirits, and Worship in the Greco-Roman World and Early Christianity* (JCT 35, SSEJC 23; London and New York, NY: T&T Clark, 2022), 39–59.

Bolt, P. G. — *Jesus' Defeat of Death: Persuading Mark's Early Readers* (SNTMS 125; Cambridge: Cambridge University Press, 2003).

Brown, R. E. — *The Death of the Messiah: From Gethsemane to the Grave. A Commentary on the Passion Narratives in the Four Gospels* (2 vols., New York, NY: Doubleday, 1994).

Burkett, D. — 'The Transfiguration of Jesus (Mark 9:2–8): Epiphany or Apotheosis?', *JBL* 138 (2019), 413–32.

Capes, D. B. — *Old Testament Yahweh Texts in Paul's Christology* (WUNT II.47; Tübingen: Mohr Siebeck, 1992).

Carter, W. — *Matthew and the Margins: A Socio-Political and Religious Reading* (JSNTSup 204; Sheffield: Sheffield Academic Press, 2000).

Carter, W. — 'Paying the Tax to Rome as Subversive Praxis: Matthew 17:24–27', *JSNT* 76 (1999), 3–31.

Cary, E. — *Dionysius of Halicarnassus: Roman Antiquities I: Books I–II* (LCL 319; Cambridge, MA: Harvard University Press, 1937).

Catchpole, D. R. — 'The "Triumphal" Entry', in E. Bammel and C. F. D. Moule (eds.), *Jesus and the Politics of His Day* (Cambridge: Cambridge University Press, 1984), 319–35.

Charlesworth, J. H. — 'Exploring the Origins of the *descensus ad inferos*', in A. J. Avery-Peck, C. A. Evans, and J. Neusner (eds.), *Earliest Christianity within the Boundaries of Judaism: Essays in Honor of Bruce Chilton* (BRLJ 49; Leiden: Brill, 2016), 372–95.

| | |
|---|---|
| Clarke, K. | *Shaping the Geography of Empire: Man and Nature in Herodotus' Histories* (Oxford: Oxford University Press, 2018). |
| Colson, F. H. | *Philo VI* (LCL 289; Cambridge, MA; Harvard University Press, 1935). |
| Dunn, J. D. G. | *The Theology of Paul the Apostle* (Grand Rapids, MI: Eerdmans, 1998). |
| Elliott, J. K. | *The Apocryphal New Testament: A Collection of Apocryphal Christian Literature in an English Translation based on M. R. James* (Oxford: Clarendon Press, 1993). |
| Evans, C. A. | 'Romulus, Roman Omens, and the Portents of the Birth and Passion of Jesus', in C. A. Evans and A. Z. Wright (eds.), *Gods, Spirits, and Worship in Christianity and the Greco-Roman World* (JCT 35; SSEJC 23; London and New York, NY: T&T Clark, 2022), 83–121. |
| Eve, E. | 'Spit in Your Eye: The Blind Man of Bethsaida and the Blind Man of Alexandria', *NTS* 54 (2008), 1–17. |
| Frank, G. | 'Christ's Descent to the Underworld in Ancient Ritual and Legend', in R. J. Daly (ed.), *Apocalyptic Thought in Early Christianity* (Holy Cross Studies in Patristic Theology and History; Grand Rapids, MI: Baker Academic, 2009), 211–26. |
| Gnuse, R. K. | *Dreams and Dream Reports in the Writings of Josephus: A Traditio-Historical Analysis* (AGJU 36; Leiden: Brill, 1996). |
| Grüll, T. | 'The Legendary Fate of Pontius Pilate', *Classica et Mediaevalia* 61 (2010), 151–76. |
| Gurtner, D. M. | *The Torn Veil: Matthew's Exposition of the Death of Jesus* (SNTSMS 139; Cambridge: Cambridge University Press, 2007). |
| Hicks, R. D. | *Diogenes Laertius I* (LCL 184; Cambridge, MA: Harvard University Press, 1925). |
| Jackson, H. M. | 'The Death of Jesus in Mark and the Miracle from the Cross', *NTS* 33 (1987), 16–37. |
| Jacobus, H. R. | 'Balaam's "Star Oracle" (Num 24:15–19)', in P. Barthel and G. van Kooten (eds.), *The Star of Bethlehem and the Magi: Interdisciplinary Perspectives from Experts on the Ancient Near East, the Greco-Roman World, and Modern Astronomy* (Leiden: Brill, 2015), 399–429. |

| | |
|---|---|
| Kim, T. H. | 'The Anarthrous υἱὸς θεοῦ in Mark 15,39 and the Roman Imperial Cult', *Bib* 79 (1998), 221–41. |
| Klostermann, E. | *Das Matthäusevangelium* (HNT 4; Tübingen: Mohr [Siebeck], 4th edn, 1971). |
| McNamer, E. | 'Philip, Julia, and the Imperial Cult', in J. H. Ellens (ed.), *Bethsaida in Archaeology, History and Ancient Culture: A Festschrift in Honor of John T. Greene* (Newcastle upon Tyne: Cambridge Scholars Publishing, 2014), 242–51. |
| Martin, B. | 'Calpurnius Siculus' "New" *aurea aetas*', *Acta Classica* 39 (1996), 17–38. |
| Newman, H. I. | 'Stars of the Messiah', in M. Kister et al. (eds.), *Tradition, Transmission, and Transformation from Second Temple Literature through Judaism and Christianity in Late Antiquity: Proceedings of the Thirteenth International Symposium of the Orion Center for the Study of the Dead Sea Scrolls and Associated Literature* (Leiden: Brill, 2015), 272–303. |
| Perrin, B. | *Plutarch Lives: Demosthenes and Cicero, Alexander and Caesar* (LCL 99; Cambridge, MA: Harvard University Press, 1919). |
| Perrin, B. | *Plutarch, Lives: Agesilaus and Pompey, Pelopidas and Marcellus* (LCL 87; Cambridge, MA: Harvard University Press, 1917). |
| Pritchard, J. B. | *Ancient Near Eastern Texts Relating to the Old Testament* (Princeton: Princeton University Press, 1969). |
| Quarles, C. L. | 'Matthew 27:51–53: Meaning, Genre Intertextuality, Theology, and Reception History', *JETS* 59 (2016), 271–86. |
| Quarles, C. L. | 'Μετὰ τὴν ἔγερσιν αὐτοῦ: A Scribal Interpolation in Matthew 27:53?' *TC: A Journal of Biblical Textual Criticism* (2015), 1–15. |
| Rowland, R. J., Jr. | 'The "Very Poor" and the Grain Dole at Rome and Oxyrhynchus', *ZPE* 21 (1976), 69–73. |
| Schmidt, T. E. | 'Mark 15.16–32: The Crucifixion Narrative and the Roman Triumphal Procession', *NTS* 41 (1995), 1–18. |
| Strickert, F. | 'The Renaming of Bethsaida in Honor of Livia, a.k.a. Julia, the Daughter of Caesar, in Josephus, *Jewish Antiquities* 18.27–28', in R. Arav and R. A. Freund (eds.), *Bethsaida: A City by the North Shore of the Sea of Galilee* (Vol. 3; Kirksville, MO: Truman State University Press, 2004), 93–113. |

| | |
|---|---|
| Talbert, C. H. | *Reading Luke: A Literary and Theological Commentary on the Third Gospel* (Reading the New Testament; New York, NY: Crossroad, 1982). |
| Trumbower, J. A. | 'Jesus' Descent to the Underworld', in *Rescue for the Dead: The Posthumous Salvation of Non-Christians in Early Christianity* (Oxford Studies in Historical Theology; Oxford: Oxford University Press, 2001), 91–108. |
| van Henten, J. W. | 'The World Leader from the Land of the Jews: Josephus, *Jewish War* 6.300–315; Tacitus, *Histories* 5.13; and Suetonius, *Vespasian* 4.5', in P. Barthel and G. van Kooten (eds.), *The Star of Bethlehem and the Magi: Interdisciplinary Perspectives from Experts on the Ancient Near East, the Greco-Roman World, and Modern Astronomy* (Leiden: Brill, 2015), 361–86. |
| Wasserman, T. | 'The "Son of God" was in the Beginning (Mark 1:1)', *JTS* n.s. 62 (2011), 20–50. |
| Winter, B. W. | *Divine Honours for the Caesars: The First Christians' Responses* (Grand Rapids, MI: Eerdmans, 2015). |

CHAPTER 3

# Ethics and Eschatology in the Synoptic Tradition: A Theological-Moral Response to N. T. Wright's Gifford Lectures

David J. Neville

The 2018 Gifford Lectures were delivered at the University of Aberdeen by N. T. Wright, the first New Testament (NT) scholar to be invited to give the Giffords since Rudolf Bultmann in 1954–55.[1] Wright presented eight public lectures under the title, 'Discerning the Dawn: History, Eschatology and New Creation'. These lectures were subsequently published in 2019 by both Baylor University Press and SPCK as *History and Eschatology: Jesus and the Promise of Natural Theology*.[2] In response to Wright, this study probes a point of tension between ethics and eschatology in his proposal about the eschatology

---

1  Bultmann, *History and Eschatology*.
2  Several reviews of Wright's *History and Eschatology* have been published, without broaching the critical concern of this study. For a brief discussion of Wright's eschatology, taking his Giffords into account, see Mitchel, 'New Testament Eschatologies', 237–40. For a differently focused appraisal of Wright on Jesus' eschatology and ethics, with an appreciative response by Wright, see Perrin, 'Jesus' Eschatology and Kingdom Ethics', 92–114.

of Jesus in the Synoptic Gospels, which is that Jesus' future-oriented sayings featuring the 'Son of Man' and/or the kingdom of God pertained to the destruction of the temple in Jerusalem in 70 CE rather than presaging the 'end of the world' at Jesus' return or Parousia.

Within my own work in NT theology and ethics, one longstanding concern is the apparent discrepancy between the peaceable mode of Jesus' historic mission and expressions of violent eschatology attributed to Jesus by Gospel writers.[3] Matthew, especially, presents the historic mission and message of Jesus in largely peaceful terms *but also* depicts Jesus as anticipating future judgement on the part of the Son of Man in terms difficult to reconcile with his own peaceful mission. In this connection, it merits pondering that although violent eschatology features in the Gospels and wider NT, it is not the norm. New Testament expectations of eschatological judgement are neither inherently nor inevitably violent, implying that it is possible to envisage eschatology as cohering, theologically and morally, with the events of Jesus' mission that his NT witnesses attest as life-liberating.[4]

Wright is a prolific writer, creative interpreter, and forceful proponent of certain distinctive perspectives in NT scholarship. He is recognised as being a formative influence on the development of the so-called 'New Perspective on Paul', alongside other interpretative approaches to Paul. He champions the idea that many Second Temple Israelites considered themselves as continuing in exile, figuratively speaking, and that this mindset is important for comprehending much that we find in the NT, including Jesus' own mission and

---

3   See Neville, *A Peaceable Hope*; 'Toward a Hermeneutic of Shalom'; *The Vehement Jesus*, 219–54; 'Like Lightning?'. Informing this earlier body of work as well as this current exercise in theological interpretation are the following interlocking ideological (that is, Christian theological) convictions: (1) the theological-moral nexus found in the biblical canon or 'moral monotheism'; (2) the correlative view that what God does is good rather than that divine action is measurable against some independent moral norm or standard; (3) the general inscrutability of divine action in the world; and, most importantly, (4) the historic discernment of definitive divine disclosure in the Christ event—the life, mission, message, death, and resurrection of Jesus as remembered and presented in the biblical Gospels.
4   For a comparable perspective, composed in the register of constructive theology, see Rahner, 'Hermeneutics of Eschatological Assertions', especially theses 4–6.

message.⁵ Regarding Jesus, Wright contends that he did not prophesy his end-time return as the Son of Man. Rather, those Son of Man sayings traditionally understood as references to the Parousia of Jesus are in reality anticipations of his exaltation to God, mundanely manifested by the destruction of Jerusalem interpreted as divine judgement for Israel's failure to embrace Jesus as God's messiah. This conception of Jesus' future-oriented Son of Man sayings is neither original to Wright nor unique to him,⁶ but he is probably the most high-profile exponent of this interpretative position. He has argued for this perspective in several volumes,⁷ but the restatement of this position in his Gifford lectures provides an opportune occasion to appraise his view anew.

Since this study contests some of Wright's contentions about the eschatology of Jesus as reflected in the Synoptic Gospels, it is perhaps worth acknowledging that I consider *History and Eschatology* to be an exceptional achievement. Here Wright reflects in big-picture terms on key features of NT scholarship and the larger context of biblical criticism. Characterising the post-Enlightenment period in Western culture as 'the triumph of Epicureanism', Wright dissects key trends in critical scholarship on the Gospels and Jesus. He also teases out various meanings of 'history' and in so doing defends a nuanced epistemological stance known as critical realism. Moreover, he has valuable things to say about imponderables such as divine agency and theodicy, all in the service of reconfiguring the task of natural theology by focusing on comprehending Jesus in his historical context. Concluding the first, 'ground-clearing' half of his book, Wright presents his views on eschatology and apocalyptic in historical perspective, after which, in the second half of the book, he sets out the building blocks of his constructive argument for a holistic theology of new creation, grounded

---

5   For a recent restatement, see Wright, *Paul and the Faithfulness of God*, 139–62. For wide-ranging engagement with this signature theme, see the essays in *Exile: A Conversation with N. T. Wright*, edited and helpfully introduced by James Scott, which also includes a lead essay and concluding response by Wright.
6   Wright seems to have adopted the view of his teacher, G. B. Caird, at least with respect to Luke. See Caird, *Jesus and the Jewish Nation*, and *The Gospel of St Luke*. Cf. Wright, *Jesus and the Victory of God*, xviii–xix, and the prefatory comments to Wright, 'Jesus, Israel and the Cross', 9.
7   See especially Wright, *New Testament and the People of God*, 280–338, 459–64; *Jesus and the Victory of God*, 320–68, 612–53; *Surprised by Hope*; and *How God Became King*.

in the crucifixion and resurrection of Jesus, which, because it reaffirms but also reconfigures historic Israelite convictions about creation, cosmology, and covenant, serves as the basis for what might be termed a biblically chastened natural theology. In short, Wright's Giffords compose a creative and constructive case for taking Jesus seriously as a historical figure.

## 1. Christology, Soteriology, Eschatology, and Ethics

Since Johannes Weiss reminded his late-nineteenth-century contemporaries of the significance of eschatology for understanding the mindset of Jesus and his earliest witnesses,[8] students of the NT have been alert to the relation between eschatology and ethics, both in historically descriptive and theologically constructive senses.[9] The relation between eschatology and ethics cannot be reduced to a simple formula, however. Nor can it be claimed that all moral instruction in the NT is eschatologically conditioned,[10] although some ethical exhortations within the NT are either premised on or conditioned by eschatological expectations. 'In Matthew', for example, 'eschatology becomes a powerful warrant for moral behavior', as Richard Hays observes,[11] and in his view Luke shares Matthew's concern to encourage fitting conduct by warnings of eschatological judgement.[12] More generally, although one cannot predict what moral ramifications will follow, person to person, from end-time expectations or the absence thereof, surely that for which people ultimately hope bears on moral vision, moral convictions and commitments, and even moral decision-making here and now. In broad terms, discussion of the relation between eschatology and ethics posits this line of influence: eschatological expectation conditions moral musing and ethical exhortation. Much more rarely, by contrast, is the question of the relation between eschatology and ethics posed in such a way as to

---

8   Weiss, *Jesus' Proclamation of the Kingdom of God*. The first German edition was published in 1892.
9   For a brief overview, see Finger, 'Eschatology and Ethics', 276–79.
10  See Allison, 'Problem of the Historical Jesus', 230–34, especially his evocative coda.
11  Hays, *Moral Vision*, 106.
12  Hays, *Moral Vision*, 129.

foster consideration of ethics—NT ethics—as a criterion for assessing eschatological expectations within the NT. New Testament texts themselves do not explicitly raise this prospect, but insofar as moral teaching is traceable to Jesus in some sense, the question pertains, in my view, especially because NT soteriology is grounded in the identity and significance of Jesus as God's messianic agent of salvation.

Reference to NT soteriology prompts another preliminary point.[13] For pedagogical purposes, we separate Christology from soteriology and both Christology and soteriology from eschatology. In the NT, however, there is no neat division between Christology and soteriology; indeed, many soteriological affirmations are christologically charged, so to speak. According to Paul, for example, 'God was, through Christ, reconciling the world to Himself' (2 Cor. 5:18–19), and Luke 19:10 recalls Jesus as saying, 'For the Son of Man came to seek and to save the lost'. For such soteriological affirmations to be meaningful, certain christological convictions must be true.

A comparably close relation obtains between soteriology and eschatology. Considering what the NT affirms about the present availability, yet future consummation, of the kingdom of God, eternal life, and salvation, is there any real difference between soteriology and eschatology? One who takes history seriously must answer this question in the affirmative, but even if not identical, soteriology and eschatology are, within the NT, overlapping notions on a temporal continuum. Perhaps it is not too far-fetched to say that soteriology is present, realised, or inaugurated eschatology, whereas eschatology is yet-to-be realised soteriology.[14]

There are theological-moral ramifications of seeing soteriology and eschatology as overlapping categories, not least of which is that the moral bearing of the life-saving event *par excellence* within the NT—the mission and message of Jesus in its totality—relates to eschatological expectation no less than to soteriological affirmation. If NT

---

13  For a brief statement on the moral bearing of biblical notions of salvation, see Wright, 'Salvation', 696–98.
14  At times Paul uses the language of 'salvation' in a future-oriented, yet-to-be-realised sense (see, e.g., Rom. 5:9–10; 1 Thess. 5:8–9), confirming the close conceptual connection between soteriology and eschatology.

soteriology is realised or inaugurated eschatology, this is but another way of affirming that God's life-saving purposes are disclosed in the moral shape of Jesus' mission as presented in the biblical Gospels. If that be granted, and if eschatology is inaugurated-but-yet-to-be-realised soteriology, should not the moral mode of divine agency displayed in Jesus' historic mission and message remain constant through to God's life-saving work at the end? If not, how is it possible to affirm—with Paul, the Gospels, and much of the remainder of the NT—that God's agency in the historic mission of Jesus was efficacious in life-saving terms? To pose the question starkly, if Jesus' life and death were life-liberating, though nonviolent on Jesus' part, whence violently retributive eschatology? Borrowing a Johannine notion, I propose that the moral shape of *incarnation* serves as a criterion for evaluating expressions of violent eschatology. At least at the interpretative level, eschatological expectations, including those found within the NT itself, may be appraised in accord with moral vision grounded in the story of Jesus Messiah, whom Hebrews 13:8 attests as *constant* (and hence trustworthy) yesterday, today, and always.[15]

## 2. Wright on the Modern Myth of the 'End-of-the-World Jesus'

Although Chapter 4 of Wright's Giffords is most germane to the concerns of this essay, his discussion of scholarship on Jesus and the Gospels in Chapter 2 also pertains because he focuses on the influence of Weiss and Albert Schweitzer, especially the latter.[16] Indeed, part of his rationale for examining critical scholarship on Jesus and the Gospels is to expose the modern myth of the 'end-of-the-world Jesus' allegedly discovered by Weiss and Schweitzer. As he advises,

> I want in the present chapter to argue in particular that the idea of the literal and imminent 'end of the world' as a central

---

15 For similar ruminations, elegantly expressed, see Allison, *Night Comes*, 65–66.
16 Wright advises that Chapters 2 and 4 of *History and Eschatology* draw heavily from his 2018 article, 'Hope Deferred?'. See Wright, *History and Eschatology*, 292 n.23 and 305 n.24.

belief of first-century Jews, including Jesus and his early followers, is a modern myth. The 'end-of-the-world Jesus' has become a vital part of the argument for keeping Jesus himself off stage in theological construction, just as it was a vital part of the position advanced by Rudolf Bultmann in his Gifford Lectures and elsewhere and emphasised by his followers to this day.[17]

By the myth of the 'end-of-the-world Jesus', Wright means the view that Weiss and Schweitzer rediscovered the following points about Jesus in his historical matrix: first, that Jewish apocalyptic literature envisaged the imminent end of the world; second, that Jesus shared this apocalyptic viewpoint; and third, that Jesus' followers maintained his imminent apocalyptic outlook, albeit focused on Jesus' return, which proved to be a futile hope because the Parousia did not occur quickly and still has not occurred. For Udo Schnelle, the delay of the Parousia was the greatest internal challenge for early Christianity.[18] For Wright, however, this 'delayed Parousia' myth threatens to undermine any appeal in theological discourse to Jesus as a historical figure (p.48).[19]

The bulk of Chapter 2 in Wright's *History and Eschatology* composes his survey of developments from David Friedrich Strauss to Ernst Käsemann, focusing on notions of history, eschatology, and myth. The lengthiest section of this discussion is devoted to Schweitzer, in which Wright seeks to show that, far from being the result of careful historical study of texts from the Second Temple period, Schweitzer's 'end-of-the-world Jesus' was more probably the product of philosophical and cultural influences contemporary with Schweitzer himself, most notably Friedrich Nietzsche and Richard Wagner. In Wright's words,

> Schweitzer's understanding of the 'eschatological' Jesus owed much to the genuine historical insight that Jesus was

---

17 Wright, *History and Eschatology*, 47. Further page references to this book are provided within parentheses in the body of the text. Moreover, all italics for emphasis in citations from Wright are original to him.
18 Schnelle, *First One Hundred Years*, 388–400.
19 Apropos natural theology, Wright remarks: 'If the world is coming to an end, to be replaced by the wholly other "kingdom of God," the chance of being able to infer anything about the latter from the former is effectively nil' (p.56).

announcing not just a new or strengthened morality but a new world order. But his interpretation of Jesus' new vision owed far more to the underlying Epicurean cosmology of his culture (in which 'heaven' and 'earth' were radically incompatible) and the revolutionary ideology of his two great heroes, Nietzsche and Wagner: the moralist and the musician (p.52).

Here Wright credits Schweitzer with 'the genuine historical insight that Jesus was announcing not just a new or strengthened morality but a new world order' while also alleging that Schweitzer's 'interpretation of Jesus' new vision' is more indebted to features of his own cultural context. Indeed, Wright devotes considerable space to defending the thesis that Schweitzer's 'end-of-the-world Jesus' is, to a significant extent, the by-product of Schweitzer's immersion in a Wagnerian 'musical sub-culture whose controlling myth reached its climax in the coming end of the world' (p.53). Less nuanced is this declaration: 'The imminent end of the world was not [...] a first-century Jewish idea which Schweitzer (and Weiss) had discovered and expounded as something alien to their times. It was a glorious piece of late nineteenth-century German mythology' (p.55).[20]

Regarding Jewish apocalyptic texts on the basis of which Weiss and Schweitzer defended their depiction of an 'end-of-the-world Jesus', Wright ponders what they found in *1 Enoch*, *4 Ezra*, and *2 Baruch* that led them to think that such texts anticipated the actual end of the world, 'the world of space, time and matter' (p.57). For Wright, such texts envisage the end of socio-political situations in which God's people are suffering under foreign oppression, not the literal end of the cosmos. They compose a form of political theology in which what is anticipated is profound socio-political change *within* history, not an end to history brought about by divinely instigated cosmic catastrophe. As for NT texts that might be appealed to in support of an 'end-of-the-world Jesus', Wright concedes that 2 Peter 3:10 (re:

---

20 In *History and Eschatology* Wright focuses on Schweitzer, with only passing reference to Weiss, so it is unfair to present Weiss as susceptible to the same cultural influences as Schweitzer. As I point out in the final section of this study, Wright arguably misconstrues Weiss, which makes one wonder how fair he has been to Schweitzer.

cosmic conflagration) and John 21 (re: Jesus' return) may be read in such terms (p.65), but he makes no such concession for any other texts in the Gospels. The meaning of texts such as Mark 9:1 and parallels is addressed in Chapter 4, titled 'The End of the World? Eschatology and Apocalyptic in Historical Perspective'.

## 3. Wright on Eschatological Hope in Paul and in the Synoptic Tradition

Wright begins Chapter 4 of *History and Eschatology* by identifying two principal concerns: first, to clarify different senses of two key—and often related—terms, 'eschatology' and 'apocalyptic'; and second, to provide a historical account of the eschatological convictions of Jesus and his first-century followers. Concerning 'eschatology', Wright builds on the work of G. B. Caird.[21] After briefly surveying various understandings of eschatology, including Schweitzer's 'consistent eschatology', C. H. Dodd's 'realised eschatology', and Bultmann's demythologised 'existentialist eschatology', Wright focuses on two conceptions of eschatology readily apparent from historical research: first, the widespread Jewish notion of two ages, the present age and an age to come; and second, the early Christian modification of this Jewish two-age schema in which the age to come has already been inaugurated within the present age by virtue of the mission of Jesus, especially his death and resurrection (pp.131–32).[22] Apropos 'apocalyptic', Wright jousts with various scholarly viewpoints, but his principal concerns are: first, to dissociate the term from the idea of an imminent end to the world, understood literally; second, to rescue the term from the viewpoint that 'apocalyptic' is antithetical to history, especially salvation or covenantal history; and third, to associate his own view with the position of Caird that 'the word "apocalyptic" [...] is best used to denote a *genre*, or at least a *literary form and use*, where the writers intend to *denote* what we call this-worldly realities and to *connote* theological

---

21   Caird, *The Language and Imagery of the Bible*, Chapter 14.
22   For Wright, 'The two-age scheme summarizes the historical and political hope for the real "return from exile," the "new Exodus," and so on' (p.132).

meaning' (p.134).[23] This, for Wright, is the position most naturally associated with the practice of reading 'apocalyptic' texts responsibly in their respective historical contexts.

Whatever one decides about the central importance that Wright attaches to history for natural theology, it is difficult to argue against the importance of history, historical context, and historically conditioned hermeneutics for making sense of first-century eschatological texts. 'What matters throughout is historical exegesis', Wright writes, 'the constant effort to understand texts in their contexts' (p.135). In this respect, he maintains that 'in the sense of *what the first-century texts were actually talking about* [...] neither Schweitzer, nor Bultmann, nor Käsemann got the history itself right' (p.135). Here Wright implicitly claims to understand relevant ancient texts within their respective historical contexts better than Schweitzer, Bultmann, and Käsemann.

In a revealing paragraph under the rubric of 'The Historical Hope', Wright begins by pointing out that 'apocalyptic' literature makes use of the language of cosmic collapse to refer to political events such as the fall of Babylon or Jerusalem, yet in such a way as to convey a sense of their larger significance. But with respect to the *prophetic* texts to which he refers to substantiate this claim,[24] Wright never demonstrates that neither Schweitzer nor Bultmann nor Käsemann understood such texts in ways different from himself. More importantly, within the same paragraph on the use, within Isaiah and Jeremiah, of imagery relating to cosmic catastrophe, Wright brings the book of Daniel into the discussion, inferring that, since no one then or now would interpret Daniel's four sea-monsters in literal terms, no one should consider 'the son of man coming on the clouds' to signify a human being in flight. Daniel 7—12 differs from Isaiah and Jeremiah in generic terms, which probably deserved consideration, but both the development, during the Second Temple period, of the image of one like a son of man in Daniel 7:13 and the usage of this image within

---

23 See also Wright, *History and Eschatology*, 151, where he asserts: '"Apocalyptic" *was not a general principle about the way things happen in the world*. It was biblical language to convey the meaning of a one-off, unique event, the meaning which belonged to its *unique* and *disruptive* role *within* the narrative of creation and covenant'.

24 I accept a line of development from prophetic to apocalyptic texts, not least in the Tanakh, so my point is not to differentiate strongly between prophecy and apocalypse in generic terms.

Gospel traditions suggest that it deserves to be interpreted separately, even if not in isolation from the imagery of cosmic collapse. The image of one like a son of man is clearly decoded within Daniel 7 itself—as 'holy ones of the Most High' or 'people of the holy ones of the Most High' (7:18,21–22,25–27)—but that did not prevent this image from being subsequently developed into a heavenly redeemer figure with the divine authority to judge.[25]

Regarding the eschatological hope of Jesus and his earliest followers, Wright identifies two principal questions: 'First, do any early texts speak of an actual cosmic catastrophe? Second, how did the first Christians themselves understand the sayings which *did* have a specific time limit, such as Mark 9.1 or Mark 13.30?' (p.137).[26] For Wright, these questions are best answered by a two-stage or 'now-and-not-yet' eschatology: 'Something *had happened* to bring the expected kingdom to birth, and something *was yet to happen* through which that already-inaugurated kingdom would reach its ultimate goal' (p.139). Beginning with Pauline traditions preceding the Gospels (pp.139–44), Wright argues cogently that Paul affirmed the already-present reign of God through Jesus Messiah by virtue of his resurrection, exaltation, and enthronement, even if questions remain about his contention that Paul deliberately alludes to Daniel 7:27 in 1 Corinthinas 15:20–28, especially 15:24, alongside Genesis 1—3 and Psalms 110 and 8, which seems to be the basis for his inference that Paul had in mind the same basic idea as Gospel traditions about the coming of the Son of Man (p.141). If Wright is correct that Paul had Psalm 8 and Daniel 7 in mind when writing about the exaltation of Jesus, his description of Paul's inaugurated eschatology—as 'related specifically to the *present and future kingdom* and also to the *exaltation of the Son of Man* as something which has already taken place and whose implications are being worked out through the apostolic mission against the day when

---

25 On this development by the first century CE, see Nickelsburg, 'Son of Man', as well as Collins, 'Messiah and Son of Man'. The biblical Gospels attest to this development, as do the Parables of Enoch (*1 Enoch 37–71*) and *4 Ezra*.

26 Previously on the same page, Wright also refers to Mark 14:62 as 'closely allied' with Mark 9:1 and parallels.

every tongue will confess him as *Kyrios*' (p.143)—is understandable.²⁷ In that case, however, one wonders why the 'Son of Man' fails to feature in Paul's Christology.²⁸

While discussing Paul's inaugurated eschatology, Wright points out that, to affirm the presence of God's kingdom in power, Paul had to clarify that the present power of God's inaugurated kingdom was paradoxically displayed in weakness (p.143). On this point, Paul's understanding of God's present and continuing rule clearly coheres with ways in which the presence of the kingdom was displayed in Jesus' mission. Divine power is enacted in and through human weakness, even to the extent of suffering the humiliation of crucifixion.

After considering Paul, Wright turns to the Synoptic Gospels, focusing on the themes of the kingdom of God and the Son of Man, particularly the question of whether the kingdom had come in power in the wake of Jesus' crucifixion (p.144).²⁹ On this point, Wright announces at the outset: 'No surprises here: I shall argue that they [the Gospel writers] would have agreed with Paul' (p.144). Within this section of his chapter on eschatology and apocalyptic in historical perspective, Wright has sagacious things to say, including this central point: that the messianic figure of Jesus not only taught and enacted God's heavenly reign but also redefined the meaning of the presence

---

27 On Paul's inaugurated eschatology, both 'present exaltation ("already") and the future *parousia* ("not yet")' (p.143), Wright contends that Paul alluded to similar biblical texts in support of both realised and yet-future dimensions of his eschatology, not only the still-future Parousia. On this point, Wright contests the critique of Stephen Motyer, who allegedly takes Paul's relevant biblical allusions to refer solely to the Parousia. In his critique of Wright, however, Motyer's concern is not to deny inaugurated eschatology—indeed, he explicitly notes that biblical 'Day of the Lord' imagery is applied to three different 'comings' in the NT, namely, the historical mission of Jesus, the coming of the Holy Spirit at Pentecost, and the still-future coming of Jesus (p.21)—but to provide evidence from Paul that, in his view, makes it unlikely that Gospel traditions concerning the coming of the Son of Man refer to first-century events such as the destruction of Jerusalem and growth of the church.

28 Cf. Wright, 'Hope Deferred?', 63, where he addresses the question why, if Paul had Daniel 7 in mind, he was not more explicit about it: 'I suspect that Paul, in company with Luke, realized that his largely non-Jewish congregations might well not be able to decode the rich symbolic language of Daniel'. In *History and Eschatology*, however, Wright simply asserts that in 1 Corinthians 15 Paul refers to Daniel 7, citing in support Hewitt, *In Messiah*.

29 This is how Wright poses his question, deliberately echoing the wording of Mark 9:1: 'whether the kingdom had indeed come with power in the events which followed Jesus' death?' The inaugurated eschatology of the Synoptics, however, affirms the presence, power, and pressure of God's heavenly reign during Jesus' historic mission preceding his death.

of the kingdom. With reference to Jesus' parables, for example, Wright comments: 'The kingdom-parables all assume a meaning of the kingdom *and then explain that in fact the kingdom is indeed coming, but in a different, subversive fashion.* The hope of Israel is being fulfilled, but not in the way people had thought—a theme which permeates the texts' (p.146). Then, concerning the crucifixion of Jesus, Wright correctly observes that, 'for Mark, it encapsulates Jesus' paradoxical redefinition of power itself (10.35–45)' (p.147).[30] Although strongly affirmed, this decisive insight is not consistently upheld by Wright, in my view.

Regarding Mark 9:1, identified as a 'central saying', Wright first considers how Matthew understood this utterance, although not by discussing in detail his parallel to Mark 9:1 but rather by showing one way of understanding Matthew 16:28 when read in light of Matthew's passion narrative, bracketed by the Son of Man saying in Matthew 26:2 and 28:18–20, which in Wright's view is an unmistakable echo of Daniel 7:14. The Son of Man coming in his kingdom means the exaltation of the Son of Man into his kingdom, an interpretation confirmed by the Son of Man sayings in Matthew 26:64 and Luke 22:69, both of which can be understood along the lines of Jesus' imminent exaltation and are hence supportive of an inaugurated eschatology. As for Mark 9:1 itself, Wright explains this text largely in light of Mark 13, which he understands to refer to the destruction of the temple in Jerusalem. As he explains,

> Since my earlier contributions, the upsurge of interest in Temple-theology [...] has strengthened my view, first, that the discourse is primarily about the fall of the Temple, and second, that, since the Temple was the heaven-and-earth place, the *microcosmos*, its imminent destruction was bound to mean more than the mere failure of national hope. It was, from the Jewish point of view, the collapse of the space-time order itself —not in the sense that the literal space, time and matter would suddenly cease to exist, but that the created order of 'heaven

---

30 On the same page, concerning the cross as a key element of the Gospel writers' inaugurated eschatology, Wright makes this more general point: 'Jesus was not depoliticizing the kingdom. He was redefining power and politics themselves'.

and earth' had lost the linchpin which held it together. This line of thought goes back to Jeremiah, for whom the destruction of the Temple meant the return of creation itself to primal chaos (pp.149–50).[31]

More clearly than in prior publications, Wright here refines his view that the imagery of cosmic catastrophe that one finds in Mark 13:24–25 (and parallels) largely conveys the theological significance of political demise, especially with respect to the destruction of Jerusalem. The new dimension is that insofar as the imagery of cosmic collapse relates to the destruction of the temple, it bespeaks the end of the symbolic universe inhabited by first-century Jews, for whom the temple in Jerusalem was the dwelling place of God and hence the point of overlapping contact between heaven and earth. In Wright's view, Mark indicates a nexus between Jesus' prophecy against the temple and his own implicit kingdom-claim, namely, that his own messianic presence makes the temple redundant and hence 'ripe for destruction' (p.150). As a result, according to Wright, were it not for the presence of Mark 13:24–27, the temple focus of Mark 13 as a whole would be self-evident. Equating the content of Mark 13:24–27 with that of 9:1, Wright maintains that this is the event predicted to take place within a generation (Mark 13:30). Then these key lines:

> [E]verything we have seen so far from Paul, from Matthew and from Luke insists that we should read this language in terms of the death, resurrection and ascension of Jesus on the one hand and the fall of the Temple (the heaven-and-earth place) on the other. The crucial arguments come from the allusions to Isaiah 13 and 34 and Daniel 7 [...]. The language and imagery had been in regular use for a long time to refer to (what we call) socio-political events and to invest them with (what we might call) their 'cosmic' significance [...]. Mark has here presented a construct, retrospectively of course but quite carefully, of *how it all may have appeared from within Jesus' public career*. Mark's Jesus believes on the one hand that he will

---

[31] Among his prior discussions of Mark 13, Wright makes particular reference to his *Jesus and the Victory of God*, 320–68.

die and be raised, as the climax of his kingdom-bringing vocation, and that these events will be the reality towards which the vivid imagery of Daniel 7 (interpreted with the help of the Psalms) had been pointing. Mark's Jesus believes, too, that he is called to pronounce the Temple's doom, so that when the Temple is destroyed he will be vindicated. The two go together (pp.150–51).

Isaiah 13 is a 'Day of the Lord' oracle of judgement against Babylon, and with considerable hyperbole Isaiah 34 announces the Lord's day of vengeance against the nations, especially Edom. In both Isaianic oracles, cosmic upheaval is one aspect of a larger visionary scenario symbolising divine judgement of political entities (especially Babylon and Edom), but without reference to one like a son of man. By contrast, the dream vision of Daniel 7 features one like a son of man receiving perpetual dominion from the Ancient of Days, but without reference to the language or imagery of cosmic dissolution. Although it is possible that Jesus or the Gospel writers merged both cosmic collapse and Son of Man imagery into a creative synthesis, it is also possible that, when alluding to these biblical texts in light of their respective histories of reception, Jesus and/or the Gospel writers retained the distinction between the two sets of imagery, investing each in its own way with more universal and eschatological significance. After all, as Wright himself acknowledges,

> References to the 'son of man' in pre-Christian Jewish literature are few and far between, and there is no precedent at all for 'son of man' imagery being used *against the Temple itself*. This is a *novum* so enormous that we must postulate a context sufficiently strong to bear the weight.[32]

---

32  Wright, *Jesus and the Victory of God*, 519. For Wright, this was an innovation on the part of Jesus. In Chapters 5 and 6 of *History and Eschatology*, Wright builds on the key Jewish institutions of Temple and Sabbath to develop the idea that Temple-focused cosmology and Sabbath-grounded eschatology evoke the symbolic world for making sense of NT convictions about the inauguration of God's kingdom in the mission of Jesus, which nevertheless point forward to God's ultimate renewal of the created order. To broach a point deserving further consideration, if Wright's 'temple cosmology' is firmly grounded in first-century Jewish consciousness, it would make sense for Jesus' eschatological discourse in Matthew 24, Mark 13, and Luke 21 to associate the end of the temple with the end of things more generally, even if not the dissolution of the universe. In other words, prescience about the destruction of the temple might well have connected with more all-encompassing eschatological expectations.

## 4. Theological-Moral Appraisal

To anyone already convinced of Wright's reading of imminently anticipated kingdom of God texts and future-oriented Son of Man texts, Chapter 4 of *History and Eschatology* might well be compelling, but I remain unpersuaded. Here I am unable to delve into the debates on this point between Wright and his critics—for example, Edward Adams, Dale Allison, James Crossley, Christopher Hays, Howard Marshall, and Stephen Motyer—none of whom receives much by way of attention, if any, either in Wright's Giffords or in the journal article from which Chapters 2 and 4 were drawn.[33] Rather, after commenting on the manner in which Wright tends to address views he opposes, I identify two theological-moral incongruities associated with Wright's reading of Jesus' future-oriented sayings featuring the kingdom of God and the Son of Man.

Wright seems to coalesce various views into one eschatological construct: an imminent end of the world, understood literally; the 'dogma of delay', to wit, that what Jesus prophesied would occur within a generation failed to eventuate, thereby causing cognitive dissonance that resulted in revisionary eschatological schemas on the part of second- and third-generation followers of Jesus; eschatological perspectives different from a two-stage inaugurated eschatology; and a literal reading of the language and imagery of cosmic collapse. In this connection, Wright's reading of Weiss is tendentious. According to Wright, Weiss is the source of the myth of the 'end-of-the-world Jesus', but this can only be sustained by a selective reading of Weiss. Granted, Weiss did not hold Wright's views on Jesus' messianic self-consciousness, nor did he advocate anything like Wright's view of Jesus' future-oriented Son of Man sayings. But neither did Weiss uphold a view of Jesus' eschatology in which the arrival of God's transcendent rule equates to the literal end of the world. Rather, read in context, Weiss's statements about divine destruction of the world more plausibly imply the vanquishment of the world as ruled by Satan and God's transformation of the old

---

33 See the bibliography for studies by Adams, Allison, Crossley, Hays, Marshall, and Motyer responding to Wright. Related, albeit focused on Paul, is the exchange between Frey, 'Demythologizing Apocalyptic?', and Wright, 'Challenge of Dialogue', 743–54.

world under satanic dominion into God's new creation, centred in a restored and resplendent Israel.³⁴ Roughly two decades before Wright's Gifford Lectures, Allison had already pointed this out and indicated that his own understanding of NT language about 'the end' is not necessarily a reference to the literal 'end of the space-time universe', a phrase still used in Wright's Giffords (p.129), but rather a reference to God's 'radical transformation of the present cosmos', which necessarily implies an end to the world as we currently experience it.³⁵ Wright is well acquainted with Allison's views, having devoted a subsection in part 1 of his *Paul and the Faithfulness of God* to rebutting Allison and Adams's critique of his interpretation of Jesus' eschatology in the synoptic tradition.³⁶ Although apparently aware that at least some critics of his views on the eschatology of Jesus and Paul do not simply equate sayings about the imminent arrival of the kingdom of God or coming of the Son of Man with anticipations of God's abolishment of the world but rather of its transformation, this awareness is not reflected in *History and Eschatology*. Sometimes Wright tilts at straw figures.

Turning finally to two theological-moral incongruities in Wright's exegesis of key synoptic texts relating to Jesus' eschatology, perhaps the first thing to say is that one cannot deny that Wright's treatment of such texts is suggestive, especially when read within the interpretative matrix he provides, namely, that 'all four Gospels frame the story of Jesus in terms of the long-awaited return of Israel's God' (p.144). I also appreciate that theological and moral considerations cannot disprove either history or historical interpretation, provided Wright's interpretative scenario provides the most compelling explanatory power for the texts he considers. Allowing for the inherently theological character of such texts, however, perhaps theological and moral reflection goes some way toward counterbalancing what would seem to be an apologetic rationale for associating so closely Gospel texts about the

---

34  See Weiss, *Jesus' Proclamation, passim*, but especially his own summary on pp.129–31.
35  Allison, 'Jesus & the Victory of Apocalyptic', 128–30.
36  See Wright, *Paul and the Faithfulness of God*, 163–75, a subsection titled 'A World Transformed, Not Abolished', which accurately describes Allison's view no less than Wright's own. Within this subsection Wright expresses the hope that he will at some point provide a full response to the arguments of Adams and Allison, but such a response is not to be found either in Wright's Giffords or in 'Hope Deferred?'.

imminent advent of God's heavenly kingdom or coming of the Son of Man with the destruction of Jerusalem.[37]

For Wright, the burden of Jesus' message to Israel was to avoid the path of violent revolution against Rome. Indeed, in a study of Wright's conception of 'Jesus' Eschatology and Kingdom Ethics', Nicholas Perrin documents that, according to Wright, Jesus' call for Israel's repentance focused on its tendency toward violent militancy, which in *Jesus and the Victory of God* 'functions as a kind of national meta-sin, the repudiation of which would avert judgment and indicate the end of exile'.[38] Although the prospect of imminent divine judgement was integral to Jesus' mission and message, Jesus also identified himself with his people Israel and, as Israel's representative, took upon himself the imminent judgement about which he forewarned Israel. This is an integral, not incidental, dimension of Wright's understanding of Jesus' death on a Roman cross.[39] Yet if the crucifixion of Jesus was truly the instantiation of divine judgement on Israel's true representative, one wonders why the destruction of Jerusalem, as a further expression of divine judgement to vindicate Jesus' messianic mission, was necessary. Was not judgement poured out on Israel's innocent representative sufficient, so that more encompassing judgement needed to be visited upon Jerusalem within a generation of Jesus' crucifixion? Or is the logic of this way of putting things that, since Israel was not brought to its senses by the execution of its unrecognised representative, understood in terms of divine judgement, the crucifixion of Jesus

---

37 Wright denies an apologetic concern. See, e.g., Wright, *Jesus and the Victory of God*, 342. But to argue, as Wright does twenty pages later, that the destruction of Jerusalem *vindicates* Jesus' time-conditioned prophecies relating to the advent of God's kingdom or to the coming of the Son of Man is to compose an apology for Jesus as a prescient prophet.
38 Perrin, 'Jesus' Eschatology', 107. Cf. Wright, *Jesus and the Victory of God*, 246–58. In a brief response appended to Perrin's essay, Wright remarks: 'I still think that the nationalist dream (of Israel becoming top nation by military conquest, restoring the ancient kingdom of David and Solomon) did function as a kind of meta-sin [...]' (p.113).
39 See, e.g., Wright, *How God Became King*, especially chapter 9, in which Wright emphasises that the suffering and death of Jesus as Israel's messianic representative are the means by which God's sovereign reign is established. See also Wright, 'Jesus, Israel and the Cross', 31. Written for the annual SBL meeting in 1985, this paper is identified by Wright as one of several stimulants for his *Jesus and the Victory of God*. For a study of ways in which the mission and message of Jesus are illuminated by comprehending the close conceptual nexus between eschatology and violence within Second Temple Judaism, see Nickel, *Things that Make for Peace*, a revised doctoral thesis supervised by Wright.

failed to achieve its objective and thus needed to be replicated, albeit on a much grander scale?

At a historical level, one can readily connect Israel's recalcitrance against Rome to the destruction of Jerusalem and its temple—leaving aside the inestimable collateral damage inflicted on countless Galileans and Judeans, the majority of whom probably shared Jesus' view on the folly of revolt against Rome. But the interpretative judgement that the overwhelming violence of Roman forces against Jerusalem and its surrounds, including the destruction of the temple, constituted the historical correlate of divine vindication of Jesus by means of his exaltation to God implies a mismatch between divine agency displayed in Jesus' public mission and divine agency displayed in the vindication of that self-same mission.[40] To use 'Wright-speak', God became king by means of Jesus' nonviolent mission but vindicated that mission by means of the kind of violence eschewed by Jesus.

This brings into focus the central concern of this study—the discrepancy between what Wright affirms about the presence of God's kingdom in Jesus' public mission and what he claims about God's validation and vindication of Jesus' mission. For Paul, Mark, Matthew, and Luke, Wright maintains that, as part of their inaugurated eschatology (reflective of Jesus' own), to affirm the *present* power of God's kingdom required a corresponding reconfiguration of the meaning of power. Seen in light of Jesus' mission, the power of God—divine agency effecting change for good—is qualitatively different from conventional conceptions of power. Wright emphasises this point. But if he is correct that the referent of Jesus' future-oriented Son of Man

---

40 Why exaltation (allegedly) demonstrated by Jerusalem's destruction displays God's vindication of Jesus' mission and message better than the simple confession of Jesus' resurrection by God and exaltation to God, as affirmed by Jesus' witnesses in Acts, remains a puzzle to me—apart from precedents in Luke's Gospel and, more subtly, perhaps also in Luke's canonical counterparts. Paul was a visionary with the gift of prophecy, but a vision of Jerusalem's impending destruction as divine judgement on Israel for rejecting Jesus as Messiah and also as the mundane manifestation of God's vindication-by-exaltation of Jesus' mission was apparently not vouchsafed to him. Wright correctly interprets the resurrection of Jesus as God's reaffirmation of creation (pp.199–205), but the resurrection of Jesus was first and foremost God's vindication of Jesus and his way in the world. In the synoptic tradition, the resurrection of Jesus 'reiterates' by means of divine action what the divine voice affirms of Jesus at his baptism and his transfiguration. This is my way of affirming what Wright asserts in 'Whence and Wither', 149: 'The resurrection means what it means because it is the resurrection *of this Jesus*, not of someone else'.

sayings is the destruction of Jerusalem and its temple, as the historical demonstration of God's vindication of Jesus' mission, the fulfilment of Jesus' future-oriented Son of Man sayings simply realigns divine power with standard displays of forceful, coercive, and violent power. The messianic mission of Jesus is vindicated by divine vindictiveness.

While I agree with much of what Wright argues about the inaugurated eschatology of Paul and the synoptic evangelists, perhaps something may be gained by applying the ethics of the kingdom discerned to have been inaugurated by Jesus' mission to interpretations of his future-oriented eschatological sayings.[41] If one accepts the theological intuition that the mission and message of Jesus definitively disclosed and displayed the nature or character of that which he inaugurated (see Luke 17:20–21; John 1:14–18), and if inaugurated eschatology is coextensive with soteriology, or largely so, then the moral character of future eschatology should conform to and cohere with what has been inaugurated in Jesus' historic mission, including his kingdom-oriented moral vision. Regarding divine rescue by means of Jesus' crucifixion, Wright asserts: 'This is the real victory over the real enemy' (p.147).[42] If that be the case, however, surely divine agency displayed in that life-saving event serves as the historical benchmark and interpretative criterion for evaluating all other claims to discerning the continuation and completion of God's life-saving work in the world.

David J. Neville
St Mark's National Theological Centre / Charles Sturt University

---

41 If, as I consider, the phrase, 'inaugurated eschatology of new creation', encapsulates Wright's sense of the eschatological outlook of Paul and the synoptic evangelists, this phrase neatly expresses the necessary nexus between soteriology and eschatology grounded in Christology marked by the discernment of God's life-liberating presence and paradoxical power in the historic mission and message of Jesus.

42 Cf. Wright, *History and Eschatology*, 276, where, in his conclusion to the book as a whole, Wright says of the death of Jesus on a Roman cross: 'God himself has revealed himself right there, at the dead end, simultaneously unveiling his true character and rebuking any attempt to find it by other means'. See also Wright, 'Whence and Whither', 152, where, in speaking about the mission of the church, he identifies the cross as 'the means of victory, the *only* means by which genuine kingdom victories are won'. My question to Wright is: If 'Christ crucified' reveals divine agency in the world, why not adopt the historic Christ event as our criterion for discerning God's handiwork, both in relation to historical events like the destruction of Jerusalem and also with respect to divine action in the future?

## Bibliography

Adams, E. — *The Stars Will Fall from Heaven: Cosmic Catastrophe in the New Testament and its World* (London: T&T Clark International, 2007).

Allison, D. C., Jr. — *Constructing Jesus: Memory, Imagination, and History* (Grand Rapids, MI: Baker Academic, 2010), especially Chapter 2, 'More Than a Sage: The Eschatology of Jesus'.

Allison, D. C., Jr. — 'Jesus & the Victory of Apocalyptic', in C. C. Newman (ed.), *Jesus & the Restoration of Israel: A Critical Assessment of N. T. Wright's Jesus and the Victory of God* (Downers Grove, IL: InterVarsity Press, 1999), 126–41, 310–13.

Allison, D. C., Jr. — *Night Comes: Death, Imagination, and the Last Things* (Grand Rapids, MI: Eerdmans, 2016).

Allison, D. C., Jr. — 'The Problem of the Historical Jesus', in D. E. Aune (ed.), *The Blackwell Companion to the New Testament* (Chichester: Wiley-Blackwell, 2010), 220–35.

Bultmann, R. — *History and Eschatology: The Presence of Eternity* (Waco, TX: Baylor University Press, 2019).

Caird, G. B. — *The Gospel of Luke* (Harmondsworth, Middlesex: Penguin Books, 1963).

Caird, G. B. — *Jesus and the Jewish Nation* (London: Athlone, 1965).

Caird, G. B. — *The Language and Imagery of the Bible* (London: Duckworth, 1980).

Collins, J. J. — 'Messiah and Son of Man', in A. Y. Collins and J. J. Collins, *King and Messiah as Son of God: Divine, Human, and Angelic Messianic Figures in Biblical and Related Literature* (Grand Rapids, MI: Eerdmans, 2008), 75–100.

Crossley, J. G. — *The Date of Mark's Gospel: Insight from the Law in Earliest Christianity* (London: T&T Clark International, 2004), especially Chapter 2.

Finger, T. — 'Eschatology and Ethics', in J. B. Green, et al. (eds), *Dictionary of Scripture and Ethics* (Grand Rapids, MI: Baker Academic, 2011), 276–79.

| | |
|---|---|
| Frey, J. | 'Demythologizing Apocalyptic? On N. T. Wright's Paul, Apocalyptic Interpretation, and the Constraints of Construction', in C. Heilig, J. T. Hewitt, and M. Bird (eds.), *God and the Faithfulness of Paul: A Critical Examination of the Pauline Theology of N. T. Wright* (Tübingen: Mohr Siebeck, 2016), 489–531. |
| Hays, C. M., et al. | *When the Son of Man Didn't Come: A Constructive Proposal on the Delay of the Parousia* (Minneapolis, MN: Fortress, 2016), especially the chapters by Hays. |
| Hays, R. B. | *The Moral Vision of the New Testament—Community, Cross, New Creation: A Contemporary Introduction to New Testament Ethics* (San Francisco: HarperOne, 1996). |
| Hewitt, J. T. | *In Messiah: Messiah Discourse in Ancient Judaism and 'In Christ' Language in Paul* (Tübingen: Mohr Siebeck, 2019). |
| Marshall, I. H. | 'Political and Eschatological Language in Luke', in C. G. Bartholomew, J. B. Green, and A. C. Thiselton (eds), *Reading Luke: Interpretation, Reflection, Formation* (Grand Rapids, MI: Zondervan; Milton Keynes: Paternoster, 2005), 157–77. |
| Mitchel, P. | 'New Testament Eschatologies', in S. McKnight and N. K. Gupta (eds.), *The State of New Testament Studies: A Survey of Recent Research* (Grand Rapids, MI: Baker Academic, 2019), 224–52. |
| Motyer, S. | *Come, Lord Jesus! A Biblical Theology of the Second Coming of Christ* (London: APOLLOS, 2016). |
| Neville, D. J. | *A Peaceable Hope: Contesting Violent Eschatology in New Testament Narratives* (Grand Rapids, MI: Baker Academic, 2013). |
| Neville, D. J. | 'Like Lightning? Luke 17:22–37 Revisited in Interfaith Perspective', in A. Rees (ed.), *Things that Make for Peace: Traversing Text and Tradition in Christianity and Islam* (Lanham, MD: Lexington Books, 2020), 13–24. |
| Neville, D. J. | 'Toward a Hermeneutic of Shalom: Reading Texts of Teleological Terror in Peace Perspective', *Word & World: Theology for Christian Ministry* 34 (2014), 339–48. |
| Neville, D. J. | *The Vehement Jesus: Grappling with Troubling Gospel Texts* (Eugene, OR: Cascade Books, 2017). |

Nickel, J. P.     *The Things that Make for Peace: Jesus and Eschatological Violence* (Berlin/Boston: de Gruyter, 2021).

Nickelsburg, G. W. E.     'Son of Man', in D. N. Freedman et al. (eds), *The Anchor Bible Dictionary*, Vol. 6 (New York, NY: Doubleday, 1992), 137–50.

Perrin, N.     'Jesus' Eschatology and Kingdom Ethics: Ever the Twain Shall Meet', in N. Perrin and R. B. Hays (eds.), *Jesus, Paul and the People of God: A Theological Dialogue with N. T. Wright* (Downers Grove, IL: IVP Academic, 2011), 92–112.

Rahner, K.     'The Hermeneutics of Eschatological Assertions', in K. Rahner, *Theological Investigations,* Vol. IV (trans. K. Smyth; London: Darton, Longman & Todd, 1966), 323–46.

Schnelle, U.     *The First One Hundred Years of Christianity: An Introduction to Its History, Literature, and Development* (trans. J. W. Thompson; Grand Rapids, MI: Baker Academic, 2020).

Scott, J. M.     'N. T. Wright's Hypothesis of an "Ongoing Exile": Issues and Answers', in J. M. Scott (ed.), *Exile: A Conversation with N. T. Wright* (Downers Grove, IL: IVP Academic, 2017), 3–16.

Scott, J. M., ed.     *Exile: A Conversation with N. T. Wright* (Downers Grove, IL: IVP Academic, 2017).

Weiss, J.     *Jesus' Proclamation of the Kingdom of God* (translated and edited by R. H. Hiers and D. L. Holland; Philadelphia, PA: Fortress, 1971; reprinted, Chico, CA: Scholars, 1985).

Wright, J. W.     'Salvation', in J. B. Green et al. (eds), *Dictionary of Scripture and Ethics* (Grand Rapids, MI: Baker Academic, 2011), 696–98.

Wright, N. T.     'The Challenge of Dialogue: A Partial and Preliminary Response', in C. Heilig, J. T. Hewitt, and M. Bird (eds.), *God and the Faithfulness of Paul: A Critical Examination of the Pauline Theology of N. T. Wright* (Tübingen: Mohr Siebeck, 2016), 711–68.

Wright, N. T.     *History and Eschatology: Jesus and the Promise of Natural Theology* (London: SPCK; Waco, TX: Baylor University Press, 2019).

| | |
|---|---|
| Wright, N. T. | 'Hope Deferred? Against the Dogma of Delay', *Early Christianity* 9 (2018), 37–82. |
| Wright, N. T. | *How God Became King: Getting to the Heart of the Gospels* (London: SPCK, 2012). |
| Wright, N. T. | 'In Grateful Dialogue: A Response', in C. C. Newman (ed.), *Jesus & the Restoration of Israel: A Critical Assessment of N. T. Wright's Jesus and the Victory of God* (Downers Grove, IL: InterVarsity Press, 1999), 244–77, 316–19. |
| Wright, N. T. | *Jesus and the Victory of God* (London: SPCK; Minneapolis, MN: Fortress, 1996). |
| Wright, N. T. | 'Jesus, Israel and the Cross', in N. T. Wright, *Interpreting Jesus: Essays on the Gospels* (London: SPCK, 2020), 9–36. |
| Wright, N. T. | *The New Testament and the People of God* (London: SPCK; Minneapolis: Fortress Press, 1992). |
| Wright, N. T. | *Paul and the Faithfulness of God* (2 vols; London: SPCK; Minneapolis, MN: Fortress, 2013). |
| Wright, N. T. | 'Responding to Exile', in J. M. Scott (ed.), *Exile: A Conversation with N. T. Wright* (Downers Grove, IL: IVP Academic, 2017), 305–332. |
| Wright, N. T. | *Surprised by Hope* (London: SPCK, 2007). |
| Wright, N. T. | 'Whence and Whither Historical Jesus Studies in the Life of the Church?', in N. Perrin and R. B. Hays (eds.), *Jesus, Paul and the People of God: A Theological Dialogue with N. T. Wright* (Downers Grove, IL: IVP Academic, 2011), 115–58. |
| Wright, N. T. | 'Yet the Sun Will Rise Again: Reflections on the Exile and Restoration in Second Temple Judaism, Jesus, Paul, and the Church Today', in J. M. Scott (ed.), *Exile: A Conversation with N. T. Wright* (Downers Grove, IL: IVP Academic, 2017), 19–80. |

CHAPTER 4

# The 'New Covenant' Debate Revisited
Mary J. Marshall

## Abstract
Interest in reviewing debate on the 'New Covenant' was sparked by Jonathan Klawans' 2019 volume *Heresy, Forgery, Novelty: Condemning, Denying, and Asserting Innovation in Ancient Judaism.* Yet rather than focusing on heresiology, the present study considers the interpretation of the relevant term in the Dead Sea Scrolls and the New Testament, and its relationship with Jeremiah 31:31–34. It builds on the finding of the author's previous research that the Last Supper was held on Wednesday 1 April 33 C.E. in an Essene household where Jesus' brother James was the *mebaqqer*. Examination of the Gospels indicates that although Jesus' injunction to love one's enemies is innovative, his teaching did not abrogate Mosaic Law. Review of pertinent New Testament epistles reveals that Paul's reference to 'new covenant' in 2 Corinthians 3:18 confirms the finding concerning the Dead Sea Scrolls, that in its original context, Jeremiah 31:31–34 is focused on repentance, and that it relates to *renewal* of the Sinai covenant. In contrast, usage in Hebrews of supersessionist language and an amended form of the Jeremianic passage distorts the meaning of the text. It is observed that Jesus' teaching on love of enemies relates to the ethic of hospitality and is therefore

relevant to his typical status as a guest at meals, including the Last Supper. The interpretation of 'new covenant' as 'renewed' rather than 'new' is applied to Jesus' words over the cup, hence supporting the proposed scenario at his last meal, with his brother James as host.

## 1. Introduction

My interest in revisiting the 'New Covenant' debate was kindled by Jonathan Klawans' 2019 volume, *Heresy, Forgery, Novelty: Condemning, Denying, and Asserting Innovation in Ancient Judaism*. Whereas Klawans' primary focus in that work is to explore whether heresiology was associated initially with Christianity, or evolved from Jewish precedents, the present study undertakes a review of the debate concerning interpretation of the term 'new covenant' in the Dead Sea Scrolls and the New Testament, and whether or how it relates to Jeremiah 31:31–34. Klawans himself does not discern Essenic influence on the historical Jesus, but following Joseph, I consider it certain that Jesus and his family had some association with the Essenes and their beliefs.[1] Consequently, this essay builds on my previous research, which concluded that the Last Supper took place in southwest Jerusalem on 1 April 33 C.E. in an Essenic household of which Jesus' brother James was the *mebaqqer*.[2]

The occasion of Jesus' last meal is of central significance as we endeavour to determine whether he may have inferred by his words and actions that he was inaugurating a covenant in some sense different from that established at Sinai.[3] Exploration of the concept of such a 'new' covenant inevitably raises the issue of supersessionism, that is, the erroneous belief that Christianity replaced Judaism.[4] It will therefore be necessary to move beyond the confines of the Gospels and Acts—in particular to

---

1 See Joseph, *Jesus, the Essenes, and Christian Origins*, 164–66.
2 The Hebrew term for 'guardian', deriving from the verb בקר and the participle as a noun, has the meaning *inspector* or *overseer*. See בקר I, mng. 2, in Clines, *CDCH*, 54; Marshall, 'Essenic Influence on Jesus', 54–55.
3 Exodus 32—34.
4 See Svartvik, 'I Have Come Not to Abolish'; Donaldson, *Jews and Anti-Judaism*, 20–21; Bibliowicz, *Jewish–Christian Relations*, 141-42; Thistlethwaite, 'The Bible is Active', 169–70; Levine and Brettler, *Bible With and Without Jesus*, 171.

## 2. The Term 'New Covenant'

Klawans begins discussion on 'new covenant' by referring to Jeremiah 31:31–34 and its prominence in debate concerning interpretation of the term. To highlight the conundrum as to whether it relates to innovation or restoration, he refers to the fact that renewal is cyclical, and focuses on the semantics of *chadash* (new), and *chodesh* (month), noting that the latter indicates the *renewal* of the lunar cycle.[5] Some further instances where the verb form חדש denotes renewal[6] relate to the restoration of kingship (1 Sam. 11:14); sanctuary renovation undertaken by Jehoash (2 Chr. 24:4,12); and Jeremiah's plea for renewal of 'days of old' (Lam. 5:21).[7] Klawans also refers to other forecasts of renewal in Ezekiel (18:31; 36:26) and Deutero-Isaiah (65:17). Together with the expectation of renewal are warnings in Deuteronomy (4:2; 12:32) against adding to, or subtracting from, the laws given by God, thus resulting in the traditional belief that the Mosaic law was never to be superseded.[8]

The dilemma is underlined in light of: the occurrence of the term 'new covenant' in the Damascus Document (CD 6.19); and in accounts of the Last Supper;[9] the value seemingly assigned to newness in other New Testament writings such as 2 Corinthians 3:1–18; and the association of the term in Hebrews with the emergence of supersessionist critique.[10] Each of these instances will be investigated in order to gain an accurate assessment of the term's meaning.

---

5   Klawans, *Heresy*, 3.
6   *CDCH* 'חדש I', 109; Holladay, 'חד: piel', *Hebrew and Aramaic Lexicon*, 96, meaning *make new, restore*.
7   Klawans, *Heresy*, 3. See also Ps. 104:30; 51:12; and Isa. 61:4 (*CDCH* 'חדש I', 109).
8   Klawans, *Heresy*, 1–3.
9   Both Paul and Luke feature it in the cup saying (1 Cor. 11:25; Luke 22:20).
10  Klawans, *Heresy*, 3–7.

## 3. 'Covenant' in Essenic Documents

Reference to the 'new covenant' in CD 6.19 has led to much speculation and to 'Christianisation' of the scrolls.[11] Klawans quotes VanderKam on the matter: 'The *Damascus Document* introduces the phrase "the new covenant in the land of Damascus" ... which apparently designates the renewed covenant that had been described [in Jeremiah 31]'.[12] Summarising VanderKam's view, he observes that both the Jeremianic text and CD 6.19 refer not to a *new* covenant, but a *renewed* one.[13] Thus Jeremiah's prophecy, like CD 6.19, refers to a 'renewed covenant between God and his people in which he would place his "law within them"'.[14] As Matthew Black understood, the prophecy is about repentance and God's merciful response: 'I will forgive their iniquity' (citing Jer. 31:34).[15]

Examination of the Qumran scrolls provides further support for the finding.[16] There is a probable reference to 'new covenant' in *Pesher Habakkuk*, its meaning being about renewal or restoration, rather than novelty.[17] Any disclosure of sacred things is viewed as merely revealed from *ancient* texts, especially Torah and the Prophets.[18] Moreover, the many copies of the pseudepigraphic work *Jubilees* found at Qumran testify to its significance for the community. This document features the concept of a single covenant repeatedly renewed, with an annual ceremony taking place at Shavuot (Pentecost).[19]

A further element in the Qumran corpus is that of the Two Ways, as described in the *Rule of the Community* (3.13–21)—the dualistic conflict between light and darkness, good and evil. Members of the

---

11 Klawans, *Heresy*, 85.
12 Klawans, *Heresy*, 85, citing VanderKam, 'Covenant'. Cf. Hultgren, *From the Damascus Covenant*, 492, who sees '"the new covenant" (in the land of Damascus) ... as a specific movement in Second Temple Judaism', i.e. the parent of the Qumran community.
13 Klawans, *Heresy*, 86, citing Talmon, et al. Klawans expresses some doubt about the connection between the Damascus Document reference and Jeremiah 31 (*Heresy*, 86n.22), but I find VanderKam's view totally convincing.
14 VanderKam, 'Covenant in the Hebrew Scriptures'; and 'Covenant'—referring specifically to Jer. 31:31–34.
15 Black, *Scrolls and Christian Origins*, 92. See also Klawans, *Heresy*, 87, citing Hultgren, *From the Damascus Covenant*, 77–112.
16 I.e. that the 'new covenant' reference in CD 6.19 concerns renewal (Klawans, *Heresy*, 99).
17 Klawans, *Heresy*, 94. On the reliability of the reconstruction of the relevant text, 1QpHab 2.3, see Klawans, *Heresy*, 83, and nn.11,13; and Hultgren, *From the Damascus Covenant*, 60–61.
18 Klawans, *Heresy*, 94.
19 Klawans, *Heresy*, 100–101.

community regarded themselves as 'sons of light' and children of righteousness, ruled by the Prince of Light, over against 'children of injustice', who were ruled by the Angel of Darkness.[20] As Klawans observes, this concept is timeless and always eternal, and was anticipated to endure until a 'renewal' (חדשה; 1QS 4.25) at the Last Day.[21] The *War Scroll* contains similar references,[22] as does the Damascus Document.[23]

Klawans concludes that the few references to a 'new covenant' and renewal of covenant are offset by frequent acknowledgement of only a single covenant from the beginning unto eternity—ברית עולם.[24] This covenant may be renewed, and its hidden truths revealed, but it is not to be superseded.[25] We will turn now to the Gospel accounts of Jesus' teaching, to determine whether there is evidence of novelty.

## 4. Examination of the Gospel Accounts

At the outset, it is necessary to explain that Klawans' aims differ from my own here. While he is looking for indications of novelty in the *accounts* of Jesus' ministry, I am seeking to discern the actual content of Jesus' teaching, and whether it involves innovation.[26] Klawans focuses first on Mark's account of Jesus' teaching in the synagogue in Capernaum, and the surprise expressed by the audience, who perceive it as 'new' and authoritative.[27] Similar comments are made concerning audience response in Matthew's and John's narratives.[28] Klawans then discusses the command to love one another (John 13:34; 15:12–17), and the 'double love command' (Matt. 22:34–40; Mark 12:28–34; Luke 10:25–28).[29] The juxtaposition in Mark 12:28–34 (and parallels) of the 'love of God' and 'love of neighbour' commands (Deut. 6:5; Lev.

---

20  Klawans, *Heresy*, 104–106. See also Bibliowicz, *Jewish–Christian Relations*, 62–63.
21  Klawans, *Heresy*, 105.
22  1QM 1.1–3; 10.10; 13.7–8; 14.8–10, cited in Klawans, *Heresy*, 105.
23  Klawans, *Heresy*, 105–106.
24  Klawans, *Heresy*, 109.
25  Klawans, *Heresy*, 109.
26  Klawans firmly acknowledges Jesus' Jewishness, but is sceptical of J. P. Meier's assertion that 'The historical Jesus is the halakic Jesus', although Meier's findings are similar to his own; Klawans, *Heresy*, 128, 128 n.39, quoting Meier, *Marginal Jew*, 4:1–25.
27  Klawans, *Heresy*, 129, on Mark 1:21–22 and par. Luke 4:31–32.
28  Klawans, *Heresy*, 129–30, citing Matt. 7:28–29; John 7:14–39.
29  Klawans, *Heresy*, 130–31.

19:18) is found by both Klawans and Meier to be novel.[30] In contrast, while Klawans considers John's love command is presented 'in a fashion to highlight that the time for innovation is at hand',[31] Meier concludes, and I concur, that 'it does not go back to the historical Jesus'.[32]

Klawans next considers the Sermon on the Mount (Matthew 5:1—7:28), working through the topics of divorce, *lex talionis*, love of enemies, anger, adultery, oaths,[33] and concluding that 'the cumulative impact of the Sermon's antitheses is ineluctable. Scripture falls short in important ways'.[34] Yet while it is true that this teaching is audacious, I agree with Meier and Loader that Jesus did not abrogate Mosaic Law. In his discussion of Matthew 5:17–48,[35] Meier observes that this section is 'a creation of Matthew or his church'.[36] Likewise, Loader notes that 'Jesus brings something new' but that 'the new is not abrogation of the old'.[37] He emphasises that the teaching is meant primarily for the Matthaean community, not for outsiders,[38] and that it 'places greater demands on adherents of the Law'.[39] Klawans' treatment of Matthew 5:43–48 is relatively brief,[40] but he finds the injunction for 'love of enemies' to be authentic and novel.[41] It is significant, and we will return to it in section 7.

Klawans' further exploration of the Gospels did not reveal any information about novelty in the teaching of Jesus that is of relevance to our study.[42] However, his discussion of Hebrews is significant, and will be considered in section 6.2.

---

30  Klawans, *Heresy*, 131; Meier, *Marginal Jew*, 4:501–528 (p.528) on Mark 12:28–34. As noted by Klawans, parallels are found in the *Testaments of the Twelve Patriarchs*, but these are Christian pseudepigraphs. See Klawans, *Heresy*, 131 n.51.
31  Klawans, *Heresy*, 131.
32  Meier, *Marginal Jew*, 4:558–72 (p.572).
33  Klawans, *Heresy*, 131–138.
34  Klawans, *Heresy*, 138.
35  Meier, *Marginal Jew*, 4:40–47.
36  Meier, *Marginal Jew*, 4:41.
37  Loader, *Jesus' Attitude*, 168.
38  Loader, *Jesus' Attitude*, 182.
39  Loader, *Jesus' Attitude*, 179. See also Bibliowicz, *Jewish–Christian Relations*, 78.
40  Klawans, *Heresy*, 136–37.
41  Klawans cites Meier's 'exhaustive review' which finds Jesus' directive to 'Love your enemies' to be authentic and without parallel. See Klawans, *Heresy*, 137 and n.73, and Meier, *Marginal Jew*, 4:528–51.
42  Klawans, *Heresy*, 144–49.

## 5. Embrace of Novelty in Christianity

One of Klawans' aims is to fathom how Christianity came to embrace innovation so enthusiastically, whereas Jewish society traditionally condemned novelty. The clue to understanding this is to be found in Bibliowicz's study *Jewish–Christian Relations: The First Centuries*. His thesis is highly complex, but basically surmises that the division between different factions that is evident in the New Testament is not between Jews and Christians as such, but between the *original* Jewish followers of Jesus, and the later mainly Gentile believers who were influenced by Pauline thought and theology.[43] Whereas the early members of the movement—the 'Jerusalem faction'—embraced Jesus' teaching and were committed to Torah observance,[44] the so-called 'Pauline faction' claimed to have replaced the Jewish people as God's chosen, and to be the 'New Israel'.[45]

According to Bibliowicz, writings linked to the Jerusalem faction are James, Q, the M material of Matthew, the Pharisees featured in Acts 15:1,5, and the *Didache*.[46] The Epistle of James is particularly significant because the ethical concerns it expresses cohere with those of the historical Jesus, as exemplified in the Sermon on the Mount, Q, M, and the narrative of the rich young ruler.[47] It is noteworthy that while James refers to forgiveness of sins (5:15), there is nothing in the epistle about atonement theory, thus indicating that the author's affinities lie with 'the pre-Gentile strata of the Jesus movement'.[48] It is my belief that even if the epistle were not actually written by James the brother of Jesus, its contents are consistent with the views espoused by him.[49]

Bibliowicz's 'Pauline faction' includes: Paul's seven undisputed letters; Mark; Luke-Acts; and Hebrews,[50] all of which are characterised by their emphasis on 'Jesus' death and resurrection' over against his

---

43 Bibliowicz, *Jewish–Christian Relations*, 19.
44 Bibliowicz, *Jewish–Christian Relations*, 21.
45 Bibliowicz, *Jewish–Christian Relations*, 25.
46 Bibliowicz, *Jewish–Christian Relations*, 79. Note that several works of the church fathers are also included, but are not relevant to this study.
47 Bibliowicz, *Jewish–Christian Relations*, 75. See Mark 10:17–31 and par. Matthew 19:16–30; Luke 18:18–30.
48 Bibliowicz, *Jewish–Christian Relations*, 75.
49 Following Bibliowicz, *Jewish–Christian Relations*, 76.
50 Bibliowicz, *Jewish–Christian Relations*, 26.

life and ministry.⁵¹ It is important to note that Bibliowicz focuses on 'the controversial, polemical, rhetorical Paul—the originator of the anti-Jewish strand, according to traditional scholarship'.⁵² He does so in order to highlight the damage done by centuries of scholarship in which Paul's writings were wrongly interpreted as anti-Judaic.⁵³ However, he also discusses at length the so-called 'revisionist Paul',⁵⁴ reflecting efforts made in recent decades to view Paul as 'grounded in first-century Judaism', and as a 'torah-observant Jew who was opposed to demanding Torah observance from Gentiles'.⁵⁵

Unlike Klawans, Bibliowicz perceives many parallels between the early Jesus movement and Qumran.⁵⁶ He sees the similarities as reflecting 'that the Qumran sect and the pre-Gentile Jesus movement were contemporaneous sectarian Jewish streams',⁵⁷ though he observes that the Essenes were distinctive with regard to 'strict application of purity rules and discipline'.⁵⁸ What is not generally appreciated is that at the time of Jesus' death, the Essenic renewal movement had existed for well over a century, its members focusing on repentance and forgiveness, and seeing their prayers and study of Torah as a substitute for sacrificial offerings.⁵⁹ The Jesus movement, similarly, is one of renewal, with an emphasis on repentance, prayer, and Torah observance, but requiring a more stringent level of righteousness, in accordance with the double love command, and enjoining the love of enemies. The latter requirement marks a distinct departure from Essenic adherence to the *Two Ways* concept, which involved *enmity* between its members ('sons of light') and all others, deemed 'sons of darkness'.⁶⁰ It appears that Matthew 5:43, stating, 'You have heard that it was said, "You shall love your neighbor and hate your enemy"' (NRSV), reflects Qumranic

---

51 Bibliowicz, *Jewish–Christian Relations*, 25–26, 46.
52 Bibliowicz, *Jewish–Christian Relations*, 46.
53 Bibliowicz, *Jewish–Christian Relations*, 48, 54–55, 57–58.
54 See the discussion on 'Paul in Modern Scholarship' in Bibliowicz, *Jewish–Christian Relations*, 54–57.
55 Bibliowicz, *Jewish–Christian Relations*, 56.
56 Bibliowicz, *Jewish–Christian Relations*, 63–65, listing twenty-one parallels.
57 Bibliowicz, *Jewish–Christian Relations*, 65.
58 Bibliowicz, *Jewish–Christian Relations*, 62.
59 Joseph, *Jesus, the Essenes, and Christian Origins*, 146.
60 See Klawans, *Heresy*, 104–105, citing 1QS 3.13–21; Martínez, *Dead Sea Scrolls Translated*, 6.

influence,[61] since the *Rule of the Community* decrees that members are to 'love all the sons of light', ... and 'to detest all the sons of darkness' (1QS 1.9–10).[62] To put this point in context, I surmise that over the decades from when the scrolls were originally written until the early 30s, there was likely to have been some evolution of rules, as it became clear over several generations that the last days were considerably extended. Hence, while Essenic influence on Jesus is not in doubt, strict compliance with the *Rule of the Community* is not implied; conversely, Jesus evidently chose to strengthen some aspects of Torah, in keeping with his anticipation of the coming of the kingdom.

## 6. The 'New Covenant' in the Epistles

In this section we consider the reference to 'new covenant' in each of three epistles: 2 Corinthians 3:1–18; Hebrews 8:13; 9:15; and 1 Corinthians 11:25. Though the third of these is the earliest written, in approximately 56 C.E.,[63] it is held over until last because it is treated alongside the corresponding text in Luke 22:20.

### 6.1  2 Corinthians 3:1–18

In his discussion of 2 Corinthians 3:1–18, Klawans makes some significant points, noting that Paul's reference to 'new covenant' in 3:6 is the earliest datable usage, that is, in about 57 C.E.[64] He also observes that this is the first time that the 'new' and 'old' covenants are contrasted,[65] but emphasises that Paul is not implying that the new covenant is 'of the Spirit' while the old is 'of the letter'.[66] However, Klawans' overall assessment is unsatisfactory in that his use of the traditional translation

---

61  Note that Klawans regards it as a scriptural misquotation (*Heresy*, 136).
62  See Martínez, *Dead Sea Scrolls Translated*, 3. For similar sentiments in the *War Scroll* (1QM), see Joseph, *Jesus, the Essenes, and Christian Origins*, 122–23.
63  Brown, *Introduction to the New Testament*, 512. In contrast, Barton, '1 Corinthians', 1315 suggests 54–55 C.E.
64  Brown, *Introduction to the New Testament*, 542, with an alternative date of 55–56 C.E.; regarding Pauline chronology see also 428–29.
65  Klawans, *Heresy*, 124.
66  Klawans, *Heresy*, 125.

of the passage results in ambiguity,[67] and also leads to a supersessionist reading, which indeed appears to be the implied meaning of the standard text.[68] Similarly, Avery-Peck interprets the passage according to the traditional view of Paul, reaching the stark conclusion that the law is 'an aspect only of the "old" and deficient covenant that God made with the Jews, a covenant entirely superseded by the "new" covenant God made available to those who believe in Jesus'.[69] To avoid such an interpretation it is necessary to utilise an alternative translation for the crucial verb καταργέω that features in 3:7,10, and 13–14. Antoinette Wire, in her 2019 in-depth study of Second Corinthians,[70] does this most efficaciously, as well as incorporating several other exegetical strategies.

First, Wire interprets the text in relation to Exodus 32—34, the focus being on Moses' second descent from Sinai, especially Exodus 34:29–35,[71] describing the renewal of the covenant which had been established at the time of his first descent. However, she observes that Paul's reference to 'death' in verses 4–7 likely draws on the account in Exodus 32, where the breaking of the law resulted in death.[72] In contrast, the new covenant, foretold in Jeremiah 31:31–34 and Ezekiel 11:19, is exemplified in the Spirit-filled work being done by the Corinthian believers.[73] Second, instead of translating καταργέω as 'set aside' or 'abolish',[74] Wire renders it 'eclipse', asserting that: 'the verb καταργεῖν means in this context not that the glory is fading or canceled but that it is something like being suspended, as when one brightness eclipses another and makes it no longer separately visible'.[75] Third, Wire rightly explains that the term 'Lord' (κύριος) in 3:16, which Paul quotes from Exodus 34:34 LXX, refers not to Jesus Christ,[76] but to

---

67  Klawans, *Heresy*, 125, 127.
68  Klawans, *Heresy*, 125–26. He comments on 3:14: 'The implication, apparently, is that if the veil were to be removed—if the Israelites in question were to become "in Christ"—then the unveiled would see clearly' (pp.125–26).
69  Avery-Peck, 'Second Corinthians', 315.
70  Wire, *2 Corinthians*.
71  Wire, *2 Corinthians*, 60–61.
72  Wire, *2 Corinthians*, 52, 60.
73  Wire, *2 Corinthians*, 51–52.
74  See e.g. Avery-Peck, 'Corinthians', 320.
75  Wire, *2 Corinthians*, 55. See also further discussion on p. 63.
76  Wire, *2 Corinthians*, 64, 69.

the Spirit of God, the divine presence, 'perhaps parallel to Wisdom'.[77] Importantly, she notes that in 3:16, Paul alters the verb used in Exodus 34:34 LXX from εἰσπορεύομαι ('to go in') to ἐπιστρέφω ('to turn back').[78] The substitution of ἐπιστρέφω—drawn from Exodus 34:31 LXX[79]—is highly significant, given the metaphorical connection between turning back, and repentance.[80] The resultant interpretation enables Paul's 'we all' (ἡμεῖς δὲ πάντες) in 3:18 to be understood as referring to the transformation of all '"into the same image" of the one seen ... the Lord who is the Spirit (3:17–18)', to whom both Moses and Christ turn, and whom they reflect as in a mirror.[81] Such transformation is accepted by Wire as incorporating all—Jews and Gentiles alike—who 'turn with Moses to the Spirit of God'.[82] It is envisaged as a process in which God's glory is taken on and spread 'from glory to glory'.[83] Wire observes that while Christ is identified in 2 Corinthians 4:4,6, with God's image, Paul had already asserted Moses as the paradigm for those who turn to Yhwh.[84]

Given that at face value, the standard translation of 2 Corinthians 3:1–18 appears decidedly supersessionist, Wire's insightful exegesis is highly significant, and gives rise to three important findings. First, the 'revised' Paul is exonerated of any supersessionist trait. This means that from my viewpoint, clarification is required for Bibliowicz's definition of 'the Pauline faction'. It refers not to Paul himself but to 'Gentile followers of Paul',[85] and to his 'immediate successors, and maybe some of his contemporaries, [who] used his epistles to discredit Jesus' Jewish followers'.[86]

Second, the correlation of the passage with Exodus 34:29–35 demonstrates that Paul is referring not to a *different* covenant but a *renewal* of the Sinai covenant. From this we can affirm with Stendahl

---

77 Wire, *2 Corinthians*, 53, 64 n.26. See also Cover, *Lifting the Veil*, 276.
78 Wire, *2 Corinthians*, 64. See also Cover, *Lifting the Veil*, 274.
79 See Cover, *Lifting the Veil*, 274.
80 Wire, *2 Corinthians*, 64.
81 Wire, *2 Corinthians*, 55–56.
82 Wire, *2 Corinthians*, 65, following Marlene Crüsemann. See 65 n.29.
83 Wire, *2 Corinthians*, 56.
84 Wire, *2 Corinthians*, 69.
85 Bibliowicz, *Jewish–Christian Relations*, 25.
86 Bibliowicz, *Jewish–Christian Relations*, 21.

that Paul in no way visualises a 'two-covenant model ... one for Jews and one for Gentiles'.[87] Stendahl saw such a notion as 'an expression of "misplaced concreteness"',[88] and regarded the salvation of Jews as 'a mystery', as did Paul.[89] Notably, Wire regards 2 Corinthians 3:7–18 as functioning in a way comparable to Romans 9—11, with Paul affirming 'God's faithfulness to Israel'.[90]

Third, Wire's interpretation draws on an understanding of Jeremiah 31:31–34 that coheres with our findings in section 3—that in its original context it focuses on repentance. Paul's deliberate use of ἐπιστρέφω in place of εἰσπορεύομαι in 3:16 indicates this understanding.[91] Importantly, the 'turning (back)' to Yhwh is applicable to both Jews and Gentiles. Paul speaks 'not only of Israel turning to the Spirit of God but of the Corinthians incorporated through Christ within Israel's experience of God's presence'.[92]

Fourth, although interpreting 2 Corinthians 3:4–18 as *fulfilment* of Jeremiah 31:31–34,[93] Wire stops short of suggesting the renewed covenant as superior to the old. Rather, her translation of καταργέω allows her to view 3:7–11 in terms of God's glory at Sinai being 'outshone by an overriding glory of God in Christ'.[94] Yet Paul's exegesis does contain what Cover terms 'the seeds of later Christological developments',[95] as exemplified in the next section.

## 6.2 The Letter to the Hebrews

We turn now to Hebrews' extensive utilisation of Jeremiah 31:31–34, which is central to its author's argument toward a high Christology. Klawans describes Hebrews as 'the clearest, boldest articulation of the concept of a new covenant in the entire New Testament',[96] surprisingly appearing

---

87   Stendahl, *Final Account*, x.
88   Stendahl, *Final Account*, x.
89   Stendahl, *Final Account*, 7.
90   Wire, *2 Corinthians*, 65 n.29.
91   Note Wire's reference to the exegetical principle of Meir Sternberg that 'every quotation is a recontextualization of meaning in the new situation'; *2 Corinthians*, 64 n.23.
92   Wire, *2 Corinthians*, 57.
93   Wire, *2 Corinthians*, 51.
94   Wire, *2 Corinthians*, 52.
95   Cover, *Lifting the Veil*, 274–75.
96   Klawans, *Heresy*, 138.

to treat the work as if it offered an accurate portrayal of Christian belief at the time it was written.[97] In contrast, I follow Bibliowicz's theory that the letter marks a turning point in relations between Gentile and Jewish Christians, moving beyond Pauline theology, and involving supersessionism and denigration of Jews and Judaism.[98] The letter is frequently regarded as 'the New Testament's most anti-Jewish text'.[99] Attempts have been made by scholars to interpret Hebrews innocuously,[100] but as Klawans points out, these fail to convince.[101]

Thompson considers the author to be exhorting Christians to faithful endurance during a time of hardship,[102] while Eisenbaum, commenting on 10:29, asserts that the letter is addressed to 'Christians who commit apostasy'.[103] With Bibliowicz, I consider the addressees to be Gentile Christians whose faith is in opposition to that of the founding fathers.[104] That they are Gentiles coheres with the references to 'those from Italy' (13:29), and the fact that the earliest citation of Hebrews is from Clement of Rome.[105] A precise date for Hebrews is not calculable but the majority view is 60–90 C.E.,[106] and this aligns with 2:3, which indicates that the author and readers are second generation Christians.[107] Bibliowicz proposes a date about two decades after Paul, hence approximately contemporary with the Synoptic Gospels.[108]

The thrust of the epistle is to contend that Christ, having been exalted to a seat at God's right hand, is superior to all other beings,

---

97  See Klawans, *Heresy*, 138–43, esp. 143, where he notes that 'valorization of the new coupled with the condemnation of the old' differs from the stances of Tertullian and Josephus.
98  Bibliowicz, *Jewish–Christian Relations*, 144.
99  Eisenbaum, 'Hebrews', 406.
100 Eisenbaum, 'Hebrews', 407.
101 Klawans, *Heresy*, 143 n.96, citing e.g. Richard Hays as failing to mitigate the supersessionist character of the text. See also Thompson, 'Hebrews', 568.
102 Thompson, 'Hebrews', 568.
103 Eisenbaum, 'Hebrews', 420. See also Thompson, 'Hebrews', 569. Eisenbaum, 'Hebrews', 420, emphasises that it should not be interpreted as addressed to Jews who did not accept Jesus as Messiah.
104 Bibliowicz, *Jewish–Christian Relations*, 145. See also Lohse, *Formation of the NT*, 199–200.
105 Eisenbaum, 'Hebrews', 406. See also Lohse, *Formation of the NT*, 198, in regard to earlier documentation in Pantaenus, cited by Eusebius.
106 Bibliowicz, *Jewish–Christian Relations*, 146; see also Brown, *Introduction to the New Testament*, 696–97, favouring the 80s.
107 Thompson, 'Hebrews', 569.
108 Bibliowicz, *Jewish–Christian Relations*, 144.

and to all heroes of the Bible.[109] The remainder of the letter builds on the introductory verses (1:1–4), with the references to time periods in 1:1–2 foreshadowing the subsequent contrasting of old and new,[110] with a focus on the term 'covenant', which features nineteen times in all, mainly in Chapters 8—10.[111] The author also repeatedly utilises the literary device of comparison to argue for the superiority of Christ, and of the new covenant over the old.[112] The word 'better' features eleven times (NRSV), including references to a 'better hope' (7:19), and twice to a 'better covenant' (7:22; 8:6).

The quotation of Jeremiah 31:31–34 appears in 8:8–12. It is drawn from the LXX (38:31–34) with some noteworthy amendments.[113] Two of the preceding verses (vv.6–7) introduce the passage with highly supersessionist language, suggesting that had the first covenant been adequate, a second one would not have been required.[114] Verse 8 leads into the quote with the words: 'He [God] finds fault with them when he says … ', setting the stage for criticism of Israel. In verse 9, where the MT has (in 31:32) 'though I was their husband', the text reads 'I had no concern for them'.[115] The citation ends with 'I will remember their sins no more' in verse 12. Verse 13 follows with the astounding assertion that in speaking of a new covenant he [that is, God] had made the first one—the Sinai covenant as discussed in Jeremiah 8:8–12—obsolete.[116] In taking the Jeremianic text out of its original context, the author absurdly appears to imply that 600 years earlier, Yhwh himself had called for the 'old' covenant to be replaced, and a new one to be established with Gentile believers.[117] In addition he argues in verse 13b that the old would soon be gone.

The term 'covenant' occurs again in Hebrew 9:15, where Christ is identified as 'the mediator of a new covenant'. This statement

---

109 Eisenbaum, 'Hebrews', 406; Thompson, 'Hebrews', 568. For the significance of Christ's place at God's right hand, and the quotations from Psalm 110, see Thiselton, 'Hebrews', 1455.
110 Eisenbaum, 'Hebrews', 407.
111 Thiselton, 'Hebrews', 1453.
112 Thompson, 'Hebrews', 568.
113 Eisenbaum, 'Hebrews', 416.
114 Eisenbaum, 'Hebrews', 416.
115 Eisenbaum, 'Hebrews', 416.
116 Eisenbaum, 'Hebrews', 416.
117 Bibliowicz, *Jewish–Christian Relations*, 151.

follows from the use of a *qal vahomer* argument in verses 11–14 that the blood of Christ is far more powerful than that of goats and bulls.[118] 'Covenant' (διαθήκη) is used in verses 15–17 with the meaning of both 'covenant' and 'will', to make the point that a will is one's last testament, not taking effect until death has occurred.[119] Verses 18–22 then focus on the utilisation of blood for the inauguration of the Mosaic covenant, citing Exodus 24:8 in verse 20, and concluding with the claim that 'without the shedding of blood there is no forgiveness of sins'. Then follows a description of the uniqueness of Christ's sacrifice, ending in verse 28 with a reference to the anticipation of his appearing 'a second time'.

The arguments in this part of the letter may be critiqued on several points. First, it is not correct that there must necessarily be shedding of blood for the ratification of a covenant.[120] The inauguration of the Sinai covenant was by means of blood, as described in Exodus 24, and was followed by Moses' destruction of the two tablets after the Golden Calf incident,[121] but, as related in Exodus 34, the covenant was *renewed* without animal sacrifice.[122] Second, as Levine and Brettler explain, it is not true that according to Jewish tradition, atonement requires the shedding of blood.[123] Third, there are several inaccuracies in the account of rituals used and the items required.[124] Fourth, the notion of a second coming of the Messiah is not in accordance with Jewish tradition.[125]

In Hebrews 10:1–18, the basic tenets of the author's argument are repeated, with verses 11–17 containing a summary of themes from 8:1—9:28.[126] In verses 5–9 the quote from Psalm 40:6–8 is from the LXX, with the words 'a body you have prepared for me' in place of the MT version 'ears you have dug for me'.[127] The relevant lines, taken

---

118 Eisenbaum, 'Hebrews', 417.
119 Eisenbaum, 'Hebrews', 417.
120 E.g. the covenant Yhwh made with Abra(ha)m in Gen. 15 required animal sacrifice, but not that made in Gen. 17.
121 See Exod. 31:18—32:35, the destruction of the tablets occurring in 32:19.
122 See esp. Exod. 34:10–28.
123 *Bible With and Without Jesus*, 245–47.
124 Eisenbaum, 'Hebrews', 418. For anomalies in 9:1–10, see Thiselton, 'Hebrews', 1467–68.
125 Eisenbaum, 'Hebrews', 418.
126 Thiselton, 'Hebrews', 1469.
127 Eisenbaum, 'Hebrews', 418–19. The meaning of the Hebrew phrase ('ears you have dug for me' in Ps. 40:6) is uncertain but possibly relates to an emphasis on obedience; Thiselton, 'Hebrews', 1469.

out of context, are treated in Hebrews as if Jesus is addressing God.[128] The occurrence here of the word 'body' (σῶμα) fits the author's purpose well and he employs it in an *inclusio* in verses 5–10. As Bibliowicz states: the claim is being made that 'God himself acknowledged the inadequacies of the Levitical sacrifices (10:8–10)'.[129]

The summary continues with a paraphrase of Jeremiah 31:33–34, spoken by the Holy Spirit, thus reinforcing verse 10.[130] Variations include that instead of the covenant being made with 'the house of Israel', it is 'with them', and the words 'their lawless deeds' are added.[131] Reference to 'forgiveness' is moved to verse 18 with the assertion that 'there is no longer any offering for sin', and that according to Thiselton, 'no "supplement" to the work of Christ remains conceivable'.[132]

In addition to weaknesses already observed in the author's argument, the notion that there can be no second repentance in the case of apostasy (6:4–6; 10:26; 12:17) flies in the face of Jewish tradition concerning God's forgiveness of the penitent,[133] and our findings above. Despite scholarly arguments concerning a distinction between wilful and unwitting sin,[134] I concur with Luther that the idea is 'contrary to all the Gospels and the Letters of Paul'.[135]

Klawans appears to overlook errors in the author's argument, and simply to accept the interpretation of Jeremiah 31 as a *novum*.[136] In contrast, Nanos rightly finds it 'confused, and confusing' and 'finally incoherent',[137] and describes the true meaning of Jeremiah 31:31–34 as a matter of fact: 'After all, Scripture described a new agency that renews the covenant partners' capability to be loyal to the teaching, Torah written on the heart ... rather than a new Torah'.[138]

---

128 Eisenbaum, 'Hebrews', 419, and 409 in regard to Heb. 2:13.
129 *Jewish–Christian Relations*, 153.
130 Eisenbaum, 'Hebrews', 419.
131 Eisenbaum, 'Hebrews', 419.
132 Thiselton, 'Hebrews', 1469.
133 See e.g. Levine and Brettler, *Bible With and Without Jesus*, 241–44.
134 Eisenbaum, 'Hebrews', 419.
135 Lohse, *Formation of the NT*, 202.
136 Klawans, *Heresy*, 142–43.
137 Nanos, '*New* or *Renewed* Covenantalism?' 187.
138 Nanos, '*New* or *Renewed* Covenantalism?' 185.

## 6.3 The Cup Sayings

Klawans notes the difficulty of assessing the authenticity of the words 'new covenant' in 1 Corinthians 11:25 and Luke 22:20,[139] despite their eventual prominence in Christian ideology.[140] He queries the inclusion of 'new' in the cup saying, giving five reasons: (1) its absence from Mark's and Matthew's versions; (2) the word order in the Greek, which differs from what would be expected for translation from Aramaic; (3) the absence of 'new covenant' from Jesus' sayings; (4) the lack of comparisons of new and old, or of valuing the new more highly; (5) and the fact that Hebrews, despite its supersessionist character, does not describe the covenant as 'new' in 9:20.[141] While Klawans' remarks on the cup sayings are sound, they do not take into account the significance of the venue in which I contend the Last Supper took place, or of Jesus' commensals at the meal. These factors will be discussed in section 7.

## 7. Application of Relevant Findings

In sections 2 and 3, exploration of the term 'new covenant' and its occurrences in the Dead Sea Scrolls showed that it referred to *renewal*, and that the Essenes regarded the Mosaic covenant as eternal. Jeremiah 31:31–34 was understood to have inspired renewal movements grounded on its focus on repentance. The assessment of Jesus' teaching in section 4 indicated that he was Torah-observant, and enjoined his followers to adhere to more stringent commandments, notably love of enemies. In section 5, the embrace of innovation in the New Testament was shown to be the result of the division that evolved between Jesus' original *Jewish* followers, and the later *Gentile* Christians who wrongly regarded themselves as the 'new covenant' people. While examination of 2 Corinthians 3:1–18 in section 6 demonstrated that Paul was not supersessionist, Hebrews, with its false claims, evidently brought about a distortion in Christian theology, and adversely influenced

---

139 I follow the scholarly trend in accepting the authenticity of Luke 22:19b–20. See esp. Billings, 'Disputed Words'.
140 Klawans, *Heresy*, 122.
141 Klawans, *Heresy*, 122–24.

contemporaneous and subsequent writers.[142]

Returning now to Jesus' injunction to 'love of enemies', this phrase translates literally into Greek as the term φιλοξενία, i.e. 'hospitality'.[143] As explicated in my previous writings, hospitality—'love of strangers or enemies'—was crucial for Jesus' and his disciples' itinerant ministry, as they were reliant on householders for food and shelter.[144] It was also relevant to the Last Supper, when, as I assert, Jesus had sought his brother James' permission to join the Essenic household together with his followers for the Passover meal, held in accordance with the Qumran calendar.

## 8. Conclusion

The findings have led me to the conclusion that at the Last Supper, when Jesus spoke the words over the cup, he used the Aramaic equivalent of the word καινή (perhaps חדתא)[145] in reference to the covenant, and that it would have been interpreted by those present as meaning *renewed*, with a sense of heartfelt commitment to Torah. In whatever form it was transmitted to Paul (1 Cor. 11:23–25), we can certainly surmise that he understood it to signify covenant *renewal*. The similarity of Luke's version (22:20) to 1 Corinthians 11:25 strongly suggests that it derives from Paul. However, in view of the adverse influence of Hebrews, the Greek term καινή may well have been misunderstood as meaning 'new' by the time that the Gospel was written (probably c. 85 C.E.).[146]

It is important to note that in Paul's version, there is no reference to 'pouring out' and that in Luke's, it is the *cup* that is poured out, *not* 'the blood'. Also, in Luke 22:20 in the Greek, there is no *copula* (likely indicating its antiquity), and an appropriate translation would therefore be: 'This cup that is poured out for you *signifies* the *renewed* covenant in my blood.'

---

142  Bibliowicz, *Jewish–Christian Relations*, 158–59, 360 n.527.
143  BDAG, 683.
144  Marshall, 'Glutton and Drunkard?', esp. 47–57; Marshall, *Dichotomy*, 311–19.
145  As suggested by Klawans, *Heresy*, 123.
146  E.g. as suggested by Bibliowicz, *Jewish–Christian Relations*, 27, and generally accepted by scholars.

In my opinion, Mark (14:24) and Matthew (26:27–28) both appear to have erred in their renditions of the cup saying. Moreover, while I previously considered Mark 14:25 (the so-called 'eschatological prospect') to be authentic,[147] I am now suspicious about the inclusion of the word 'new'. The parallel in Luke 22:17–18 is therefore to be preferred.

The study has demonstrated that there is no evidence in Jesus' teaching or in his words at the Last Supper that it was his intention to inaugurate a 'new covenant' that was in any sense a replacement of the Mosaic covenant. On the contrary, his words over the cup, recalling Jeremiah's prophecy of a time of renewal, indicated his ongoing, heartfelt support of Torah. The cup saying termed the 'eschatological prospect' (Luke 22:17–18) expresses Jesus' anticipation of the final covenant renewal which would occur at the eschatological banquet. Hence the findings cohere with the proposed scenario regarding Jesus' last meal, with his brother James as the Essene host.

Mary J. Marshall
Murdoch University

---

147  See Marshall, 'Re-examining the Last Supper Sayings', 210–12.

## Bibliography

Avery-Peck, A. J. — 'The Second Letter of Paul to the Corinthians', in A.J. Levine and M. Z. Brettler (eds.), *The Jewish Annotated New Testament: New Revised Standard Version Bible Translation* (New York, NY: Oxford University Press, 2011), 315–31.

Barton, S. C. — '1 Corinthians', in J. D. G. Dunn, and J.W. Rogerson (eds.), *Eerdmans Commentary on the Bible* (Grand Rapids, MI: Eerdmans, 2003), 1314–1352.

Bibliowicz, A. M. — *Jewish–Christian Relations: The First Centuries* (rev. edn; Coppell, TX: Mascarat, 2019).

Billings, B. S. — 'The Disputed Words in the Lukan Institution Narrative (Luke 22:19b–20): A Sociological Answer to a Textual Problem', *JBL* 125.3 (2006), 507–26.

Black, M. — *The Scrolls and Christian Origins* (Studies in the Jewish Background of the New Testament; London: Nelson, 1961).

Brown, R. E. — *An Introduction to the New Testament* (ABRL; New York, NY: Doubleday, 1997).

Clines, D. J. A. (ed.) — *Concise Dictionary of Classical Hebrew* (Sheffield: Sheffield Phoenix Press, 2009).

Cover, M. — *Lifting the Veil: 2 Corinthians 3:7–18 in Light of Jewish Homiletic and Commentary Traditions* (BZNW 210; Berlin: de Gruyter, 2015).

Danker, F. W. et al. — *Greek-English Lexicon of the New Testament and Other Early Christian Literature* (3rd edn; Chicago, IL: University of Chicago Press, 2000).

Donaldson, T. L. — *Jews and Anti-Judaism in the New Testament: Decision Points and Divergent Interpretations* (London: SPCK, 2010).

Eisenbaum, P. — 'The Letter to the Hebrews', in A.-J. Levine, and M. Z. Brettler (eds.), *The Jewish Annotated New Testament: New Revised Standard Version Bible Translation* (New York, NY: Oxford University Press, 2011), 406–26.

García Martínez, F. — *The Dead Sea Scrolls Translated: The Qumran Texts in English* (2nd edn; Grand Rapids, MI: Eerdmans, 1996).

Holladay, W. L. (ed.) — *A Concise Hebrew and Aramaic Lexicon of the Old Testament* (Grand Rapids, MI: Eerdmans, 1988).

Hultgren, S.     *From the Damascus Covenant to the Covenant of the Community: Literary, Historical, and Theological Studies in the Dead Sea Scrolls* (STDJ 66; Leiden: Brill, 2007).

Joseph, S. J.     *Jesus, the Essenes, and Christian Origins: New Light on Ancient Texts and Communities* (Waco, TX: Baylor University Press, 2018).

Klawans, J.     *Heresy, Forgery, Novelty: Condemning, Denying, and Asserting Innovation in Ancient Judaism* (New York, NY: Oxford University Press, 2019).

Levine, A.-J and M. Z. Brettler     *The Bible With and Without Jesus: How Jews and Christians Read the Same Stories Differently* (New York, NY: HarperCollins, 2020).

Loader, W. R. G.     *Jesus' Attitude towards the Law* (WUNT Reihe 2, 97; Tübingen: Mohr Siebeck, 1997).

Lohse, E.     *The Formation of the New Testament* (3rd edn.; Nashville, TN: Abingdon, 1981 [German: 1972]).

Marshall, M. J.     'Essenic Influence on Jesus, his Brothers, and the Early Church', in P. G. Bolt (ed.), *The Future of Gospels and Acts Research* (Macquarie Park, NSW: SCD Press, 2021), 51–76.

Marshall, M. J.     'Jesus: Glutton and Drunkard?', *JSHJ* 3.1 (2005), 47–60.

Marshall, M. J.     'Re-examining the Last Supper Sayings in Light of the Hebrew Scriptures', in T. Hägerland (ed.), *Jesus and the Scriptures: Problems, Passages and Patterns* (Library of Historical Jesus Studies 9; Library of New Testament Studies 552; London: Bloomsbury T&T Clark, 2016), 193–214.

Marshall, M. J.     'The Hospitality–Inhospitality Dichotomy in Continuum', in T. Holmén (ed.), *Jesus in Continuum* (WUNT 289; Tübingen: Mohr Siebeck, 2012), 299–322.

Meier, J. P.     *A Marginal Jew: Rethinking the Historical Jesus.* Vol. 4: *Law and Love* (New Haven, CT: Yale University Press, 2009).

Nanos, M. D.     '*New* or *Renewed* Covenantalism? A Response to Richard Hays', in R. Bauckham et al., (eds.), *The Epistle to the Hebrews and Christian Theology* (Grand Rapids, MI: Eerdmans, 2009), 183–88.

Stendahl, K.     *Final Account: Paul's Letter to the Romans* (Minneapolis, MN: Fortress, 1995).

| | |
|---|---|
| Svartvik, J. | '"I Have Come Not to Abolish but to Fulfil": Reflections on Understanding Christianity as Fulfilment without Presupposing Supersessionism', [https://www.jcrelations.net/articles/article/i-have-come-not-to-abolish-but-to-fulfil.html]. |
| Thiselton, A. C. | 'Hebrews', in J. D. G. Dunn and J. W. Rogerson (eds.), *Eerdmans Commentary on the Bible* (Grand Rapids, MI: Eerdmans, 2003), 1451–82. |
| Thistlethwaite, S. B. | 'The Bible is Active in Politics Today: A Christian Response to Contesting Texts', in M. D. Knowles et al. (eds.), *Contesting Texts: Jews and Christians in Conversation about the Bible* (Minneapolis, MN: Fortress Press, 2007), 165–72. |
| Thompson, J. W. | 'Hebrews, Epistle to the', *EDB*, 568–70. |
| VanderKam, J. C. | 'Covenant', in L. H. Schiffman and J. C. VanderKam, (eds.), *The Encyclopedia of the Dead Sea Scrolls* (2 vols.; New York, NY: Oxford University Press, 2000), 1.151–55. |
| Wire, A. C. | *2 Corinthians* (Wisdom Commentary 48; Collegeville, MN; Liturgical Press, 2019). |

CHAPTER 5

# Wicked Wizards of the East:
# The μάγοι in Historical Context and Ambiguity as Narrative Technique in Matthew 2

Jonathan Thambyrajah

## 1. Introduction

In Matthew's infancy narratives, the μάγοι play a major role, and it is no secret that they have been subject to a lot of misinterpretation over the centuries. This has led to the current state of research on the μάγοι, where the strong (and rightful) emphasis is on understanding them in the historical context of the Gospels. However, there is a problem: the ancient evidence itself provides a variety of conflicting views. It is not immediately clear which ancient view is the most relevant for our understanding of the μάγοι in Matthew. Ultimately, we will argue, the Gospel wishes to present the μάγοι as positive figures. However, in order to do so we must deal with the reputation of the μάγοι.

The Gospel's presentation of the μάγοι cannot entirely be separated from literary allusions to Numbers 24, and a nexus of texts consisting of Isaiah 60 (esp. v.6), 1 Kings 10, and Psalm 72:10. However, these two sets of allusions, if applied to the μάγοι, present strikingly different pictures of the μάγοι. On the one hand, they are compared to the wicked

Balaam, on the other to foreign monarchs submitting to God's king.

By understanding the role of ambiguity in Matthew's narrative, we can understand how the Gospel manages the reputation of the μάγοι and how it is able to draw on such contradictory allusions to do so.

## 2. Historical Ambiguity: The μάγοι in Historical Context

According to one approach, the μάγοι are Parthian kingmakers and ambassadors, who come to recognise the birth of a new king in the West: the μάγοι should, therefore, be understood in the context of the political relationship between Rome and Parthia. The primary point of comparison is the visit of the μάγοι to Nero.[1] According to another approach, the μάγοι are primarily priests or astrologers.[2] They may or may not be connected with Parthia.[3] Particularly of note is the view that the μάγοι are not necessarily gentiles, but Jewish occultists.[4] This view has the potential to view the μάγοι in a more negative light, because if they are liberated from the role of Parthian priest, they can more easily be understood as charlatans. A third view, not necessarily incompatible with the former two, emphasises how the presence of the μάγοι in the Gospel relates to two passages from the Hebrew Bible, Numbers 2, Isaiah 60 (esp. v.6), 1 Kings 10, and Psalm 72:10.[5]

The most important Persian source for the μάγοι is the Behishtun

---

1 Beck, 'Greco-Roman Astrologers'; Horsley, *The Liberation of Christmas*, 55–57; de Jong, 'Matthew's Magi as Experts on Kingship'; Kim, 'The Worship of Jesus', 231–32; Trost, 'Herod the Great, the Magi, and Parthia'. As a variation on this approach, Ossendrijver, 'The Story of the Magi', compares the Magi incident to Alexander and the Chaldeans; Schniewind, *Das Evangelium*, 16–17.
2 Albright and Mann, *Matthew*, 14; Bonnard, *L'évangile*, 25; Brown, *The Birth of the Messiah*, 167; Davies and Allison, *Matthew*, 1:228–30; Hare, *Matthew*, 13; France, *Matthew*, TNTC 1, 81; France, *Matthew*, NICNT, 66; Harrington, *Matthew*, 42; Hagner, *Matthew 1–13*, 26; Horsley, *The Liberation of Christmas*, 53–60; Horsley, *Jesus and Magic*, 38–42; Keener, *Matthew*, 98; Lagrange, *Évangile*, 21; Luz, *Matthew 1–7*, 112; Meier, *Matthew*, 11; Morris, *Matthew*, 35; Osborne, *Matthew*, 86; Turner, *Matthew*, 79. See also Delling, 'μάγος', *TDNT* 4:356–59.
3 Schmid describes them as 'Babylonian Magi', which is to say 'Chaldeans'. Schmid, *Matthäus*, 46. However, we should not confuse the two distinct offices.
4 Sim, 'Gentiles or Jews?'
5 Brown, *Birth of the Messiah*, 51 n.25, 117, 168, 187, 190–96; Davies and Allison, *Matthew*, 1:230–31, 249–51; Bruns, 'The Magi Episode in Matthew 2'; France, *Matthew*, TNTC 1, 80, 84; Hare, *Matthew*, 13; Harrington, *The Gospel of Matthew*, 42, 44; Lohmeyer, *Matthäus*, 20–22; Meier, *Matthew*, 11–12; Morris, *Matthew*, 41; Trost, 'Herod the Great', 100; Turner, *Matthew*, 79.

Inscription, in which Darius claims that he put down a *magu-* usurper (*DB* I.36–71). Subsequently, he slaughtered them. It is difficult to extricate history from the royal ideology that is presented in the Behishtun Inscription,[6] but references to the '*magophonia*' continue nevertheless throughout the sources for centuries.[7] Whatever the truth of Darius' rise to power, his official version of events seems to have become the dominant one. Both within the Persian Empire and beyond, the *magu-* tribe was remembered for their coup d'état. Nevertheless, Parthian and later Zoroastrian sources seem, unsurprisingly, more positive.[8]

Much of the Graeco-Roman evidence has already been covered by van Kooten and de Jong. As a generalisation, van Kooten tends to emphasise the positive depictions of μάγοι (or at least, positive interpretations of neutral evidence).[9] De Jong is more conscious of the pejorative overtones found in most of the evidence.[10] I do not intend to repeat all of the evidence that is summarised in these works. However, it is necessary to give a sense of some of the Graeco-Roman evidence.

Among the earliest references is a fragment of Heraclitus, where the μάγοι appear in a list of suspicious semi-religious figures: τίσι δὴ μαντεύεται Ἡ. ὁ Ἐφέσιος; νυκτιπόλοις, μάγοις, βάκχοις, λήναις, μύσταις·[11] Similarly, in the Derveni papyrus, the μάγοι appear as ritualists, performing sacrifices.[12] Even among relatively early sources, we can find references to the μάγοι as charlatans and cheats.[13] However, from the classical period, there are also more neutral, or even positive descriptions: Plato mentions them in passing as involved in the education of kings.[14] In *Histories*, despite some

---

6   See Kuhrt, *The Persian Empire*, 135–39.
7   Diodorus Siculus, 11.57 and 16.47; Herodotus, *Histories*, 3.79; Josephus, *AJ*, 11.3; Polybius, *Histories*, 5.43.
8   Shaphur 32; Avesta Y. 65.7.
9   van Kooten, 'Matthew, the Parthians, and the Magi', 496–646.
10  de Jong, *Traditions of the Magi*, 387–413; de Jong, 'Matthew's Magi'.
11  Heraclitus fragment (found in Clement's *Protrepicus* 22.2).
12  Derveni Papyrus col. VI. See Janko, 'The Derveni Papyrus'.
13  Aeschines, *Against Ctesiphon* 3.137; Euripides, *Orestes*, 1498; Sophocles, *Oedipus Tyrannus*, 387.
14  Plato, *Republic*, 572e–573a. In the context, Plato is discussing the 'descent' from king to timocrat to oligarch to democrat to tyrant. Here, the μάγοι hope to restrain democracy, hoping for the 'higher' orders of government but resulting in tyranny. Later, however, others would claim that the μάγοι were one of two groups responsible for choosing the king. Cf. Apuleius, *Apology*, 25–26; Cicero, *De divinatione*, 1.91; Philo, *On the Special Laws* 3.100–101; Strabo, *Geography*, 11.9.

wariness,[15] Herodotus mostly treats them as priests of a particular tribe, particularly involved in interpreting dreams and predicting the rise of Cyrus.[16] Xenophon too focuses on their ritual role.[17] Occasionally, they are mentioned as a source of philosophy.[18]

Later Greek and Latin sources tend to be more negative, focusing on the fact that μάγοι lie.[19] The involvement of the μάγοι in 'magic,' particularly telling the future, also becomes more prominent.[20] Cicero is interested in, but at times quite critical of Magian religion.[21] Yet even at this stage, some authors limit themselves to description, with less negativity.[22] Plutarch describes their role within (proto-)Zoroastrian religion, mostly as a topic of interesting conversation for the educated.[23] Particularly prominent in the classical sources is the idea that Tiridates, a *'magus'*—actually the king of Armenia—made a trip to visit Nero.[24]

While on the topic of Graeco-Roman evidence, it is worth saying something about the Greek word μάγος.[25] The word is transparently a loanword from an Iranian language, on semantic grounds. However,

---

15   Herodotus, *Histories*, 1.140.
16   Herodotus, *Histories*, 1.101, 1.107, 1.108, 1.132, 3.61, *inter alia*. In particular, it seems that the μάγοι (except during the annual commemoration of the *magophonia*) would travel abroad. Herodotus, *Histories* 3.79. This role as predictors of kings is also noted by Keener, *The Gospel of Matthew*, 102, who points to Pliny, *NH* 1.47, 30.6.
17   Xenophon, *Cyropedia*. μάγοι are called by Cyrus to select appropriate gifts for the gods. (4.5.14, 51, 7.3.1, 8.3.11); μάγοι interpret the will of the gods (4.5.51); the μάγοι collect the part of the booty that belongs to the gods (5.3.4, 7.5.35); after the siege of Babylon, the μάγοι have the first opportunity to select locations for sanctuaries for the gods (7.5.35); the μάγοι direct sacrifices to local (non-Persian) gods (7.5.57, 8.1.23, 8.3.24–25). Cf. Herodotus, *Histories*, 7.43, 7.191.
18   Apuleius, *Apology*, 31; Cicero, *De finibus*, 5.7; Diogenes Laertius, *Democritus*, 9.7.
19   Appian, *Syrian War*, 9.58; Catullus, 90; Cassius Dio, *Historiae Romanae*, 46.4, 72.8, 78.18; Cicero, *De legibus*, 2.26; Lucian, *Demonax*, 23; Lucian, *Philopsuedes sive incredulus*, 12; Lucian, *De Mercede*, 27; Lucian, *Alexander*, 6, 21; Acts 8:9–11; 13:6ff.
20   Chariton, *Callirhoe*, 5.9.5; Cicero, *De divinatione*, 1.46–47; Pliny the Elder, *Natural History*, 30.2. It is particularly interesting to note that Pliny believes there is a group of μάγοι who are Jewish, particularly to be associated with Cyprus in more recent times (cf. Acts 8:9–11, Acts 13:6ff; Josephus, *AJ*, 20.141.)
21   Cicero, *De divinatione*, 1.43, 46–47; *De legibus*, 2.26; *De natura deorum*, 1.43; *Tusculanae disputationes*, 1.108.
22   Clement of Alexandria, *Protrepicus*, 5.1.66; 4.58.3.1; 2.22.2.2; 5.65.1.1ff.
23   Plutarch, *Roman Questions*, 26; Plutarch, *On Isis and Osiris*, 46, 47; Plutarch, *On the Defect of the Oracles* 10; Plutarch, *On Envy and Hate*, 3. Particularly amusing is that Plutarch relates that the Magi fear mice.
24   Dio Cassius, *Roman History*, 63; Pliny, *Natural History*, 30; Suetonius, *Nero*, 13, Tacitus, *Annals*, 15.1–32.
25   BDAG, s.v. 'μάγος'; *LSJ*, s.v. 'Μάγος'.

it must be a loanword of considerable age by the time it is used in the Gospels: it is attested from the fourth century, which means that it was not borrowed from Parthian, but Old Persian, *magu-*,²⁶ during the first stage of Irano-Hellenistic contact. Given that the word is so established in the Greek language, we must assume that it had probably undergone significant semantic development over the centuries, which explains how it has come, in the Graeco-Roman sources, to refer to magicians and charlatans, especially in the derived forms like μαγεύω and μαγικός. However, as we have seen, the connection with eastern 'Persian' priests is not forgotten in the Graeco-Roman sources. Rather, by the time of Matthew, as we have seen, the word μάγος has developed a decided ambiguity: it might refer to a common charlatan *or* to a Persian, or by this stage Parthian, priest. Even when it refers to a Parthian priest, this is not necessarily positive, depending on the author's perception of the Parthian empire.

Finally, we reach the early Jewish evidence. Sometimes they appear in a *relatively* neutral way, as officials. Thus, Persian מגושיא appear as witnesses to a contract in Elephantine, scribed by the presumably Jewish Mauziah, the son of Nathan, the son of Ananiah.²⁷ This kind of evidence suggests that the מגושא were likely known to Jewish communities in the Persian period, throughout the Persian empire, even in distant border towns like Elephantine. This provides some context for the use of Μάγος in the Greek translations of Daniel to refer to wise officials/sorcerers in the king's court.²⁸ Likewise, the Peshitta uses ܡܓܘܫܐ in Daniel and Isaiah in contexts that refer to various kinds of sorcerers.²⁹

---

26 Kent, *Old Persian*, 201. Cf. Durkin-Meisterernst, *Dictionary of Manichean Middle Persian and Parthian*, s.v. 'mgbyd'; Gharib, *Soghdian Dictionary*, s.vv. 'myw', 'mywpt', 'mwγ', etc.; Nyberg, *A Manual of Pahlavi*, 2:122. Soghdian and Pahlavi both attest both *mag-* and *mog-* forms of the word. Nyberg suggests that the *mag-* spellings are archaising, whereas *mog-* was the current form. However, since the Greek borrowed the word in the Old Persian period, it is unsurprising that it reflects the *mag-* form. It is particularly striking that even though the word was borrowed into Greek in the 4th century BCE at the latest, and even though it underwent significant semantic development, the word retains its association with Iran, even in the first centuries CE.
27 *TAD* B 3.5.
28 In Daniel, Theodotion consistently uses μάγος isomorphically where MT has, אַשָּׁף 'sorcerer' (1:20, 2:2, 2:10, 2:27, 4:4, 5:7, 5:11, 5:15). OG Daniel only uses μάγος twice, both times that MT reads, אַשָּׁף 'sorcerer' (2:2, 2:10).
29 The Peshitta uses ܡܓܘܫܐ at Isa. 19:3, 47:9, 47:12, Dan. 2:2, 4:4, 5:7, and 5:11. It appears to correspond to a variety of different words in MT. See also, Keener, *The Gospel of Matthew*, 99.

However, frequently the μάγοι/ מגושא are seen in a negative light.[30] The targum of pseudo-Jonathan refers at Exodus 7:15 to Pharaoh engaging in divination on the water 'like a female Magian'.[31] As with the Greek sources, it appears that מגוש comes to refer to a practitioner of magic, even beyond the Persian priesthood. The Talmud is particularly negative towards the מגושא, viewing them as wicked purveyors of foolishness and strange beliefs.[32]

## 3. Narrative Ambiguity: The μάγοι in Matthew's Narrative

Based on such differences of opinion, we cannot claim the predominance of one view or another on the μάγοι, since we have no way of knowing how representative our sources are. Rather, we should note the variety of ancient opinions on the μάγοι.

Given such variety, the Gospel of Matthew cannot assume its readers' stance towards the μάγοι. Therefore, the Gospel itself must guide the readers' impressions of the μάγοι as they read. As readers progress through the narrative, the character of the μάγοι is gradually revealed. Nonetheless, the narrative is highly tolerant of ambiguity.

One of the best examples of ambiguity in Matthew 2 is the very introduction of the μάγοι as 'from the East'. At this point, the Gospel could have easily cleared up much of the ambiguity around the μάγοι by specifying that they were from Parthia or from Babylon, or by providing some other point of clarification.[33] However, the Gospel proves reticent on this point. Even at the end of the narrative, it is genuinely possible for the reader to interpret the text as referring to Parthia or

---

30 Cf. France, *The Gospel of Matthew*, 66–67.
31 The reference to Pharaoh's use of Magi is interesting in light of a passing reference in Cassius Dio, *Historiae Romanae*, 72.8 to an Egyptian Magus.
32 *b.Shabb.* 139a, where the Magi serve as examples of people even more proud than the proud; *b.Sot* 22a, where the Magus mumbles memorised chants, but does not understand the meaning of what they say; *b.BB* 58a, where the Magi rummage through graves; *b.San.* 39a, where the Magi's beliefs are ridiculed.
33 Even today, there is a great veriety of opinion: Brown, *Birth of the Messiah*, 168–170; Davies and Allison, *Matthew*, 1:228; Hagner, *Matthew 1–13*, 27; Keener, *The Gospel of Matthew*, 99; Osborne, *Matthew*, 86–87; Schneiwind, *Matthäus*, 16–17; Zahn, *Das Evangelium*, 90–95.

Babylon or some other location: it is genuinely ambiguous.³⁴ Judging by the variety of ancient views on the μάγοι, it must have been ambiguous for the ancient reader too. Nor is there any attempt by the Gospel to resolve this particular ambiguity. However, according to the dynamics of reading, there are certain 'ambiguities' that are resolved as the narrative progresses. What seemed ambiguous becomes clear and previous events are revisited, or rather re-evaluated, as the reader encounters new information.³⁵

## 4. Ambiguity in the Narrative Progression of Matthew 2
### 4.1 The Star and Balaam

If their point of origin is the first *datum* for the characterisation of the μάγοι, the next is the appearance of the star and its apparent use for astrology. Although astrology is not *typically* one of the activities of Parthian μάγοι, there may be a degree of confusion in later non-Parthian sources of Chaldeans (famed astrologers) with μάγοι.³⁶ Some readers may have found the use of astrology off-putting, given Leviticus 19:26 and Deuteronomy 18:9–12.³⁷

The star, in conjunction with reference to 'the East', raises the possibility of an allusion to Balaam in Numbers 24—a reading that is popular in the commentaries,³⁸ but divisive in other scholarship. Though

---

34 On ambiguity, see: Rimmon-Kenan, 'Ambiguity and Narrative Levels'; Sternberg, 'Gaps, Ambiguity, and the Reading Process'; Vöhler, 'Modern and Ancient Concepts of Ambiguity'.
35 On the sequentiality of narrative and reader judgements, see: Grabes, 'Sequentiality'; Phelan, *Experiencing Fiction*; Phelan, 'Rhetorical Narratology'; Rimmon-Kenan, *Narrative Fiction*, 48–53, 123–26.
36 E.g. Philostratus, *Life of Apollonius*, 1.2, 1.18, 1.25ff. However, it may be that these are Parthian Magi, who simply happen to be located in Parthian Babylon. Both Greek translations of Daniel and the Peshitta seem to refer, anachronistically, to Magi in Dan. 2:2, set in pre-Persian Babylon, as well as other parts of the book. It seems that this must reflect a degree of confusion between different types of religious official, since the translator would (presumably) not have thought that Persian officials would be present in Nebuchadnezzar's court.
37 Cf. Keener, *The Gospel of Matthew*, 421; Trost, 'Herod the Great', 101–2.
38 Brown, *Birth of the Messiah*, 117, 168, 187, 190–96; Davies and Allison, *Matthew*, 1:230–31; France, *Matthew*, TNTC 1, 82; Harrington, *The Gospel of Matthew*, 42; Meier, *Matthew*, 11; Trost, 'Herod the Great', 100; Turner, *Matthew*, 79.

references to Balaam as a μάγος in Philo[39] suggest that an ancient reader may have easily identified the connection between μάγοι and Numbers 24, there is nothing in the narrative itself that compels the reader to make the connection. There is no explicit statement of fulfilment of prophecy.[40] Moreover, any connection with Numbers 24 is made more complex, because the sense of the ἀνατελλ- word group appears to be altered.[41] This has caused some scholars to reject any possibility of an allusion. However, to reject the allusion on these grounds has a much too low view of the literary skill of the Gospel—a Gospel that is full of subtle and complex allusions that would not meet these criteria. Rather, we observe that the Gospel leaves the possibility of a connection with Balaam open to the reader, especially in view of the choice to refer to the 'East' rather than a more specific point of origin. The possibility of an allusion to Balaam is also made difficult by the fact that it would seem to conflict with the possible allusions to Sheba. However, we will return to this point, below.

In addition, it is much less clear how a reader is supposed to take the reference: Balaam himself had a dubious reputation in antiquity. Comparing the μάγοι to him does little to disambiguate their characterisation. Thus, the Gospel continues to maintain the ambiguity at this point: the readers are unsure whether the μάγοι are friend or foe.

## 4.2 The μάγοι as a Threat

As the story develops, the picture of the μάγοι is drawn out. As they begin to interact with Herod (2:3), they begin to emerge as figures of potential threat. It is unsurprising that Herod is terrified by the μάγοι. However, we should not gloss over the fact that they are perceived as

---

39  *Mos.* 1.276. Cf. Brown, *Birth of the Messiah*, 36; van Kooten, 'Matthew, the Parthians, and the Magi', 583 n.97; Sim, 'Gentiles or Jews?', 990–91.
40  van Kooten, 'Matthew, the Parthians, and the Magi', 602–9; see also: Davies and Allison, *Matthew*, 1:235.
41  van Kooten, 'Matthew, the Parthians, and the Magi', 605–8.

dangerous not just by Herod, but by all of Jerusalem.⁴² The inhabitants of Jerusalem act as a proxy for the Jewish/Jewish-Christian audience of the Gospel in this pericope. Confronted with Jerusalem's reaction, such an audience might be inclined to assume that the Gospel is presenting the μάγοι in the light of their negative reputation in the ancient world. At this point of the narrative, there are no characters within the text that have reacted positively to the μάγοι. It does not *compel* a negative reading, but puts the plausibility of a positive reading under considerable strain.⁴³

As if to confirm that the μάγοι are such threatening figures, Herod seeks to use them clandestinely to flush out the hidden king. This plays exactly into the more negative stereotypes about μάγοι: Herod's actions put him in a role similar to Astyages in Herodotus' account of the birth of Cyrus. The μάγοι run the risk, in the eyes of the readers, of fulfilling their stereotypical role of being unwitting (or willing?) stooges to a king. Their involvement in Herod's plot, limited as it may be, does little to commend them to the readers.

---

42  Some commentators attempt to explain away the fear of Jerusalem as belonging only to the religious leaders (so Turner, *Matthew*, 81, following Horsley, *The Liberation of Christmas*, 49–52). However, if the Gospel wished to limit the fear to only the leaders, it would not have any trouble expressing itself: within the pericope, the religious leaders are a discernible group (2:4), distinct from the rest of the population of Jerusalem. Lagrange, *Évangile*, 24, suggests that ταράσσειν might mean a disturbance of fear in the case of Herod, but one of hope in the case of the populace. However, the zeugma is awkward. Moreover, that ταράσσειν could denote positive emotion seems to require further proof. Cf. *BDAG*, s.v. 'ταράσσω'; Davies and Allison, *Matthew*, 1:38. Bonnard, *L'évangile*, 26, suggests that Jerusalem might fear, expecting backlash against them from Herod. However, there is no hint of this motive in the text, which reads: ὁ βασιλεὺς Ἡρῴδης ἐταράχθη καὶ πᾶσα Ἱεροσόλυμα μετ' αὐτοῦ. It is implausible that the city's fear would be described as μετ' αὐτοῦ, 'alongside Herod' if the situation were that Herod feared the Magi, but the city feared Herod. Harrington, *The Gospel of Matthew*, 41, is right to note that 'all' is totalising—while the whole city is in view, that does not need to imply every last individual. Luz, *Matthew 1–7*, 113, correctly identifies that Matthew intends the whole city, not just the leadership, but explains this as Matthew's tendency to view Jerusalem as the 'the city of Jesus' murder'. So also, Davies and Allison, *Matthew*, 238. However, Matthew is not so black-and-white: Jerusalem is also, at times, supportive of John's ministry and Jesus', especially early on in the Gospel (e.g. 3:5, 4:25).

43  Here, we note the so-called 'primary' effect, by which the reader will attempt to hold on to their initial assumption until it is no longer tenable. Rimmon-Kenan, *Narrative Fiction*, 124.

### 4.3 The μάγοι as Foolish Wise Men

As Powell has argued, the μάγοι are contrasted with the king's wise men in their interactions with Herod.[44] It seems that, for supposed experts, the μάγοι know far less than the Jewish experts: they have followed their astrology, but they do not know where to go, or apparently, much about the nature of the king they seek. In contrast, the Biblical prophecy, identified by the Jewish priests and scribes is able to guide them precisely to the correct location. It may not be that we should conclude (as Powell does) that the μάγοι are 'foolish'[45]—though it is tempting. Such a reading would put them squarely in the ancient vein of thought that viewed μάγοι as charlatans. However, this reading would obscure the fact that the μάγοι have correctly identified the star in the first place. Instead, what appears to be going on here is that the great, if potentially sinister, wisdom of the μάγοι provides a foil for the even greater wisdom of the prophet, Micah.[46]

### 4.4 The Reappearance of the Star

At this stage, the Gospel has not compelled its readers one way or the other. However, it must be admitted that so far, the Gospel has flirted much more with presenting these μάγοι in a very negative light. The reader who wishes to read them as positive figures has faced several more challenges to that interpretation than the reader who reads them as threatening. It is at the reappearance of the star that the situation begins to be reversed.[47]

It is worthy of note that up until this point, the reader has been denied any insight into the internal thoughts or emotions of the μάγοι: they have been forced to form a view on the μάγοι based only on the information available to them, namely their own perceptions of their actions and the reactions of Herod and the Jerusalemites. This lack of information about the internal thought of the μάγοι is the

---

44  Powell, 'The Magi as Wise Men'.
45  Powell, 'The Magi as Wise Men', 8.
46  Cf. Brown, *The Birth of the Messiah*, 167–68.
47  On the Messianic symbolism of the star itself, see: Hannah, 'The Star of the Magi and the Prophecy of Balaam', 433–34; Newman, 'Stars of the Messiah'.

largest part of what creates ambiguity in the first half of the pericope. The reader is forced to evaluate them based on external appearances alone. This changes with the reappearance of the star, where the Gospel says that the μάγοι were overwhelmed with joy, stressing the extent of their joy very fully: ἐχάρησαν χαρὰν μεγάλην σφόδρα.[48] The Gospel, here, provides the first authorial statement on the internal thoughts of the μάγοι, and characterises them objectively.

### 4.5 *Proskynesis* to the King

Once the Gospel has shown its hand, the characterisation of the μάγοι continues to develop along similar lines: straightaway they perform *proskynesis* to the one born king of the Jews. Their reaction to the Messiah proves their intent: they are not wicked charlatans, but rather they genuinely seek to honour the king of the Jews.

For all that Matthew has nodded to the formidable reputation of the μάγοι, it is difficult to deny that in the end they are positive figures because of their joy at discovering Jesus, and because of their response to that joy. This realisation prompts a re-interpretation of events to this point:[49] where previously the μάγοι might have appeared sinister, they now become models of the correct response to the unveiling of the hidden Messiah. Indeed, they are the first such models in Matthew's Gospel. Only now that the μάγοι have been transformed is it 'safe' for the reader to identify with the pagan μάγοι, instead of the more obvious candidates within the narrative pericope, namely the Jerusalemites.

The light in which the μάγοι stand at the end of the narrative rules out, retrospectively, a number of the views about μάγοι that might have been plausible based on the ancient evidence: they cannot be sinister, because of their response to Jesus. Nor can the μάγοι be charlatans, because their astrology did eventually lead them to the king. If they are Parthian priests, they are not acting in a ritual role. Rather, the

---

48  See Turner, *Matthew*, 85 n.11.
49  For a reader, the most recent information overrides older information, 'the recency effect'. This can force the reader to re-evaluate their initial assumptions. Grabes, 'The Processualities of Literature'; Rimmon-Kenan, *Narrative Fiction*, 124–26.

view that is most consonant with the *end* of the pericope is that they act as ambassadors to a new king. This role also helps build Matthew's theology.

The combination of the *proskynesis* of the μάγοι with gifts of gold, frankincense, and myrrh has prompted comparison with kings of Sheba and Saba in Isaiah 60, Psalm 72:10 and the queen of Sheba in 1 Kings 10.[50] There is also significant objection to such a comparison.[51] However, when the role of the μάγοι is understood as being ambassadors of kings, the allusion is much stronger. In the logic of this allusion, the μάγοι play the role of gentiles, who come, on the behalf of the Parthian king, to offer their wealth to the Christ. In this they are similar perhaps to the Queen of Sheba (who surely stands behind the reference to the kings of Sheba and Saba in Isaiah 60), but instead they offer their wealth to one greater than Solomon, as the Gospel will pick up again in 12:42.[52]

---

50 Brown, *Birth of the Messiah*, 51 n.25, 187–88; Davies and Allison, *Matthew*, 1:249–51; France, *Matthew*, TNTC, 84; Harrington, *The Gospel of Matthew*, 44; Lohmeyer, *Das Evangelium*, 20–22; Meier, *Matthew*, 12; Morris, *Matthew*, 41; Newman, 'Stars of the Messiah', 276; Trost, 'Herod the Great', 100. Cf. Keener, *The Gospel of Matthew*, 105. Each of the gifts can be associated with divine worship, as well as kingly honour: Derrett, 'Further Light on the Narratives of the Nativity', 103–5. Distinguishing between the two might be a distinction only felt by modern readers. Hagner, *Matthew 1–13*, 28; Osborne, *Matthew*, 87. See also Luz, *Matthew 1–7*, 139; Schmid, *Das Evangelium*, 48.

51 One objection is that the Magi are not kings (van Kooten, 'Matthew, the Parthians, and the Magi', 615; cf. Powell, 'The Magi as Kings'). This is true, but Magi function as ambassadors/servants of the king. Powell agrees, but thinks that this constitutes a failure of the prophecy ('The Magi as Kings', 472–73). However, though they are not the Parthian king, in Matthew 2 they *represent* the Parthian king. Powell argues that there is no indication in the text that they act as anyone's representative. However, the indication is in their identity: they are representatives, because that is what Magi do ('The Scriptures are *not* fulfilled, and that is the point', Powell, 'The Magi as Kings', 472). In either case, as Powell recognises, the reader is supposed to be thinking of these texts from the Hebrew Bible. Another objection is that Matthew does not use a fulfilment motif (van Kooten, 'Matthew, the Parthians, and the Magi', 615–17; Sim, 'Gentiles or Jews?', 997): but as we argued with Numbers, Matthew often alludes to the Hebrew Bible without the use of the motif. Matthew 2:11 functions as allusion to Isaiah 60, without necessarily rising to the level of a specific fulfilment of prophecy.

52 Bruns, 'The Magi Episode', 52–53.

## 5. Ambiguity and Maximal Interpretation: Balaam *and* Sheba

On the surface, however, there is a conflict between the allusion to Balaam and the allusion to the kings/queen of Sheba. In the allusion to Balaam, the μάγοι play the role of the wicked prophet. In the allusion to Sheba, they play the role of subjects to the prophesied king. In Balaam, they are compared to a negative character, in Sheba an admirable one. Understanding the role of ambiguity in the narrative and in the characterisation of the μάγοι solves this problem.

In wanting to refer to the μάγοι, Matthew is faced with the not insignificant problem of their bad reputation in antiquity. As several scholars have pointed out, Matthew does himself no favours by including them and their (perhaps temporary) acknowledgement of the Messiah, which may indicate that he is relying on an earlier tradition that he does not feel at liberty to omit.[53] Equally, however, he is not at liberty to ignore the very widely-held view that μάγοι are dangerous and not at all trustworthy. The Gospel's strategy for dealing with this is ambiguity.

The first half of the pericope is given over to acknowledging the probable situation that the readers of the Gospel would be inclined to doubt the trustworthiness of the μάγοι. However, in this section, there is nothing that commits the Gospel or its readers to that understanding. Matthew acknowledges their involvement in astrology and that they terrified the Jerusalemites. It is in this context that he alludes to Balaam, who epitomises this type of figure of distrust.

However, the Gospel then presents the readers with the reappearance of the star, and the first authorial statement about the internal thoughts and feelings of the μάγοι. This has the effect of forcing a re-evaluation. One effect of this re-evaluation is that the allusion to Balaam is recontextualised: parallels between the μάγοι and Balaam himself must be rejected. The force of the allusion is thereby limited to the eschatological imagery of the star. The Gospel moves from one matrix of allusion to another, taking the reader along with it: from Balaam to Sheba.

---

53 France, *Matthew*, TNTC 1, 81; France, *Matthew*, NICNT, 64–65; Horsley, *The Liberation of Christmas*, 57. See also: Derrett, 'The Narratives of the Nativity'; Keener, *The Gospel of Matthew*, 81–83.

This way of proceeding allows Matthew to have it both ways: he can acknowledge the bad elements of the reputation of μάγοι *and* use them as exemplars.[54] He can draw on eschatological imagery from both Numbers 24 *and* Isaiah 60, despite their apparent incompatibility. This allows Matthew to make a variety of eschatological claims: Jesus is the eschatological star arising and conquering Israel's enemies, as in Numbers 24. However, Jesus is *also* the eschatological king, to whom the nations flock with their wealth, in Isaiah 60.

## 6. Conclusion

According to the evidence, ancient attitudes towards μάγοι were highly varied, though frequently negative. Too often, however, those who would study the μάγοι in the context of Matthew have ignored the diversity of opinion in the ancient sources—a diversity that Matthew's narrative needed to address. More importantly, scholars have tended to evaluate Matthew's attitude to the μάγοι based only on the evidence of when they reach the house in Bethlehem, where they are revealed as positive figures. This overlooks the fact that in many parts of the pericope, Matthew alludes to the more negative aspects of their reputation. However, by maintaining a high degree of ambiguity, especially in the first half of the pericope, Matthew can have it both ways. The Gospel is able to acknowledge the dubious reputation of the μάγοι *and* use them as exemplars. He can draw on the imagery of Numbers 24 and also Isaiah 60, even where the imagery is conflicting. Jesus is the star, arising to conquer Israel's enemies, as in Numbers 24. However, Jesus is also the king to whom the nations flock in Isaiah 60.

Jonathan Thambyrajah
Broken Bay Institute. The Australian Institute of Theological Education

---

54 Note that there is no *inherent* problem with Matthew making use of socially undesirable characters, even as exemplars (Cf. Zahn, *Matthäus*, 104–105). Indeed, he often does so (e.g. Matt. 9:9–13; 15:21–28, etc.). I note that the Gospel employs a similar dynamic in such episodes, wherein reason to doubt the character is introduced at first (e.g. 9:11; 15:24), before the Gospel instead remodels them as exemplars.

## Bibliography

Albright, W. and C. Mann  *Matthew: Introduction, Translation, and Notes* (AB 26; Garden City, NY: Doubleday, 1971).

Beck, R.  'Greco-Roman Astrologers, the Magi, and Mithraism', in G. H. van Kooten and P. Barthel (eds.), *The Star of Bethlehem and the Magi: Interdisciplinary Perspectives from Experts on the Ancient Near East, the Greco-Roman World, and Modern Astronomy* (Themes in Biblical Narrative 19; Leiden: Brill, 2015), 286–96.

Bonnard, P.  *L'évangile selon Saint Matthieu* (Neuchâtel, Delachaux & Niestlé, 1963).

Brown, R.  *The Birth of the Messiah: a Commentary on the Infancy Narratives in the Gospels of Matthew and Luke* (updated edn; ABRL; New York, NY: Doubleday, 1993).

Bruns, J. E.  'The Magi Episode in Matthew 2', *CBQ* 23 (1961), 51–54.

Davies, W. D. and D. C. Allison  *A Critical and Exegetical Commentary on the Gospel According to Saint Matthew* (3 vols; ICC; London: T&T Clark, 1988).

Derrett, J. D. M.  'Further light on the Narratives of the Nativity', *NovT* 17 (1975), 81–108.

Durkin-Meisterernst, D.  *Dictionary of Manichean Middle Persian and Parthian* (Corpus Fontium Manichaeorum; Turnhout: Brepols, 2004).

France, R. T.  *The Gospel of Matthew* (NICNT; Grand Rapids, MI: Eerdmans, 2007).

France, R. T.  *Matthew: an Introduction and Commentary* (TNTC 1; Nottingham: IVP, 1985).

Gharib, B.  *Soghdian Dictionary* (Tehran: Farhangan, 1995).

Grabes, H.  'The Processualities of Literature', *Journal of Literature and Art Studies* 3 (2013), 1–8.

Grabes, H.  'Sequentiality', in P. Hühn et al. (eds), *The Living Handbook of Narratology* (Hamburg: Hamburg University, 2014). http://www.lhn.uni-hamburg.de/article/sequentiality.

Hagner, D.  *Matthew 1–13* (WBC 13a; Dallas, TX: Word Books, 1993).

| | |
|---|---|
| Hannah, D. | 'The Star of the Magi and the Prophecy of Balaam in Earliest Christianity, with Special Attention to the Lost Books of Balaam', in G. H. van Kooten and P. Barthel (eds.), *The Star of Bethlehem and the Magi: Interdisciplinary Perspectives from Experts on the Ancient Near East, the Greco-Roman World, and Modern Astronomy* (Themes in Biblical Narrative 19; Leiden: Brill, 2015), 433–62. |
| Hare, D. | *Matthew* (IBC; Louisville, KY: John Knox, 1993). |
| Harrington, D. | *The Gospel of Matthew* (Sacra Pagina 1; Collegeville, MN: Liturgical, 1991). |
| Horsley, R. A. | *The Liberation of Christmas: The Infancy Narratives in Social Context* (Eugene, OR: Wipf and Stock, 1989). |
| Horsley, R. A. | *Jesus and Magic: Freeing the Gospel Stories from Modern Misconceptions* (Cambridge: James Clarke, 2015). |
| Janko, R. | 'The Derveni Papyrus (Diagoras of Melos *apopyrgizontes logoi?*): a new translation', *Classical Philology* 96 (2001), 1–32. |
| de Jong, A. | 'Matthew's Magi as Experts on Kingship', in G. H. van Kooten and P. Barthel (eds.), *The Star of Bethlehem and the Magi: Interdisciplinary Perspectives from Experts on the Ancient Near East, the Greco-Roman World, and Modern Astronomy* (Themes in Biblical Narrative 19; Leiden: Brill, 2015), 271–85. |
| de Jong, A. | *Traditions of the Magi: Zoroastrianism in Greek and Latin Literature* (Leiden: Brill, 1997). |
| Keener, C. | *A Commentary on the Gospel of Matthew* (Grand Rapids, MI: Eerdmans, 1999). |
| Kent, R. | *Old Persian: Grammar, Texts, Lexicon* (New Haven, CT: American Oriental Society, 1950). |
| Kim, H. C. | 'The Worship of Jesus in the Gospel of Matthew', *Biblica* 93 (2012), 227–41. |
| Kuhrt, A. | *The Persian Empire: a Corpus of Sources from the Achaemenid Period* (London: Routledge, 2007). |
| Lagrange, M.-J. | *Évangile selon saint Matthieu* (Paris: J. Gabalda, 1923). |
| Lohmeyer, E. | *Das Evangelium des Matthäus* (Göttingen: Vandenhoeck & Ruprecht, 1958). |

| | |
|---|---|
| Luz, U. | *Matthew 1—7: a commentary* (trans. W. C. Linss; Hermeneia; Minneapolis, MN: Fortress, 2007). |
| Meier, J. | *Matthew* (New Testament Message 3; Wilmington, DE: Michael Glazier, 1980). |
| Morris, L. L. | *The Gospel According to Matthew* (PNTC; Grand Rapids, MI: Eerdmans, 1992). |
| Newman, H. | 'Stars of the Messiah', in George H. van Kooten and Peter Barthel (eds.), *The Star of Bethlehem and the Magi: Interdisciplinary Perspectives from Experts on the Ancient Near East, the Greco-Roman World, and Modern Astronomy* (Themes in Biblical Narrative 19; Leiden: Brill, 2015), 272–303. |
| Nyberg, H. | *A Manual of Pahlavi* (2 vols.; Wiesbaden: Otto Harrassowitz, 1974). |
| Osborne, G. | *Matthew* (Zondervan Exegetical Commentary on the New Testament; Grand Rapids: Zondervan, 2010). |
| Ossendrijver, M. | 'The Story of the Magi in the Light of Alexander the Great's Encounters with Chaldeans', in G. H. van Kooten and P. Barthel (eds.), *The Star of Bethlehem and the Magi: Interdisciplinary Perspectives from Experts on the Ancient Near East, the Greco-Roman World, and Modern Astronomy* (Themes in Biblical Narrative 19; Leiden: Brill, 2015), 217–30. |
| Phelan, J. | *Experiencing Fiction: Judgments, Progressions, and the Rhetorical Theory of Narrative* (Columbus, OH: Ohio State University, 2007). |
| Phelan, J. | 'Rhetorical Narratology', in D. Herman et al. (eds.), *Routledge Encyclopedia of Narrative Theory* (London: Routledge, 2005), 500–504. |
| Powell, M. | 'The Magi as Wise Men: Re-examining a Basic Supposition', *NTS* 46 (2000), 1–20. |
| Rimmon-Kenan, S. | 'Ambiguity and Narrative Levels: Christine Brooke-Rose's Thru', *Poetics Today* 3 (1982), 21–32. |
| Rimmon-Kenan, S. | *Narrative Fiction: Contemporary Poetics* (2nd edn; London: Routledge, 2005). |
| Schmid, J. | *Das Evangelium nach Matthäus* (Regensburg: F. Pustet, 1965). |
| Schniewind, J. | *Das Evangelium nach Matthäus* (Göttingen: Vandenhoeck & Ruprecht, 1950). |

| | |
|---|---|
| Sim, D. | 'The Magi: Gentiles or Jews?', *HTS* 55 (1999), 980–1000. |
| Sternberg, M. | 'Gaps, Ambiguity, and the Reading Process', in *The Poetics of Biblical Narrative: Ideological Literature and the Drama of Reading* (Bloomington, IN: Indiana University Press, 1985), 186–229. |
| Trost, T. | 'Herod the Great, the Magi, and Parthia', *Hen* 38 (2016), 89–110. |
| Turner, D. | *Matthew* (BECNT; Grand Rapids, MI: Baker Academic, 2008). |
| van Kooten, G. | 'Matthew, the Parthians, and the Magi: A Contextualization of Matthew's Gospel in Roman-Parthian Relations of the First Centuries BCE and CE, in G. H. van Kooten and P. Barthel (eds.), *The Star of Bethlehem and the Magi: Interdisciplinary Perspectives from Experts on the Ancient Near East, the Greco-Roman World, and Modern Astronomy* (Themes in Biblical Narrative 19; Leiden: Brill, 2015), 496–646. |
| Vöhler, M. | 'Modern and Ancient Concepts of Ambiguity', in M. Vöhler, T. Fuhrer, and S. Frangoulidis (eds.), *Strategies of Ambiguity in Ancient Literature* (Trends in Classics Supplementary Volumes 114; Berlin: de Gruyter, 2021), 1–10. |
| Zahn, T. | *Das Evangelium des Matthäus* (Leipzig: Deichert, 1922). |

CHAPTER 6

# The Function of John's Baptism in Matthew's Gospel: A Dramatised Declaration of the Coming Judgement

Daniel W. McManigal

According to Ben Witherington, 'John the Baptist called his audience to repentance. One major theme of John's preaching was that Yahweh's eschatological wrath would soon fall on Israel. What is not clear is the relationship between John's preaching of repentance and his baptismal practice.'[1] Joan Taylor summarises, 'The meaning of John's active immersion of another person remains unclear.'[2] Years earlier, Charles Scobie opined that source information concerning the meaning of John's baptism is 'meager', and 'contradictory.'[3]

---

1   Witherington, 'John the Baptist'.
2   Taylor, 'Baptism'.
3   In Matthew and Luke, John's baptism contrasts with an eschatological figure who baptises in the Holy Spirit and fire. For Mark, his baptism was a ritual, 'for the forgiveness of sin'. Josephus characterises John as a popular leader of moral piety, presumably initiated by baptism; Scobie, *John the Baptist*, 91. Unlike the Gospels which frame the meaning of John (and his baptism) by way of comparison to Jesus, Josephus nowhere mentions any such connection. So, Nepper-Christensen, 'Die Taufe im Matthäusevangelium', 190.

One of the virtually indisputable pieces of information drawn from the source material is that John baptised with water. His baptism was so well-known that the Gospels and Josephus (*Ant.* 18.116) could refer to him as a 'Baptiser' or, 'Baptist'. That he baptised, there is no good reason to doubt. NT scholarship, to a great degree, grants that John was performing a ritual action with water, in which was contained a symbolic meaning, or meanings, but the precise meaning(s) is a matter that remains difficult to establish.[4]

## Water Symbolism

The semantic range of βαπτίζω covers both physical and metaphorical actions and meanings. Namaan ἐβαπτίσατο seven times in the Jordan (2 Kgs 5:14). John baptised the crowds with water (Matt. 3:11). Josephus uses βαπτίζω for the drowning of ships (*Life* 3, *Ant.* 3.9,10; 9.10; *War* 3.8) and the drowning of the high priest Aristobulus (*Ant.* 15.3; *War* 1.22).[5] The metaphorical meaning is used in Isaiah 21:4, 'lawlessness overwhelms (βαπτίζει) me; my soul has turned to fear'. In Josephus a city's utter destruction is its ἐβάπτισαν (*War* 1.27; 2.20; 3.7; 4.3). Likewise, after Simon slaughtered his family, he submerged (baptised) the sword into his flesh and died (*War* 2.18).

By the time the Gospels were written both uses were in circulation as evidenced by the contrast between John's water baptism and the coming one's Spirit-baptism. The symbolism of this water ritual, as it has come to be exemplified in the Gospels (Matt. 3:11; Mark 1:4,8;

---

[4] A number of scholars have adopted the view that John's baptism was an initiatory rite derived, perhaps, from pre-existing proselyte baptisms. While not denying that John may have been influenced in 'at least some measure' by Qumran, it is nevertheless doubtful that John's baptism developed within wider, proselyte, baptising movements. As Dunn, *Jesus Remembered*, 357, asked, 'If there was an already well recognized practice of "baptism", why would John be picked out as "the Baptist"?'. The arguments for Jewish proselyte baptism predating John's have been vigorously debated. For proselyte baptism in the first century ce, see Rowley, *From Moses to Qumran*, 211–35; Jeremias, *Infant Baptism*, 24–29. For an overview of arguments against proselyte baptism see especially Webb, *John the Baptizer*, 122–30. For comparisons with the ritual washings at Qumran see Taylor, *The Immerser*, 64–88; Brownlee, 'John the Baptist'; Smith, 'Jewish Proselyte Baptism'; Flusser, 'The Baptism of John'; Robinson, 'The Baptism of John'.

[5] As the lexicons point out, βάπτω and βαπτίζω convey the meanings of 'to dip, plunge, wash, purify, or immerse'.

Luke 3:16; John 1:33), can be traced out under two broad headings: purification and punishment.

Typically, associations with purification are drawn from several places in the OT. The psalmist writes, 'Purge me with hyssop, and I shall be clean; wash me, and I shall be whiter than snow' (Ps. 51:7). Ezekiel 36 contains an eschatological promise that God will pour clean water upon his people to purify them. And in a parallel thought, God will put his Spirit in them (Ezek. 36:24–27; cf. Isa. 44:3; 52:15).[6] One could say that John's baptism functioned as an 'eschatological sacrament'.[7]

On the other hand, there have been those who find the exact opposite analogy to John's baptism in the OT water judgements, of which the flood, and the drowning of Pharaoh, stand in archetypal fashion to later crises (Gen. 7; Exod. 14; Ps. 69:2). In Isaiah, God's judgement at the hand of the Assyrians is pronounced by the use of liquid imagery: 'The Lord is bringing up against them the waters of the river, mighty and many, the king of Assyria and all his glory. And it will rise over all its channels and go over all its banks' (Isa. 8:7). Likewise, in Hosea 5:10 God promises, 'I will pour out my wrath like water' upon the princes of Judah (cf. 2 Sam. 22:5; Ps. 66:10–12; 69:1–2; Job 22:11; Isa. 30:27–28).

Connecting the symbolism of John's baptism to ritual and spiritual cleansing is by far the most widely held interpretation in the secondary literature: ancient to modern. After all, purity is the point in dispute between John's disciples and an unnamed Jew (John 3:25). Furthermore, John speaks of his purpose as baptising *for repentance*—so Matthew (Matt. 3:11), and for the forgiveness of sins—so Mark and Luke (Mark 1:4; Luke 3:3).

---

6   Nolland, 'In Such a Manner', 69, correctly observes that OT water rituals have to do with ritual purification and not with sin and guilt. But one wonders if Levitical prescriptions for ritual purification washings would not be connected in the worshippers' minds to the horizontal dimensions imbedded in those ceremonies. The scrolls made such a connection between ritual purification and sin explicit, 'And it is by the holy spirit of the community, in its truth, that he is cleansed of all his iniquities. And by the spirit of uprightness and of humility his sin is atoned. And by the compliance of his soul with all the laws of God his flesh is cleansed by being sprinkled with cleansing waters and being made holy with the waters of repentance' (1QS 3.7–9; cf. 1QS 4.20–22; 5:13–14).
7   Reiser, *Jesus and Judgment*, 185–86; Otto, *The Kingdom of God*, 77. More cautiously, Beasley-Murray thinks it 'not impossible' that John's baptism was sacramental in character as a prophetic action: *Baptism in the New Testament*, 43.

On the other hand, the accounts of John's preaching put a heavy emphasis upon the approaching wrath. Moreover, the notion of baptism as a form of judgement and death is close at hand. In Mark and Luke, Jesus speaks of his approaching death as a baptism (Luke 12:50; Mark 10:38). True, John baptises with water for repentance, but if John's baptism functioned as a sign of punishment (for sin), this could also be a strong motivation to repent.[8]

## Outline of the Argument

The question we wish to pursue is whether or not there are other factors that would lend support to the understanding of John's baptism as a sign of approaching calamity. We will proceed by looking briefly at John's identity, outlining the sign acts of the OT prophets, and finally by connecting this meaning to his baptism and to his preaching in Matthew 3.

## John as Prophet

The Greek term, προφήτης occurs thirty-seven times in Matthew, and is usually descriptive of the OT prophets and their books. No ambiguities are resolved by locating the few, general occurrences of προφήτης to any sources outside of the OT.[9] For Matthew, the prophets are those men of the OT who are connected to the Law, so, 'the Law and the Prophets' (Matt. 7:12; 11:13; 22:40). They are spokesmen sent by God to foretell the future, both positive and negative (Matt. 3), and to share a similar fate at the hands of Israel (Matt. 23).

---

8   While wrongly locating John's baptism against a Persian, rather than Jewish background, Kraeling's analysis of the symbolism is on target: 'If we are permitted by the word about the two baptisms to assume that this conception of judgment by a fiery torrent was a part of John's eschatological imagery, it becomes possible to suggest a basis for the inauguration by him of a rite of immersion that had eschatological associations. The suggestion is simply this, that the water of baptism represents and symbolizes the fiery torrent of judgment, and that the individual by voluntarily immersing himself in the water enacts in advance before God his willing submission to the divine judgment the river of fire will perform'; *John the Baptist*, 117. See the additional discussions in Davies and Allison, *Matthew I-VII*, 317; Dunn, 'Spirit-and-Fire Baptism'.
9   For a detailed survey see McManigal, *A Baptism of Judgment*, 90–93.

The uncontroversial understanding of the canonical Gospels is that John was a prophet.[10] This is especially characteristic of Matthew's account. Jesus asks the crowds what they went out into the wilderness to see. A prophet? 'Yes, I tell you and more than a prophet' (11:9–14). Herod hesitates to put John to death because he feared the people, 'for they held him to be a prophet' (14:5). Likewise, the chief priests and elders do not wish to publicly object to John's baptism because, again, the crowds held him to be a prophet (21:26).[11] Both in public and in private John is identified as the Elijah who is to come (Matt. 11:13–14; 17:11–13), of which the descriptions of his clothing of camel's hair, leather belt, and thundering call for Israel to repent is reminiscent of the prophet Elijah (Matt. 3:2,4).

## Signs of the Prophet

Having sketched the way Matthew situates John's identity as an OT prophet, we next move to his activity as a baptiser. In this section and the next I will build on the insights of Lampe,[12] Dunn,[13] Brooks,[14]

---

10 Flemington, *The New Testament Doctrine of Baptism*, 13–23; Trilling, 'Die Täufertradition bei Matthäus', 271–89; Scobie, *John the Baptist*, 117–30; Wink, *John the Baptist*; Ladd, *A Theology of the New Testament*, 35–36; Hengel, *The Charismatic Leader*, 34–37; Sanders, *Jesus and Judaism*, 91–92; Vos, *Redemptive History*, 299–300; Davies and Allison, *Matthew*, 1.295; Meier, *Mentor, Message, and Miracles*, 21, 29–40; Davies and Allison, 'John the Baptist in Matthew's Gospel', 394; Witherington, 'John the Baptist'; Becker, *Jesus von Nazaret*, 56–58; Reiser, *Jesus and Judgment*, 167, 252; Evans, 'The Baptism of John', 45–61; Carter, *Matthew and the Margins*, 91–92; Charlesworth, 'John the Baptizer and the Dead Sea Scrolls', 10; Turner, *Israel's Last Prophet*, 129–50; Keener, *Matthew*, 116–19; Nolland, *Matthew*, 136–37; France, *Matthew*, 97–98; Dapaah, *Relationship*, 49. According to Cooper, *Incorporated Servanthood*, 78, by presenting John as a 'present-day' prophet, Matthew implies John's reliability. For Q's evaluation of John as a prophet see Kloppenborg, *The Formation of Q*, 105; and Rothchild, *Baptist Traditions*, 34.
11 For socio-historical studies of the prophets of the first century ce see Blenkinsopp, 'Prophecy and Priesthood in Josephus'; Barnett, 'The Jewish Sign Prophets', 679–97; Aune, *Prophecy in Early Christianity*; Horsley, '"Like One of the Prophets of Old"'; Feldman, 'Prophets and Prophecy in Josephus'; Grabbe, 'Thus Spake the Prophet Josephus'; Webb, *John the Baptizer and Prophet*, 346–47. This historical methodology undoubtedly illuminates various sociological aspects of the prophets of the first century ce and their movements, but in the case of Josephus' de-eschatologising of (ignorance of?) John, it is doubtful that he and Matthew would have understood the program of the Baptist in the same way.
12 Lampe, *The Seal of the Spirit*, 19–31.
13 Dunn, *Baptism in the Holy Spirit*, 17.
14 Brooks, *The Drama of Decision*, 30–32.

Hooker,[15] Bergin,[16] and Kline,[17] that John's baptism, while related to future Christian baptism, is also related to the past sign acts of the OT prophets.[18] Where most of the aforementioned scholars view John's baptism as a prophetic sign pointing to spiritual cleansing, I will argue that in Matthew's account of John's sign act with water, the symbolism lends itself most readily to eschatological judgement.[19]

## Two Types of Signs

In the OT there are, broadly speaking, two types of signs performed: extraordinary and ordinary signs. The signs that Moses performed in Egypt were of the former, while the signs of Isaiah, Jeremiah, and Ezekiel respectively, were of the latter. The latter prophets typically used ordinary items and actions that extended referential meaning to something else in the sign–referent relationship.[20] To illustrate, when Pharaoh saw the signs displaying the power of Yahweh, he had no need to ask, 'What do these signs mean?' The river of blood, darkness, death of the firstborn, *et cetera* were manifestations of the divine displeasure that Moses warned of. But in the case of Ezekiel, the people asked, 'What do these things mean?' (Ezek. 17:12; 24:19; 37:18).

---

15  Hooker, *The Signs of a Prophet*, 9–13, esp. 12. Hooker, 'John's Baptism'.
16  Bergin, *O Propheticum Lavacrum*, 111–42.
17  Kline, *By Oath Consigned*, 55–62.
18  Beasley-Murray, *Baptism*, 43.
19  Additionally, *if* it could also be established that John's baptism functioned as a protest against the sin offerings of the temple it would fit comfortably under the work of the latter prophets in their rebuke of Israel. Cf. Isa. 1:10–12; Jer. 7:4. For a survey and analysis of John's sign see McManigal, *A Baptism of Judgment*, 121–40.
20  Friebel, 'A Hermeneutical Paradigm for Interpreting Prophetic Sign-Actions'.

## Sign Act Taxonomy

As we proceed to survey the 'ordinary' signs of the latter prophets we will group them into three categories: individual, relational, and national. Undoubtedly, there are other ways of collating the data which would produce different taxonomies. Organising the signs in this way should not be misunderstood as a rejection of certain levels of overlap. Obviously, the sign acts are given to Israel as a nation precisely because the nation had a relationship with Yahweh, being bound to the covenant. Likewise, in the case of individual destinies, the sign act could have implications for the future of nations (e.g. Joash, the northern kingdom, and Syria in 2 Kgs 13:14–19; of the crown placed upon Joshua's head as a sign of hope for Israel in Zechariah 6:9–15).[21]

*Individual* Some of the OT sign acts visualised the future particularly of certain leaders of Israel. Though not performed by a prophet, when Saul tore Samuel's robe, the message was: '...The Lord has torn the kingdom of Israel from you ...' (1 Sam. 15:28). In a similar manner, the prophet Ahijah tore his own garment into twelve pieces. After giving ten pieces to Jeroboam he explains the symbolic meaning: Jeroboam will rule over the ten northern tribes (1 Kgs 11:30–31).[22]

*Relational* The second category of sign acts were given to illustrate the relationship between God and Israel. In the case of Hosea naming his children, they are signs of the broken relationship: 'No Mercy, and Not My People'. W. D. Stacey comments,

> Just as marriage, on the historical level, was a dramatic action of many years' duration, so the naming of children was a long-lasting sign. Wherever the children went and whenever their names were spoken, the drama was re-enacted.[23]

*National* In the third place—and this is by far the most common category—OT signs acts were given to reveal aspects of national futures:

---

21 These are secondary observations, important though they may be, and one suspects that no artificial arrangement would have non-porous category boundaries.
22 For additional examples see 2 Kgs 13:14–17 (striking arrows on the ground) and Zech. 6:9–15 symbolising a coming king who will build the temple of the Lord.
23 Stacey, *Prophetic Drama*, 103–4.

either judgement, or restoration. Setting aside the false predictions of Zedekiah and Hananiah,[24] there are *approximately*[25] twenty-eight sign acts relating to the future of nations:[26] one in Isaiah (Ch. 20), two in Zechariah (6:9–15; 11:4–17), and the remaining twenty-six in Jeremiah and Ezekiel. These prophets often use ordinary objects and gestures that would only be appropriate in certain situations. Jeremiah buys a field (32:1–15), but also buries stones in the palace of Egypt (43:8–13). Many of Ezekiel's signs are strange: he digs through a wall (12:1–16), shaves his head and slashes one-third with a sword, burns the second third, and tosses the remainder into the wind (Ezek. 5:1–12), and when his wife dies he does not mourn (24:15–24).

With these sign acts of the prophets, God previewed future events. The potter's clay was a sign—God is shaping disaster against Israel (Jer. 18:1–12). The cup Jeremiah gives the nations to drink symbolises God's wrath against the nations (Jer. 25:15–29). Isaiah's nakedness is a sign of Egypt and Ethiopia's humiliation at the hands of Assyria (Isa. 20:16). Ezekiel lying on his left side for 390 days and on his right for forty days was a sign of the punishing years to come upon Israel. After writing 'favour' and 'union' on his two sticks, Zechariah says, 'What is to be destroyed, let it be destroyed. And let those who are left devour the flesh of one another'. Zechariah then breaks the staff labelled Favour—as a visual enactment of the future (Zech. 11:7–14).

There is one more important observation to make about the national, prophetic sign acts. There are twenty-eight of these sign acts in Isaiah, Jeremiah, Ezekiel and Zechariah. Twenty-six of the twenty-eight have to do with God's wrath against his people. It is also significant that the two merciful signs—Jeremiah's purchase of a field, and Ezekiel's joining of two sticks—are premised upon Israel's destruction and exile. By way of summary, we can surmise that when God sent his prophets to Israel and gave them signs to perform, judgement was in the near future.

---

24  Zedekiah—with his iron horns as a sign of Israel's victory over the Arameans (1 Kgs 22:11) and Hananiah's breaking of the yoke carried by Jeremiah (Jer. 28:10–11).
25  Scholarly opinions diverge with Ezek. 2:8—3:3, Isa. 7:3,10–17; 8:1–4; Mic 1:8.
26  Most of the sign acts are performed for Israel, even when referring to other countries as in the case of Jer. 43:8–13; Isa. 20:1–6.

To summarise the sign acts of the prophets, their OT signs: 1) corresponded to the prophetic word; 2) were carried out by human actions and ordinary items; 3) conveyed information through the visual channel, giving God's assessment and/or intentions; and 4) were predominantly concerned with judgement.

As these findings relate to John the Baptist, the category most reasonably descriptive of his baptism is the third (national sign/future outlook). As a prophet, John was sent to Israel not to individuals (Matt. 3:5). His water baptism was a sign performed before large numbers of people from Jerusalem and the region of Judea. He proclaimed the future, speaking of a coming kingdom and a mysterious figure who would come to conduct a baptism *not by means of water*.[27] As Jeremiah and Ezekiel incorporated people into their sign acts,[28] so also John baptised the crowds, giving them a sign to see and participate in. Finally, John's baptism, as a sign act, is amplified and explained by preaching that is similar in outlook to that of the OT latter prophets.

## John's Sign Act and Preaching

Like the OT prophets, John gave the nation a multifaceted sign to consider. Unlike the signs of Jesus, John's was singular, repeated, and ordinary.[29] Matthew gives us two summary statements. In Matthew 3:6, John baptised the crowds in the Jordan River. The summary of John's preaching is found in verse 2 and his first word is one of warning, μετανοεῖτε. Israel must repent and the reason for their repentance is immediately given. Rather than saying, 'Repent because of your sins',

---

27 Lang views a divine identity as incongruent with John's loosing of the coming one's sandals statement: οὗ οὐκ εἰμὶ ἱκανὸς τὰ ὑποδήματα βαστάσαι (3:11): 'Erwägungen zur eschatologiischen Verkündigung Johannes des Täufers', 470. It is questionable whether or not John's detail of the coming one's sandals is meant to be taken literally. More likely, it belongs to the descriptive category of 'anthropomorphic' (Deut. 26:8; Ps. 75:8; Jer. 47:6).
28 E.g. Jeremiah placing the cup of wine before the Rechabites in the presence of those in the temple (Jer. 35:1–11).
29 'An action performed more than once does not thereby eliminate it for consideration ... Some prophetic actions are repeated': McKnight, 'Jesus and Prophetic Actions', 221. Isaiah walking naked for 3 years (Isa. 20:1–6), Jeremiah prohibited from marrying, mourning, and feasting (Jer. 16), Ezekiel lying on his sides 390+ 40 days (Ezek. 4:4–8), and his eating the proscribed unclean food while lying for 390 days on his left side (Ezek. 4:9–17).

as true as that statement would be, John says, 'Repent because the kingdom of the heaven is at hand' (3:2).[30]

It is unlikely that Matthew's deliberate pairing of ἡ βασιλεία with the genitive plural οὐρανῶν is a circumlocution for the divine name since he does not entirely avoid the familiar 'kingdom of God' (12:28; 19:24; 21:31,43)[31] and refers to God directly as θεός no fewer than fifty-eight times.[32] Matthew 3:2 contains the first of fifty-five plurals, suggesting that οὐρανῶν might have special significance.[33] Through a careful study of various OT texts (Deut. 10:14; 1 Kgs 8:27; Neh. 9:6; Ps. 148:4; 2 Chr. 2:5 [MT]; 2 Chr. 6:18; cf. 2 Cor. 12:2) and Second Temple writings (Judith, 2 and 3 Maccabees, *Psalms of Solomon* and *Prayer of Manasseh*), Jonathan Pennington has persuasively demonstrated that 'the kingdom of the heavens' serves a rhetorical and polemical purpose in Matthew as the divine realm standing over and against the kingdoms of the world and their antithetical values, ethics and beliefs.[34] 'In contrast with the singulars used in heaven and earth pairs and in reference to the visible world, the plural forms in Matthew refer to the invisible realm, usually explicitly God's realm or speaking of God indirectly through metonymy'.[35] Thirty-two of the fifty-five plurals are the stock phrase of Matthew 3:2, ἡ βασιλεία τῶν οὐρανῶν, and unambiguously refer to God's kingdom or rule. 'The

---

30  Matthew drops Mark's εἰς ἄφεσιν ἁμαρτιῶν and relocates it to the institution of the eucharist (26:28). His reason, according to Meier, *A Marginal Jew*, 53, is due to Matthew finding the phrase offensive as a description of John's baptism. This conclusion is unnecessary for several reasons. First, repentance would be a meaningless act apart from forgiveness. Second, it would be difficult to imagine that John the Baptist, or Matthew, would have understood that forgiveness could be effected, either in the present or future, by the waters of baptism (note Matt. 3:8, 10/ Luke 3:8–9). Third, the context of John's baptism and call to repentance is God who shows mercy and provides a way of escape (Matt. 3:7). Fourth, repentance presupposes forgiveness of sins in both the OT and NT. Finally, if forgiveness of sins is too closely associated to baptism, why does Matthew reproduce Mark a few verses later? Καὶ ἐβαπτίζοντο ὑπ' αὐτοῦ ἐν τῷ Ἰορδάνῃ ποταμῷ ἐξομολογούμενοι τὰς ἁμαρτίας αὐτῶν (Mark 1:5); καὶ ἐβαπτίζοντο ἐν τῷ Ἰορδάνῃ ποταμῷ ὑπ' αὐτοῦ ἐξομολογούμενοι τὰς ἁμαρτίας αὐτῶν (Matt. 3:6).
31  The variant reading in Matt. 6:33 τὴν βασιλείαν οὐρανῶν καὶ τὴν δικαιοσύνην αὐτοῦ has scant support: *l* 858 (Clement) in comparison to the witnesses for τὴν βασιλείαν τοῦ θεοῦ καὶ τὴν δικαιοσύνην αὐτοῦ L W Δ Θ 0233* (0233c omit αὐτοῦ) f1 f13 28 33 157 180 205 565 579 597 700 892 1006 1010 1071 1241 1243 1292 1342 1424 1505 *Byz*.
32  Gundry, *Matthew*, 43.
33  Matthew uses the plural fifty-five times and the singular twenty-seven times.
34  Pennington, *Heaven and Earth*, 313–14, 339, 342.
35  *Heaven and Earth*, 140.

ultimate point of the important expression kingdom of heaven is that God's kingdom is very unlike earthly kingdoms, both in their Jewish and Roman manifestations, and will eschatologically replace them'.[36] While such a nuanced understanding could not possibly be discerned on a 'first reading' of the preaching of John the Baptist, the plural form does stand out, drawing readers' attention to the unusual expression which will be regularly repeated in contrast to the kingdoms of the world. The warning of the kingdom's arrival and—through the use of the plural—its opposition, is directed solely at Israel in Matthew 3.

Secondly, there is a literary connection between the coming kingdom and the baptism of John. John tells the crowds to *repent* because God's kingdom was drawing near. In parallel fashion, John tells them why he baptised, namely, *for repentance*. In other words, both the coming kingdom and John's baptism are aimed at repentance.[37]

After identifying John as the Isaianic voice and the responses of the crowds in baptism, Matthew turns from the general 'crowds' to the more specific 'Pharisees and Sadducees' Ἰδὼν δὲ πολλοὺς τῶν Φαρισαίων καὶ Σαδδουκαίων ἐρχομένους ἐπὶ τὸ βάπτισμα αὐτοῦ.[38] In Luke the crowds receive the brunt of John's warning and they respond in desperation. But unlike Luke's crowds, Matthew focuses in verse 7 upon these religious leaders who will not repent (Matt. 21:25) and will later win over a crowd to crucify Jesus (Matt. 27:20). There is no one in this Gospel who stands in greater opposition to the kingdom of heaven than the religious leaders. By reinforcement through the use of repetition, Matthew illustrates that the religious leaders fail to produce the fruits of repentance that John stresses (Matt. 3:8). Though their response to John's ultimatum is temporarily left unanswered, from this point in Matthew's narrative, he will provide multiple examples to show

---

36 *Heaven and Earth*, 342.
37 A further, more obvious parallel between John's baptism in water with the Coming One's baptism in the Holy Spirit and fire is drawn in v.11. Ἐγὼ μὲν ὑμᾶς βαπτίζω ἐν ὕδατι εἰς μετάνοιαν . . . αὐτὸς ὑμᾶς βαπτίσει ἐν πνεύματι ἁγίῳ καὶ πυρί.
38 From a literary perspective, 'Those who comprise the Jewish leaders are the Pharisees, the Sadducees, the chief priests, the elders, and the scribes... the rhetorical effect of the way in which these several groups are presented is such as to make of them a monolithic front opposed to Jesus, they can, narrative-critically, be treated as a single character' (Kingsbury, 'The Developing Conflict', 58.

that the religious leaders have not redirected their thinking and living according to the aims and demands of the kingdom (Matt. 5:11; 9:32–34; 12; 15:1–9; 16:1–6; 19:1–9; 20:17–19; 21:14–17,23–27,33–46; 22:15,23–33; 23; 26:3,14–16,57–68; 27:1–2,12,20,62–66; 28:11–15).

They are the offspring of serpents, γεννήματα ἐχιδνῶν (Matt. 3:7), and seen from this perspective John's sign act turns against them as a symbolic act of the coming kingdom. What this kingdom does (symbolised through the prophetic sign of water baptism) is explained through the verbal channel. It is wrath to come (v.7), it is the axe laid at the root of the tree (v.10), it is baptism in the Holy Spirit and fire (v.11), and like those being submerged in the waters by John,[39] there is no chance of the chaff escaping the fires of eschatological judgement, from which no one rises (v.12).

In the Matthean context, John's sign act by water can be understood as a prophetic enactment that prefigures the fate of unbelieving Israel. In OT prophetic practice, the sign visually illustrates the preaching of John the Baptist: trees and chaff tossed into the fire and standing between these two eschatological acts, the baptism of fire and Holy Spirit.

Venturing beyond the warning of chapter 3, John's bitter words are not only found on the lips of Jesus (Matt. 12:34), they are amplified in the seven woes.

> [33] You serpents, you brood of vipers, how are you to escape being sentenced to hell? [34] Therefore I send you prophets and wise men and scribes, some of whom you will kill and crucify, and some you will flog in your synagogues and persecute from town to town, [35] so that on you may come all the righteous blood shed on earth, from the blood of righteous Abel to the blood of Zechariah the son of Barachiah, whom you murdered between the sanctuary and the altar. (Matt. 23:33–35)

Not surprisingly, after Jesus laments over Israel's desolate house, he compares the coming destruction and judgement upon Jerusalem, to the flood of Noah (24:36–44).

---

39 Curiously the novelty of John's baptism might be that he administered it rather than self-immersion as was practised by various groups of the first century CE.

## Conclusion

John's eschatological outlook for Israel: embodied in his preaching and sign is one of national urgency in the shadow of the approaching eschatological calamity. Matthew, as did John, saw and expected (Matt. 11:2–3) that the future for the nation would be largely catastrophic. But for those who did respond in repentance to the preaching and baptising of John, there would be a place for them in the eschatological kingdom of heaven. There would be trees spared the axe, and wheat not cast into the fire. But for the Pharisees, Sadducees, and all who would side with them, John's sign, like the prophets of the OT, was an enactment of the coming eschatological judgement. If the accent of baptism can be symbolic for cleansing and renewal for the repentant, it could also be a sign of overwhelming destruction for the unrepentant.[40]

In conclusion, the following parallels can now be summarised: 1) The OT prophets were sent from God, likewise John the Baptist. 2) Prophets were recognised by the people as authentic prophets—so also John. 3) Prophets preached that Israel must turn and repent because of God's approaching judgement. They summoned Israel to seek God's mercy. John preached repentance and return to God in order to seek his mercy. 4) Certain latter prophets gave signs of the future which were almost universally actions conveying coming destruction. As a prophet, John gave a sign that was flexible and adaptable to his listeners and onlookers, having points of contact with *both* OT cleansing and wrath. For the aforementioned reasons, it would be reasonable to resist the interpretive urge to flatten John's baptism, having only to do with purification, or only about judgement. According to the logic of Gospels and the prophets, it can bear the weight of both.

Daniel W. McManigal
Belhaven University (adjunct Professor of Biblical and Theological Studies)

---

[40] While OT prophetic signs do not ordinarily convey a dual outcome (but see Zech. 11:7–10), the institution of the eucharistic supper (Matt. 26—29) does. See further, Moule, 'The Judgment Theme in the Sacraments, 464–81.

## Bibliography

Aune, D. E. — *Prophecy in Early Christianity and the Ancient Mediterranean World* (Grand Rapids, MI: Eerdmans, 1991).

Barnett P. W. — 'The Jewish Sign Prophets—AD 40-70: Their Intentions and Origin', *NTS* 27.5 (1981), 679-97.

Beasley-Murray, G. R. — *Baptism in the New Testament* (Grand Rapids, MI: Eerdmans, 1962).

Becker, B. — *Jesus von Nazaret* (Berlin: Walter de Gruyter, 1996).

Bergin, L. — *O Propheticum Lavacrum: Baptism as Symbolic Act of Eschatological Salvation* (Analecta Gregoriana 277; Rome: Gregorian University, 1999), 111-42.

Blenkinsopp, J. — 'Prophecy and Priesthood in Josephus', *JJS* 25.2 (1974), 239-62.

Brooks, O. S. — *The Drama of Decision: Baptism in the New Testament* (Peabody, MS: Hendrickson, 1987).

Brownlee, W. — 'John the Baptist in Light of the Ancient Scrolls', in K. Stendahl (ed.), *The Scrolls and the New Testament* (New York, NY: Crossroad, 1992), 33-53.

Charlesworth, J. H. — 'John the Baptizer and the Dead Sea Scrolls', in J. H. Charlesworth (ed.), *The Bible and the Dead Sea* Scrolls (vol. 3 of *The Scrolls and Christian Origins*; Waco, TX: Baylor University Press, 2006).

Cooper, B. — *Incorporated Servanthood: Commitment and Discipleship in the Gospel of Matthew* (London: T&T Clark, 2013).

Dapaah, D. S. — *The Relationship between John the Baptist and Jesus of Nazareth: A Critical Study* (Lanham, MD: University Press of America, 2005).

Davies, W. D., and D. C. Allison, Jnr — *Matthew I-VII* (ICC; Edinburgh: T&T Clark, 1988).

Dunn, J. D. G. — *Baptism in the Holy Spirit: A Re-examination of the New Testament Teaching on the* Gift *of the Spirit in Relation to Pentecostalism Today* (Philadelphia, PA: Westminster Press, 1970).

Dunn, J. D. G. — *Jesus Remembered: Christianity in the Making* (vol. 1; Grand Rapids, MI: Eerdmans, 2003).

| | |
|---|---|
| Dunn, J. D. G. | 'Spirit-and-Fire Baptism', *NovT* 14 (1972), 81–92. |
| Evans, C. A. | 'The Baptism of John in a Typological Context', in S. E. Porter, and A. R. Cross, (eds.), *Baptism, The New Testament and the Church* (JSNTSup 171; Sheffield: Sheffield Academic Press, 1999). |
| Feldman, L. H. | 'Prophets and Prophecy in Josephus', in M. H. Floyd, and R. D. Haak (eds.), *Prophets, Prophecy, and Prophetic Texts in Second Temple Judaism* (New York, NY: T&T Clark, 2006), 210-39. |
| Flemington, W. F. | *The New Testament Doctrine of Baptism* (London: SPCK, 1948). |
| Flusser, D. | 'The Baptism of John and the Dead Sea Sect', in C. Rabin, and Y. Yadin, (eds.), *Essays on the Dead Sea Scrolls: In Memory of E. L. Sukenik* (Jerusalem: Hehal Ha-Sefer, 1961), 209–38. |
| Friebel, K. G. | 'A Hermeneutical Paradigm for Interpreting Prophetic Sign-Actions', *Didaskalia* 12.2 (2001), 25-45. |
| Grabbe, L. L. | 'Thus Spake the Prophet Josephus...: the Jewish Historian on Prophets and Prophecy', in M. H. Floyd, and R. D. Haak, (eds.), *Prophets, Prophecy, and Prophetic Texts in Second Temple Judaism* (New York, NY: T&T Clark, 2006), 240-47. |
| Gundry, R. H. | *Matthew: A Commentary on His Literary and Theological Art* (Grand Rapids, MI: Eerdmans, 1982). |
| Hengel, M. | *The Charismatic Leader and His Followers* (trans. J. Greig; Spring Valley, NY: Crossroad, 1981). |
| Hooker, M. D. | 'John's Baptism: A Prophetic Sign', in G. Stanton, B. W. Longenecker, and S. C. Barton, (eds.), *The Holy Spirit and Christian Origins: Essays in Honor of James D. G. Dunn* (Grand Rapids, MI: Eerdmans, 2004), 22–40. |
| Hooker, M. D. | *The Signs of a Prophet: The Prophetic Actions of Jesus* (Harrisburg, PA: Trinity Press, 1997). |
| Horsley, R. A. | '"Like One of the Prophets of Old": Two Types of Popular Prophets at the Time of Jesus', *CBQ* 47 (1985), 435–63. |
| Jeremias, J. | *Infant Baptism in the First Four Centuries* (Philadelphia, PA: Westminster, 1960). |

| | |
|---|---|
| Keener, C. S. | *A Commentary on the Gospel of Matthew* (Grand Rapids, MI: Eerdmans, 1999). |
| Kingsbury, J. D. | 'The Developing Conflict between Jesus and the Jewish Leaders in Matthew's Gospel', *CBQ* 49 (1987), 57-73. |
| Kline, M. G. | *By Oath Consigned* (Grand Rapids, MI: Eerdmans, 1968). |
| Kloppenborg, J. S. | *The Formation of Q: Trajectories in Ancient Wisdom Collections* (Harrisburg, PA: Trinity Press International, 1987). |
| Kraeling, C. H. | *John the Baptist* (New York, NY: Charles Scribner's Sons, 1951). |
| Ladd, G. E. | *A Theology of the New Testament* (Grand Rapids, MI: Eerdmans, 1974). |
| Lampe, G. W. H. | *The Seal of the Spirit: A Study in the Doctrine of Baptism and Confirmation in the New Testament and the Fathers* (London: SPCK, 1967). |
| Lang, F. | 'Erwägungen zur eschatologiischen Verkündigung Johannes des Täufers', in G. Strecker (ed.), *Jesus Christus in Historie und Theologie: Festschrift für Hans Conzelmann zum 60* (Tübingen: Mohr 1975), 459-73. |
| McManigal, D. W. | *A Baptism of Judgment in the Fire of the Holy Spirit: John's Eschatological Proclamation in Matthew 3* (LNTS 595; London: Bloomsbury/T&T Clark, 2019). |
| McKnight, S. | 'Jesus and Prophetic Actions', *BBR* 10.2 (2000), 197-232. |
| Meier, J. P. | 'John the Baptist in Matthew's Gospel', *JBL* 99.3 (1980), 383-405. |
| Meier, J. P. | *Mentor, Message, and Miracles* (vol. 2 of *A Marginal Jew: Rethinking the Historical Jesus*; New York, NY: Doubleday, 1994). |
| Moule, C. F. D. | 'The Judgment Theme in the Sacraments' in W. D. Davies, and D. Daube (eds.), *The Background of the New Testament and its Eschatology* (Cambridge: Cambridge University Press, 1964), 464-81. |
| Nepper-Christensen, P. | 'Die Taufe im Matthäusevangelium im Lichte der Traditionen über Johannes den Täufer', *NTS* 31 (1985), 189-207. |
| Nolland, J. | '"In Such a Manner It Is Fitting for Us to Fulfill All Righteousness": Reflections on the Place of Baptism in the Gospel of Matthew', in S. E. Porter, and A. R. Cross (eds.), |

| | |
|---|---|
| | *Baptism, The New Testament and the Church* (JSNTSup 171; Sheffield: Sheffield Academic, 1999), 63-80. |
| Otto, R. | *The Kingdom of God and the Son of Man: A Study in the History of Religions* (London: Lutterworth, 1943). |
| Pennington, J. | *Heaven and Earth in the Gospel of Matthew* (Grand Rapids, MI: Baker, 2007). |
| Reiser, M. | *Jesus and Judgment: The Eschatological Proclamation in Its Jewish Context* (trans. L. M. Maloney; Minneapolis, MN: Fortress, 1997). |
| Robinson, J. A. T. | 'The Baptism of John and the Qumran Community: Testing a Hypothesis', *HTR*, 50:3 (1957), 175-92. |
| Rothchild, C. K. | *Baptist Traditions and Q* (WUNT 190; Tübingen: Mohr Siebeck, 2005). |
| Rowley, H. H. | *From Moses to Qumran: Studies in the Old Testament* (New York, NY: Association Press, 1963). |
| Sanders, E. P. | *Jesus and Judaism* (Minneapolis, MN: Fortress, 1985). |
| Scobie, C. H. | *John the Baptist* (Philadelphia: Fortress, 1964). |
| Smith, D. | 'Jewish Proselyte Baptism and the Baptism of John', *ResQ* 25 (1982), 13-32. |
| Stacey, W. D. | Prophetic *Drama in the Old Testament* (London: Epworth, 1990). |
| Taylor, J. E. | 'Baptism', *NIDB*, 1.392. |
| Taylor, J. E. | *The Immerser: John the Baptist within Second Temple Judaism* (Grand Rapids, MI: Eerdmans, 1997). |
| Trilling, W. | 'Die Täufertradition bei Matthäus', *BZ* 3 (1959), 271-89. |
| Turner, D. L. | *Israel's Last Prophet: Jesus and the Jewish Leaders in Matthew 23* (Minneapolis, MN: Fortress, 2015). |
| Vos, G. | *Redemptive History and Biblical Interpretation* (ed. R. B. Gaffin; Phillipsburg, NJ: Presbyterian & Reformed, 1980). |
| Webb, R. L. | *John the Baptizer and Prophet: A Socio-Historical Study* (JSNTSup 62; Sheffield: Sheffield Academic, 1991). |
| Wink, W. | *John the Baptist in the Gospel Tradition* (Cambridge: Cambridge University Press, 1968). |
| Witherington, B. | 'John the Baptist', *DJG*, 386. |

CHAPTER 7

# 'Like the angels'?: Embodiment and eschatology in Matthew's Gospel

Timothy P. Bradford

## Abstract

This article investigates the possible meaning and background of the comparison that the resurrected will be 'like the angels' (ὡς ἄγγελοι, Matt. 22:30, Mark 12:25). The depiction of angelic bodies in the Old Testament and Second Temple Judaism is considered afresh amidst the interpretation that Jesus' angelic comparison indicates the erasure of sexual differentiation in the resurrection. The tradition of comparing humans to angels or describing individuals with angelic characteristics found throughout the Old Testament and literature of Second Temple Judaism is also considered. Additional angelic comparisons in Matthew's Gospel, such as the vindication of the righteous in the Parable of the Weeds (Matt. 13:43) and the transfiguration (Matt. 17:2) are discussed before concluding that comparing humans to angels or describing humans with angelic features serves not to signal the transformation of the human body at the resurrection, but to describe the hope of human nature raised from the dead and glorified in the presence of God.

## Introduction

According to the Nicene Creed (A.D. 381), the church looks forward to 'the resurrection of the dead and to the life of the world to come'. The hope of resurrected life captures the Christian imagination. We wonder what aspects of our present experience will continue in the resurrection and what aspects will cease. Since our current experience is so thoroughly tied to our bodies, we naturally wonder what the resurrection body will be like? One passage that has often perplexed interpreters is Jesus' insistence that 'at the resurrection, they neither marry nor are given in marriage, but are like the angels (ὡς ἄγγελοι) in heaven' (Matt. 22:30, cf. Mark 12:25). This angelic comparison has frequently been interpreted as indicating the transcendence or even transformation of bodily sex in the new creation.[1] Yet what precisely does it mean to be 'like the angels' and what are the implications for our understanding of future embodiment? Will we be raised as men and women or does the comparison to the angels indicate the end of sexed embodiment? Does the Gospel of Matthew indicate that there is a future for male and female bodies? This essay seeks to contribute to current theological debates pertaining to the body by considering afresh the portrayal of angelic bodies in the Old Testament and Second Temple Jewish literature as well as the tradition found in this same literature and the Gospel of Matthew that compares human beings to angels, or describes human beings with angelic features.

## History of Interpretation

Jesus' comparison to the angels featured regularly in the early church's discussions of the resurrected body.[2] As early as the second century A.D., Justin Martyr felt compelled to address those who claimed that 'there is no resurrection of the flesh' because 'the angels, say they, have neither flesh, nor do they eat, nor have sexual intercourse' (*On the Resurrection,* 2). Justin argued for the resurrection of a physical and sexed body, defending the inherent goodness of the created body against those 'who think meanly of the flesh and say that is not worthy

---

1  For example, Looy and Bouma, 'The Nature of Gender', 176. Martin, *Sex and the Single Saviour,* 87.
2  See esp. Bynum, *Resurrection of the Body,* and Lehtipuu, 'No Sex in Heaven', 22–39.

of the resurrection' (*On the Resurrection*, 7). For Justin it was the 'acts of our fleshly members', and not the womb and penis *per se*, that would be abolished in the world to come (*On the Resurrection*, 3). Similarly, Tertullian's *On the Resurrection of the Flesh* was a response to certain 'heretics' who 'single out what parts of our bodies may suit them', in this case, the sexual anatomy of men and women, 'for the purpose of upsetting the resurrection (*On the Resurrection*, 61). According to Tertullian, God would raise the sexed body and clothe it with 'that garment of incorruptibility' (*On the Resurrection*, 60.2–3).[3] While apologists of the early Church, such as Justin and Tertullian, argued for the resurrection of the sexed body, the issue was far from settled. Origen believed the resurrection body would be distinguished from the human body and instead be a transformed 'spiritual body' which 'adorns the angels of God' (*On First Principles*, 2.2.2).

Intriguingly, the history of interpretation reveals that Jesus' angelic comparison has often been marshalled as evidence for both those who have emphasised the continuity between the present body and resurrected body and those who have emphasised discontinuity.[4] This discussion often reveals how the church's pre-existing perceptions of the body have influenced what aspects of the body different generations of the church deemed 'worthy of the resurrection'. An extreme example of this can be seen from the fifth–eighth century Christian work, *The First Apocryphal Apocalypse of John*:

> In the resurrection, what form (will they take) when they arise? And I heard a voice saying to me, 'Listen, righteous John… those in the resurrection will all be human. They will be neither fair of skin, nor red of skin, nor black of skin; neither will they be (like the) Ethiopian with different facial features: but all will rise in one appearance and one stature. The whole of humanity will rise bodiless, just as I told you, "In the resurrection, they neither marry nor are given in marriage, but are like angels of God."' (*First Apocryphal Apocalypse of John*, 10)

---

3   For the strands of contradictory statements in Tertullian, see Kuefler, *The Manly Eunuch*, 228–230.
4   Lehtipuu, 'No Sex in Heaven', 25.

Similar prejudices can be found in modern interpretations.[5] The history of interpretation reveals the importance of returning to the thought-world of the first century. How might the depiction of angels in the Old Testament and literature of Second Temple Judaism contribute to our understanding of embodiment in the age to come?

## Angelic bodies in the Old Testament and Second Temple Judaism

Discerning precisely what is meant by the comparison 'like the angels' (Matt. 22:30) is made difficult by the wide and, at times, competing traditions regarding angels in the Old Testament and wider literature of Second Temple Judaism. Angels frequently appear in human form in the Old Testament.[6] Two of the three men visiting Abraham (Gen. 18:2) are later identified as 'two angels' (שְׁנֵי הַמַּלְאָכִים, Gen. 19:1). Jacob struggled with a 'man' (Gen. 33:24) that the prophet Hosea identifies as an 'angel' (מַלְאָךְ, Hos. 12:5 MT, ἄγγελος Hos. 12:4 LXX). Ancient Jewish and Christian literature regularly interpreted the incident in Genesis 6:1–4, where the 'sons of God' procreate with the 'daughters of men', as referring to 'the angels of God' (οἱ ἄγγελοι τοῦ θεοῦ, Gen. 6:2 LXX, cf. 1 En. 6:1--2; 15:2–7; *Jub.* 4:22; 5:1–2, cf. Josephus, *Ant.* 1.3.1, Jude 6). The sexual capacity of such angels is consistent with the portrayal of heavenly creatures, such as the seraphim and cherubim, as sexed. Isaiah's seraphim use their wings to cover their 'feet' (Isa. 6:2), a euphemism for genitals (cf. Isa. 7:20; Exod. 4:25, Judg. 3:24).[7] In Ezekiel, the sexed body of the human-like cherubim (1:5; 10:8) is implied by the wings covering its body (1:11). In Zechariah 5:9, there appear to be 'female' heavenly creatures.[8] The sexed embodiment and procreative potential of these heavenly creatures was accepted in the ancient world where the heavenly pantheon engaged in sexual intercourse and reproduction.[9]

---

5   Consider Oepke, 'γυνή', 785: 'In holding out the prospect of sexless being like that of the angels in the consummated kingdom of God [...] He indirectly lifts from woman the curse of her sex and sets her at the side of man as equally a child of God'.
6   For example, Gen. 18:2, Jos. 5:13, Judg. 13:3–6
7   Clements, *Isaiah 1—39*, 74.
8   Meyers and Meyers, *Haggai, Zechariah 1—8*, 305.
9   Wenham, *Genesis 1–15*, 140.

Beliefs about the bodily nature of angels developed and diversified during the Second Temple period.[10] The literature of Second Temple Judaism regularly expands upon the Watchers' ability to procreate (*1 Enoch* 15:3–7), even explaining that the Jewish practice of circumcision originated in the circumcision of the angels of the presence (*Jub.* 15:25–27). Yet, at the same time, angels could be described as 'bodiless' (*2 Enoch* 29:3), 'incorporeal' (*T. Abraham* 4:9), shape-shifting (*2 Baruch* 49:1; 51:5) and capable of transforming into men (*T. Reuben* 5.6).

As a result of these diverse descriptions of angels in the Old Testament and literature of Second Temple Judaism, there is also a variety of descriptions of the resurrection life and future embodiment. For some, the image of angels is an 'unsettling category' destabilising 'fixed notions of two sexes/genders'[11] or even indicating the erasure of sexual difference in the age to come.[12] While the portrayal of angels as capable of sexual embodiment and even procreation in the Old Testament and literature of Second Temple Judaism problematises this interpretation, I will argue that the comparison to the angels is not necessarily a bodily comparison in the first place.

## Synoptic Comparison (Matt. 22:30, Mark 12:25, Luke 20:36)

Jesus' comparison to the angels forms part of his response to the Sadducees (Matt. 22:23–33, Mark 12:18–27, Luke 20:27–40). Upon entering the temple, Jesus is approached by a succession of Jewish groups attempting to challenge his authority (Matt. 21:23—22:40). The Sadducees, who do not believe in the resurrection (μὴ εἶναι ἀνάστασιν, v.23), attempt to expose belief in the resurrection as absurd by constructing an elaborate scenario of levirate marriage (vv.25–28, cf. Deut. 25:5–6). After seven childless marriages end in death, the Sadducees cynically ask: 'At the resurrection, whose wife of the seven will she be?' (τίνος τῶν ἑπτὰ ἔσται γυνή; v.28).

---

10  Bautch, 'Heavenly Beings', 105–128.
11  Vander Stichele, 'Like Angels in Heaven', 232. Hester, 'Eunuchs and the Postgender Jesus', 39.
12  For Dale Martin, Jesus' comparison to the angels (Matt. 22:30) is one piece in a supposed trajectory through scripture towards the abolition of dimorphic sexuality. Martin, *Sex and the Single Savior*, 87.

In reply, Jesus accuses the Sadducees of error. They are ignorant (μὴ εἰδότες) of Israel's Scriptures and the power of God (v.29).[13] Jesus corrects the Sadducees' caricature of resurrection life by undermining the foundation of their hypothetical scenario by revealing 'at the resurrection they neither marry nor are given in marriage, but are like the angels in heaven' / οὔτε γαμοῦσιν οὔτε γαμίζονται ἀλλ' ὡς ἄγγελοι ἐν τῷ οὐρανῷ εἰσιν (Matt. 22:30).[14]

The assumption is often made by interpreters that the cessation of marriage is explained by the comparison to the angels.[15] On this reading, the reason why marriages will cease is because the resurrected will have a bodily nature similar to the angels.[16] But reading the comparison ὡς ἄγγελοι as an explanation for why marriages cease is more than the text explicitly says. Such a reading would most naturally require the conjunction connecting the clauses οὔτε γαμοῦσιν οὔτε γαμίζονται and ὡς ἄγγελοι ἐν τῷ οὐρανῷ εἰσιν to be explanatory, such as γάρ. However, the conjunction connecting the clauses is the adversative ἀλλά (Mark 12:25, Matt. 22:30).[17] The contrastive conjunction is part of a longer construction οὔτε... οὔτε... ἀλλά indicating that the dissolution of marriage and the comparison to the angels serve as separate descriptions of the resurrected life. The first description, 'they neither marry nor are given in marriage'/ οὔτε γαμοῦσιν οὔτε γαμίζονται denies the premise behind the Sadducees' scenario, namely, that resurrection life would simply be a continuance of present relationships. Jesus reveals that marriage will cease at the resurrection.[18] The second description, 'Instead they are like the angels in heaven'/ ἀλλ' ὡς ἄγγελοι ἐν τῷ οὐρανῷ εἰσιν does not explicitly explain the cessation of marriage. It seems unlikely that the angelic comparison could function to explain the cessation of marriage when the literature of the Old

---

13 Hagner, *Matthew 14—28*, 641.
14 Matthew 22:30 is virtually identical to Mark 12:25 in recording Jesus' dissolution of marriage and the comparison to the angels. The differences between the accounts are minor and indicate no difference in meaning.
15 Sailhammer, *The Pentateuch*, 120. Mathews, *Genesis*, 327.
16 Robbins, *Jesus the Teacher*, 192.
17 LSJ, 67–68. BDAG, 44.
18 Ben Witherington has argued that existing marriages will in fact continue in the resurrection but that there will be no new marriages. Witherington, *Women in the Ministry*, 34–35.

Testament and Second Temple Judaism portrays angels as capable of human appearance and procreation.

In the Third Gospel, the dissolution of marriage is explained by the resurrection to eternal life. According to Luke, the reason why those regarded as worthy of the resurrection neither marry nor are given in marriage is, 'because they are no longer able to die' / οὐδὲ γὰρ ἀποθανεῖν ἔτι δύνανται (Luke 20:36a).[19] Humanity will no longer be plagued by death 'because they are equal to the angels' (ἰσάγγελοι γάρ εἰσιν, 20:36b). Luke's angelic comparison, ἰσάγγελοι, functions as a qualitative comparison of experience as opposed to a bodily comparison of nature.[20]

It is more likely that angels, by virtue of their heavenly location (ἐν τῷ οὐρανῷ, v.30) explain the nature of resurrected life. In Matthew's cosmology, angels are located in the presence of God and continually see the face of the Father (Matt. 18:10 cf. *1 En.* 14:23, Jub. 30:18).[21] William Loader believes that the first audiences of the angelic comparison 'could hear a statement about becoming like angels as referring to being like them in holy space'.[22]

In all three Synoptics Gospels, the angelic comparison features in a discussion of the change brought about by the resurrection. While sexual relationships will be transcended at the resurrection, there is nothing explicit to indicate that the sexed bodies of men and women will be transcended or transformed at the resurrection. This line of reasoning has often been assumed and read into the texts.

Moreover, an obvious challenge to those interpreting the angelic comparison to indicate the abolition of dimorphic sexuality or the transformation of the human body into an angelic or asexual body is the context of the discussion. The Sadducees have issued a challenge to the belief in resurrection. The transformation of a human body into an angelic body would cease to be a resurrection and would not cohere with Matthew's wider eschatology. The eschatology of the First Gospel is in continuity with the Old Testament's hope of resurrection

---

19  Bock, *Luke 9:51—24:53*, 1623.
20  Fitzmyer, *Luke (X—XXIV)*, 1305.
21  Bendoriatas, *'Behold, the Angels Came'*, 155.
22  Loader, 'Sexuality and Eschatology', 49.

(Isa. 26:19; Dan. 12:2,13) and renewal (Isa. 65:17–25; 66:22).[23] Jesus speaks of a general resurrection from the dead for judgement (Matt. 12:41–42) and Gehenna as the destiny of the wicked (Matt. 10:28; 23:15). At the end of the age, the righteous, by contrast, will 'shine like the sun in the kingdom of their Father' (Matt. 13:43). In addition to the hope of resurrection, Matthew's eschatological descriptor παλιγγενεσία (19:28) reflects the Old Testament's expectation for the renewal of creation (Isa. 65:17–25; 66:22).[24] While English translations often provide vague descriptions like 'Messianic Age' (HCSB) or 'New World' (RSV, ESV), elsewhere παλιγγενεσία is used to describe Noah and his family's task of restoring humanity's dominion (Philo, *De Vita Mosis* 2.65), the reproductive potential to create anew (Hermes, *Heiros Logos* 3.3), the restoration of the land (Josephus, *Antiquities* 11.66), revival (Lucian, *Muscae Encomoium* 7), or, in the second-century medical literature, avoiding relapse (Galen 13.83). These examples reveal a consistent nuance of recovery or restoration. The idea that the resurrection would indicate the transformation of the human body into an angelic body ceases to cohere with Matthew's own expectations of resurrection and the renewal of creation. Furthermore, in the Gospel accounts of Jesus' own resurrection, the disciples do not perceive that Jesus' bodily sex has been transcended or transformed (Matt. 28:8–10, Luke 24:13–35,36–49, John 20:14–28).

## Angelic Comparisons in the Old Testament and Second Temple Judaism

Jesus' comparison of human individuals to angels is not without precedent. Human beings have been compared to angels or portrayed with angelic characteristics in the Old Testament and wider Jewish literature.[25] Two prominent examples include the Old Testament's

---

23 For an examination of this hope in Jewish literature see esp., Stephens, *Annihilation Or Renewal?*, 19–45. Wilkinson, *Christian Eschatology*, 64.
24 Sim, 'The Meaning of Palingenesia', 3–12. Pennington, 'Heaven, Earth, and a New Genesis', 40–43. Russell, *The 'New Heavens, and New Earth'*, 156.
25 See, e.g. Gieschen, *Angelomorphic* Christology; Fletcher-Louis, *Luke-Acts*; Sullivan, *Wrestling with Angels*.

depiction of Moses and David.[26] The Old Testament tradition of comparing humans to angels, which is developed in the literature of Second Temple Judaism, provides important background for our investigation of the meaning of Jesus' comparison to the angels (Matt. 22:30) and the implications for future embodiment.

Upon descending Mt Sinai, Moses' face was 'glorified' (δοξάζω, Exod. 30:29 LXX) causing the Israelites to be afraid to approach him. According to Sirach, God made Moses 'equal in glory to the holy ones'/ ὡμοίωσεν αὐτὸν δόξῃ ἁγίων (Sir. 45.2). On three separate occasions David is compared to 'an angel of God'/ כְּמַלְאַךְ אֱלֹהִים because of his blameless character (1 Sam. 29:9) and wisdom (2 Sam. 14:17; 19:27). In Pseudo-Philo's retelling of David's conflict with Goliath, there is the inclusion that the 'Philistine looked and saw an angel' (*Biblical Antiquities*, 61.8–9).

The portrayal of Moses with angelic features and the comparison of David to an angel does not indicate a fundamental transformation of their human bodies but instead serve to emphasise their exalted status in Israel's history. It would appear that these angelic descriptions developed in time to articulate the hope of the righteous. The prophet Zechariah anticipated that one outcome of YHWH's future salvation would include an exaltation of God's people. Even the weakest within Jerusalem, 'the stumbler', would become 'like David', and 'the whole house of David will be like God, like the angel of the LORD' (כֵּאלֹהִים כְּמַלְאַךְ יְהוָה) / ὡς ἄγγελος Κυρίου, 12:8). In Zechariah's vision, the angelic comparison serves not to indicate a transformation of the human form so much as an elevation of their status. Such a comparison complements the eschatology of Daniel 12 where the hope of resurrection and angelic comparison converge. Once awakened from sleeping in the dust, the wise will shine 'like the brightness in the heavens' and 'like the stars' (12:3, cf. Job 38:7).[27]

---

26  For further examples in the Old Testament and Second Temple Jewish literature see Sullivan, *Wrestling with Angels*, 85–141.
27  Angels were often identified as, or associated with, stars in Jewish thinking. For e.g., Judg. 5:20; Job 38:7; *1 En.* 86:1; *2 Bar.* 51:5. See further Allison, *Studies in Matthew*, 17–41, and Thiessen, 'Buried Pentateuchal Allusion, 278–282.

The literature of Second Temple Judaism follows this trajectory by applying angelic comparisons to the righteous more generally. In *1 Enoch*, the righteous are encouraged to persevere until the day of the great judgement with the promise that they will 'shine like the lights of heaven' (104:2). In the future state, the face of the righteous will 'shine like the sun', and be 'like the light of the stars, being incorruptible from then on' (*4 Ezra* 7:97). This angelic comparison is also found in *2 Baruch* where the resurrected 'will be like the angels and be equal to the stars' (51:10).

## The Parable of the Weeds (Matt. 13:24–30, 37–43), and the Transfiguration (Matt. 17:1–8)

Jesus' comparison of humanity to angels (Matt. 22:30) is not an isolated event in the first Gospel. On at least two additional occasions the righteous are either compared to angels or described with angelic features.

The first example can be found in the Parable Discourse. The Parable of the Weeds (Matt. 13:24–30) and its explanation (vv.37–43) is unique to the Gospel of Matthew. This parable provides a cosmic explanation of human history and an itinerary for 'the end of the age' (v.40). The field stands for the world with good seed, the people of the kingdom, co-existing alongside weeds, the people of the evil one (vv.38–39). 'Just as the weeds are pulled up', so the Son of Man will initiate a judgement at the end of the age so thorough that everything that causes sin and lawlessness will be weeded out of his kingdom and thrown into a furnace of fire (vv.40–42). The righteous, by contrast, 'will shine like the sun (ὡς ὁ ἥλιος) in the kingdom of their Father' (13:43). As seen above, shining 'like the sun' is a common description of the eschatological glory of the righteous (*4 Ezra* 7:97) and can serve as a description of angels (*2 Bar.* 51:5,10). This imagery also features in Matthew's account of the transfiguration.

Matthew's account of the Transfiguration (17:1–8) follows directly on from Peter's confession of Jesus as the 'Messiah, the Son of the living God' (16:16). 'From that time on' (ἀπὸ τότε ἤρξατο, 16:18), as Matthew indicates, Jesus began preparing his disciples for his coming suffering and death in Jerusalem (Matt. 16:21). As a way of reassuring his disciples at the news of his coming death and the prospect of the disciples own suffering, Jesus promises that some of the disciples 'will not taste death before they see the Son of Man coming in his kingdom' (16:28). The following account of the transfiguration (17:1–8) is linked to the confession at Caesarea Philippi by the chronological reference 'after six days' (17:1). One result of Jesus' transfiguration (μεταμορφόω) is that his face shines 'like the sun' (ὡς ὁ ἥλιος, 17:2). The transfiguration provides a 'vision' (ὅραμα, v.9) of the eschatological glory of the Son of Man (16:27–28) in order to reassure the disciples of Jesus' identity and certain vindication after suffering.[28] But the repetition of such a specific a comparison as 'like the sun' demands a connection between the transfiguration and the Parable of the Weeds. Since the Parable of the Weeds indicated that the righteous would shine 'like the sun' (13:43), the transfiguration also serves to indicate the eschatological glory of the Messiah's followers and provides a 'glimpse of what eschatological resurrection will mean'.[29] The transfiguration of Jesus provides an example of the righteous being raised from the dead not with a different angelic body but with a glorified human body.

In his study of Matthew's transfiguration account, A. D. A. Moses believes: 'Matthew has blended Moses–Sinai (Exod. 34:29–35) and Danielic (12:3) motifs'.[30] It seems plausible, however, that these are not separate motifs but are, in fact, cut from the same cloth. The imagery used to describe the vindicated righteous (Matt. 13:43), the appearance of the transfigured Jesus (Matt. 17:2), and the comparison of the resurrected to the angels (Matt. 22:30), can all be traced back to the tradition found within the Old Testament and developed in Second Temple Jewish literature of comparing humans to angels or describing humans with angelic features. Comparing the resurrected to the angels (Matt. 22:30) then is not an isolated incident in Matthew but consistent with the eschatological expectations of the first Gospel.[31]

In the worldview of the Old Testament, humanity was made 'a little lower than the heavenly beings' (אֱלֹהִים, ἄγγελος, Ps. 8:6). What

---

28  Bendoraitis, *'Behold, the Angels came'*, 126. Davies and Allison, *Matthew 8—18*, 431, 688.
29  Davies and Allison, *Matthew 8—18*, 688.
30  Moses, *Matthew's Transfiguration*, 126.
31  Sim, *Apocalyptic Eschatology*, 142–145.

better way to describe the elevated glory of resurrected life enjoyed in the presence of God than to compare humanity to being 'like the angels' (Matt. 22:30; Mark 12:35) or 'equal to the angels' (Luke 20:36)? Angels were associated with life (Luke 20:36), brilliant light (Matt. 28:3; John 20:12) and the presence of God (Matt. 18:10).[32] By contrast, Matthew utilises Isaiah's imagery of 'darkness' and 'the shadow do death' to describe the human predicament: 'The people dwelling in darkness saw a great light, And on those dwelling in the region and in the shadow of death a light has dawned' (Matt. 4:16). Matthew's description of humanity blurs 'the line between the living and the dead'.[33] Becoming 'like the angels' could have been heard as a way of describing life no longer haunted by death but enjoyed in the presence of God. The angelic comparison contributes to Matthew's understanding of salvation, which progressively unfolds throughout the first Gospel. In addition to the promise of salvation from sin (Matt. 1:21), Matthew also shows that the Old Testament's hope for resurrection and renewal is found in Jesus, the Son of David, Son of Abraham, including the glorification of humanity, shining like the sun, in the kingdom of the Father.

## Conclusion

As the history of interpretation has revealed, cultural presuppositions have, at times, influenced what aspects of the body the church has deemed worthy of the resurrection. The church's eschatological imagination needs, on the one hand, to be aware of these trappings and, on the other hand, to be content to imagine within the confines of Scripture's own presentation. Matthew's wider eschatological emphasis of resurrection and renewal challenge the cultural influences that deem aspects of the physical body as 'not worthy of the resurrection'.

Jesus' angelic comparison stands within a tradition, stretching back into the Old Testament's portrayal of Moses and David and continuing through the literature of Second Temple Judaism. Originally serving to

---

32  Loader, 'Sexuality and Eschatology', 47–49.
33  Clark-Soles, *Death and the Afterlife*, 159.

emphasise the significant roles Moses and David performed in Israel's history, this tradition developed as a way of describing the eschatological hope of the righteous. While Moses and David are portrayed with angelic characteristics, there is no indication that their bodies underwent significant transformation. Since there is no evidence of a bodily transformation in these examples, there is no precedent for suggesting the comparison to the angels indicates the transcendence or transformation of bodily sex in the future. Rather, comparing humans to angels or describing humans with angelic features serves to describe tangibly the hope of human nature raised from the dead and glorified in the presence of God. In keeping with the hope of the righteous glorified (Matt. 13:43), the transfiguration provides a preview of humanity glorified. As the church looks forward to the resurrection and the life of the world to come, the church can gaze at the vision of Jesus glorified knowing they too will be raised as men and women and glorified like him.

Tim Bradford
PhD Candidate, Sydney College of Divinity

## Bibliography

Allison, D. C. — *Studies in Matthew: Interpretation Past and Present* (Grand Rapids: Baker Academic, 2005).

Bautch, K. C. — 'Heavenly Beings in the Enoch Traditions and Synoptic Gospels', in L. T. Stuckenbruck and G. Boccaccini, (eds.), *Enoch and the Synoptic Gospels: Reminiscences, Allusions, Intertextuality* (Atlanta, GA: Society of Biblical Literature, 2016), 105–127.

Bendoraitis, K. A. — *'Behold, the Angels Came and Served Him': A Compositional Analysis of Angels in Matthew* (London: T&T Clark, 2018).

Bock, D. L. — *Luke. Volume 2: 9:51—24:53* (Baker Exegetical Commentary on the New Testament; Grand Rapids, MI: Baker, 1996).

Bynum, C. W. — *Resurrection of the Body in Western Christianity, 200–1336* (Lectures on the History of Religions, 15; New York, NY: Columbia University Press, 1995).

Clark-Soles, J. — *Death and the Afterlife in the New Testament* (New York: T&T Clark, 2006).

Clements, R.E. — *Isaiah 1—39* (New Century Bible Commentary; Grand Rapids, MI: Eerdmans, 1982).

Davies, W. D., and D. C. Allison — *A Critical and Exegetical Commentary on the Gospel According to Saint Matthew: Matthew 19–28* (ICC; London: T & T Clark, 2004).

Fletcher-Louis, C. H. T. — *Luke–Acts: Angels, Christology and Soteriology* (WUNT 2:94; Tübingen: Mohr–Siebeck, 1995).

Fitzmyer, J. A. — *The Gospel according to Luke (X–XXIV)* (Anchor Bible 28A; Garden City, N.Y.: Doubleday, 2015).

Gieschen, C. A. — *Angelomorphic Christology: Antecedents and Early Evidence* (Leiden: E. J. Brill, 1998).

Hagner, D. A. — *Matthew 14–28* (Word Biblical Commentary, 33B; Dallas, TX: Word Books, 1982).

Hester, J. D. — 'Eunuchs and the Postgender Jesus: Matthew 19.12 and Transgressive Sexualities', *Journal for the Study of the New Testament* 28.1 (2005), 13–40.

Isherwood, L., and E. Stuart — *Introducing Body Theology* (Introductions in Feminist Theology 2; Sheffield: Sheffield Academic, 1998).

Kuefler, M. — *The Manly Eunuch: Masculinity, Gender Ambiguity, and Christian Ideology in Late Antiquity* (Chicago: University of Chicago Press, 2001).

Lehtipuu, O. — 'No Sex in Heaven—Nor on Earth?: Luke 20:27–38 as a Proof-Text in Early Christian Discourses on Resurrection and Asceticism', *Bodies Borders, Believers: Ancient Texts and Present Conversations* (Eugene, OR: Pickwick, 2015), 22–39.

Loader, W. — 'Sexuality and Eschatology: In Search of a Celibate Utopia in Pseudepigraphic Literature', *Journal for the Study of the Pseudepigrapha* 24.1 (2014), 43–67.

Looy, H. and Bouma, H. — 'The Nature of Gender: Gender Identity in Persons who are Intersexed or Transgendered', *Journal of Psychology and Theology* 33.3 (2005), 166–178.

Martin, D. B. — *Sex and the Single Savior: Gender and Sexuality in Biblical Interpretation* (Louisville, KY: Westminster John Knox, 2006).

Mathews, K. A. — *Genesis 1–11.26* (The New American Commentary, 1A; Nashville, TN: Broadman and Holman, 1996).

Meyers, C. L., and E. M. Meyers — *Haggai, Zechariah 1–8* (Anchor Bible 25B; New York, N.Y: Doubleday, 1987).

Moses, A. D. A. — *Matthew's Transfiguration Story and Jewish-Christian Controversy* (London: A&C Black, 1996).

Oepke, A. — 'γυνή', in G. Kittel (ed.), *Theological Dictionary of the New Testament. Volume I A-G* (translated and edited G. W. Bromiley; Grand Rapids, MI: Eerdmans, 1964), 776–789.

Pennington, J. T. — 'Heaven, Earth, and a New Genesis: Theological Cosmology in Matthew', in J. T. Pennington and S. M. McDonough (eds.), *Cosmology and New Testament Theology* (London, T&T Clark, 2008), 28–44.

Robbins, V. K. — *Jesus the Teacher: A Socio-Rhetorical Interpretation of Mark* (Philadelphia, PA: Fortress, 1984).

Russell, D. M. — *The 'New Heavens, and New Earth': Hope for the Creation in Jewish Apocalyptic and the New Testament* (Studies in Biblical Apocalyptic Literature; Philadelphia, PA: Visionary Press, 1996).

Sailhammer, J.H.  *The Pentateuch as Narrative: A Biblical–theological Commentary* (Grand Rapids, MI: Zondervan, 1992).

Sim, D. C.  'The Meaning of Palingenesia in Matthew 19.28', *Journal for the Study of the New Testament* 50 (1993), 3–12.

Sim, D. C.  *Apocalyptic Eschatology in the Gospel of Matthew* (SNTSMS 88; Cambridge: Cambridge University Press, 1996).

Stephens, M. B.  *Annihilation Or Renewal?: The Meaning and Function of New Creation in the Book of Revelation* (Tübingen: Mohr-Siebeck, 2011).

Thiessen, M.  'A Buried Pentateuchal Allusion to the Resurrection in Mark 12:25', *The Catholic Biblical Quarterly* 76.2 (2014), 273–290.

Vander Stichele, C.  'Like Angels in Heaven: Corporeality, Resurrection, and Gender in Mark 12:18–27', in *Begin with the Body: Corporeality Religion and Gender* (Louvain, 1998), 215–232.

Sullivan, K. P.  *Wrestling with Angels: A Study of the Relationship Between Angels and Humans in Ancient Jewish Literature and the New Testament* (Leiden: Brill, 2004).

Wenham, G. J.  *Genesis 1–15* (Word Biblical Commentary; Nashville, TN: Nelson, 1987).

Wilkinson, D.  *Christian Eschatology and the Physical Universe* (London: T&T Clark, 2010).

Witherington, B.  Women in the Ministry of Jesus: A Study of Jesus' Attitudes to Women and Their Roles as Reflected in His Earthly Life (Cambridge: Cambridge University Press, 1984).

CHAPTER 8

# The Markan Alphabet Theory: Eschatological Origins of Mark's Gospel

Michael Modini

## Abstract

If the epoch-defining events which contributed to the composition of the earliest Gospel can be regarded as 'last things' or 'end times', then there is an eschatological component to the synthesis of the three alphabetical sequences which, according to the Markan Alphabet theory, provided the foundations of Mark's Gospel. This essay explores some areas where alphabet and eschatology converge.

The Markan Alphabet theory[1] is a hypothesis which posits that the Hebrew (Aramaic) alphabet was utilised by the author of the earliest Gospel—named after the disciple John Mark—as a means of referencing, sequencing, and exploring key themes and moments in the Gospel's three major sequences: (i) the miracle narratives, (ii) the dominical discourses, and (iii) the Passion-Resurrection narrative. It is premised on

---

1   For more detail, see https://frequens.wordpress.com/2021/08/24/the-markan-alphabet-theory/.

the facts that the word אות (oth) can be translated as 'letter', 'sign', or 'miracle', and that twenty-two—the number of letters in the Hebrew (Aramaic) alphabet—represents a cycle of completion and perfection.

In all probability, the three alphabetical sequences predated the composition of the Gospel. It was Mark's task as evangelist to weave them into a single narrative.[2] Though the account of the Passion and Resurrection (and probably the sequence of miracle narratives) post-dates the life of Jesus, it's possible that the use of the Hebrew (Aramaic) alphabet as a mnemonic technique or preaching aid was first used by Jesus himself; the same system would then have been used by followers or witnesses of his deeds to enumerate and narrate these other aspects of his ministry. In addition to assisting believers in retaining and transmitting both sayings and narratives during the pre-Greek, oral phase of the Gospel's development, the divine perfection of the alphabetical system bolstered claims that the Master who employed it—in word, in deed, and in the manner and circumstances of his death—was indeed the Son of God. Yet, while first-century Jews would have recognised the Hebrew (Aramaic) word-clues of the alphabetical sequences, it was concealed by the Greek of Mark's Gospel; thus the evangelists Matthew and Luke, who borrowed extensively from Mark, neglected to retain it.

Though it may seem obvious from a twenty-first century perspective that the life and death of a 'prophet mighty in word and deed' (Luke 24:19) deserves an informative biography, this was not necessarily the expectation in the first century of the Common Era. It was Mark's genius to combine—comprehensively, cohesively and in Greek—the oral traditions relating to Jesus that were known to him. In synthesising these traditions, the evangelist had necessarily

---

2   The only episodes in Mark which are not comprised by one of the three alphabetical sequences are the baptism of Jesus by John the Baptist (1:1–11), the temptation of Jesus in the wilderness (1:12–13) and the death of the Baptist (6:14–29). It's probable that the accounts of the beginning of Jesus' ministry (1:14–15), the calling of the fishermen (1:16–20), the calling of Levi (2:13–14), the choosing of the Twelve (3:13–19) and various descriptions of Jesus' ministry including his preaching style and entry into Jerusalem (1:35–39; 2:1–17; 3:7–12; 6:1–4; 11:1–33) also represent biographical material originally separate from the alphabetical sequences, but in the hands of the evangelist they have become incorporated into material associated with other narratives and discourses.

to interweave one sequence with another; thus, while the Passion-Resurrection account remains intact as the Gospel's conclusion, elsewhere Mark interspersed Jesus' sayings with accounts of his miracles and other stories about the Baptist and the disciples. It is this interspersing of the discourses with miracle narratives and other biographical material which both provides us with clues to the author's insights about Jesus' ministry, and essentially determines the Gospel's structure. That this written synthesis came into being around the year 70 C.E. suggests that the magnitude of current events—epoch-changing to the extent that we can refer to them as 'eschatological'—provided an impetus for the Gospel's formation.

Some areas where 'eschatology' and 'alphabet' converge include: the welcoming of the Gentiles as an eschatological event; the significance of the number twenty-two in the realisation of eschatology as the end-time equivalent and complement of protology; some specifically eschatological themes in the sequence of discourses; the duality of some of the discourses; the Mosaic origins of alphabet and Torah; the development of the miracle narratives around Mosaic and Elianic themes; the inclusion among the miracle narratives of some specific place names; the curious inversion of two particular miracles; the inclusion of the crucifixion among the sequence of miracles; and the combination of the three alphabetical sequences as an expression of realised eschatology. These eschatological factors may help to explain some of the discrepancies in the evangelised (in the sense of 'turned into Gospel') version of the three sequences, to the extent that the combination of the three sequences in itself might be regarded as an event on the eschatological 'spectrum'.

That the 'end-times' featuring the fulfilment of prophecies around the Messiah as 'Son of Man' would also welcome the (pagan) Gentiles into a (monotheistic) Jewish fold is known from a number of Old Testament texts.[3] The period of national emergency now generally referred to as the first Jewish War (66–73 C.E.) was 'eschatological' to the extent that it witnessed the destruction of the second Temple and threatened the existence of the Jewish nation; tradition also tells us

---

3   E.g. Ps. 86:9; Isa. 9:2; 49:6; 55; 60:3; Dan. 7:14; Hos. 2:23; Mal. 1:11.

that Simon Peter was martyred around this time in Rome. The regard for Jewish ideas, however, and the inclusion of Gentiles into table-fellowship around the memory of Jesus, necessitated a foundation document in the *lingua franca* of the eastern Empire. Thus the eschatological emergency contributed to the collation and unification of the oral alphabetical sequences in a single Greek text.

If the end-times can be seen as a renewal of God's creative activity, then it is to be expected that the coming of the Messiah would in some shape or form provide an end-time mirror-image of—or complement to—the beginning of time. The first chapters of Genesis tell us that the world was created in seven days, and while this sevenfold structure isn't specifically retained in Mark,[4] there is an allusion to it in the narrative around Passion Week (i.e. seven days plus one). According to the *Book of Jubilees* (2:15), the 'works of creation' mentioned by Genesis include seven wrought on the first day, one on the second, four on the third, three on the fourth, three on the fifth, and four on the sixth. And while *Jubilees* doesn't specifically list these 'works', the total of twenty-two is a clear allusion to the number of letters in the alphabet, whose structure is then incorporated into the record of the deeds of the Messiah—as compiled by Mark—in triplicate. It's interesting to speculate that if Mark (or his sources) intended to follow the pattern established by the author of *Jubilees*, the narratives would occur in a series replicating the number of works performed on each of the six days of creation—that is to say, in conceptual groupings of seven, one, four, three, three, and four (in that order). The corpus of miracle narratives provides a hint of such an ordering, although not according to time. Instead, the *locations* in which the miracles take place are arranged according to just such a schema: the first seven works (Aleph to Zayin) take place in Galilee; the episode of the Gerasene swine (Cheth) is an isolated incident in an isolated location; the raising of Jairus' daughter (Theth) coincides with the healing of the bleeding woman (Yod); the three healings represented by Ayin, Peh, and Tsaddi take place after Jesus' return from the region of Tyre; and the final four are placed on the road to and in Jerusalem.

---

4   Cf. the Gospel of John, where the structure of seven 'days' is more explicit.

If the eschaton is heralded by the appearance of Jesus and his fate, a complete account of Jesus' sayings—the discursive *oeuvre* or arsenal representing the verbal component of his ministry, or stock-in-trade speeches that he employed as he went from table to table, lake to synagogue, developing the theme of the kingdom of God—must therefore include some which refer to end-time events. In Mark's account we find that at least two and perhaps even four of the last six sayings (all recorded as having been delivered in Jerusalem) refer to relevant topics: the cleansing (צַדִּיק, *tsadiq*) of the Temple (Tsaddi), the practice of *qorban* (קָרְבָּן, Qoph), and the prophet Daniel's 'abomination of desolation' (שִׁקּוּץ, *shiquts*: Shin; and תּוֹעֵבָה, *to'evah*; Tau).

The implicit duality of some of the discourses may also conceal an eschatological intention. The so-called Alphabet of Rabbi Akiva, a sequence of discursive headings attributed to the famous historical and religious figure who lived c. 50–135 C.E., is comparable to that of Jesus' discourses, and is particularly notable for featuring in one of its versions a 'good' and a 'bad' aspect for each of the letters. Such duality would make sense at a time when citizens were called upon to join the ranks of either the righteous or the unclean. Granted, identifying the 'topic headings' of Jesus' sequence of discourses isn't always straightforward, and often where one heading is obvious, an alternative (or 'dual') heading isn't as readily decipherable. Nevertheless, it is possible to discern an attempt at this in the Aleph passage's statement that 'the son of man (דְמָא, *adam*) is lord (אֲדֹנָי, *Adonai*) of the Sabbath', while the Beth passage's contrast between the 'house' (Beth) of the strong man and 'Beelzebul' is more clearly diametrical.

The Hebrew (Aramaic) alphabet itself is, of course, the Palestinian variety of what we might today call the Phoenician or Central Semitic alphabet, but Jewish tradition saw it as providing the basis for the language that was used by Moses to compose the Torah (and preserve the ten Commandments) and by God to bring the world into existence. Jesus' employment of the alphabet as a preaching aid or mnemonic thus made an implicit appeal to the 'man of God'; while those who recorded his miracles, marvelling that 'even the wind and waves obey him' (Mark 4:41), saw in him a thaumaturge made from the same mould as Moses. That the miracles represented a kind of appropriation of the alphabet can be discerned from the fact that in approximately a third of cases the key word directly references the name for the letter itself (e.g. *Beth*, 'house'; *Yod*, 'hand').

As a prophet of the eschaton, furthermore, Jesus is heralded by the appearance of Moses and Elijah. The account of the Transfiguration is thus a key event in the Messianic trajectory, and the Markan Alphabet theory includes this event as the nineteenth (Qoph) miraculous 'sign' (אוֹת, *oth*). The work of Karl Ludwig Schmidt, Emil Wendling, Paul Achtemeier, Joanna Dewey, Burton Mack, and others on the core structure of the miracle *opus* posits a *catena* of five events recalling the deeds of Moses and Elijah: a walking across water and a feeding of a multitude (Moses) framing three healing stories (Elijah), one of which concerns a woman, and one of which is an exorcism. The tradition that it was Moses the miracle-worker who designed the alphabet was possibly a factor in convincing the originators of the list of twenty-two miracles to expand upon the already widely-recognised miracles of the *catena* to reach a number equivalent to that of the Messianic discourses. The interchangeability of some letters in Hebrew and Aramaic (Samekh, Tsaddi and Shin, for example) may go some way to explaining why the same miracle may be retold, albeit with variations.

Remarkable among the list of miracle narratives are three which refer to topographical names with the correlating information that Jesus worked miracles at these places. If our working theory is that the list of twenty-two is founded upon three or four renditions of the five-event *catena*, then clearly some additional 'fillers' were needed to complete the list. While 'Galilee' is an obvious insertion for Gimel, less clear are the references to 'the villages' (כְּפָרִים, *kaferim*)[5] for Kaph, and Gennesareth (נֶגֶד, *neged*, the 'other side') for Nun. In the process of turning the three alphabetical sequences into Gospel, the evangelist seems to have misread—or else deliberately combined—*kaferim* with *kafirah*, thus making 'denial' or 'unbelief' (Mark 6:6) one of the phenomena attributable to an eschatological prophet on the basis of a proverbial saying (Mark 6:4). The reference to villages, nevertheless, remains in the second part of verse 6 as the location for Jesus' 'teaching'.

---

5   Another possibility here is that Jesus' 'own country' (Mark 6:1) was Capernaum (*Kafar-Nahum*).

Eschatological factors might also help to explain one of the glaring discrepancies in the list of miracle narratives. As it stands, the healing of the deaf-mute (Mark 7:31–37) is placed *before* the feeding of the 4000 (Mark 8:1–10), whereas if the evangelist were adhering strictly to alphabetical order the reference to Peh ('mouth' and *Ephphratha*) should come *after* Ayin (עֲצֶרֶת, *etseret*, 'assembly', or עוֹדֶף, *odeph*, 'surplus'). That this is the only inversion in the entire category of miracles as preserved by Mark suggests that it merits an explanation. It is possible, of course, that the evangelist wished to associate the deaf-mute with a place closer to the location of Samekh miracle (Tyre or *Sur*)—Pella and Philadelphia are possibilities—but since these places are in the region of the Decapolis, which is itself the location of the Ayin miracle (Mark 8:1–10), it seems unlikely that the order of the two miracles would be reversed just for this reason. What seems more likely is that in the list's original form Ayin stood for the healing of a blind man (*Ayin* meaning 'eye' just as *Peh* represents 'mouth') and that the arrival of the end-time necessitated the accommodation into the list of the story of the feeding of a Gentile crowd in order to complement that of the Jewish crowd which had previously been fed with the bread of Lamed (Mark 6:30–44). We can assume from this that accounts of both versions of crowd-feeding were in circulation before the Gospel was compiled; and since the feeding of a Gentile crowd must necessarily take place in a location with a substantial Gentile population, it required positioning between the miracles relating to Samekh (Tyre) and Tsaddi (Bethsaida). The healing of the blind man which the feeding of the 4000 replaced was so unforgettable, however, that it was relocated to Bethsaida, where it displaced a (hypothetically) original healing of a cripple whose story is preserved in the Gospel of John, where the pool of Bethzatha or Bethesda (5:2) replaces the linguistically similar Bethsaida. The order of the miracles of Ayin and Peh were reversed, then, to retain the close association between the 'eye' of Ayin and the blind man of Tsaddi.

A narrative featuring a Messiah composed around the time of the destruction of the second Temple must of necessity have its hero refer to this structure. Mark does this by placing Jesus in the Temple shortly before his arrest, thereby implicitly linking the crucifixion with the rending of the curtain. The cross, as a physical representation of the Tau, was almost certainly the last in the original sequence of twenty-two wondrous signs, but the institution of the Passion-Resurrection narrative, among which an account of the crucifixion must necessarily be included, led to its substitution in the Tau position by an account of the miracle of the (ripe) fig (תְּאֵנָה, *te'enah*). In the evangelist's hands, the final (Tau) miracle of the reworked sequence is thus one which both evokes the cleansing of the Temple and looks forward to the rending of the curtain which accompanies the crucifixion and evokes not only the Temple's destruction but the elimination of barriers between Jews and Gentiles and between people and God.

The incorporation of the alphabet into the Messianic ministry—even if only in the form of a meta-narratival mnemonic—invests that ministry with a kind of validity which, in its appeal to the origins of language, reaches towards the sacred. In combining the three alphabetical traditions known to him, Mark found value in the alphabetical model. That the language—and the twenty-two sounds of that language—used by Moses to write the Torah and by God to create the world could now be used to delineate a new paradigm clearly appealed to the evangelist whom tradition calls the Second but whom we know to have been the first, and who saw in the trio of alphabetical sequences (and in the work he would do in combining them) an inherently divine sanction which spoke to him of the 'last things'. Though the Hebrew (Aramaic) alphabetical clues have been lost over time and with Mark's translation into other languages, on a metalinguistic level these memories are activated—as is so much with the Gospel—each time the story is told.

Michael Modini
mmodini@mlmc.vic.edu.au

CHAPTER 9

# The Eschatological Coherence of Jesus' 'Random Sayings on Faith, Prayer, and Forgiveness' in Mark 11:22–25(26)

Peter G. Bolt

## Abstract

In the 'rising action' of the closing chapters of Mark's Gospel, after entering Jerusalem to cries of Hosanna, and clearing the temple of traders, Jesus curses a fig tree before reflecting upon these dramatic events with a series of sayings on faith, prayer, and forgiveness which are usually treated as rather random (11:22–25[26]). After carefully analysing these sayings in their own right, this essay reads them in the context of the narrative-movement towards Jesus' end, and against apocalyptic expectation of the movement of the world towards God's kingdom. Rather than being random, these sayings are found to have a profound eschatological coherence focused upon the End.

Mark 11:22–25(26) has been called the most difficult and the most neglected paragraph in Mark's Gospel.[1] If we immediately dispense with v.26, which is most probably an interpolation from Matt. 6:15,[2] the paragraph consists of four sayings. These are usually deemed to be originally independent, rather loosely connected to each other, and, although addressing major issues of interest to later Christian generations—faith, forgiveness, and prayer—very poorly connected to the Markan context. At a time when source-critical judgements were common in Gospels scholarship, these originally independent sayings were deemed to have been collected together by some kind of 'catchword' association, whether in Mark's source or by his own activity. However, even after decades of narrative-reader criticism has revealed Mark to be an artfully-constructed narrative, carefully oriented towards the persuasion of its readers, this legacy of previous scholarship continues in these sayings being treated as rather random intrusions into one of the most carefully-structured sections of Mark's Gospel.[3]

Part of Mark's rising action, i.e. as the narrative movement gathers pace towards its climax—and Jesus' End—these sayings appear as the final section of an intercalation (11:12–14; 15–19; 20–25). This oral-communicative device[4] for which Mark is famous structures the hearing/reading experience so that two stories sandwiched together become mutually interpretive—in this instance, Jesus' cursing of the fig tree and his action in the temple. But this feature of the sayings' immediate context is also part of a larger narrative movement, structured temporally across three successive days and by movement and topography, as Jesus repeats the same daily journey from Bethany,

---

1 See Dowd, *Prayer*, 2–5; cf. Voelz, *Mark*, 829.
2 Metzger, *Textual Commentary*, 93. The commentaries do not dispute its inauthenticity.
3 Montefiore, *Synoptic Gospels*, 1.270, furnishes an example from the tail-end of the source-critical era, declaring connection to the fig tree 'awkward' and 'artificial', and the whole passage 'incoherent', due to being 'utterances of Jesus which were not originally connected with [the fig tree]'. Later commentaries continue to echo such conclusions: e.g. Branscomb, *Mark*, 206–207; Taylor, *St Mark*, 466; Best, 'Preservation', 42–43; Lane, *Mark*, 409; Telford, *Barren*, 56; Evans, *Mark*, 185; Juel, *Mark*, 160; Hooker, *Mark*, 269–270; Gundry, *Mark*, 654; France, *Mark*, 448; Harrington and Donahue, *Mark*, 329; Beavis, *Mark*, 171; Black, *Mark*, 244; Kirk, 'Fig Tree', 509, 523–24; Strauss, *Mark*, 497–498; Keener, 'Mountains', 53–54. Making the same point, see the survey in Berge, 'Jesus', 1–4.
4 Achtemeier, 'Omne Verbum Sonat', 21.

across the Mount of Olives, to arrive at Jerusalem and her temple, and back again (Day One: 11:1–11; Day Two: 11:12–19; Day Three: 11:20—13:37).[5] Despite the fact that such careful patterning has generated the occasional attempt to find an inner logic that binds the sayings into a meaningful paragraph, the influence of previous scholarship is nevertheless apparent in the tendency to propose a coherence that is linked more to its meaning for later generations, than for Jesus' life and ministry in its original setting, as portrayed by Mark.[6]

This essay seeks to overcome this legacy of fragmentation and to expose the coherence of these supposedly 'random sayings on faith, prayer, and forgiveness' within the context of Mark's narrative portrayal of Jesus' eschatological significance.[7]

If any such coherence might emerge, the lexical, grammatical, or syntactical ambiguities encountered at almost every turn must first be negotiated.

## 1. Ἔχετε πίστιν θεοῦ

The bulk of this essay will be given to Jesus' foundational saying (v.22), which is arguably the most significant and also the most problematic. Consisting of only three words, the saying presents difficulties in regard to lexical denotation, grammar, and syntax. However, despite these exegetical difficulties, the saying is commonly deemed to be so straightforward that any alternative to the proclaimed consensus is rarely acknowledged and often quickly dismissed. Since it is apparently

---

5   The close of the third day is not narrated (but cf. 14:3). Although the journey home begins, it pauses on the Mount of Olives (13:1,3) where Jesus delivers his extended 'apocalyptic discourse'.
6   That is, notions of the replacement of the prayers in the temple with those of the (Christian) 'eschatological community', and/or efficacious miracle-working commands; see Marshall, *Faith*, 163–174; Kirk, 'Time for Figs', 524–525; Voelz, *Mark*, 855–856 (drawing upon Berge, 'Jesus'); Keener, 'Mountains', 54, 57–58.
7   Since 1991 I have published several brief notes challenging the consensus on this paragraph (*Narrative Integrity*, 47 n.86 [original: 1991]; *Jesus' Defeat of Death*, 244–245; *Cross*, 88; 'Faith', 250–255). The present essay bolsters the argument with further evidence and refines the conclusions.

a clause with only one known analogy[8] in biblical (Rom. 3:3, τὴν πίστιν τοῦ θεοῦ) and surrounding literature,[9] the force with which such dismissals are delivered seems unwarranted,[10] especially since, as indicated both in the ancient textual tradition and across the entire

---

[8] Sylva, 'Review', took me to task for using the adjective 'unusual' for the expression ('Faith', 252), despite having precedent (Hooker, *St Mark*, 269) and evidently missing my comment that Rom. 3:3 is 'the only comparable expression' (p.250), claiming it was a 'very generous adjective'. My full statement was: 'Now, although the occurrence of this phrase is unusual, its theological truth is not'. See below for further support of the latter.

[9] On closer analysis, the references supplied at BDAG 2.a. πίστις θεοῦ also prove to be non-analogous. In Jos. *Ant*. 17.179 πίστιν τοῦ θείου is more likely 'a pledge to God' than a reference to the faith of Salome (cf. 17:284, ἐπὶ δεξιαῖς καὶ πίστει τοῦ θείου; and, for πίστις = [covenantal] political fidelity, see 19:289, and LSJ IV, Plb. 20.9.10; 3.30.1; 6.17.8; and Jos. *Ap*. 2:218 [see below in this note]); in 1 Theoph. 7, ἐν τῇ καρδίᾳ πίστις καὶ φόβος ὁ τοῦ Θεοῦ the masculine article shows that the genitive modifies fear, not both fear and faith; and 1 Cl. 3:4; 27:3, as in other Christian literature the phrase (or similar) is used for 'the faith of God/Christ' (Ig. *Eph*. 16:2; *Rom*. 1:0; Herm. *Shep*. 63:6; 93:5; possibly also 43:9), that is, orthodox Christianity, following e.g. Acts 6:7; 13:8; 14:22; 16:5; Gal. 1:23; 2 Cor 13:5; etc., which is also the meaning of ἡ πίστις τοῦ θεοῦ in Acts 19:20 D. The translation 'firm loyalty of God' for τοῦ δὲ θεοῦ τὴν πίστιν ἰσχυράν in Jos. *Ap*. 2:218 is analogous to the translation suggested in this article. No other analogous case is yielded by searches of LXX (apart from the spurious 1 Sam. 21:3, see n.22), Pseudepigrapha, Philo, Josephus, Apostolic Fathers, Apologists, Apocryphal Acts, Athanasius, or Eusebius. At this point, I have not systematically searched the wider Greek literature, but neither have I come across anyone else providing such occurrences.

[10] E.g. Cranfield, *Mark*, 361: *in loc*, 'the suggestion that the genitive is subjective, "have the sort of faith God has" is surely a monstrosity of exegesis'. Retorting Cranfield's invective, Robinson, '"The Faith"', 139, noted that 'it could mean "be firm" and in Mark 11:22 "be firm as God is firm"'. For further dismissals: France, *Gospel of Mark*, 448: 'surely forced' (cf. Sanday and Headlam, *Romans*, dismissal of Haussleiter (1891) reading the subjective genitive at Rom. 3:22, with its implications for other passages, as 'forced'). After suggesting some kind of psychoanalysis is required for those with views other than his own in the *pistis theou* debate (which, he implies, arise from 'ignoring or minimizing the obvious and indisputable'), Silva, 'Review', declares on Mark 11:22 that 'virtually every standard commentary and translation understands this clause to mean "Have faith in God"'—and relegates the alternative to 'a fanciful preacher here and there'. Perhaps he can be excused by overlooking the much earlier Australian studies of Hebert, '"Faithfulness"' (1955), and Robinson, '"The Faith"' (1970), but even by 2010, there were commentators who had foregone sarcasm and extremity of language, to deal instead with evidence and argument: e.g. Lane, *Mark*, 409–410, treats the possibility seriously: 'The brief saying in verse 22 is commonly interpreted as an exhortation to have faith in God. It is possible that it should be understood as an encouragement rather than an exhortation: you have the faithfulness of God (cf. Hab. 2:4). On this understanding the solemnly introduced assurances of verses 23–24 are grounded explicitly on God's faithfulness and not on the ability of a man to banish from his heart the presumption of doubt'. Hooker, *St Mark*, 269, has it both ways: 'The use of the unusual expression in Mark 11:22 serves to remind us that the exhortation to have faith in God is in fact based on God's own faithfulness'; cf. Marcus, *Mark 8–16*, 785; Keener, 'Mountains', 56.

history of English Bible translation,[11] the underlying problems have been long-recognised.

As the first of its difficulties, the second person plural form ἔχετε introduces a morphological ambiguity.[12] Although it also does duty for the indicative (as in 4:40),[13] modern interpreters quickly parse ἔχετε as an imperative. However, in the textual tradition, the addition of the particle εἰ before the verb, even if an imported solution from another Gospel (cf. Luke 17:6 or Matt. 21:21),[14] certainly indicates a scribal discomfort with the imperative, if not an attempt to clarify the mood as indicative. For the problems with reading the expression imperativally are significant.[15] In particular, if Jesus was really commanding his disciples to put their faith in God, he doesn't use any of

---

11  Even in 2010, Silva, 'Review' (see previous note), should have been aware of the following translations, which he presumably dismisses as not 'standard': Wycliffe (1382): 'Have ye the faith of God'; Douay-Rheims (1582) and *Geneva Bible* (1599): 'Have the faith of God' (unchanged by *Revised Geneva Translation*, 2019); *Young's Literal Translation* (1898): 'Have faith of God'; *Bible in Basic English* (1965): 'Have God's faith'; *Complete Jewish Bible* (1998): 'Have the kind of trust that comes from God!'. It is also relevant to note in relation to the *Pistis Christou* discussion, that 'the Authorized Version regularly rendered the phrase in question "the faith of Jesus Christ", not "faith in Jesus Christ", before modern versions, with one accord, opted for the latter interpretation', Robinson, '"The Faith"', 130; cf. KJV Rom. 3:22; Gal. 2:16 (x2); 3:22; Eph. 3:12; Phil. 3:9; Rev. 14:12 [see also Phil. 1:27; Col. 2:12; 2 Thess. 2:13].
12  Voelz, *Mark*, 829; cf. Dowd, *Prayer*, 60
13  Despite several commentators declaring the usage at 4:40 'decisive' for that at 11:22 (Sylva, 'Review'; Voelz, *Mark*, 831; Keener, 'Mountains', 56), this is not usually extended to the mood.
14  Although some witnesses (ℵ D Θ 0233$^{vid}$ $f^{13}$ 28 33$^c$ 565 700 1071 it$^{a, b, d, i, r}$$^1$ syr$^{s, palmss}$ arm geo$^1$) including the usually respectable ℵ, insert εἰ before the verb, this is most probably an assimilation to Luke 17:6 or Matthew 21:21, and the reading without this particle (A B C L W Δ Ψ $f^1$ 33* 157 180 205 579 597 892 1006 1010 1241 1243 1292 1342 1424 1505 *Byz* [E G H N Σ] *Lect* it$^{aur, c, f, ff2, k, l, q}$ vg syr$^{p, h, palmss}$ cop$^{sa, bo}$ eth slav) is original. For discussion, Metzger, *Textual Commentary*, 92.
15  It is unusual enough to find πίστις as the object of the verb ἔχω 'I have'. Apart from those texts similar to Mark 11:22 (Matt. 17:20; 21:21; Luke 17:6; 1 Cor. 13:2), the NT has only eight further clear cases (Mark 4:40; Acts 14:9; Rom. 14:22; 1 Tim. 1:19; Phlm. 5; Jas 2:1,14,18; and perhaps cf. 1 Tim. 3:9, if the genitive is epexegetic. The LXX has but two examples (Jer. 15:18; 4 Macc. 16:22), see n.23.

the usual ways that this relationship is expressed.¹⁶ In particular, the use of the simple genitive to supply the object of trust is extremely rare—if it occurs at all.¹⁷

Linguistically, when two nouns are brought into relationship with each other by way of a genitive, the exact relationship has to be specified from the reader's contextual or historical knowledge, and the reader's lexical knowledge, especially of the first noun.¹⁸ However, the noun πίστις introduces its own ambiguities. For one thing, its Greek lexical family is difficult to render into English, where Latin influence creates fine distinctions between intellectual assent (*fides*) or personal trust (*fiducia*), whereas the one Greek lexical family covers both.¹⁹ In addition, πίστις could denote concepts usually captured by the translation 'faith' (e.g. 5:36), or those captured by 'faithfulness' (e.g. Matt.

---

16 In relation to faith in God, see: Heb. 6:1 πίστις ἐπὶ θεόν; 1 Thess. 1:8 ἡ πίστις ὑμῶν ἡ πρὸς τὸν θεόν (cf. 4 Macc. 16:22). More generally, πίστις followed by εἰς (Acts 20:21; 24:24; 26:18; Col. 2:5). Although ἐν is used to express an object of faith (see Rom. 3:25), in the NT this not always straightforward. Several instances (Gal. 3:26; Eph. 1:15; Col. 1:4) most probably refer to 'the faith' which is found 'in Christ', as indicated by the clearer analogies at (1 Tim. 1:14; 3:13; 2 Tim. 1:13; 3:15), a usage that became more popular in early Christian literature; see n.9. Given the paucity of evidence, it is not clear how France, *Mark*, 448, can so confidently declare that: "Ἔχετε πίστιν θεοῦ is a more arresting expression for πιστεύετε θεῷ, but does not differ in meaning". Robinson, "'The Faith'", 139, notes that πιστεύω 'in its transitive form is never used with an objective genitive, but always with the prepositions *eis*, *en* or with *peri*, or occasionaly with the accusative object'.

17 The majority of the NT instances of a genitive following πίστις indicate the one who possesses the faith, not the one in whom it is exercised. For a pro/nominal genitive following πίστις used of the person exercising the faith, see: Matt. 9:2,22,29; 15:28; Mark 2:5; 5:34; 10:52; Luke 5:20; 7:50; 8:25,48; 17:19; 18:42; 22:32; Rom. 1:8,12; 4:5 (cf. 4:9 = Gen. 15:6 Ἐλογίσθη τῷ Ἀβραὰμ ἡ πίστις εἰς δικαιοσύνην); 4:11,12 (cf. 4:16); 1 Cor. 2:5; 15:14,17; 2 Cor. 1:24; 10:15; Phil. 2:17; Col. 1:4; 2:5; 1 Thess. 1:8; 3:2,5,6,10; 2 Thess. 1:3,4; 3:2; 2 Tim. 2:18; Phlm. 6; Jas 1:3; 2:18; 1 Pet. 1:9,21; 2 Pet. 1:5; 1 John 5:4; Rev. 2:13; 2:19; 13:10. All instances usually cited for a genitive following πίστις indicating the object of faith can be disputed, such as the eight texts at the heart of the *Pistis Christou* debate (Gal. 2:16 twice; 2:20; 3:22; Rom. 3:22,26; Phil. 3:9; Eph. 3:12), as well as Acts 3:16; Phil. 1:27; Col. 2:12; 2 Thess. 2:13; Jas 2:1; Rev. 2:13; 14:12. See Robinson, "'The Faith'", 138–142, who also notes that neither LSJ 9 nor Moulton and Milligan cites a case of an objective genitive after πίστις, justifying the supposition that the objective genitive was not found in general Greek usage (p.139).

18 Silva, 'Faith', 220, cf. 227.

19 For a philosophical discussion of the two terms and their related concepts, see Hick, *Faith and Knowledge*, 3–4, although Hick's primary concern is with *fides*, an epistemological term denoting assent to propositions or creeds, whereas the biblical usage denotes predominantly *fiducia*, trust between persons, whether human or divine. The two conceptions can be traced in the Gospel of John, with *fides* corresponding to *pisteuō hoti* (e.g. 20:31), and *fiducia* to *pisteuō eis* (4:39) or *en* (3:15), or simply *pisteuō* plus the dative (5:24). See also Marshall, *Faith*, 54–56.

23:23)—which is its predominant usage in wider Greek.[20] However, although this particular issue has generated some heat in the 'Pistis Christou Debate' within Pauline scholarship,[21] it is important to resist the dichotomy between πίστις as the capacity of faith (trust) that is exercised, or as the quality of faithfulness that is displayed. To properly understand Jesus' difficult expression, the interpreter must bear in mind all possibilities presented by the broad semantic range of πίστις, which extends 'from subjective confidence to objective basis for confidence' (BDAG).

In particular, because of its clear debt to the Old Testament, the New Testament's usage of this Greek word-family must be read against the Hebrew that it seeks to render into the 1st century vernacular. In this regard, the Septuagint had already paved the way for New Testament usage. Apart from observing that Jesus' exact phrase does not occur,[22] two important observations can be made about its evidence. First, the LXX does not use πίστις of human beings trusting God, and with one exception, neither does it speak of '*having faith*' (i.e. using ἔχω) at all.[23] In terms of the current dichotomy, it is instructive that the Septuagint predominantly uses πίστις for 'faithfulness', rather than 'personal trust'.[24] Second, carefully tracking the πίστις vocabulary in the LXX allows the conceptualities expressed by the underlying Hebrew terms to emerge, which affords great assistance in understanding Jesus' phrase.

Although there are a number of Hebrew terms that may denote 'faith', the LXX uses the πιστ- family exclusively for words related

---

20 For an early discussion of this issue, see Hebert, '"Faithfulness"'. See also Robinson, '"The Faith"', 135–136, who, noting that even the Septuagint 'probably never uses *pistis* in our sense of "faith" or "trust"', concludes that 'the term *pistis* designates a quality of firmness or fixity or constancy' (p.142).
21 Robinson, '"The Faith"', 130–134, traces the early stages of this debate. For a recent collection of contributions, see Bird and Sprinkle, *The Faith of Jesus Christ*.
22 Apart from the spurious reference 1 Sam. 21:3, which first renders the Hebrew אֶל־מְקוֹם פְּלֹנִי אַלְמוֹנִי as ἐν τῷ τόπῳ τῷ λεγομένῳ Θεοῦ πίστις, which appears to be an attempt to translate אַלְמוֹנִי as a place name, and then follows it with a transliteration of the awkward phrase: Φελλανι Αλεμωνι.
23 πίστιν ἔχειν only occurs twice: for the false stream 'which does not "contain what it promises"' (Jer. 15:18; for contrast see Isa. 33:16); Weiser, 'πιστεύω, κτλ', 184. 4 Macc. 16:22 is more relevant, but it uses a more usual prepositional phrase: ὑμεῖς οὖν τὴν αὐτὴν πίστιν πρὸς τὸν θεὸν ἔχοντες.
24 See Hebert, '"Faithfulness"'; Robinson, '"The Faith"'; Voelz, *Mark*, 831.

to the stem אמן, which, when used in relation to God, is particularly related to the covenant relationship between YHWH and Israel.²⁵ Or, in reverse, when the LXX usage is examined, the πιστ- family almost invariably renders a member of the אמן family, which is 'essential and basic in relation to the OT view of faith'.²⁶ Jesus explicitly draws on this family in his use of ἀμήν in the solemn introductory formula introducing the saying in v.23 explicitly and that of v.24 implicitly.²⁷ This being so, that Jesus' phrase in v.22 also draws upon his significant OT family (as being argued here) finds support in the immediate context.

Given the strong links with YHWH's covenant promises in the usage of אמן/πιστ-, it may be useful to approach Jesus' use of πίστις from a New Testament outlier, since it also provides access to some relevant ancient Hellenistic-Jewish exegetical discussion. Although the New Testament uses πιστόω (another verb from this lexical family) but once (2 Tim. 3:14, translate: 'were grounded in'), in translating the Hebrew the Septuagint uses it in relation to God's promises to Israel and especially to David, and the covenant that is based upon those promises.²⁸ Given the significance of God's promises for biblical theology, in that the promises generated the expectations Jesus declared to have been fulfilled in him (e.g. Mark 1:15), as we approach the clause in Mark 11:22, it is worthwhile exploring the segment of the πιστ- semantic range suggested by this verb.

As also represented in New Testament usage (e.g. Heb. 11:1; 1 Tim. 5:12; perhaps 2 Tim. 4:7), πίστις can denote 'that which gives

---

25  See Weiser, 'πιστεύω, κτλ', 182–196. As terms related to 'faith', he deals with בטח (pp.191–192); חסה (pp.192–193); חכה יחל קוה (pp.193–196). Noting that אמן is more significant for OT thought than the merely statistical evidence might indicate (pp.183, 196), Weiser concluded that 'the LXX and NT were right when they related their term for faith (πιστεύειν) to the OT stem אמן for in this word is expressed the most distinctive and profound thing which the OT has to say about faith'. In summarising the OT usage, Bultmann, 'πιστεύω, κτλ', 197 n.78, reiterates the strong septuagintal relationship between πιστ- and אמן and its derivatives.

26  Weiser, 'πιστεύω, κτλ', 183. Weiser notes the family's origin in the ancient promise-covenant structure of YHWH's relationship with Israel (pp.190–191), and that, as recognised by the LXX and NT's usage of πιστ-, 'the concept אמן in this sense was closest to the unique relation between Yahweh and Israel and very quickly came to express the specifically OT divine relationship preserved in the covenant tradition' (p.196).

27  The expression διὰ τοῦτο λέγω ὑμῖν in v.24 is sufficient to ensure that the reader brings it over from the fuller expression in v.23.

28  2 Sam. 7:16//1 Chron. 17:14; 2 Sam. 7:25//1 Chron. 17:23; 1 Kgs 1:36; 8:26//2 Chron. 6:17; 2 Chron. 1:9, cf. 1 Kgs 3:6–9; Psa. 77:8, 37; 92:5. In relation to political friendship, cf. 2 Macc. 7:24.

confidence' (LSJ II), hence 'assurance, pledge of good faith, guarantee' (LSJ II.1).²⁹ In this usage, the noun is closely associated with the giving of oaths, as illustrated by Herodotus, who talks of πίστιν καὶ ὅρκια ποιέεσθαι 'make a treaty by exchange of *an assurance* and oaths' (Hdt. 9.92; cf. 3.8; 3.74; 9.106), as part of the transactions involved in the making of political 'friends' (3.8, cf. Gen. 15:7–21; 3.74; cf. 2 Macc. 7:24 πιστόω). Given the nature of these transactions, it is unsurprising that πίστις was also used metonymously for the resultant state of affairs, that is, 'political *protection* or *suzerainty*' (LSJ IV; see Plb. 20.9.10, εἰς τὴν Ῥωμαίων πίστιν 'into the good faith of the Romans'; 3.30.1 εἰς τὴν τῶν Ῥωμαίων πίστιν; 6.17.8 εἰς τὴν ταύτης πίστιν; and Jos. *Ap.* 2:218; *Ant.* 19:289). Such political alliances were, of course, well-known to the Biblical world, and analogous to Israel's covenantal relationship with Yhwh, which was created by, and continued to be operative upon, his promises to their ancestors. Just as such promises of political alliance in the wider world were bound by oaths, Yhwh's covenant with Israel was famously confirmed by his own oath, because, with no-one greater to swear by, he was required to swear by himself (Gen. 22:15–18; Heb. 6:13–18).

In discussing why this was necessary (*Legum* 3.203–207), Philo provides a parallel, not only to the discussion in Hebrews, but also to the conception lying behind Jesus' expression in Mark 11:22.³⁰

> ἔφασαν δέ τινες, ὡς ἀνοίκειον ἦν ὀμνύναι· ὁ ὅρκος γὰρ πίστεως ἕνεκα παραλαμβάνεται πιστὸς δὲ μόνος ὁ θεὸς καὶ εἴ τις θεῷ φίλος, καθάπερ Μωυσῆς λέγεται "πιστὸς ἐν παντὶ τῷ οἴκῳ" γεγενῆσθαι. ἄλλως τε καὶ οἱ λόγοι τοῦ θεοῦ εἰσιν ὅρκοι καὶ νόμοι τοῦ θεοῦ καὶ θεσμοὶ ἱεροπρεπέστατοι τεκμήριον δὲ τῆς ἰσχυρότητος αὐτοῦ, ὃ ἂν εἴπῃ γίνεται, ὅπερ ἦν οἰκειότατον ὅρκῳ· ὥστ' ἀκόλουθον ἂν εἴη λέγειν, ὅτι πάντες οἱ τοῦ θεοῦ λόγοι εἰσὶν ὅρκοι βεβαιούμενοι ἔργων ἀποτελέσμασι. (Legum 3:204)

---

29 See, briefly, Bultmann, 'πιστεύω, κτλ', 176–177.
30 This passage also provides counter-evidence to Bultmann's claim that for Philo, taking 'trust' as the basic meaning of πίστις and following Platonic tradition, 'Turning to God is not a response to His Word or to His acts in history. It rests on contemplation of the world, and is a disposition of the soul'; 'πιστεύω, κτλ', 202.

Some have said, how inappropriate he [God] was to swear, for the oath is taken for the sake of assurance (πίστεως ἕνεκα), and God alone is faithful [cf. Deut. 32:4]—along with whoever might become a friend of God, just as it is said of Moses 'faithful in all his house'. Above all the words of God are oaths, both laws and ordinances of God most reverent, and the proof (τεκμήριον) of his strength is this:[31] whatever he says comes about (ὃ ἂν εἴπῃ γίνεται), which would be precisely[32] most akin to an oath: such that the thing conforming to what is spoken might exist (ὥστ' ἀκόλουθον ἂν εἴη λέγειν),[33] for all the words of God are oaths, being confirmed in the completion of [his] works. (my translation)

In the exposition that followed, Philo explained why it was appropriate for God to swear by himself, utilising the verb πιστόω:

(3.206) οὐδὲν τῶν δυναμένων πιστοῦν δύναται παγίως περὶ θεοῦ πιστῶσαι, οὐδενὶ γὰρ ἔδειξεν αὐτοῦ τὴν φύσιν [...] ἀλλὰ περί γε ἑαυτοῦ μόνος ἰσχυριεῖται, ἐπεὶ καὶ μόνος ἀψευδῶς τὴν ἑαυτοῦ φύσιν ἠκρίβωσε. (3.207) βεβαιωτὴς οὖν ἰσχυρότατος ἑαυτοῦ τὸ πρῶτον, ἔπειτα καὶ τῶν ἔργων αὐτοῦ μόνος ὁ θεός, ὥστ' εἰκότως ὤμνυε καθ' ἑαυτοῦ πιστούμενος ἑαυτόν, ὃ μὴ δυνατὸν ἦν ἄλλῳ. [...] (3.208) ἱκανὸν γὰρ τῷ γενητῷ πιστοῦσθαι καὶ μαρτυρεῖσθαι λόγῳ θείῳ· ὁ δὲ θεὸς αὐτοῦ πίστις ἔστω καὶ μαρτυρία βεβαιοτάτη.

No-one *establishing* the possibilities is able without reservation to *establish* [the things] concerning God, for he shows his nature to no-one. [...] But surely concerning himself only he prevails, since also only he unlyingly makes his own nature exact. The strongest guarantor of himself, then, is first, God

---

31 Cf. LSJ II.2: 'τεκμήριον δέ as an independent clause, *now the proof of it is this* (which follows), *take this as a proof*. Given that τεκμήριον was 'proof (properly of an argumentative kind, opp. direct evidence)' (LSJ II), Philo is transforming its meaning to suit the empirical context of Israel's God revealing himself in history, just as Luke will also do (Acts 1:3).
32 ὅπερ ἦν, cf. LSJ II.5b, according to Aristotle's more technical sense of ὅπερ ἐστί expressing identity.
33 Neither Colson and Whitaker, *Philo*, nor Yonge, *Works*, translates this difficult sentence, replacing it with a connecting phrase that misses the logic and so obscures Philo's meaning.

alone, and then his works, with the result that appropriately he swore by himself *establishing* himself, which was not possible for another. [...] for it is enough for the created being that he should *be assured* and have testimony borne [to him] by the Divine word: but let God be his own most sure guarantee (πίστις) and testimony. (my translation)

In sections of the Septuagint without Hebrew parallel, πιστόω is used for making assurances in both political (2 Macc. 7:24; 12:25; 3 Macc. 4:19) and personal (Sir. 27:17; 29:3) contexts.[34] In the sections translating the Hebrew, the verb is used for establishing the covenant with Israel, despite the faithlessness of their ancestors (Ps. 77[78]:5–8,37), and especially in relation to YHWH's promises to David to establish his house and throne, as well as the Lord's own house (Ps. 92[93]:5; 2 Sam. 7:16//1 Chron. 17:14 [וְהַעֲמַדְתִּיהוּ]; 2 Sam. 7:25 [הָקֵם]//1 Chron. 17:23; 1 Kgs 1:36–37; 8:26 //2 Chron. 6:17; 2 Chron. 1:9 [cf. 1 Kgs 3:6–9]). In these verses, πιστόω regularly translates the verb אמן. The two exceptions, alternatives between Samuel-Kings and the Chronicler (shown above by the alternative verb being listed in brackets), also prove to be mutually illuminating, for אמן is correlated with the Hiphil forms of עמד and קום, both yielding a sense of 'cause to stand, establish'. If πιστόω can be used in this way for God bringing into reality what he has previously promised, then it seems clear that similar overtones could also be expressed by Jesus' (and Paul's) use of the noun, and that πίστιν θεοῦ could therefore refer to the activity of God in assuredly bringing into existence what he had previously promised.

Although the usage of the entire אמן family[35] lies behind Jesus' πίστις θεοῦ (v.22), since it formally correlates with the אמן nouns,

---

34  Classically, πιστόω 'means "to make someone a πιστός, namely, a. one who is bound by an oath, contract, pledge, etc., and who may thus be relied on'; Bultmann, 'πιστεύω, κτλ', 178–179.
35  For which see Weiser, 'πιστεύω, κτλ', 183–191.

אֱמוּנָה has particular significance.³⁶ Tracking the pronominal suffixes referring to God in the first, second, or third person provides ample analogies for Jesus' genitival construction in Mark 11:22.³⁷ Jesus' succinct phrase allows him to invoke one of the Old Testament's core fundamentals: that the God of Israel not only makes promises to his people, but he can be trusted to keep them because of his אֱמוּנָה, his trustworthiness. Not only is Israel's God 'the God of faithfulness' (Deut. 32:4: אֵל אֱמוּנָה),³⁸ but because of this fact, it is abundantly possible for the Israelite to speak of 'the faithfulness of God'.

This is confirmed by turning to the adjective πιστός. The Septuagint of Deuteronomy 32:4 renders its credal statement as θεὸς πιστός, introducing a correlative expression utilising the adjective to show that God has the quality of being faithful (Deut. 7:9; 32:4; Isa. 49:7; cf. 3 Macc. 1:9; *Pss.Sol.* 14:1; 1 Cor. 1:9; 10:13; 2 Cor. 1:18; 1 Thess. 5:24; 1 Pet. 4:19; 1 John 1:9; and for the same statement

---

36   The noun אֱמוּנָה occurs 49 times in the MT, and is translated by the LXX 19 times by πίστις or πιστός (marked */** respectively below). Although it is used to describe a quality of human beings 23 times (Exod. 17:12; 1 Sam. 26:23*; 2 Kgs 12:16*; 22:7*; Isa. 59:4; Jer. 5:1*,3*; 7:28; 9:2*; Hos. 2:22*; Ps 37[LXX 36]:3; 119[LXX 118]:30; Prov. 12:17*,22*; 28:20; 1 Chron. 9:22*,26*,31*; 2 Chron. 19:9; 31:12*,15*,18*; 34:12*), this is derivative of it being, 26 times, an attribute of God: Deut. 32:4**; Isa. 25:1; 33:6; Hab. 2:4*; Ps 33:4 [LXX 32:4*]; 36[LXX 35]:6 [ET 5]; 40[LXX 39]:11 [ET 10]; 88[LXX 87]:12 [ET 11]; 89[LXX 88]:2–3,6,9,25,34,50 [ET 1–2,5,8,24,33,49]; 92[LXX 91]:3 [ET 2]; 96[LXX 95]:13; 98[LXX 97]:3; 100[LXX 99]:5; 119[LXX 118]:90; 143[LXX 142]:1; Lam. 3:23;—or indeed, an attribute of one of his attributes: God afflicting the Psalmist (Ps. 119[LXX 118]:75); God's commands (Ps. 119[LXX 118]:86); God's decrees (Ps. 119[LXX 118]:38; God's Messiah (Isa. 11:5; cf. Ps. 89 above). See also the nouns אֹמֶן Deut. 32:20*; אֲמָנָה Neh. 10:1*; and אֵמוּן Prov. 13:17**; 14:5**; 20:6**.
37   First: Ps. 89[LXX 88]:25,34 [ET 24,33]; Second: Ps. 36[LXX 35]:6 [ET 5]; 40[LXX 39]:11 [ET 10]; 88[LXX 87]:12 [ET 11]; 89[LXX 88]:2–3,6,9,50 [ET 1–2, 5, 8,49]; 92[LXX 91]:3 [ET 2]; 119[LXX 118]:90; 143[LXX 142]:1; Lam. 3:23; Third: Ps. 96[LXX 95]:13; 98[LXX 97]:3; 100[LXX 99]:5. The famously difficult Hab. 2:4 is also to be placed here (cf. the Old Greek resolving the ambiguity in the right direction, LXX ἐκ πίστεώς μου; contra Weiser, 'πιστεύω, κτλ', 190 n.54), whether the third person refers directly to YHWH (see Keil and Delitzsche, *Commentary*, in loc.), or (more likely) indirectly to him by referring to the vision/his revealed plan; See the discussion in Anderson, *Habakkuk*, 211, cf. 5 'by its trustworthiness'.
38   Deut. 32:4: θεός, ἀληθινὰ τὰ ἔργα αὐτοῦ, καὶ πᾶσαι αἱ ὁδοὶ αὐτοῦ κρίσεις· θεὸς πιστός, καὶ οὐκ ἔστιν ἀδικία, δίκαιος καὶ ὅσιος κύριος (MT:הַצּוּר תָּמִים פָּעֳלוֹ כִּי כָל־דְּרָכָיו מִשְׁפָּט אֵל אֱמוּנָה וְאֵין עָוֶל צַדִּיק וְיָשָׁר הוּא).

of Jesus Christ: 2 Thess. 3:3; 2 Tim. 2:13).³⁹ Not only is the adjective used 'of God as the One in whom we can have full confidence' (BDAG; also citing Pind., *N.* 10, 54; Philo, *Her.* 93, *Sacr.* 93, *Legum* 3.204; 1 Clem. 60:1; Ig., *Trall.* 13:3), but he is, in particular, faithful to his promises (Ps. 144:13a; *Pss.Sol.* 7:10; Heb. 10:23; 11:11; 1 Clem. 27:1; 2 Clem. 11:6; cf. Ps. 144:13a). But if God is adequately described with the adjective 'faithful', it is perfectly possible in Greek to use the cognate noun to speak of 'the faithfulness of God', and, even if rarely done, to nevertheless communicate clearly.

Thankfully, as already noted above, the New Testament itself has a second example of Jesus' expression in Romans 3:3. Although the analogy between these two verses has often been denied, there are no good linguistic reasons for doing so. Apart from the addition of the article to both nouns, which changes nothing, the formal expression in Romans 3:3 is exactly the same as that in Mark 11:22, and, negating 1 Samuel 21:3, these are the only two places the expression occurs.⁴⁰ Despite the frequency with which it is done, the analogy cannot be denied on contextual grounds, for, in fact, the context in both Mark and Romans is exactly the same.⁴¹ Utilising Greek to draw upon his Hebraic and OT understanding of one of God's core characteristics, the apostle Paul uses this syntax to declare that the un-faithlessness (ἡ ἀπιστία) of Israel will not nullify (μὴ ... καταργήσει) 'the faithfulness of God' (τὴν πίστιν τοῦ θεοῦ). Turning to the context of Mark 11:22, the analogy continues to be perfect, in which Jesus dramatically indicts the leadership of Israel for their un-faithfulness (11:17–18;

---

39 Philo, *Mut.* 182, cites Deut. 32:4 as a credal affirmation: 'For he says that the belief which man has once conceived ought to be so firm as in no respect to differ from that which is entertained of the truly living God and which is complete in every part; for Moses, in his greater hymn, says, "God is faithful, and there is no unrighteousness in him ("θεὸς πιστός, καὶ οὐκ ἔστιν ἀδικία ἐν αὐτῷ.")'. This presumably also lies behind his other similar affirmations, e.g. 'God is the only faithful being' [πιστὸς δὲ μόνος ὁ θεός] (*Legum* 3.204); and his argument shared with the writer to the Hebrews (cf. Heb. 6:13–18) that whereas men must have recourse to an oath, God's word already has the status of an oath and can be believed, as he is the 'only faithful one' [μόνῳ πιστῷ] (*Sacr.* 93; cf. *Her.* 93).
40 Rom. 3:3 is usually regarded as a clear case of the subjective genitive. For 1 Sam. 21:3, see above n.22. Although Dowd, *Prayer*, 60, takes πίστις τοῦ θεοῦ in Acts 19:20 D as objective, see my comment in n.9.
41 Robinson, '"The Faith"', 139–140: 'Romans 3:3 certainly speaks of God's *pistis*, his fidelity which is contrasted with the infidelity of Israelites. The subject matter is closely parallel to that of the incident of the withering of the fig tree. "God's *pistis*" must be kept as a live option for Mark 11'.

12:1–12) which has caused Israel to be unprepared for the last days' harvest (11:12–14). In combination with ἔχετε taken not as an imperative but as an indicative,[42] the expression is perfectly capable of permitting Jesus to make exactly the same assertion as Paul, but in the positive: 'You have the faithfulness of God'.

A further difficulty with Jesus' clause arises from the need to disambiguate the verb 'have', since it is another troublesome lexeme with 'an astonishing range of meaning'.[43] By the use of the indicative, Jesus is not saying that the faithfulness of God is something the disciples possess internally in some mystical fashion.[44] It is perfectly possible and quite usual for the verb to have a more external nuance, depending upon the object to be possessed: such as having custodians assigned for security (Matt. 27:65); 'salt among yourselves' (Mark 9:50); the reputation of commendable persons (Phil. 2:29); and even 'the faith of our Lord Jesus' (Jas 2:1) referring to an external orthodoxy that is handed on in order to be held onto by others.

Josephus, *Ant.* 19:16, provides a relevant example for the present discussion, in which πίστις is the object of ἔχω in its sense of 'pledge, assurance, guarantee' (LSJ II.1) with the combination yielding the sense of an objective assurance (πολλὴν ἔχει πίστιν τοῦ θεοῦ τῆς δυνάμεως, 'great assurance of the power of God' [Yonge]).[45] Although utilising the verb, *Ap.* 2.218 also expresses the same concept, where a person, 'having their conscience bearing witness' (τὸ συνειδὸς ἔχων μαρτυροῦν), 'is assured' (πεπίστευκεν). After the subordinated reference to the internal witness of the conscience, Josephus then reveals

---

42  So Lane, *Mark*, 409: 'It is possible that it should be understood as an encouragement rather than an exhortation: "you have the faithfulness of God" (cf. Hab. 2:4)'. Although opting for 'faithfulness' and a subjective genitive, Robinson, '"The Faith"', 78–79, maintains the imperative, offering the translation: 'be firm as God is firm'.

43  Hanse, 'ἔχω, κτλ', 816. Cf. Aristotle, *Met.* 5.23; *Cat.* 15. Mark's own 62 uses of ἔχω display its wide variety of relations.

44  Cf. The misunderstanding of Sylva, 'Review': 'Is there any other example of people being said to "have" a comparable divine attribute (e.g., You have the kindness of God, or We have the patience of God)?'. Even though this is not the sense in Mark 11:22, there are, in fact, several expressions in which human beings 'have' a characteristic of God: the love of God (John 5:42); jealousy of God (Rom. 10:2); righteousness of God (Phil. 3:9); his eternal life (1 John 5:13).

45  It is 'objective' because what would supply this assurance is Josephus' accurate account of this matter (*Ant.* 19:15: δι' ἀκριβείας τὸν πάντα περὶ αὐτοῦ λόγον, 'a full account of this matter particularly' [Yonge]).

that this assurance comes externally: 'not only through the prophesying of the [our] lawmaker, but also through the strong assurance of God' (τοῦ μὲν νομοθέτου προφητεύσαντος, τοῦ δὲ θεοῦ τὴν πίστιν ἰσχυρὰν παρεσχηκότος).[46]

Turning to potential Old Testament connections, Hebrew, like other Semitic languages, has no word for 'to have' and no equivalent for the Greek ἔχω.[47] As the LXX also does very occasionally, Jesus is using the verb ἔχω here with the sense of the Hebrew expression of existence, יֵשׁ.[48] Even if Jesus was using ἔχετε as an imperative, he would be commending the faithfulness of God as a reality that stands ready for his disciples to see, to take account of, to grasp the significance of—to have. But in answering Peter's question, through the indicative Jesus now offers a reminder of the most fundamental feature of Israel's God (Deut. 32:4), now brought to a head with the coming of Jesus (cf. 1:15). After hundreds of years of dealing with Yhwh, the living God who declared his name to Moses as 'I will be whom I will be' (Exod. 3:14), and after hundreds of years of reading the OT accounts of Yhwh working towards fulfilling his promises, the people of Israel should already know the facts. As Jesus assures his disciples, now gazing at the fig tree cursed by the one they have already declared to be the Christ (8:29), in the history of Israel, written down in the Scriptures, the faithfulness of God is plain for everyone with eyes to see, and the promises that shaped that history are now coming to their

---

46 To complete the sentence, the content of the assurance is then given: 'that to those who carefully guard the laws even if it might be necessary to die for them, God willingly granted [them] to die both to come into existence again and to receive a better life from the revolutionary change' (ὅτι τοῖς τοὺς νόμους διαφυλάξασι κἂν εἰ δέοι θνήσκειν ὑπὲρ αὐτῶν προθύμως ἀποθανεῖν ἔδωκεν ὁ θεὸς γενέσθαι τε πάλιν καὶ βίον ἀμείνω λαβεῖν ἐκ περιτροπῆς), my translation.

47 Hanse, 'ἔχω, κτλ', 817.

48 Strictly speaking, the LXX uses ἔχω to render only three of the 129 occurrences of יֵשׁ in the MT (Gen. 23:8; 44:19; Num. 22:29). In Gen. 23:8 אִם־יֵשׁ אֶת־נַפְשְׁכֶם is rendered Εἰ ἔχετε τῇ ψυχῇ ὑμῶν. In Gen. 43:7, when Joseph's brothers report his inquiry as to whether their father is still alive (הַעוֹד אֲבִיכֶם חַי) and whether they have a brother (הֲיֵשׁ לָכֶם אָח), the LXX renders the two sentences: Εἰ ἔτι ὁ πατὴρ ὑμῶν ζῇ; εἰ ἔστιν ὑμῖν ἀδελφός, whereas, in Gen. 44:19 when the brothers report back to Joseph himself and truncate the same query (הֲיֵשׁ־לָכֶם אָב אוֹ־אָח), the LXX translates Εἰ ἔχετε πατέρα ἢ ἀδελφόν, before translating their report of their reply to Joseph Ἔστιν ἡμῖν πατὴρ πρεσβύτερος καὶ παιδίον γήρως νεώτερον αὐτῷ; and in Num. 22:29: לוּ יֶשׁ־חֶרֶב בְּיָדִי is translated as εἰ εἶχον μάχαιραν ἐν τῇ χειρί μου. However, Isa. 43:8 and Prov. 13:7 are also relevant, for although ἔχω does not translate יֵשׁ, in both it is used to translate a parallel expression. For more on the LXX translation of יֵשׁ, see n.51.

fulfilment: 'you have the trustworthiness of God'.[49]

But, if so, the question is raised: what promises did Jesus have in mind here, just days before he ended his life on this earth?

## 2. Moving *This* Mountain (v.23)

²³ ἀμὴν λέγω ὑμῖν ὅτι
  ὃς ἂν εἴπῃ τῷ ὄρει τούτῳ,
    Ἄρθητι καὶ βλήθητι εἰς τὴν θάλασσαν,
  καὶ μὴ διακριθῇ ἐν τῇ καρδίᾳ αὐτοῦ
  ἀλλὰ πιστεύῃ
    ὅτι ὃ λαλεῖ γίνεται,
  ἔσται αὐτῷ.

By utilising his famous introductory formula derived from the אמן family, ἀμὴν λέγω ὑμῖν, 'Truly I say to you', Jesus opens his second saying with a further reminder of 'the faithfulness of God'.[50]

Consisting of only two words, the future indicative of εἰμί used impersonally and a personal pronoun as its indirect object, the main clause abruptly states a future existent reality, 'it will be for him' (ἔσται αὐτῷ)—which, on the precedent of the Septuagint, is a parallel expression to the ἔχετε of v.22.[51] The one for whom (αὐτῷ) this existent reality will come about, that is, the antecedent of the pronoun, is provided by the lengthy three-part relative clause that opens the saying by introducing an indefinite subject (ὃς ἂν) of three subjunctive verbs describing that subject's potential activities. The first subjunctive describes

---

49 Note the translation reported by Robinson, '"The Faith"', 130: 'Reckon on God's fidelity'. Cf. 1 Cor. 1:24; 2 Tim. 1:19. Jesus' encouragement therefore operates in a similar way to Hab. 2:4, which also speaks of God's faithfulness, as clarified by the LXX by the addition of μου; see e.g. Baker, 'Habakkuk', 843, more emphatically than Baker, *Nahum*, 59. Lane, *Mark*, 409–410: 'the assurances of vv.23–24 are grounded explicitly on God's faithfulness and not on the ability of a man to banish from his heart the presumption of doubt'.
50 Weiser, 'πιστεύω, κτλ', 185, אמן 'is a concept which expresses the fact that the totality of the elements in the command (curse, doxology) is to be fulfilled', and this is confirmed by the LXX translating it fourteen times with γένοιτο and transliterating ἀμήν just thrice.
51 The LXX regularly translates יֵשׁ with the verb εἰμί followed by a personal pronoun in the dative (e.g. Gen. 33:9,11; 39:4–5,8; 43:7; 44:19; cf. related prepostional expressions, e.g. Num. 13:20), or in the future tense (e.g. Num. 9:20). Cf. n.48. For a comparison of both clause and concept in a similar exegetical context, see above and below, Philo, *Legum* 3.204 (ὥστ' ἀκόλουθον ἂν εἴη λέγειν).

the main (potential) action, whereas the second and third consist of two opposing (potential) actions combined to reveal the appropriate manner in which the main action is to be performed to ensure that it becomes future existent reality.

In context, the indefinite subject (ὃς ἂν) includes Jesus himself, since he is replying to Peter's observation about the fig tree he cursed, as well as his disciples who are (presumably) part of the conversation, but both of these parties are representative of a broader group of 'anyone' who 'might say (εἴπῃ) to this mountain, "be taken up and cast into the sea"'. Before returning to this potential statement further below, the appropriate manner in which Jesus commends it be said will first be explored.

The statement strongly opposes (μή ... ἀλλά ..., 'not ... but ...') an activity taking place in the subject's 'heart' (ἐν τῇ καρδίᾳ αὐτοῦ)—which denotes the centre of their inner life and the seat of the emotional, rational, volitional, and moral capacities that provide their life-direction;[52] their secret life manifest only to God, rather than their external life manifest to other human beings (1 Sam. 16:7)[53]—with the positive activity of 'believing', utilising πιστεύω, a cognate verb to πίστις (v.22).

Although English Bibles usually translate the inner activity to be negated (μὴ διακριθῇ) as 'doubting', this is almost certainly a mistranslation for it assumes that the Greek verb διακρίνομαι has a special meaning within the New Testament that it bears nowhere else in Greek literature. Whereas the active verb, διακρίνω (Matt. 16:3; Acts 11:12; 15:9; 1 Cor. 4:7; 6:5; 11:29,31; 14:29), is usually translated in conformity with classical/Hellenistic Greek, 'discern, decide, or separate', the instances of the middle/passive, διακρίνομαι, are rendered to suggest hesitation or doubt (Matt. 21:21; Mark 11:23; Acts 10:20; 11:2; Rom. 4:20; 14:23; Jas 1:6 [2x]; 2:4; Jude 9:22; and some manuscripts for Acts 11:12 and Luke 11:38). As demonstrated by Spitaler, however, rather than supporting the 'semantic shift' usually invoked to

---

52 For the semantic range, see Baumgärtel and Behm, 'καρδία, κτλ'. Marshall, *Faith*, 31, notes it is the 'seat of faith'.
53 Cf. God as ὁ καρδιογνώστης, 'the One who knows the heart' (Acts 15:8; cf. 1:24; and more broadly: Luke 16:15; Rom. 8:27; 1 Thess. 2:4; Rev. 2:23 [of Christ]; LXX: 1 Kgs 8:39; 1 Chron. 28:9; Ps. 7:10; Jer. 11:20; 17:10; Sir. 42:18–20).

justify this special New Testament meaning, the evidence suggests that the translation 'doubt' was an interpretive rendering introduced as the New Testament began to be translated into Latin.⁵⁴ Rather than 'hesitating', 'wavering', or 'doubting', Jesus commends that 'being divided in heart',⁵⁵ 'separating oneself', or even 'disputing, quarrelling' (BDAG 2, 5ab; cf. διάκρισις BDAG 2, LSJ III) should be rejected in favour of the positive action of 'believing'.⁵⁶

Because the verb is followed by a ὅτι clause, the 'believing' that Jesus urges is not simply a general attitude of trust, but a belief in a particular item of content, which is given in the form of another verb of existence (γίνεται) with a relative clause as its subject (ὃ λαλεῖ). The imperfective aspect of the present tense-form of γίνεται indicates the action is being viewed as occurring simultaneously with the speaker's statement to the mountain, 'it is coming into existence'. This therefore provides an intermediate step between the address to 'this mountain' and its outcome in the commanded state of affairs representing future existent reality (ἔσται αὐτῷ). But what is it exactly that is 'coming into existence'?

The subject of the verb in the relative clause (ὃ λαλεῖ) is regularly interpreted to be the speaker addressing the mountain, with the antecedent of the neuter relative pronoun being the address itself, making the content of his belief a confidence that his own command is coming about. This 'power of positive thinking' may perhaps sound credible in contrast to the notion of 'doubt', but it becomes less probable, if not

---

54  Spitaler, 'Διακρίνεσθαι', shows by that 'if, indeed, a semantic shift took place, [Greek patristic and medieval authors] show no awareness of that movement' (p.1,2). His argument has been accepted by Voelz, *Mark*, 833; Berge, 'Jesus', 69, 179; Keener, 'Mountains', 56. As further and earlier support, despite claiming (post-Spitaler, wrongly) that 'διακρίνεσθαι in the sense "to doubt" is a product of Greek speaking Christianity' (p.948), not found in the fathers (pp.948–949), and an illustration of 'the constructive force of the gospel in the linguistic sphere' (p.949), Büchsel, 'κρίνω, κτλ', 950, noted that there is much in the OT regarding the rejection of God's word, but little concerning doubt, comparing Mark 11:23 instead to the censuring in later Judaism of 'pusillanimity in prayer' (Sir. 7:10).
55  As a pointer to 'the way in which the OT itself would have the attitude of faith understood', Weiser, 'πιστεύω, κτλ', 188, notes the divided heart (Hos. 10:2) as opposed to the required whole heart service of God reflecting the 'exclusiveness of the divine relation'. See, for example, Deut. 6:5; 1 Sam. 12:20,24; Mark 12:29–30.
56  For a similar opposition to that of Jesus here, as Psalm 78 rehearses the waywardness of Israel from the exodus and wilderness generation up to Yhwh's promises to David, it notes that a misaligned heart is opposite to being established in Yhwh's covenant: Ps. [LXX] 77 [Heb 78]:37 ἡ δὲ καρδία αὐτῶν οὐκ εὐθεῖα μετ᾽ αὐτοῦ, οὐδὲ ἐπιστώθησαν ἐν τῇ διαθήκῃ αὐτοῦ (cf. v.8).

nonsensical, in contrast to the notion of 'separating oneself from', or 'disputing'. By treating the verse as a self-contained unit, such a reading also reinforces the sense that this saying is disconnected from the preceding saying (v.22), whereas a more integrated reading arises from exploring another possibility of the grammar and syntax.

Since the unstated subject of λαλεῖ needs to be supplied from the context, the other possibility already mentioned is God himself (v.22),[57] whose 'reliability' or 'faithfulness' in 'establishing his promises' is not only demonstrated in his dealings with Israel, but is something that, with Jesus standing in front of them, is there in the disciples' present experience. Variants of this relative clause can be found in Old Testament passages already referred to above, in regard to God's promises to David and his determination to most certainly establish (πιστόω) them forever:[58]

**2 Sam. 7:25** καὶ νῦν, κύριέ μου κύριε, <u>τὸ ῥῆμα, ὃ ἐλάλησας</u> (Heb: הַדָּבָר אֲשֶׁר דִּבַּרְתָּ) περὶ τοῦ δούλου σου καὶ τοῦ οἴκου αὐτοῦ, <u>πίστωσον</u> ἕως αἰῶνος, κύριε παντοκράτωρ θεὲ τοῦ Ισραηλ· καὶ νῦν <u>καθὼς ἐλάλησας</u>... (NB Heb: וַעֲשֵׂה כַּאֲשֶׁר דִּבַּרְתָּ)

And now, my Lord, O Lord, <u>the word that you spoke</u> concerning your slave and his house, <u>confirm it</u> forever, O Lord Almighty, O God of Israel, and now <u>as you said</u>, ... (NETS)

**1 Chron. 17:23** καὶ νῦν, κύριε, <u>ὁ λόγος σου, ὃν ἐλάλησας</u> (Heb: הַדָּבָר אֲשֶׁר דִּבַּרְתָּ) πρὸς τὸν παῖδά σου καὶ ἐπὶ τὸν οἶκον αὐτοῦ, <u>πιστωθήτω</u> (יֵאָמֵן) ἕως αἰῶνος (Heb: וַעֲשֵׂה כַּאֲשֶׁר דִּבַּרְתָּ)

---

57 So Bird, 'Some γάρ Clauses', 178, noting that, '*ho lalei ginetai* is a quotation—believe that what the Lord says, comes to pass'; Berge, 'Jesus', 52, 68, 179, 185 (and Jesus his agent); Voelz, *Mark*, 834, 851.
58 For the expression more generally, see also Gen. 23:16; Exod. 4:12, 30; 14:12; 16:23; Lev. 10:11; Num. 22:8,20,35, 38; 23:26; Deut. 1:14; 13:3; 18:20–22; 23:24; Josh. 14:6; 21:45; 23:15; 24:27; 1 Sam. 9:6; 15:16; 16:4; 18:24; 20:23; 2 Sam. 14:19; 1 Kgs 2:27,38; 8:20,25; 12:15; 13:3,11,32; 15:29; 16:12,34; 17:16; 18:24; 22:14,38; 2 Kgs 1:17; 2:22; 10:17; 14:25; 23:16; 18:13; Esth. 2:1; Tob. 14:8; 2 Macc. 12:14; Ps. 17:1; Job 19:4; *Pss.Sol.* 11:8; Jonah 3:2; Isa. 16:13; Jer. 5:14; 18:10; 19:2,15; 23:25; 26:13; 28:12; 33:8,13,19; 39:42; 42:17; 43:31; 49:19–20; Bar. 2:7; Ezek. 36:36; 38:17; Dan. 9:6,12; 10:11.

> 'And now, Lord, let <u>the word</u> <u>you spoke</u> to your servant and concerning his house be <u>confirmed</u> forever, ...' (NETS)
>
> **1 Kgs 8:26** καὶ νῦν, κύριε ὁ θεὸς Ισραηλ, <u>πιστωθήτω δὴ τὸ ῥῆμά σου</u> τῷ Δαυιδ τῷ πατρί μου. (יָאָמֶן נָא דְּבָרֶיךָ [דְּבָרְךָ] אֲשֶׁר דִּבַּרְתָּ)[59]
>
> And now, O Lord God of Israel, do <u>let your word</u> to my father David <u>be confirmed</u>. (NETS)
>
> **2 Chron. 6:17** καὶ νῦν, κύριε ὁ θεὸς Ισραηλ, <u>πιστωθήτω δὴ τὸ ῥῆμά σου</u>, <u>ὃ ἐλάλησας</u> τῷ παιδί σου τῷ Δαυιδ. (יִשְׂרָאֵל יֵאָמֵן דְּבָרְךָ אֲשֶׁר דִּבַּרְתָּ)
>
> 'And now, Lord, God of Israel, <u>let your utterance indeed be confirmed</u>, <u>which you spoke</u> to your servant David ...' (NETS)

Moving beyond the Scriptures to an ancient exegete of them, Philo provides a remarkable parallel for this clause, both lexically and conceptually. As we have already seen above, in *Legum* 3:204 Philo states:

> Above all the words of God are oaths, both laws and ordinances of God most reverent, and the proof (τεκμήριον) of his strength is this:[60] <u>whatever he says comes about</u> (ὃ ἂν εἴπῃ γίνεται), which would be precisely[61] most akin to an oath: such that <u>the thing conforming to what is spoken might exist</u> (ὥστ' ἀκόλουθον ἂν εἴη λέγειν), for all the words of God are oaths, being confirmed in the completion of [his] works.

Similarly, as already seen above, Josephus (*Ap.* 2:218) also speaks of the inner testimony of the conscience that 'is established' (πεπίστευκεν) externally by scripture ('[our] lawmaker') and by God's own activity ('the strong assurance of God', τοῦ δὲ θεοῦ τὴν πίστιν ἰσχυράν).

---

59 This is therefore one of the connections of Jesus's sayings with Solomon's stress on God's faithfulness in 1 Kgs 8; Berge, 'Jesus', 52, 68 n.51.
60 Cf. LSJ II.2: 'τεκμήριον δέ as an independent clause, *now the proof of it is this* (which follows), *take this as a proof*. Given that τεκμήριον was 'proof (properly of an argumentative kind, opp. direct evidence)' (LSJ II), Philo is transforming its meaning to suit the empirical context of Israel's God revealing himself in history, just as Luke will also do (Acts 1:3).
61 ὅπερ ἦν, cf. LSJ II.5b, according to Aristotle's more technical sense of ὅπερ ἐστί expressing identity.

With this rich scriptural background, already recognised by ancient exegetes, Jesus is commending persistent believing that 'what God says will come into existence', rather than separating oneself from such a commitment or inwardly disputing that this is an entailment of his nature.[62] Although this is to be the appropriate manner adopted by the one who addresses 'this mountain' in order to see their command become future existent reality, Jesus is not commending them to place overweening confidence in their own word so that it might come about, but to continue to hold on to God's promises, because it is his nature to do exactly what he says: 'You have the faithfulness of God'.[63] This then raises the further question, what has he said about 'this mountain' ending up in the sea? With God himself being the subject of the verb, and not the hypothetical commander of the mountain, the question then becomes: what is the promise that he is speaking that should not be disputed but believed—especially now that Jesus is operating in the zone when 'the time is fulfilled and the Kingdom of God has drawn near' (Mark 1:15).

Usually under the influence of the legacy view that the four sayings were originally independent, some interpret Jesus' mountain as generic, on analogy with his saying about commanding a sycamore to be planted in the sea (Luke 17:6; *G.Thom.* 48, 106), and Paul's saying about having 'all faith resulting in moving mountains' (1 Cor. 13:2, καὶ ἐὰν ἔχω πᾶσαν τὴν πίστιν ὥστε ὄρη μεθιστάναι), which both employ a similar hyperbolic image, even if their language is not that of Mark (cf. also Rev. 8:8).[64] This 'proverbial saying' then becomes a promise that faith can lead to unusual and powerful outcomes and accomplish much.[65]

---

62 Despite acquiescing in the usual rendering of 'doubt', Büchsel, 'κρίνω, κτλ', 947, properly identified the problem as 'not [standing] firm on the promise of God'.
63 Lane, *Mark*, 409–410.
64 To bolster the proverbial nature of the saying, appeal has long been made (e.g. Str.B. I.759; Salmond, *St Mark*, 272; Nineham, *St Mark*, 305; Strauss, *Mark*, 499; Keener, 'Mountains', 52 n.37, 58) to Jewish and rabbinic parallels (e.g., *T.Sol.* 23:1; *b.Ber.* 64a; *b.Sanh.* 24a; *b.B.Bat.* 3b; *Lev.Rab.* 8.8 on Lev 6:13). However, 'none of these examples offers a close parallel beyond the general idea of moving mountains'; Evans, *Mark*, 189.
65 See e.g. Marshall, *Faith*, 66, 166, 175, 229; Collins, *Mark*, 534–535; France, *Mark*, 449; Strauss, *Mark*, 498, 499, 501; Bock, *Mark*, 295; Keener, 'Mountains', 47, 51. Frequently, the generic assumption leads to Jesus' singular mountain being pluralised; e.g. Marshall, *Faith*, 167, 233, 239; Keener, 'Mountains', 51.

However, whatever else might be going on in Mark 11:23, Jesus' use of the demonstrative pronoun shows that he most certainly does *not* speak of a generic mountain, but assumes his hearers would recognise that he has a *particular* mountain in mind.[66] The indefinite person in his promise speaks 'to *this* mountain' (τῷ ὄρει τούτῳ). The next question is immediately obvious: *which* mountain does Jesus have in view, and especially in relation to any promises that the trustworthy God is currently bringing about as Jesus is speaking?

Usually because of a purported temple critique in the wider narrative, many take Jesus as referring to 'the temple mount'.[67] However, not only is there no association between the temple and a mountain in Mark's narrative,[68] a plain reading controlled by what is on the narrative surface shows that, rather than Jesus' critique being directed against the temple structure or institution,[69] it was directed specifically at Israel's corrupt leadership.[70] Not only does this draw upon Mark's wider theme that Jesus clashed with Israel's corrupt leadership (3:6; Herod: 6:14–29; religious leaders: 3:22–30; 7:1–13,18; noting 8:15, and 6:34 [Num. 27:17 and Ezek. 34:5, and, in fact, Ezek. 34—36]), but it is also consistent with the Old Testament passages that (may) lie

---

66 As recognised by Gundry, *Mark*, 653; Berge, 'Jesus', 62, 64–65, 173. Rather strangely, sometimes the particularisation provided by the demonstrative pronoun is acknowledged, only to be ignored; see France, *Mark*, 449; Evans, *Mark*, 188–189.
67 For discussion and convenient lists of supporters, see e.g. Evans, *Mark*, 189; Voelz, *Mark*, 833; Kirk, 'Time for Figs', 522–523, 526.
68 As noted by France, *Mark*, 449, despite his interest in the temple.
69 Historically, *pace* Sanders, *Jesus*, 61–76, Evans, 'Evidence of Corruption', 319–320, noted that 'there is no evidence whatsoever that a messiah or prophet or any other eschatological figure was expected to destroy the Temple as the necessary prelude to building a new one'.
70 See my previous discussion, 'Mark 13', 16–20; *Jesus' Defeat of Death*, 244–253; *Cross*, 86–90; 'Faith of Jesus Christ', 250–255; *Narrative Integrity*, 46–49. Historically, *pace* Sanders' denial, Evans, 'Evidence of Corruption', 337–338, draws together 'significant and [...] substantial evidence' (p.320) that, up to and including Jesus' time, 'the temple establishment' (that is, Israel's religious leadership) was widely regarded as corrupt. See also Evans, 'Prophetic Criticism'. Sharing this view, Mark's account indicates that both Jesus and Mark operated within the apocalyptic views that also expected the corrupt priesthood would be replaced by the Messiah (see, e.g., the 'wicked priest' in 1QpHab; *Jub.* 23:21 and *T. Levi* 14:1–8; 16:1–5; 17—18; *Pss. Sol.* 17–18; T.Dan 5:6–13; *1 Enoch* 89–90; 93:9–10 and 91:12–17 [Apocalypse of Weeks]; 11QMelch [11Q13]); *T.Moses* 7.

behind Mark's account.⁷¹

On Jesus' second day in Jerusalem, he performed two actions (11:12–19). After cursing the fig tree (11:14) for having no early figs—a prophetic action depicting Israel as fruitless and not ready for the harvest of the last days because of their corrupt leadership (Mic. 7:1–7; note vv.3–4)—he cast out the traders from the temple (cf. Zech. 14:20–21) and accused the temple authorities of making the house of prayer for the nations into a den of robbers (11:17–18 'you'; cf. Isa. 56.7; Jer. 7.11). Rightly perceiving that his critique was directed at them, this group then steps up efforts to destroy him (11:18; 12:12; cf. 3:6). The final part of the intercalation (11:20–25), reporting on the opening of the third day, begins to assist the reader to reflect upon these two events, both of which signalled Jesus' confrontation with Israel's corrupt leadership and foreshadowed their judgement to come.⁷²

Rather than the 'Temple Mount',⁷³ the most obvious candidate for 'this mountain' is the mountain that is already deeply embedded in the tightly structured narrative movement of Mark 11—13. At the opening and close of this section, the mountain that sits between Bethany and Jerusalem is specifically named as the Mount of Olives (11:1; 13:3; and then 14:26). Jesus' daily journey takes him over and down the Mount of Olives in the morning (11:1–11a; 11:12,15; 11:20,27), and up and over the Mount of Olives in the evening (11:11b; 11:19; 13:1,3; then cf. 14:3). From the midst of this very specific topography, no other mountain springs to mind as the readers hear Jesus' demonstrative pronoun (11:23), evoking the mental picture of him indicating

---

71 Each of the suggested background passages indict Israel's leadership for the nation's problems, with no immediate reference to the temple: Hos. 9:10—10:2 (see 9:15), Jer. 8 (see vv.1–3, 8–10), or Mic. 7 (see v.3). Similarly, when Jesus reissued Isaiah's parable of the vineyard (Mark 12:1–11), already the devastation of Israel in Isaiah 5 had been blamed upon the leadership Isa. 3:13–15, before Jesus indicted 'the builders' and the religious leadership had recognised themselves the target of his parable (12:10,12). See also the texts discussed in Evans, 'Prophetic Criticism'. This critique of Israel and/ or their leadership is often noted, before being subordinated to Mark's supposedly more significant critique of the temple; see, e.g. Kirk, 'Time for Figs', 515 (on Isa. 56:7, noting v.10), 518–519 (on Jer. 7:11, directed towards 'people'), 521 (on Mic. 7:1, 'looming judgement on the people').
72 This forced reflection is the aim of the entire third day, preparing the reader for the next narrative movement which begins with 14:1.
73 The suggestion that it might be the Herodium (Edwards, *Mark*, 347) has even less support from Mark's narrative.

with a wave of his hand, *this* mountain.[74]

A search for promises particularly associated with the Mount of Olives arrives solely at Zechariah 14:4 (cf. 4:7).[75] Reflection on God's miraculous intervention in the past (e.g. Psalm 114) generated imagery that was then used to express Israel's hopes for the eschatological future, and the removal of mountains was part of this imagery (e.g. Isa 40:3–5; 45:2; 49:11; cf. 54:10; *Pss.Sol.* 11:4; Bar 5:7).[76] However, by Zechariah's apocalyptic picture of the End, this more general background imagery had become sharply focused on a particular mountain—the Mount of Olives.

When his leadership was challenged by his son Absalom, King David, the bearer of the promises of God, left Jerusalem weeping by way of the Mount of Olives (2 Sam. 15:30–32). Similarly in Ezekiel's vision, when the glory of the Lord left the city due to its inhabitants' wickedness (which had also defiled this mountain: 1 Kgs 11:7–8; 2 Kgs 23:13), it departed over the same mountain (Ezek. 11:23) and, as part of the future restoration, Ezekiel therefore expected the glory of the Lord to return by the same route (Ezek. 43:1–5). After the exile, Zechariah developed this earlier prophetic expectation to make the Mount of Olives the place where God's 'feet would stand' in the final battle of the last days (Zech. 14:4–5).[77] According to his climactic vision, 'on that day' (vv.4,6,8,9,13,20,21),[78] the mountain

---

[74] For discussion and convenient lists of supporters, see e.g. Evans, *Mark*, 188; Gundry, *Mark*, 649, 652, 654. Remarkably, Marshall, *Faith*, 168, declares the identification 'unlikely' because Mark usually mentions the Mount of Olives by name. Similarly, Berge, 'Jesus', 174, minimises the significance of the Mount of Olives because it is explicitly mentioned only three times. However, the explicit naming of this mountain (and no other) within the temporal framework and movement of this highly structured section of Mark, along with other allusions to Zechariah, keeps the reader on track as to its significance as 'the eschatological mountain' of Zech. 14:4.

[75] For those identifying Zechariah 14 as the background of this saying, see Manson, *Jesus the Messiah*, 29–30, 39–40; Lane, *Mark*, 410; Grant, *Miracle*, 167, and 'The Coming of the Kingdom', 300. Dowd, *Prayer*, 72–73, discusses this interpretation, without finally agreeing.

[76] Evans, *Mark*, 189, 195, notes these texts add an 'eschatological hue' to Mark's saying. Other texts could be added, e.g. Isa. 5:25; 41:15; 64:3; Jer. 4:24; Ezek. 38:20; Hos. 10:8; Mic. 1:4; Nah. 1:5; Hab. 3:6–10; Zech. 4:7 (Kirk, 'Time for Figs', 523).

[77] In later Jewish thought, these expectations led to the association of the mountain with the resurrection of the dead and the coming of the Messiah. Cf. *AJ* 20.169 [20.8.6] = *BJ* 2.262 [2.13.5]; Targum to Cant. 8:5; *Sepher Elijahu*. These expectations may have already been held at Jesus' time; see Lane, *Mark*, 394 n.13.

[78] This is language frequently associated with the Day of the Lord; Petterson, *Zechariah*, 285.

will be split from the east 'to the west'—or, translating more literally, 'from/towards the sea',[79] which not only identifies the sea as the Mediterranean,[80] but also explains Jesus' dramatic restatement of this prophecy, as Jesus tweaks and escalates the image to have the mountain itself being dramatically thrown into the sea in order to create this eschatological plain.[81]

In Zechariah, the two halves then move north and south (14:4), providing a great valley as an escape route, just as God had opened an escape route for his people through the depths of the sea in the exodus from Egypt (v.5; cf. Exod. 14:21–22; see also Isa. 40:4–5, cf. Ezek. 43:1–5).[82] Whereas most translations are probably wrong to translate verse 10 so that the whole land becomes 'like a plain', instead of 'like the Arabah' (v.10),[83] they nevertheless capture the imagery. In biblical times 'the Arabah' referred to the rift valley that runs from the Sea of Galilee down to the Gulf of Aqaba, a broad plain enclosed with steep escarpments on either side. Zechariah pictures the Mount of Olives splitting and the two halves moving to the north and the south to such an extent that the valley is so wide that the whole land becomes 'as the Arabah' (vv.4,10). Here Zechariah adds a twist to older idealistic imagery relating the mountains surrounding Jerusalem to YHWH's

---

79 Verse 4: MT 'from the east and towards the sea' (מִזְרָחָה וָיָמָּה); LXX: 'towards the sea' (πρὸς θάλασσαν). Although v.8 also speaks of the 'first sea' and 'the last sea', i.e. the eastern to the western sea, the valley opening up in the Mount of Olives is clearly oriented from the east, towards the (western) sea (v.4). If there is any Galilean colour to Jesus' saying (cf. Montefiore, *Synoptic Gospels*, 1.273: 'The mountain and the lake suggest Galilee rather than Jerusalem'), perhaps the (roughly) East/West valley of Jezreel has also coloured Jesus' more colourful re-issue of Zechariah's vision.
80 With this disambiguation the interpretation of the saying no longer depends upon the Dead Sea being visible from the Mount of Olives on a clear day.
81 Dismissing the allusion because Zechariah's mountain is not thrown into the sea, Marshall, *Faith*, 168, and France, *Mark*, 449, or because the mountain moves north/south, Marcus, *Mark*, 785, with Dowd, *Prayer*, 72, not only miss the subtlety of the actual language (see n.79), but constrains Jesus' communicative creativity with a demand for excessive literalism.
82 Petterson, *Zechariah*, 290; Webb, *Zechariah*, 178–79.
83 This is perhaps another way of saying the same thing as depicted by Ezekiel's final vision of the new temple that exceeded the dimensions of the land itself, which may also be reflected in the Targum to Isaiah 56:5, see Evans, 'Prophetic Criticism', 429–430. The presence of God would no longer be symbolically combined to a mere building, but it would be all encompassing and experienced by all the people of God. For Ezekiel's influence on Zechariah 14, see Zimmerli, *Ezekiel 2*, 513–516; Petterson, *Zechariah*, 292, but also Eden (v.8, Gen. 2:10–14); Webb, *Zechariah*, 179, 180.

protective presence with Israel (cf. Ps. 125:1–2). Just as the Arabah plain is surrounded by its steep protective escarpments, Zechariah's eschatological imagery depicts the whole land as a plain dominated by the protective security of Jerusalem, now raised up high above (vv.10–11), as the Eden-like eschatological mountain (cf. vv.14,16; and Isa. 2:1–4; Ezek. 40:1–2; Mic. 4:1–5).[84]

In Mark 11:23, Jesus adds his own dramatic colour and flavour to Zechariah's vision of the removal of the Mount of Olives to leave a broad plain for people to escape the last battle on 'that Day', by speaking of his generic person commanding 'this mountain' to be taken up and cast into the Mediterranean. In combination with the saying in v.22, Jesus is assuring his disciples that, because of God's trustworthiness, Zechariah's eschatological promises of God concerning the End are so certain, that they can be called upon—or even commanded. Any person standing on God's trustworthiness, without disputing God's promise but believing that he does what he says, who then speaks such a word of command, *will* experience 'the End' becoming a reality ('it will be for him').[85]

The final two sayings bring the generality of the first two to a particular focus.

## 3. The Disciples' Prayers are Being Answered (v.24)

The structure of the saying in v.24 clearly shows that Jesus is not moving on to another topic, but applying the generic promise of v.23 to his disciples in particular. With a stable core of correspondences to v.23, the major change in v.24 is that the 3rd person forms appropriate to the

---

84 Although differing in some details, see Petterson, *Zechariah*, 293, 295, who notes that the significant feature of the Arabah is the escarpments and its symbolic comparison with God surrounding the land (v.10: כָּעֲרָבָה is comparative 'like the Arabah'; יִסּוֹב never indicates a transformation of state, but 'surrounds'; cf. Zech. 2:4–5[8–9]), which then has clear connections with earlier notions of the inviolability of Zion (cf. v.11) and Jerusalem's Eden-like role in prophetic eschatology (cf. v.14 and Isa. 60:4–14; Ezek. 38:12–13; 39:10; Hag. 2:7–8).

85 Or, as William Manson put it long ago, this saying: 'implies the consciousness on the part of Jesus that at the moment when he and his disciples are going up to Jerusalem the phenomena of the Messianic Age (Zech. 14:4) are on the point of being fulfilled. What the prophet had predicted about the last days is about to happen'; Manson, *Jesus The Messiah*, 39–40. For the fulfilment of Zechariah's vision in the cross of Christ, see further Petterson's essay in this volume.

generic person of v.23 are now changed to the 2nd person forms appropriate to the disciples being addressed.

|  | v.23 | v.24 |
|---|---|---|
| solemn introduction | ἀμὴν λέγω ὑμῖν ὅτι | διὰ τοῦτο λέγω ὑμῖν |
| praying and the prayer's content | ὃς ἂν εἴπῃ τῷ ὄρει τούτῳ, Ἄρθητι καὶ βλήθητι εἰς τὴν θάλασσαν, | πάντα ὅσα προσεύχεσθε καὶ αἰτεῖσθε |
| believing ... | καὶ μὴ διακριθῇ ἐν τῇ καρδίᾳ αὐτοῦ ἀλλὰ πιστεύῃ | πιστεύετε |
| ... and the belief's content | ὅτι ὃ λαλεῖ γίνεται | ὅτι ἐλάβετε |
| promised result | ἔσται αὐτῷ | καὶ ἔσται ὑμῖν |

Although in slightly different form, Jesus' solemn introductory formula reprises the theme of God's faithfulness (πίστις /אמן, v.22; ἀμήν, v.23) by picking up the well-established truth that what God says comes about (v.23), in order to apply it to the disciples' current prayers: 'because of this, I say to you ...' (διὰ τοῦτο λέγω ὑμῖν).[86]

As with γίνεται in v.23, the present tense-forms in προσεύχεσθε καὶ αἰτεῖσθε should not be taken generically, but as reflecting the current reality into which Jesus is speaking.[87] The major change from the third (v.23) to the second (v.24) person also makes it clear that when Jesus refers to 'everything, as much as ...' (πάντα ὅσα ...) the disciples are 'praying and asking', that is, 'asking in prayer', he is not generalising

---

86  Cf. Voelz, *Mark*, 834, who notes that the referent for τοῦτο is the content of v.23.
87  The imperfective aspect of the present tense-form indicates that the action is 'going on, in process, without reference to its completion' (McKay, *New Syntax*, 29).

to countless future requests.⁸⁸ On the contrary, he is still referring to Zechariah's prophetic picture of the moving of the Mount of Olives and, by metonymy, to God's promises of the End, towards which Zechariah's focused picture was pointing and upon which the disciples' actual requests were focused: 'the things you are actually asking in prayer'.

As faithful Jews and even more so as those following behind the one who announced 'the times are fulfilled, the kingdom of God has come near' (1:15), the disciples are already praying and asking for the eschatological promises of God to reach their conclusion.⁸⁹ But with their concrete present situation in view, the aorist tense-form (ἐλάβετε) in the content (ὅτι) that Jesus now urges them to believe becomes even more significant and weighty. Although this is similar to a 'prophetic perfect' expressing a future eventuality as if it was already fulfilled,⁹⁰ it needs to be read with the force upon the concrete historical moment in which Jesus was speaking. Jesus is applying the trustworthiness of God and the promises of Zechariah to this particular moment in human history, provoked by the Messiah's arrival in the midst of Israel as the fulfilment of time (1:15), such that the promises were in the process of being fulfilled and the End would soon arrive (cf. 9:11–13). This is the moment that the people of Israel have been waiting for, and so: 'as you are asking in prayer about all such matters, believe that you *have* received them'.

Jesus' present imperative urges them to 'keep on believing' (πιστεύετε), answering God's trustworthiness (v.22) with their trust, not only that what he says is coming about (v.23, ὅτι ὃ λαλεῖ γίνεται), but, now that Jesus has arrived to bring the era of fulfilment, that they have already received (v.24, ὅτι ἐλάβετε) what was promised. As they

---

88 Although Berge, 'Jesus', esp. 185–189 (accepted by Voelz, *Mark*, 850), helpfully identifies connections between Jesus' saying(s) and Solomon's prayer at the dedication of the temple (1 Kgs 8; cf. 2 Chron. 6), this suggested background does not mean that Jesus is switching topics to provide some general teaching on prayer—with or without the temple. As noted by Evans, *Mark*, 191, this is really of no interest to Mark's wider narrative, even if 'prayer is a connecting motif' (pp.186, 195) in this narrative section (11:17 [Isa. 56:7],24–25; also noting 9:28–29; 13:33; 14:38). The connections with Solomon's dedicatory prayer are penultimate to his place within the unfolding purposes of God in relation to the covenant promises, and therefore also in relation to the eschatological jubilee; see (briefly) the next section of this essay and n.100.
89 In Ps. 143:1, אֲמָנָתְךָ is used in relation to the Lord hearing petitions (but not translated as πίστις).
90 Hooker, *St Mark*, 270; Evans, *Mark*, 192.

maintain the confidence in God that has always been called for from Israel, but which is now bolstered by the arrival of the Messiah, they will see (cf. 4:25) the promised and much-awaited End become the existent reality of this world (καὶ ἔσται ὑμῖν).[91]

But this fraught time of imminent fulfilment, just before the Day of the Lord and the arrival of the kingdom of God, presses a further responsibility upon the disciples, as the final saying in the paragraph reveals.

## 4. The Time for Forgiveness is here (v.25)

[25] καὶ ὅταν στήκετε προσευχόμενοι,
ἀφίετε εἴ τι ἔχετε κατά τινος,
ἵνα καὶ ὁ πατὴρ ὑμῶν ὁ ἐν τοῖς οὐρανοῖς ἀφῇ ὑμῖν τὰ παραπτώματα ὑμῶν.

Since the judgement day and the new age can be so confidently prayed for and the promise of its arrival is so assured, Jesus continues to speak into the disciples' current practice of praying, with a single imperative, instructing them that, 'whenever you stand praying' your eschatological prayers, 'forgive' (ἀφίετε).[92] Elaborating on the nature of the forgiveness required, Jesus says that it relates to anything they might hold against another (εἴ τι ἔχετε κατά τινος), and it ought to be motivated by the prospect of the heavenly Father releasing them from their own mistakes.

This is the language originally associated with both the Sabbatical and the Jubilee Years, both called 'the year of release' (ἔτος / ἐνιαυτός τῆς ἀφέσεως), which were built into the recurring patterns that were to structure the people of Israel's life together (Lev. 25:10–11,13,28,30,40,50,52,54; 27:17–18,23–24; Deut. 15:9; 31:10; Ezek.

---

91  For this paragraph, see also Bolt, *Jesus' Defeat of Death*, 246; *Cross*, 87.
92  For a fuller treatment of this saying, see Bolt, 'Forgive'; cf. *Jesus' Defeat of Death*, 245–246; Bolt, *Cross*, 88; and Manson, *Jesus the Messiah*, 39–40.

46:17).⁹³ Since such cycles naturally structured expectations for the longer-term future, it is unsurprising that the Jubilee (with the Sabbatical Year gradually blurring with it)⁹⁴ became a significant feature of prophetic eschatological expectation (for the specific language דְּרוֹר: Lev. 25:10; Isa. 61:1; Jer. 34:8,15,17 [an 'un-Jubilee'];⁹⁵ Ezek. 46:17. More generally: Isa. 58; Ezek. 40:1, cf. Dan. 12:7). Once Daniel's vision of 'seventy weeks (of years)' gave a Jubilee structure to the time remaining before the End (Dan. 9:24–27), the eschatological Jubilee became part of the earlier apocalyptic schemes (e.g. *1Enoch* 93:1–10, 91:11–17; *Jubilees*), and, by the first century A.D., had become (with variation) a firmly embedded feature of both the eschatological and messianic expectation⁹⁶—especially that linked with the Servant of the Lord (Isa. 42:7; 49:5,9; 61:1–4)⁹⁷—that formed the background to Jesus' announcement that 'the time is fulfilled' (Mark 1:15).⁹⁸

By urging the need to forgive, Jesus ties the coherent sayings of this paragraph not only to the main thrust of the ministry of John the Baptist, who came to prepare for the promised 'great and terrible day of the Lord' (1:2–8; Isa. 40:1–3; Mal. 3:1; 4:5–6), but also to his own major thrust of bringing in the kingdom of God (1:15),⁹⁹ which included bringing the eschatological Jubilee, forgiveness to the land

---

93 Although Barker, 'Time' is a good brief survey, the most thorough examination of the Jubilee in the Old Testament period through to the Qumran scrolls is now Bergsma, *Jubilee*. Given the significant role of the Jubilee in eschatological expectations of the second temple period, older discussions of the Jubilee in relation to the Gospels (e.g. Sloan, *Favourable*; Ringe, *Jesus and Liberation*) must now be seriously updated, especially studies that treat the Jubilee economically, rather than eschatologically, which was its only known role by the 1st century AD; see Bergsma, *Jubilee*, 298; Barker, 'Time', 25.

94 Barker, 'Time', 24, notes that the evidence of the LXX suggests the two had combined by the 3rd century BC, as in 11QMelch.

95 Bergsma, *Jubilee*, 298.

96 Bergsma, *Jubilee*, 302, identifies 'at least five documents from the Second Temple period (Daniel, Apocalypse of Weeks [= *1Enoch* 93:1–10, 91:11–17], *T. Levi* [17–18], *Apocryphon of Jeremiah* C [4Q383–391], 11QMelch [11Q13]) that present chronological schemes of history up to the inbreaking of the eschaton based on weeks, jubilees, and units of seven and ten'. He notes that 'the interpretations of the jubilee in Isa. 61:1–4, Daniel 9, *T. Levi*, and 11QMelchizedek, in addition to being *eschatological*, are also *messianic*; whereas those of Ezek. 40:1 et passim, the *Apocalypse of Weeks*, and *Apocryphon of Jeremiah* C (apparently) are only *eschatological*'.

97 Barker, 'Time', 24–25, noting the combination of the Servant texts and Dan 9:24–27 in 11QMelch (pp.27–28).

98 Barker, 'Time', esp. 28, and 32 'the Day of Judgment would occur within the lifetime of his hearers. This explains the urgency of his words'.

99 See Bolt, 'With a View to Forgiveness'

(2:10; ἄφεσις 'release'; see Lev. 25).[100] With the arrival of the Servant of the Lord / the Son of God, the great Day of Atonement is almost upon them (Lev. 25:10; Isa. 52:13—53:12; Mark 10:45), which will issue in the last Jubilee.[101] The Son of Man is about to come to the Ancient of Days, to receive authority over the everlasting kingdom of God, triggering the Day of Resurrection, the End, and bringing in the eternal life of the age to come.

So now, according to the rising action of Mark's Gospel, the Son of God, as Servant of the Lord, moves towards his greatest act, dying as a ransom for many (10:45) to do the impossible and bring human beings into the kingdom of God (cf. 10:27). Foreshadowing that Israel is not ready for the judgement day, Jesus cursed the fig tree. When the disciples noticed that his curse had become reality, Jesus encourages them by drawing upon the apocalyptic vision of Zechariah. Because of the trustworthiness of God, anyone can pray with confidence for the End. God's promises and their prayers are at this very moment in the process of being fulfilled: the judgement day is upon them; the kingdom of God is at hand. And so, as they stand on the cusp of the eschatological Jubilee, it is time to focus upon the Lord's great release of debts at the end of time, rather than upon the mistakes of others that they might legitimately hold against them.

Peter G. Bolt
Sydney College of Divinity

---

100 Once the connections between Jesus' sayings here and Solomon's dedicatory prayer are recognised (see n.88 above for Berge, 'Jesus', esp. 185–189; Voelz, *Mark*, 850), the foundations of that prayer in the Jubilee regulations (Lev. 25—26) must also then be acknowledged, as well as the consequential connection between the messianic promises to David and the future (at that point) Jubilee, which would end Israel's exile from the land—because of those promises and the prayers of Israel based upon them. Evans, 'Prophetic Cricisim', 437–439, notes the allusions to Solomon's prayer already in both Isa. 56:7 and Jer. 7:11 (cf. Mark 11:17), and how 'the targum of 1 Kgs 8:41–43 introduces elements that draw the passage even closer to the oracles of Isaiah and Jeremiah'. For the association between the Jubilee and Temple building/restoration, see Casperson, 'Sabbatical'; Barker, 'Time', 25–26.

101 Barker, 'Time', 25, notes that Day of the Lord was also the Day of Atonement: Deut. 32:43; *Ass. Mos.* 10; and that Dan 9:24–27 depicts 'a final Day of Atonement when prophecy and visions are fulfilled and the Anointed One appears' (pp.26–27). 11QMelch (=11Q13) looks forward to a jubilee at the end of time, after Melchizedek atones for sins on the Day of Atonement. See further, Bolt, 'Forgive'. For Mark's presentation of the atonement brought by Jesus the Servant, see my *Cross*.

## Bibliography

Achtemeier, P. J.  'Omne verbum sonat: The New Testament and the Oral Environment of Late Western Antiquity', *JBL* 109.1 (1990), 3–27.

Anderson, F. I.  *Habakkuk* (Anchor Yale Bible, 25: New Haven, CT and London: Yale University Press, 1974, 2001, 2008). Accordance electronic edition.

Baker, D. W.  'Habakkuk', D. A Carson et al. (ed.), *New Bible Commentary: 21st Century Edition* (Downers Grove, IL: InterVarsity Press, 1994). Accordance electronic edition.

Baker, D. W.  *Nahum, Habakkuk, and Zephaniah: An Introduction and Commentary* (TOTC 27; Downers Grove, IL: InterVarsity Press, 1988). Accordance electronic edition.

Barker, M.  'The Time is Fulfilled: Jesus and Jubilee', *SJT* 53.1 (2000), 22–32.

Baumgärtel, F., and J. Behm  'καρδία, καρδιογνώστης, σκληροκαρδία', *TDNT* III: 605–614.

Beavis, M. A.  *Mark* (Paideia; Grand Rapids, IL: Baker Academic, 2011).

Berge, D. J.  'Jesus, The New Temple Mark 11:20–25 in its Narrative Context' (2016). Doctor of Philosophy Dissertation. 20. https://scholar.csl.edu/phd/20.

Bergsma, J. S.  *The Jubilee From Leviticus to Qumran: A History of Interpretation* (SuppVT 115; Leiden: Brill, 2007).

Best, E.  'Mark's Preservation of the Tradition [1974]', in *Disciples and Discipleship. Studies in the Gospel according to Mark* (Edinburgh: T & T Clark, 1986, 31–48). Republished in W. R. Telford (ed.), *The Interpretation of Mark* (2nd ed.; Studies in New Testament Interpretation; Edinburgh: T & T Clark, 1995), 153–168.

Bird, C. H.  'Some γάρ Clauses in St. Mark's Gospel', *JTS* 4.2 (1953), 171–187.

Bird, M. F., & P. M. Sprinkle (eds.)  *The Faith of Jesus Christ: Exegetical, Biblical, and Theological Studies. The Pistis Christou Debate* (Peabody, MS and Carlisle: Hendrickson and Paternoster, 2009).

Black, C. C.  *Mark* (ANTC; Nashville, TN: Abingdon, 2011).

| | |
|---|---|
| Bock, D. | *Mark* (NCBC; Cambridge: Cambridge University Press, 2015). |
| Bolt, P. G. | 'Forgive Us Our Sins So That God Will Forgive You? (Mark 11:25)', in K. Barker and G. G. Harper (eds.), *It's OK Not to Forgive: A Biblical, Theological, and Pastoral Defence* (ACT Monograph Series; Eugene, OR: Wipf and Stock, 2023 [forthcoming]). |
| Bolt, P. G. | *The Narrative Integrity of Mark 13:24–27* (ACT Monograph Series; Eugene: Wipf and Stock, 2021). This is a slightly updated version of 'The Narrative Integrity of Mark 13:24–27' (MTh thesis accepted by Australian College of Theology, 1991). |
| Bolt, P. G. | 'The Faith of Jesus Christ: Synoptics & Acts', in M. F. Bird & P. M. Sprinkle (eds.), *The Faith of Jesus Christ: Exegetical, Biblical, and Theological Studies. The Pistis Christou Debate* (Peabody, MA and Carlisle: Hendrickson and Paternoster, 2009), 209–222. |
| Bolt, P. G. | *The Cross from a Distance. Atonement in Mark's Gospel* (Leicester: IVP, 2004). |
| Bolt, P. G. | *Jesus' Defeat of Death: Persuading Mark's Early Readers* (SNTSMS 125; Cambridge: Cambridge University Press, 2003). |
| Bolt, P. G. | '"With a View to the Forgiveness of Sins": Jesus and Forgiveness in Mark's Gospel', *RTR* 57.2 (1998), 53–69. |
| Bolt, P. G. | 'Mark 13: An apocalyptic Precursor to the Passion Narrative', *RTR* 54.1 (1995), 10–32. |
| Branscomb, B. H. | *The Gospel of Mark* (MNTC; London: Hodder & Stoughton, ⁶1953 [1937]). |
| Büchsel, F. | 'κρίνω, κρίσις, κρίμα, κριτής, κριτήριον, κριτικός, ἀνακρίνω, ἀνάκρισις, ἀποκρίνω, ἀνταποκρίνομαι, ἀπόκριμα, ἀπόκρισις, διακρίνω, διάκρισις, ἀδιάκριτος, ἐγκρίνω, κατακρίνω, κατάκριμα, κατάκρισις, ἀκατάκριτος, αὐτοκατάκριτος, πρόκριμα, συγκρίνω', *TDNT* III: 921–954 [διακρίνω: 946–949]. |
| Bultmann, R. | 'πιστεύω, πίστις, πιστός, πιστόω, ἄπιστος, ἀπιστέω, ἀπιστία, ὀλιγόπιστος, ὀλιγοπιστία. A. Greek Usage; C. Faith in Judaism; D. The πίστις Group in the New Testament', *TDNT* VI: 174–182, 197–202, 203–228. |

Casperson, L. W.  'Sabbatical, Jubilee, and the Temple of Solomon', *VT* 53.3 (2003), 283–296.

Collins, A. Y.  *Mark. A Commentary* (Hermeneia; Minneapolis, MN: Fortress, 2007).

Colson, F. H., and G. Whitaker  *Philo I* (Cambridge, MA and London: Harvard University Press & William Heinemann, 1929, repr. 1981). Archive.org.

Cranfield, C. E. B.  *The Gospel according to St Mark* (Cambridge: Cambridge University Press, 1959).

Dowd, S. E.  *Prayer, Power, and the Problem of Suffering. Mark 11:22–25 in the Context of Markan Theology* (SBLDS 105; Atlanta, GA: Scholars, 1988).

Edwards, J. R.  *Mark* (PNTC; Grand Rapids, MI: Eerdmans, 2002).

Evans, C. A.  'From "House Of Prayer" To "Cave Of Robbers". Jesus' Prophetic Criticism of the Temple Establishment', in C. A. Evans and S. Talmon (eds.), *The Quest for Context and Meaning. Studies in Biblical Intertextuality in Honor of James A. Sanders* (Leiden: Brill, 1997), 419–442.

Evans, C. A.  'Jesus' Action in the Temple and the Evidence of Corruption in the First-Century Temple', *Jesus and His Contemporaries. Comparative Studies* (Leiden: Brill, 1995), 319–344.

Evans, C. A.  *Mark 8:27–16:20* (WBC; Grand Rapids, MI: Zondervan, 1988). Accordance electronic edition.

France, R. T.  *The Gospel of Mark: A Commentary on the Greek Text* (NIGTC; Grand Rapids, MI: Eerdmans, 2002). Accordance electronic edition.

Grant, R. M.  *Miracle and Natural Law in Graeco-Roman and Early Christian Thought* (Amsterdam: North-Holland, 1952).

Grant, R. M.  'The Coming of the Kingdom', *JBL* 67.4 (1948), 297–303.

Gundry, R. H.  *Mark. A Commentary on His Apology for the Cross* (Grand Rapids, MI: Eerdmans, 1993).

Hanse, H.  'ἔχω, ἀντέχομαι, ἀπέχω, ἐνέχω, ἔνοχος, κατέχω, μετέχω, μετοχή, μέτοχος, νουνεχῶς, συμμέτοχος ἀνέχω, ἀνεκτός, ἀνοχή, σχῆμα, ἕξις', *TDNT* 2.816–832.

Harrington, D. J., and J. R. Donahue  *The Gospel of Mark* (SP 2; Collegeville, MN: Liturgical Press, 2002).

| | |
|---|---|
| Hebert, G. | '"Faithfulness" and "Faith"', *RTR* 14.2 (1955), 33–40. This article was also published in *Theology* 58.424 (1955), 373–379. |
| Hick, J. | *Faith and Knowledge* (London: Fontana, 1974 [1966², 1957]). |
| Hooker, M. D. | *A Commentary on the Gospel according to St Mark* (BNTC; London: A. & C. Black, 1991). |
| Juel, D. | *Mark* (ACNT; Minneapolis, MN: Augsburg, 1990). |
| Keener, C. S. | 'Casting Out Mountains—Mark 11:23', *JGAR* 5 (2021), 47–65. |
| Keil, C. F., and F. Delitzsch | *Commentary on the Old Testament* (Peabody, MA: Hendrickson Publishers, 1996). Accordance electronic edition. |
| Kirk, J. R. D. | 'Time for Figs, Temple Destruction, and Houses of Prayer in Mark 11:12–25', *CBQ* 74.3 (2012) 509–527. |
| Lane, W. L. | *The Gospel of Mark* (NICNT; Grand Rapids, MI: Eerdmans, 1974). Accordance electronic edition. |
| Lightfoot, R. | 'The Connexion of Chapter Thriteen with the Passion Narrative', *The Gospel Message of St. Mark* (Oxford: Clarendon, 1950), 48–59. |
| McKay, K. L. | *A New Syntax of the Verb in New Testament Greek. An Aspectual Approach* (SBG 5; New York, NY: Peter Lang, 1994). |
| Manson, W. | *Jesus the Messiah. The Synoptic Tradition of the Revelation of God in Christ: with Special Reference to Form-Criticism* (London: Hodder & Stoughton, 1943, rep. 1945). |
| Marcus, J. | *Mark 8—16* (Anchor Yale Bible; New Haven, CT: Yale University Press, 2009). Accordance electronic edition. |
| Marshall C. D. | *Faith as a Theme in Mark's Narrative* (SNTSMS 64; Cambridge: Cambridge University Press, 1989). |
| Metzger, B. M. | *A Textual Commentary on the Greek New Testament. Second Edition* (Stuttgart: Deutsche Bibelgesellschaft, 1994). Accordance electronic edition (2.3). |
| Montefiore, C. G. | *The Synoptic Gospels* (3 vols.; London: Macmillan, 1909). |
| Nineham, D. | *The Gospel of St Mark* (PNTC; Harmondsworth: Penguin, 1963, rev. 1969, repr. 1981). |

Petterson, A. R.     *Haggai, Zechariah & Malachi* (AOTC 25; Nottingham and Downers Grove, IL: Apollos & InterVarsity Press, 2015).

Quell, G.     'ἀλήθεια, ἀληθής, ἀληθινός, ἀληθεύω: A. The OT Term אֱמֶת', *TDNT* I: 230–237.

Ringe, S. H.     *Jesus and Liberation, and the Biblical Jubilee: Images for Ethics and Christology* (Overtures to Biblical Theology 19; Philadelphia, PA: Fortress, 1985).

Robinson D. W. B.     '"The Faith of Jesus Christ": a New Testament Debate', in E. Loane (ed.), *Donald Robinson. Selected Works.* Volume 3: *Biblical and Liturgical Studies* (Camperdown, NSW: Australian Church Record / Moore College, 2018), 130–144. Original: *RTR* 29 (1970), 71–81.

Sanday, W., and A. C. Headlam     *The Epistle to the Romans* (Edinburgh: T & T Clark, ⁵1902 [1895]).

Sanders, E. P.     *Jesus and Judaism* (Philadelphia, PA: Fortress, 1985).

Silva, M.     'Review of M. F. Bird & P. M. Sprinkle (eds.), *The Faith of Jesus Christ: Exegetical, Biblical, and Theological Studes. The Pistis Christou Debate* (Hendrickson, 2009)', *Themelios* 35.2 (2010). Online: https://www.thegospelcoalition.org/themelios/review/the-faith-of-jesus-christ-exegetical-biblical-and-theological-studies-the-pistis-christou-debate/.

Silva, M.     'Faith versus Works of Law in Galatians 2–3', in D. A. Carson et al. (eds.), *Justification and Variegated Nomism*, vol. 2: *The Paradoxes of Paul* (WUNT 2.181; Tübingen: Mohr Siebeck, 2004), 217–48.

Sloan, R. B.     *The Favourable Year of the Lord: A Study of the Jubilary Theology in the Gospel of Luke* (Ann Arbor, MI: Scholars, 1977).

Spitaler, P.     'Διακρίνεσθαι in Mt. 21:21, Mk. 11:23, Acts 10:20, Rom. 4:20, 14:23, Jas. 1:6, and Jude 22—the "Semantic Shift" That Went Unnoticed by Patristic Authors', *NovT* 49 (2007), 1–39.

Strauss, M.     *Mark* (ZECNT; Grand Rapids, MI: Zondervan Academic, 2014).

Taylor, V.     *The Gospel according to St Mark* (2nd edition; London: Macmillan, 1966; Reprint: Grand Rapids, MI: Baker, 1981).

Telford, W. R.     *The Barren Temple and the Withered Fig Tree* (JSNTSup 1; Sheffield: JSOT, 1980).

Voelz, J. W., and C. W. Mitchell     *Mark 8:27—16:20* (Concordia Commentary; St Louis, MO: Concordia, 2019).

Webb, B. G.     *The Message of Zechariah* (BST; Nottingham: IVP, 2003, repr. 2006, 2010).

Weiser, A.     'πιστεύω, πίστις, πιστός, πιστόω, ἄπιστος, ἀπιστέω, ἀπιστία, ὀλιγόπιστος, ὀλιγοπιστία. B. The Old Testament Concept', *TDNT* VI: 182–196.

Yonge, C. D. (transl.)     *The Works of Philo, Completed and Unabridged. New Updated Edition* (Peabody, MA: Hendrickson, 1993). Accordance electronic edition (1.3).

Zimmerli, W.     *Ezekiel 2: A Commentary on the Book of the Prophet Ezekiel, Chapters 25–48* (Hermeneia 26B; trans. J. D. Martin; Minneapolis, MN: Fortress, 1983). Accordance electronic edition.

CHAPTER 10

# The Apocalyptic Attack of Jerusalem by Non-Israelite Nations In Zechariah 9–14 and the Death of Jesus In Mark 13

Anthony R. Petterson

## Abstract

This essay comprises two parts. The first is a review of *Mark 13 and the Return of the Shepherd: The Narrative Logic of Zechariah in Mark,* by Paul T. Sloan, in which he argues that Mark 13 follows the eschatological 'framework' of Zechariah 13:7—14:5 to speak of Jesus' death, the destruction of the temple in A.D.70, and Jesus' Parousia. The second part argues, contrary to Sloan, that Mark's Gospel is not utilising Zechariah to provide a sequence for these events. Rather, Mark's Gospel utilises the apocalyptic language describing the attack of Jerusalem by non-Israelite nations in Zechariah 9—14 symbolically, to speak of Jesus' death alone. Other lines of support for this idea outside of Mark 13 and outside of Mark's Gospel are given.

## 1. Introduction

Paul T. Sloan in his monograph *Mark 13 and the Return of the Shepherd: The Narrative Logic of Zechariah in Mark* argues that the eschatological sequence of events in Zechariah 13—14 is fulfilled in the striking of the shepherd (Mark 14:27; cf. Zech. 13:7), the scattering and tribulation of the disciples and later attack of Jerusalem in A.D. 70 (Mark 13:5-23; cf. Zech. 13:7—14:5), and Jesus' Parousia (Mark 13:26-37; Zech. 14:5). More particularly, Sloan argues that Zechariah 13:7—14:5 is crucial background for explaining why in Mark 13, Jesus can jump from talking about the destruction of the temple to the seemingly unrelated topic of his Parousia.[1]

I begin this essay by reproducing the allusions to Zechariah that Sloan argues for and analysing his understanding of Zechariah's 'framework'. Sloan rightly demonstrates the significant place that Zechariah has in Mark's Gospel. However, rather than presenting a timeline of events from Jesus' death to his Parousia, I argue in the second part of this article that the apocalyptic-eschatological language describing the attack of Jerusalem by non-Israelite nations in Zechariah 9—14 is better understood as being utilised in Mark's Gospel symbolically, to speak of Jesus' death alone. I conclude by providing other lines of support for this thesis outside of Mark 13 and then outside of Mark's Gospel.

## 2. Mark's Use of Zechariah

A feature of Sloan's book is the extent to which he engages with Zechariah. There are many studies of the use of Zechariah 9—14 in Mark 11—16, but Sloan looks at the way that the whole Gospel of Mark engages with the whole of the book of Zechariah.

### 2.1 Use of Zechariah Outside of Mark 13

While the particular focus of his thesis is the use of Zechariah in the Olivet Discourse of Mark 13, Sloan first looks at the influence of

---

[1] For a history of interpretation of Zechariah 14, including its being fulfilled in the Maccabean revolt in the early second century B.C., or the Roman destruction of the Jerusalem temple in A.D. 70, or an 'end-time' battle at Jerusalem see Wolters, 'Dialogue', 39–56; Wolters, 'Biblical Theology', 26–85.

Zechariah outside of Mark 13. This is summarised in his chart:[2]

|      | Zechariah | Event                  | Mark          |
|------|-----------|------------------------|---------------|
| (1)  | 9:9–10    | Entry into Jerusalem   | 11:1–10       |
| (2)  | 14:21     | Jesus' Temple Action   | 11:15–19      |
| (3)  | 9:11      | Blood of the Covenant  | 14:24         |
| (4)  | 14:9      | Kingdom of God, That Day | 14:25       |
| (5)  | 13:2      | The Unclean Spirit     | 1:23, etc.    |
| (6)  | 3:2       | Rebuking Satan         | 8:33—9:9      |
| (7)  | 8:23      | Tassel of his Cloak    | 6:56          |
| (8)  | 8:6–8     | God's Power to Save    | 10:27         |
| (9)  | 13:7–9    | Disciples' Refinement  | 9:49; 14:27–31|
| (10) | 14:5      | Jesus' *Parousia*      | 8:38          |

The first four allusions in the chart are well recognised. To my mind, the sixth and seventh are possible, but the fifth and eighth are unlikely allusions.[3] Importantly, the first eight allusions in Sloan's list of Mark's use of Zechariah (whether granted or not), if they have a specific time of fulfilment, relate to Jesus' earthly ministry or his death. It is only the final two (Zech. 13:7–9; 14:5) that Sloan interprets as referring to events *after* Jesus' death, resurrection, and ascension. These will be closely considered.[4]

---

2  Sloan, *Mark 13*, 214–15. In addition, Bruce, *This is That*, 108, argues that Jesus' teaching on prayer, where he says, 'If anyone says to this mountain, "Go, throw yourself into the sea"' (Mark 11:23) should be understood against the backdrop of Zech. 14:4. Also, Bolt, *Cross*, 88; Evans, 'Messianic', 384.
3  Sloan, *Mark 13*, 73. The six elements of Zech. 13:2 that Sloan sees corresponding to Mark 1 are all better understood as deriving from elsewhere. Furthermore, in Zech. 13:2, the concept of 'the unclean spirit' is related to false prophecy, rather than demon possession. God's power to save in Mark 10:27 is a general theme that can be found across the OT.
4  Evans, 'Messianic', 388, is surely correct to argue that Jesus' actions were guided by Zechariah, rather than references to Zechariah simply being the result of the literary creativity of the Gospel writers. The latter view is suggested, for instance, by Marcus, *Way*, 159–60, when he argues that Mark uses Zechariah 9—14 because this has a special resonance for his audience going through the Jewish Revolt. Contrast Bruce, *John*, 260: 'It is probable to the point of certainty that our Lord himself had the oracle in mind [Zech. 9:9], and deliberately arranged to fulfil it'.

Sloan understands Jesus' prediction in Mark 14:27 of the disciples falling away to refer to the period beginning with their flight at Jesus' arrest and continuing until Jesus' Parousia.[5] The period from Jesus' arrest to his second coming acts as a time of refinement for God's people. To support this claim, Sloan claims Mark is following the sequence in Zechariah seen in the following table:[6]

| Zech. 13:7 = Strike the shepherd, sheep are scattered | Mark 14:27 = Jesus' arrest and death, disciples flee |
|---|---|
| Zech. 13:8—14:4 = tribulation of land, people, and Jerusalem | Mark 13:5–23 = tribulation of land, people, and Jerusalem |
| Zech. 14:5 = theophany with angels | Mark 13:26–27 = theophany with angels |

There are several problems with Sloan's interpretation of Zechariah 13:7—14:5. First, he does not adequately account for the shift between 13:9 and 14:1 (marked in the MT with a chapter break) and how this structural feature functions.[7] It is problematic to read 13:7—14:5 as presenting a strict sequence of events as Sloan does.[8] Zechariah 9—14 is best not interpreted as presenting a sequence of battles, but as giving different perspectives on one battle that will usher in God's kingdom. With each presentation there is a different focus, including what the battle will mean for the nations, for God's people, for the leaders, for the Messiah, for Jerusalem, for Judah, and for the wider creation.[9] This is similar to what happens in works classified as apocalypse (cf. Ezek. 38—39; the book of Revelation).[10] This means that in the broader flow

---

5   Sloan, *Mark 13*, 90–91. Yet Sloan later says that 'their flight is not that which fulfils their "falling away" or "scattering," because their flight happens *before* Jesus' death' (p.100). And in summary (p.111): 'the most plausible reference of the disciples' "falling away" is not their flight from Gethsemane, but their future tribulation that they endure in Jesus' absence'.
6   Sloan, *Mark 13*, 91.
7   Sloan, *Mark 13*, 185, later states: 'Zech. 14:1 is contiguous with Zech. 13:9', but this doesn't explain how the units function in relation to each other, or how they function in relation to the book.
8   Sloan, *Mark 13*, 149, explicitly argues for a 'sequential correspondence between Mark and Zechariah'.
9   See the table in Petterson, *Haggai, Zechariah & Malachi*, 258, and the discussion in Lessing, *Zechariah*, 330--32.
10  However, Zechariah 9—14 lacks many of the defining features of apocalypse, such as pseudonymity, angelic mediation, or otherworldly journey. O'Brien, *Zechariah*, 282, rightly comments that Zechariah frustrates modern scholarly attempts to classify it.

of Zechariah 9—14, Zechariah 14:1 reverts to offer a different perspective on the same battle that has been described in Zechariah 9, 10, 12, and in the oracle in 13:7-9.

Second, while there is not a strict sequence of events in Zechariah 13:7—14:5, there is a sequence in the clearly demarcated oracle of 13:7-9, the climax of which Sloan does not adequately deal with. The sequence is that the shepherd is struck (v.7) with the little ones judged and refined (vv.8-9a). This results in a new covenant relationship (v.9b). The phrase, 'They are my people [...] The LORD is our God' is a covenant formula that is found throughout the OT (e.g. Gen. 17:7-8; Lev. 26:12; Deut. 29:13; 2 Sam. 7:24; Zech. 8:8).[11] Since this restored relationship comes after national judgement (where the Shepherd is struck and the little ones are refined), it must refer to what Jeremiah calls the 'new covenant' (Jer. 31:33). This feature does not fit Sloan's sequence. He has the scattering and refinement of the disciples continuing until Jesus' Parousia, with no mention of the new covenant being established.[12] In Mark's Gospel, Jesus quotes from Zechariah 13:7 immediately after sharing the Passover with his disciples and telling them, '"This is the blood of the covenant, which is poured out for many," he said to them. "Truly I tell you, I will not drink again from the fruit of the vine until that day when I drink it new in the kingdom of God"' (Mark 14:24–25). Jesus' death establishes the new covenant of Zechariah 13:9. Therefore Sloan's view that the tribulations of Mark 13 continue after Jesus' death and resurrection until his Parousia does not actually fit the sequence in Zechariah 13:7–9 where the 'tribulation' is associated only with the striking of the shepherd before the new covenant is established.

The final passage in Sloan's table, Zechaiah 14:5, speaks of Yahweh coming with his holy ones to fight and defeat the nations who have attacked the inhabitants of Jerusalem: 'Then the LORD my God will come, and all the holy ones with him'. Sloan argues this lies behind Jesus' saying in Mark 8:38 (and 13:26): 'If anyone is ashamed of me

---

11  See Rendtorff, *Covenant Formula*. Bible quotations are from the NIV.
12  Sloan largely follows Wilcox, 'Denial', and argues against the objections to Wilcox by Moo, *Old Testament*, 216. In my view, Moo is correct to argue that Jesus' resurrection is what reconstitutes the disciples (p.217).

and my words in this adulterous and sinful generation, the Son of Man will be ashamed of them when he comes in his Father's glory with the holy angels'.[13] He argues that since the Son of Man comes with the holy angels, it 'implies a heavenly origin, and thus an earthly descent', and that the presence of shame implies the notion of a 'final judgment'.[14] Sloan notes the influence of Daniel 7:13 but argues that the presence of Zechariah 14:5 adapts the Daniel reference to refer to Jesus' second coming.

This is a crucial point in Sloan's thesis. However, the only point of connection between Zechariah 14:5 and Mark 8:38 is the reference to 'the holy angels' (τῶν ἀγγέλων τῶν ἁγίων). In the MT, it is not certain that these are heavenly beings. The coming of Yahweh in Zechariah 14:5 is to earth in order to save his people on the day of battle and the 'holy ones' are better understood as the people whom God restores to Jerusalem as a consequence of his victory.[15] Already in Zechariah 9:9, the Messiah who is later revealed to have been struck and pierced in the battle, returns to Jerusalem after the battle 'righteous, saved, and afflicted' (implying, in retrospect, his resurrection). If Mark is alluding to Zechariah 14:5 in Mark 8:38, then as background, Zechariah demands a link to the battle at Jerusalem in which the Messiah is pierced and struck.

If Mark is not alluding to Zechariah 14:5, then the allusion to Daniel should be given priority in interpretation where the Son of Man comes to the Ancient of Days to receive a kingdom, which is fulfilled in Jesus' ascension, shortly after his death and resurrection.[16] An application of Zechariah 14:5 to Jesus' ascension rather than his second coming makes greater sense of Mark 9:1 (which Sloan doesn't address), where Jesus states that 'some who are standing here will not taste death before they see that the kingdom of God has come with power'. If some will not taste death, then in cannot refer to Jesus' second coming.

---

13  Sloan, *Mark 13*, 111. See also Harriman, 'King', 286.
14  Sloan, *Mark 13*, 112.
15  So, Leske, 'Context', 677; Webb, *Zechariah*, 179; Boda, *Commentary*, 525; Petterson, *Haggai, Zechariah & Malachi*, 291; Lessing, *Zechariah*, 507.
16  So Bolt, 'Mark 13', 10–32. Bolt, *Cross*, 94–95, notes this interpretation goes back to the ante-Nicene Fathers, and is found in several places in John Calvin's commentary on Daniel.

## 2.2 Use of Zechariah in Mark 13

Sloan detects 16 instances where Mark 13 uses Zechariah.[17]

|      | Zechariah                          | Event                             | Mark            |
|------|------------------------------------|-----------------------------------|-----------------|
| (1)  | 14:4                               | Setting of Discourse              | 13:3            |
| (2)  | Zech. 13:7–9 + Θ Dan. 12           | Scattering = Tribulation          | 13:19           |
| (3)  | 13:2                               | False Prophets                    | 13:5–6, 21–22   |
| (4)  | 13:8                               | Earthquake, War, Famine           | 13:7–8          |
| (5)  | 13:9                               | Refinement                        | 9:49; 13:9–13   |
| (6)  | 14:16                              | Universal Evangelism              | 13:10           |
| (7)  | 4:6                                | God's Spirit                      | 13:11           |
| (8)  | 14:1–5                             | Attack on Jerusalem               | 13:14–23        |
| (9)  | 14:5                               | Flight to the Hills               | 13:14           |
| (10) | 14:2                               | Consequent Afflictions            | 13:14–17        |
| (11) | 14:5                               | Coming of Son of Man with Angels  | 8:38; 13:26–37  |
| (12) | Isa. 13:34; Joel 2; Zech. 14:5–6   | Cosmic Imagery and Judgment       | 13:26–27        |
| (13) | Tg. Zech. 14:4                     | Coming 'with Power'               | 13:26–27        |
| (14) | 2:10–15                            | Gathering the Elect               | 13:27           |
| (15) | 14:6,7,8,9                         | 'That day'                        | 13:32           |
| (16) | 14:7                               | Jesus' ignorance about 'that day' | 13:32           |

Before explaining these, Sloan outlines how he understands the structure of Mark 13.[18]

13:1–4   Jesus' prophecy [about the destruction of the temple] and the disciples' question regarding the timing of its fulfilment

13:5–23  Jesus' answer to the question regarding the timing of his prophecy

---

17 Sloan, *Mark 13*, 216.
18 Sloan, *Mark 13*, 150–51.

13:24–27   Prophecy regarding the subsequent coming of the Son of Man

13:28–31   Warning about the timing of the temple's destruction

13:32–37   Warning about the timing of the coming of the Son of Man

Sloan proposes Mark 13 is dealing with two issues: the timing of the temple's destruction (vv.5–23,28–31), and the coming of the Son of Man (vv.24–27,32–37). For Sloan the timing of the temple's destruction is within the lifetime of the disciples. The coming of the Son of Man is Jesus' second coming, which is more distant. This structure anticipates many of Sloan's interpretative decisions, which I will briefly summarise and evaluate.

Sloan is right to see Mark alluding to Zechariah 14:4 in the setting of the discourse 'on the Mount of Olives opposite the temple' (v.3) and that this reference alerts 'a scripturally literate reader to Zech. 14'.[19] As Sloan notes, the content of Zechariah 14 closely relates to Mark 13:

> each pertains to a successful attack on the city of Jerusalem by gentiles. In each case, the affliction predicted is that upon women and houses [Zech. 14:2; Mark 13:15–17], the only action done by those attacked is "flight to the mountains." [Zech. 14:5; Mark 13:14] Additionally, Zech. 14, like Mark, pertains to the coming reign of God.[20]

Sloan's second point argues from the shared vocabulary in Proto-Theodotion Daniel 12 and Mark 13 that the 'days of distress' in Mark 13:19 is a reference to the tribulations of Zechariah 13:7–9, however the textual connections are tenuous.

Third, Sloan notes the presence of the term 'the false prophets' (τοὺς ψευδοπροφήτας) in LXX Zechariah 13:2 (in MT, they are

---

19   Sloan, *Mark 13*, 153. Marcus, *Way*, 156, also observes that there is evidence from Josephus and rabbinic traditions that Zechariah 14:4 was read as a reference to the advent of the Messiah. He cites Josephus (*Jewish War* 2.261-263). Marcus draws here on the work of Black, 'Rejected', 144–47. See also Wright, *Victory*, 344, who notes the setting on the Mount of Olives 'can hardly be accidental [...] Jesus seems to intend an allusion to Zechariah 14.4–5'.

20   Sloan, *Mark 13*, 155.

simply 'prophets') and Mark 13:22. He then interprets the time of refining and testing in Zechariah 13:8–9a as coming with false prophets and teachers in the time between the first and second comings of Jesus.[21] However, there is no warrant for this in the flow of Zechariah. Zechariah 12 presents a battle in which one who is close to God is pierced (12:10). In the aftermath there is great mourning, but a fountain is opened to cleanse the house of David and the inhabitants on Jerusalem from sin (13:1). In 13:2–6, the cleansing of the land is further represented as the removal of idolatry and false prophecy, but there is no tribulation here. The short oracle in 13:7–9 replays these themes. In the context of Zechariah 9—14, the scattering and refining of the flock is a consequence of the attack of the nations at Jerusalem. It does not result from false prophets and teachers.

Sloan's next point sees an allusion to Zechariah 13:8 in Mark 13:7–8. He argues that the suffering 'in the whole land' (Zech. 13:8) refers to the afflictions of war, where the phrase 'cut off' often describes the death and exile as a consequence of warfare. This connection has more strength, but it is thematic, rather than lexical.

The fifth point returns to the topic of refinement in Zechariah 13:9, but this time as it relates to the trials in Mark 13:9–13. Sloan notes that the sequence of afflictions that Jesus predicts the disciples will undergo are the same afflictions Jesus himself undergoes in his arrest, trial, and death.[22] However, the lexical correspondence that supports a connection to Zechariah 13:9 (the phrase 'my name') seems tenuous.

Sloan's sixth point argues that the gospel going to 'all the nations' (Mark 13:10) reflects Zechariah 14. While initially 'all the nations' attack Jerusalem (14:2), at the end of the chapter, they either worship the God of Israel (14:16) or are punished with plagues (14:18,19). Sloan argues this is fulfilled before the destruction of the temple, but this is based on his understanding of the structure of Mark 13, rather than any programme in Zechariah.[23]

Seventh, Sloan argues for the influence of Zechariah 4:6 ('Not by

---

21  Sloan, *Mark 13*, 168.
22  Sloan, *Mark 13*, 172.
23  Sloan, *Mark 13*, 175.

might nor by power, but by my Spirit') in Mark 13:11.[24] While there is a conceptual link between these passages, the empowering of God's spokesperson by his Spirit is a prevalent theme in the OT and does not necessitate an allusion to Zechariah 4:6.

Sloan's eighth point is that Mark 13:14–23 alludes to Zechariah 14:1–5. He notes that 'the abomination that causes desolation' in Daniel (cf. 9:27; 11:31; 12:11) is 'a person or event that profanes the temple and precedes its destruction'.[25] He observes that in Mark it is associated with military conflict between the Jews and Romans with the jeopardy of women and children characteristic of war. He also argues that this is the sign that the disciples were asking for in 13:4. For Sloan, this section of Mark refers to the period leading up to the destruction of the temple in distinction to the period before Jesus' second coming in which the disciples are refined.

Sloan contends that in the context of the military campaign against Jerusalem, Jesus' imperatives and threats in Mark 13:14–17 recall those of Zechariah 14:1–5 (points 9 and 10). The flight from the city to the hills (Mark 13:14) reflects the flight from Jerusalem by 'my mountain valley' (Zech. 14:5). The threats to houses and to women (Mark 13:15,17) reflects the plunder of houses and rape of women in Zechariah 14:2. These are important observations. Sloan concludes: 'Mark's Jesus uses the prophecy to describe the *destruction* of Jerusalem and the temple'.[26] There is another possibility that I will consider in the next section, that Jesus uses Zechariah's prophecy about the destruction of Jerusalem (and implicitly the temple) to speak of his impending death.

As noted in the previous section, Sloan argues there is a change of topic in Mark 13:24 from the destruction of the temple to the second coming of Jesus, contending that Zechariah 14 justifies this change.[27] He asserts that the cosmic signs in Mark 13:24–25 accompany the Parousia. The description of these signs reflects Isaiah 13:10; 34:4, and

---

24  Sloan, *Mark 13*, 175. Mark does not contrast the disciples' speech with the Spirit but claims that the Spirit will speak through their speech.
25  Sloan, *Mark 13*, 182.
26  Sloan, *Mark 13*, 190.
27  Sloan, *Mark 13*, 192.

Joel 2:10. While not in his summary table, he also argues that the failing luminaries correspond to Zechariah 14:6.

As with Mark 8:38, Sloan contends again that the reference to the Son of Man coming with the angels in Mark 13:26 is a combined use of Daniel 7:13 and Zechariah 14:5 (point 11). The final five points seek to 'further attest to the proposed use of Zechariah'.[28] Twelfth, he notes that two of the passages that influenced Mark's description of the cosmic signs also have angels present (Isa. 13:4–5; Joel 2:10–11). Sloan concludes: 'the fact that Zech. 14 describes the Lord's coming *with angels* coincides with the imagery from texts that also describe the Lord's judgment *with his angels*'.[29] It is unclear how this point further attests the use of Zechariah in Mark 13, especially since the phrase 'with his angels' is not present in Mark 13:26.[30] Furthermore, as I noted earlier, in the Hebrew text the 'holy ones' in Zechariah 14:5 are better understood as the people whom God restores to Jerusalem in the aftermath of the battle.

Sloan's thirteenth 'allusion' is not actually an allusion, but evidence from the Targums that he believes supports an interpretative tradition seen in Mark. Sloan first argues that 'with great power' (μετὰ δυνάμεως πολλῆς) in Mark 13:26 should be translated 'with a great [angelic] army'.[31] He then notes that in Targum Zechariah 14:4 the anthropomorphism of God's feet standing on the Mount of Olives in the MT is removed and in its place is: 'And at that time he shall reveal himself in power'. For Sloan, Targum Zechariah is evidence of an interpretative tradition that collocates God's coming with power with coming with angels. This is possible, but speculative.

The fourteenth allusion notes the phrase 'the four winds of heaven' (Zech. 2:6 [MT 2:10]) occurs in Mark 13:27. Sloan also notes the command to 'flee' (Mark 13:14) occurs in Zechariah 2:6 [MT 2:10], and that God comes to live among his people (Zech. 2:10 [MT 2:15]) with many nations being joined to the Lord (Zech. 2:12 [MT 2:16]).

---

28  Sloan, *Mark 13*, 196.
29  Sloan, *Mark 13*, 199.
30  Sloan, *Mark 13*, 196, notes its absence, but argues it must be understood on the basis of its appearance in Mark 13:26–27.
31  Sloan, *Mark 13*, 197–98, following Angel, *Chaos*, 125–27.

He argues this is 'consonant with the total picture in Mark'.[32] While there are lexical links, there are also differences. In Zechariah the command is to flee from Babylon and return to Jerusalem, whereas in Mark the command is to flee Jerusalem. Sloan claims Zechariah 2 says that God will gather the people, but this idea is not actually present. Furthermore, it is only an assertion that God dwelling with his people is the same as 'the Son of Man coming in the clouds'. The theme of many nations being joined to the Lord is closer to Mark 13:10 than to anything in 13:24–27. Sloan argues that these points justify the inference that Zechariah 14:5 is present in Mark, but much of the reasoning is circular for this point.

The fifteenth allusion concerns the use of the phrase 'on that day', which occurs twenty-five times in Zechariah, predominantly in chapters 12—14.[33] Earlier Sloan comments: 'In Mark's case, the common element of occurring "on that day" may serve as the basis for applying the disparate prophecies to a single individual at a single time. Accordingly, Mark is telling his reader that in Jesus, "that day" has finally arrived'.[34] I agree with this assessment, but it stands at odds with Sloan's later argument that 'that day' refers to Jesus' Parousia and the phrase 'those days' refers to the attack on Jerusalem in 13:14–19.[35]

Finally, Sloan argues that the day which is 'known only to the Lord' (Zech. 14:7) lies behind Jesus' statement in Mark 13:32: 'But about that day or hour no one knows, not even the angels in heaven, nor the Son, but only the Father'.[36] This observation seems valid. However, since in Zechariah 'on that day' is a singular event that relates to the battle at Jerusalem in which the Messiah is pierced and struck, this seems to militate against Sloan's view that Mark 13:32–37 refers to the Parousia.

---

32  Sloan, *Mark 13*, 202.
33  Sloan, *Mark 13*, 203, claims it occurs eight times in Zechariah 14, but it only occurs 7 (14:7 is different).
34  Sloan, *Mark 13*, 86.
35  Sloan, *Mark 13*, 203–04. An inconsistency here is that Mark 13:24, which Sloan argues refers to Jesus' Parousia, uses the phrase 'those days'.
36  Sloan, *Mark 13*, 204–05.

## 3. Zechariah's Eschatological 'Framework' in Mark

Even though I find some of the links to Zechariah that Sloan sees in Mark tenuous, his thoroughness and creativity is appreciated. His book provides an excellent basis to think about how Mark's Gospel reflects the broader eschatological 'framework' of Zechariah.[37] His broader purpose in studying Mark's use of Zechariah is to demonstrate that it explains how when Jesus is asked about the destruction of the temple in Mark 13, he speaks about such seemingly unconnected topics as the persecution of the disciples, the attack on Jerusalem, and the Parousia.[38] However, I have several issues with Sloan's understanding of Zechariah's 'framework'. There are some elements of Zechariah's program and the way that they influence Mark's presentation that Sloan does not emphasise enough, especially the battle at Jerusalem and what it achieves, particularly in relation to the new covenant. In addition, as I have already noted, I remain unconvinced that Mark uses Zechariah 14:5 to speak of Jesus' Parousia, which is a key element of his overall thesis. Before commenting on these issues further, I will outline my understanding of Zechariah's 'framework'.

A major difficulty that the book of Zechariah addresses is why the restoration promised by earlier prophets had not taken place. Many of God's people had returned to Jerusalem from exile, but while God had turned to his people with mercy, his glorious presence (which Ezekiel dramatically portrayed departing from the temple on a throne chariot) had not returned to his people, nor had his blessing. What becomes clear from Zechariah is that the reason for this is that while Jerusalem had been through the experience of conquest and exile as the punishment of God, the sin which led to it remained an enduring problem

---

37 Other scholars note how Zechariah's presentation is reflected in Mark. For example, Allison, *End of the Ages*, 34–35; Wright, *Victory*, 422, 599; Pitre, *Tribulation*, 458–59; Menken, 'Striking', 39–59. In an unpublished doctoral thesis, made popular by Marcus, *Way*, 154–58, Black, 'Rejected', 7, concludes 'almost all of the gospel references to Zech. 9–14 occur during (or refer to) Jesus' final week'. He further argues that the structure of Zechariah 9–14 influenced the narrative shape of the Passion accounts in the Gospels. See the critique by Boda and Porter, 'Literature', 215–54, who conclude that while Mark and Matthew certainly utilise Zechariah, and Matthew especially so: 'No one of the Gospel writers, assuming that they follow the nine-step development posited by Black, utilizes Zechariah to create this narrative development' (p.252).

38 Sloan, *Mark 13*, 213.

among God's people.³⁹ Zechariah calls on the people to return to the Lord, to rebuild the city and temple, and he restates the earlier prophetic hope for the glorification of Jerusalem with God's return.

Yet this raised questions: How can the people be cleansed? How can covenant relationship be restored? How can gentiles share in this hope for Jerusalem and the recreation of the world in keeping with the hopes proclaimed by the earlier prophets? The solution that Zechariah provides in the latter part of the book is that Jerusalem will undergo another exile-like experience, which will result in its refinement and cleansing. Throughout Chapters 9—14, Zechariah envisages yet another attack on Jerusalem by the nations, just like earlier attacks (especially by the Babylonians in 586 B.C.), but one in which God will respond by defending and saving the inhabitants of the city by natural and supernatural means.

In this attack, Jerusalem will not be unscathed, nor will God himself. Zechariah envisages one who is pierced (12:10), a shepherd who is struck (13:7), and a king who is afflicted and saved, who rides back into Jerusalem on a donkey (9:9).⁴⁰ As Sloan notes, Mark associates each of these images, and many others from Zechariah, with the first coming of Jesus. Jesus' entry into Jerusalem on a donkey replays king David's return to Jerusalem after exile, having been humiliated and defeated by his enemies before God saved him.⁴¹ This prefigures Jesus' resurrection. Jesus driving the merchants out of the temple anticipates the cleansing of Jerusalem and Judah so that the temple's holiness will pervade the land. Jesus' death on the cross, where he is struck and pierced, is the punishment for sin that opens a fountain of cleansing and issues in a new covenant relationship between God and his people and establishes the worship of the nations. All of these undisputed quotations of Zechariah in Mark's Gospel speak of Jesus' earthly ministry and his death.

It is my contention that when Jesus speaks of an impending battle at Jerusalem in Mark 13, he is also speaking of his death. He is not speaking of the destruction of the temple in A.D. 70, nor of an

---

39  See Boda, *Severe*, 338.
40  See further, Petterson, *Haggai, Zechariah & Malachi*, 280–84, where the connections with the suffering servant of Isaiah are also traced. Also Petterson, *Behold*, 246–52.
41  See Scalise, 'Zechariah, Malachi', 274.

'end-time' battle at Jerusalem accompanying his Parousia but using the language and imagery of Zechariah and other prophets, and the broader program of Zechariah 9—14, to present his death as the battle at Jerusalem, which he symbolically endured, resulting in God's eternal kingdom. Indeed, the more traditional interpretations of Mark 13 pose interpretative problems that are not overcome by Sloan.[42]

The problem with interpreting the battle as an 'end-time' battle at Jerusalem accompanying his Parousia is Jesus' statement in Mark 13:30: 'this generation will certainly not pass away until *all* these things have happened'.[43] Concerning the Roman destruction of Jerusalem and the temple in A.D. 70, it is difficult to see how this relates to 'the Son of Man coming in a cloud with power and great glory' (13:26). It is also difficult to see how the Roman destruction of the temple in A.D. 70 eclipses all crises of human history: 'unequaled from the beginning, when God created the world, until now—and never to be equaled again' (13:19).[44] These problems are why interpreters like Sloan often seek a combination of referents, but on a plain reading of Mark 13, Jesus is speaking to his followers about an imminent time of tribulation.

These difficulties dissolve if Jesus is drawing on the apocalyptic language of Zechariah 9—14 (and elsewhere in the OT) that depicts another attack of Jerusalem and exile of its inhabitants and uses this language to depict the judgement that he will undergo in his imminent death. In other words, since Jesus embodies both the temple and the city of Jerusalem, he adopts the language that the OT uses to speak of their destruction to speak of his impending death.

It is not my intention here to provide a full exegetical study of Mark 13, nor to survey the history of interpretation, just to argue for an approach that is consistent with the background and program of Zechariah.[45] From the way that Mark draws on other aspects of

---

42 Bolt, 'Mark 13', 12, notes how the traditional interpretations do not attempt 'to understand Mark 13 in the literary context of Mark's Gospel'.
43 Green, *Luke*, 742, like most, attempts to circumvent this problem by arguing 'this generation' refers 'not to a set number of decades or to people living at such-and-such a time, but to people who stubbornly turn their backs on the divine purpose'. But this seems to have Jesus simply stating the obvious.
44 Bolt, *Cross*, 102.
45 For a survey of interpretative approaches, see Berry, 'Destruction', 62–74.

Zechariah 9—14 in his presentation of Jesus' ministry, it is evident that Jesus is not strictly following a sequence. For instance, the cleansing of the temple comes in the final verses of Zechariah. As I have argued, the flow of the material in Zechariah 9—14 is not sequential, but its apocalyptic style replays the same event, exploring different perspectives. Zechariah envisages one battle at Jerusalem on the day of the Lord which ushers in God's kingdom on earth in all its glory. Mark draws on the language and imagery from this battle to speak of Jesus' death.[46]

This approach is not new, but it is under-represented. It is the approach of Bolt, who argues:

> once it is admitted that the language is 'a generalized picture ... as imaginatively presented by the prophets' its fulfilment is open to question, for it need not be to a political catastrophe for the city at all. Rather than being a prediction that *the events of 586 will be repeated,* it may well be that the theological language of Jerusalem's destruction in 586 is *applied symbolically to another event with similar theological import.*[47]

Gray also notes the way that Mark 13 'uses the eschatological language of the prophets, drawn primarily from their oracles against Jerusalem.'[48] He continues: 'By identifying the false messiahs, wars and rumors of war, famine, and earthquakes as the "beginning" (ἀρχή) of the birth pangs (ὠδίνων), Mark effectively paints all these things (ταῦτα) as divine judgment, using the language of Israel's prophetic tradition.'[49] However, Gray argues that this language refers to the destruction of the temple in A.D. 70.

Shively notes the close connection in Mark between Jesus' crucifixion and the destruction of the temple:

> In Mark's narrative context, nothing is more of a sacrilege than the rejection of God's own Son (cf. 3:28–29; 12:8–10,

---

46 Again, this raises the historical question of the extent to which Mark reflects Jesus' own teaching. See footnote 2.
47 Bolt, 'Mark 13', appendix. Italics original. His quote is from Dodd, 'Fall', 52, who also says: 'So far as any historical event has coloured the picture, it is not Titus's capture of Jerusalem in A.D. 70, but Nebuchadnezzar's capture in 586 B.C. There is no single trait of the forecast which cannot be documented directly out of the Old Testament'.
48 Gray, *Temple*, 117.
49 Gray, *Temple*, 120.

where Jesus is likened to the rejected cornerstone of the temple). [...] Moreover, Mark connects the crucifixion with the temple's destruction at the end of the passion narrative. Upon Jesus' death the veil of the temple is torn in two from top to bottom, portraying its symbolic destruction (15:37–38).[50]

Similarly, Wright argues that the language of Mark 13 refers not to the end of the world, but 'the death, resurrection, and ascension of Jesus on the one hand and the fall of the Temple (the heaven-and-earth place) on the other'.[51]

While Gray, Shively, and Wright argue that the death of Jesus leads to the temple's end, I am arguing that in Mark, Jesus appropriates Zechariah's attack on Jerusalem by the nations (with the destruction of the temple as occurred in 586 B.C. implicit) to speak of his death. Of course, the death of Jesus later leads to the destruction of the Jerusalem temple by the Romans in A.D. 70, but this is not Mark's concern.

While Jesus' claim to be the temple of God is commonly recognised (e.g. Matt. 21:42; Mark 12:10; Luke 20:17; John 1:14; 2:19–21),[52] there are also grounds for seeing Jesus representing, and to some extent embodying, the city of Jerusalem. Indeed, in Zechariah 14 the temple and the city of Jerusalem merge into one reality (14:4, 20–21; cf. 2:4–5). In this way, the attack on Jerusalem and the warfare and exile language of Zechariah (and elsewhere) can be understood as being employed symbolically by Jesus to speak of his death in which he bears the punishment of God.[53] Wright argues in various places that Jesus brings the end of Israel's exile,[54] but when the OT background is traced more fully, the NT presentation is better expressed as Jesus undergoing a recapitulation of exile in his death on the cross.[55]

Interpreting Zechariah's description of a future attack on Jerusalem

---

50  Shively, *Apocalyptic*, 197.
51  Wright, *History & Eschatology*, 150. Wright notes the 'fascinating suggestion' of Bolt in footnote 62 (p.307).
52  Greene, 'Heavenly Temple', 425–46.
53  Dodd, *More*, 73–74, particularly noted that the word 'desolation' (Luke 21:20) is commonly used in the Septuagint to refer to the Babylonian destruction of Jerusalem.
54  For instance, Wright, *Victory*, 126–31.
55  On the recapitulation of exile, see Petterson, 'Exile', 41–67. Ezekiel 38—39 also envisions another attack on Jerusalem by the nations after Israel has returned from exile. God will defeat the nations and pour out his Spirit on his people.

as fulfilled symbolically in the death of Jesus is also consistent with the way that Mark reports the other apocalyptic signs in the passion narratives: 'At noon, darkness came over the whole land until three in the afternoon' (Mark 15:33; cf. Zech. 14:6), and 'the curtain of the temple was torn in two from top to bottom' (Mark 15:38; cf. the earthquake in Matt. 27:54; Zech. 14:5).[56] Sloan even notes how these signs fit with the destruction of a city (cf. 2 Sam. 22:8; Ps. 17:8 (LXX); Isa. 13:13; Jer. 10:10).[57] It also explains the description of Jesus' followers deserting him at his arrest, appropriate given the imminent attack on the city (Mark 14:50–51; cf. Zech. 13:7–9).

That Jesus understood his death in terms of the attack by the nations on Jerusalem finds support in other places. In the third prediction of the passion in Mark's Gospel, Jesus says:

> 'We are going up to Jerusalem,' he said, 'and the Son of Man will be delivered over to the chief priests and the teachers of the law. They will condemn him to death and will hand him over to the Gentiles' (Mark 10:33).

The phrase 'handed over to the Gentiles [nations]' recalls the covenant curses of the Torah (Lev. 26:32–33,38), which were realised in the Assyrian and Babylonian exiles (cf. Ps. 106:41; Ezra 9:7).[58] Understood against this background, Jesus is anticipating his own experience of warfare and exile.

The parable of the tenants (Mark 12:1–12; cf. Matt. 21:33–46; Luke 20:9–19) speaks of the son being 'cast out' (ἐκβάλλω) of the vineyard and killed. The LXX uses the same vocabulary to describe the Babylonian exile (Deut. 29:27; Isa. 22:17–18; Jer. 12:14–15; 22:28; Zech. 7:14). In the parable, Jesus is foreshadowing the cross as exile.

Most commentators rightly interpret the cup that Jesus drinks against the backdrop of the OT, identifying it as the cup of God's

---

56 In relation to the apocalyptic signs in Matthew's Gospel, see Wardle, 'Resurrection', 666–81. Sloan, *Mark 13*, 170, rightly notes the earthquake in Zechariah 14:5 is connected lexically to Mark 13:7. He argues this relates to the destruction of the temple.
57 Sloan, *Mark 13*, 171.
58 It is a concept that is also found in the Maccabean period (e.g., 2 Macc. 10:4; 13:11; 14:42). Bolt, *Cross*, 56–58.

wrath (Mark 14:36; cf. Matt. 20:22-23; 26:39,42; Luke 22:42). Yet in Isaiah the cup is more specifically a cup that Jerusalem will drink, namely, its destruction by the Babylonian army and subsequent exile of its inhabitants (Isa. 51:17,22). This is another link between an attack on Jerusalem by the nations and the death of Jesus.

There are other lines of support outside of Mark for the idea that the attack of Jerusalem by the nations and the people of Judah is fulfilled symbolically in Jesus' death. In Matthew 28:18, the coming of the Son of Man is explicitly connected with Jesus' resurrection and ascension, rather than his second coming, when the risen Jesus says 'All authority in heaven and on earth has been given to me', alluding to Daniel 7:14. Similarly, in Acts 7:55-56, Stephen sees heaven opened and the Son of Man presently standing at the right hand of God, in the position of all authority (cf. Luke 22:69). This is not in any way to deny Jesus' second coming, which is clearly taught elsewhere (e.g. 1 Thess. 4:15-17; 1 Cor. 15:22-23). My argument is that the coming of the Son of Man in Mark 13:26 refers to Jesus' ascension.

In Luke's apocalyptic discourse, the reference to Daniel's 'abomination that causes desolation' is replaced with a clear reference to Zechariah: 'When you see Jerusalem being surrounded by armies, you will know that its desolation is near' (Luke 21:20; cf. Luke 19:43-44). This supports the view that Daniel's abomination that causes desolation involves a military attack of Jerusalem as presented in Zechariah.

In Luke 23:46, Jesus quotes Psalm 31:5 from the cross, 'Father, into your hands I commit my spirit'. In the wider context of the psalm, the Psalmist either likens or describes his time of trouble as being 'in a city under siege' (v.21). An individual symbolising a city under siege has precedent elsewhere in the OT. In Job 19:12, God's troops advance against Job, build a siege ramp against him, and enemies surround his tent. So too, Jeremiah is made a fortified city to stand against the land (Jer. 1:18-19; 15:20). This is all consistent with Jesus quoting Psalm 31:5 to indicate that in his death he represents symbolically the city of Jerusalem under attack by the nations and the people of Judah (Zech. 12:2; 14:14).

A final line of support for the attack on Jerusalem by the nations being fulfilled in Jesus' death is found in Acts 4 and Luke's use of

Psalm 2.[59] The raging, plotting, and rebellion of the nations and their kings against the Lord and his Messiah in Psalm 2, which sounds like some kind of military campaign, is seen as fulfilled in the plotting of Herod and Pontius Pilate along with the Gentiles and the people of Israel 'in this city' (i.e., Jerusalem). This raging, plotting, and rebellion of the nations and their kings against the Messiah in Jerusalem, ultimately brought about Jesus' death, but it also proved to be the day of salvation for God's people.

## 4. Conclusion

The apocalyptic discourse in Mark 13 poses many difficult issues for the interpreter. Sloan is right to argue that Zechariah 9—14 is crucial background. He helpfully identifies many ways in which Zechariah is used. However, I have identified what I think are problems with his understanding of Zechariah's 'framework'. Rather than referring to the destruction of the Jerusalem temple and Jesus' Parousia, in Mark's Gospel Jesus uses Zechariah's prophecy of an attack of Jerusalem by the nations and the exile of its inhabitants symbolically to speak of his impending death. This is the same attack in Zechariah in which the Messiah is pierced and struck, and that issues in the kingdom of God. This interpretation overcomes the difficulties many have found interpreting Mark's apocalyptic discourse. It explains how Jesus sees the coming tribulation as imminent and can say, 'this generation will certainly not pass away until all these things have happened' (13:30). It also gives Jesus's death the significance that it deserves since the imminent crisis is described as 'unequalled from the beginning, when God created the world, until now—and never to be equalled again' (13:19). There is no greater tribulation than that which Jesus endured on the cross for his people.

Anthony R. Petterson
Morling College, Australian College of Theology

---

59  See further, Petterson, *Haggai, Zechariah & Malachi*, 268; Stead, *Zechariah*, 200.

## Bibliography

Allison, D. C. — *The End of the Ages Has Come: An Early Interpretation of the Passion and Resurrection* (Philadelphia: Fortress, 1985).

Angel, A. — *Chaos and the Son of Man: The Hebrew Chaoskampf Tradition in the Period 515 BCE to 200 CE* (LSTS, 60; London: T&T Clark, 2006).

Berry, E. — 'The Destruction of Jerusalem and the Coming of the Son: Evangelical Interpretations of the Olivet Discourse in Luke', *SBJT* 16 (2012), 62–74.

Black, M. C. — 'The Rejected and Slain Messiah who is Coming with his Angels: The Messianic Exegesis of Zechariah 9–14 in the Passion Narratives' (unpublished doctoral dissertation; Emory University, 1990).

Boda, M. J. — *Haggai, Zechariah* (NIVAC; Grand Rapids, MI: Zondervan, 2004).

Boda, M. J. — *A Severe Mercy: Sin and Its Remedy in the Old Testament* (Winona Lake, IN: Eisenbrauns, 2009).

Boda, M. J., and S. E. Porter — 'Literature to the Third Degree: Prophecy in Zechariah 9–14 and the Passion of Christ', in R. David and M. Jinbachian (eds.), *Translating the Hebrew Bible: From the Septuagint to the Nouvelle Bible Segond* (Montreal: Médiaspaul, 2004), 215–54.

Bolt, P. G. — 'Narrative Integrity of Mark 13.24–27' (MTh thesis; Australian College of Theology, 1991). Now published as *The Narrative Integrity of Mark 13:24–27* (ACT Monograph Series; Eugene, OR: Wipf & Stock, 2021).

Bolt, P. G. — 'Mark 13: An Apocalyptic Precursor to the Passion Narrative', *RTR* 54 (1995), 10–32.

Bolt, P. G. — *The Cross from a Distance: Atonement in Mark's Gospel* (NSBT 18; Leicester: IVP, 2004).

Bruce, F. F. — *This is That* (Exeter: Paternoster, 1968).

Bruce, F. F. — *The Gospel of John* (Grand Rapids, MI: Eerdmans, 1983).

Dodd, C. H. — 'The Fall of Jerusalem and the "Abomination of Desolation"', *The Journal of Roman Studies* 37 (1947), 47–54.

| | |
|---|---|
| Dodd, C. H. | *More New Testament Studies* (Manchester: The University Press, 1968). |
| Evans, C. A. | 'Jesus and Zechariah's Messianic Hope', in B. Chilton and C. A. Evans (eds.), *Authenticating the Activities of Jesus* (Leiden: Brill, 1999), 373–88. |
| Gray, T. C. | *The Temple in the Gospel of Mark: A Study in its Narrative Role* (Grand Rapids, MI: Baker Academic, 2010). |
| Green, J. B. | *The Gospel of Luke* (NICNT; Grand Rapids, MI: Eerdmans, 1997). |
| Greene, J. | 'Jesus as the Heavenly Temple in the Fourth Gospel', *BBR* 28 (2018), 425–46. |
| Harriman, K. R. | 'The King Arrives, but for What Purpose? The Christological Use of Zechariah 13–14 in Mark 13', *JTI* 10 (2016), 283–98. |
| Leske, A. M. | 'Context and Meaning of Zechariah 9:9', *CBQ* 62 (2000), 663–78. |
| Lessing, R. R. | *Zechariah* (Concordia Commentary; Saint Louis, MO: Concordia, 2021). |
| Marcus, J. | *The Way of the Lord: Christological Exegesis of the Old Testament in the Gospel of Mark* (Edinburgh: T&T Clark, 1993). |
| Menken, M. J. J. | 'Striking the Shepherd. Early Christian Versions and Interpretations of Zechariah 13,7', *Biblica* 92 (2011), 39–59. |
| Moo, D. | *The Old Testament in the Gospel Passion Narratives* (Sheffield: The Almond Press, 1983). |
| O'Brien, J. M. | *Nahum, Habakkuk, Zephaniah, Haggai, Zechariah, Malachi* (Nashville, TN: Abingdon, 2004). |
| Petterson, A. R. | *Behold Your King: The Hope for the House of David in the Book of Zechariah* (LHBOTS 513; New York: T&T Clark, 2009). |
| Petterson, A. R. | *Haggai, Zechariah & Malachi* (AOTC 25; Nottingham: Apollos, 2015). |
| Petterson, A. R. | 'Exile and Re-exile in the Book of the Twelve', in G. Athas, et al. (eds.), *Theodicy and Hope in the Book of the Twelve* (LHBOTS 705; New York, NY: T&T Clark, 2021), 41–67. |

| | |
|---|---|
| Pitre, B. | *Jesus, the Tribulation, and the End of Exile: Restoration Eschatology and the Origin of the Atonement* (Tübingen: Mohr Siebeck, 2005). |
| Rendtorff, R. | *The Covenant Formula: An Exegetical and Theological Investigation* (trans. M. Kohl; OTS; Edinburgh: T&T Clark, 1998). |
| Scalise, P. J. | 'Zechariah, Malachi', *Minor Prophets II* (Peabody, MA: Hendrickson, 2009), 177–366. |
| Shively, E. E. | *Apocalyptic Imagination in the Gospel of Mark: The Literary and Theological Role of Mark 3:22–30* (BZNW 189; Berlin/Boston: De Gruyter, 2012). |
| Sloan, P. | *Mark 13 and the Return of the Shepherd: The Narrative Logic of Zechariah in Mark* (LNTS, 604; London: T&T Clark, 2019). |
| Stead, M. R. | *Zechariah: The Lord Returns* (Reading the Bible Today; Sydney South: Aquila Press, 2015). |
| Wardle, T. | 'Resurrection and the Holy City: Matthew's Use of Isaiah in 27:51–53', *CBQ* 78 (2016), 666–81. |
| Webb, B. G. | *The Message of Zechariah: Your Kingdom Come* (BST; Leicester: Inter-Varsity Press, 2003). |
| Wilcox, M. | 'The Denial-Sequence in Mark 14:26–31', *NTS* 17 (1971), 426–36. |
| Wolters, A. | 'Zechariah 14: A Dialogue with the History of Interpretation', *Mid-America Journal of Theology* 13 (2002), 39–56. |
| Wolters, A. | 'Zechariah 14 and Biblical Theology', in C. G. Bartholomew (ed.), *Out of Egypt: Biblical Theology and Biblical Interpretation* (Bletchley: Paternoster Press, 2004), 261–85. |
| Wright, N. T. | *Jesus and the Victory of God* (London: Society for Promoting Christian Knowledge, 1996). |
| Wright, N. T. | *History & Eschatology: Jesus and the Promise of Natural Theology* (Waco, TX: Baylor University Press, 2019). |

CHAPTER 11

# Mark 13: Literary Impetus to the Passion Narrative and Christian Faith for All Generations

## Michele A. Connolly

## Introduction

'The good news must first be proclaimed to all nations.' (Mark 13:10)

How can Christians successfully proclaim the gospel? In particular, how did the first believers in Jesus make him and his message known to succeeding generations who would never know Jesus in the flesh? How could this first generation ensure that they preached in such a way that the faith of those later generations was—and was held to be—as authentic an engagement with the risen Jesus of Nazareth as that of Peter, James, and John?

How does first generation, eye-witness faith in Jesus of Nazareth, risen from the dead, become second and later generation unseeing, non-tactile yet faith-filled discipleship of the one not held by the tomb, Jesus Messiah?

This chapter argues that Mark 13 is the literary engine that drives this transfer of faith from the first generation of Jesus' disciples, those who knew him in the flesh, able to see him, touch him, and hear his voice, to all the generations beyond them who could only know and believe in Jesus by other means, including hearing about him from those who already believed. The task of the Gospel of Mark is to ensure that this faith of the generations succeeding those who first believed in Jesus was as grounded in reality as that of the first generation.

## Time and Space in the Markan Narrative

Mark 13 plays with time and space. This essay will focus on the way Mark 13 uses time to carry the audience into the Passion Narrative and into the time beyond the resurrection. The chapter sits between two large blocks of material in Mark: the account of Jesus' public ministry of proclaiming the reign of God by words and actions in Mark 1—12 and the account of Jesus' suffering, death, and resurrection in Mark 14—16. In Mark 13 the Gospel writer takes the reader for a moment into a new place and time, separate from the other place and time in which the final six chapters of the Gospel are set, namely the city of Jerusalem in the last days of Jesus' earthly life. That is, with regard to space, while Mark 13:1–2 shows Jesus in Jerusalem commenting on the stones of the Temple, the very next verse shows him, without any explanation about his movement outside the city, seated on the Mount of Olives (v.3).

In terms of time, Jesus' extended speech in 13:5–37 moves from the past tense narration of the Gospel narrative to future tense prediction. In 13:35 close to the end of the chapter, a new system of naming time is introduced, which will be used to construct the chronology of the Passion Narrative. From this new location and time perspective, Mark 13 allows Jesus to look forward into a future of God's making, for which all disciples need to be prepared. As I will argue, the disciples for whom Jesus' speech is narrated in Mark 13 are both those within the story world of Mark and those who will be disciples beyond that world, beyond the point of time at which Mark stops narrating. I will show that the role that Mark 13 plays in the Markan management of time appeals not only to the originally envisaged audience, if there was such a thing, but also to all potential audiences. The way in which Mark 13, together with the rest of the narrative, makes this appeal provides a way for all audiences, of any time, to become disciples of Jesus entering into the mystery of the Reign of God.

## Methodologies: Historical, Narrative and Performance Criticisms

The primary methodology I will use is a literary reading of Mark 13 as it connects with Mark 14—16, the Passion Narrative and the life beyond Mark 16:8. In this process I will draw on insights from both narrative and performance criticisms. I am not trying to press the text to tell me things it does not offer. I will offer no major argument about the very disputed timing of events predicted at Mark 13:14 (the identity and timing of the abomination of desolation) and at Mark 13:24–27 (the final coming of the Son of Man). I recognise Joel Marcus' insistence that the Gospel of Mark and other New Testament texts were composed not as 'timeless philosophical treatises or works of art but messages on target'.[1] It is a perfectly legitimate intellectual exercise to try to identify who the false prophets and messiahs may have been (vv.5–6, 21–23) or what was the 'desolating sacrilege set up where it ought not to be' (13:14). However, while the original audience of Mark may have known the specific details of the references to the 'abomination of desolation' and the necessary flight to the mountains (Mark 13:14), the knowledge of those seemingly allusive references is now lost to us.[2] I note that Craig Evans argues against the scholarly attempt to identify specific events, saying,

> Proposed correspondences invariably prove inaccurate and sometimes occasion embarrassment. It is enough to be reminded that until the kingdom of God has come in its fullness, evil still poses a danger and may some day rise up in an unprecedented manifestation.[3]

---

1 Marcus, *Mark 1—8*, 36–37.
2 See Evans, *Mark 8:27–16:20*, 324 for the explanation that 'Jesus has provided his disciples with more information than in all probability they cared to hear. They have been warned of a spiraling series of dangers and threats. The key event is not the destruction of the temple, the very thing they had asked about in the first place, but seeing "the abomination of desolation" standing where he must not. Mark knows his readers will understand what or who this is. Today we are not so sure.'
3 Evans, *Mark 8:27–16:20*, 324.

## Time of Writing of the Gospel of Mark

With regard to the time of writing of the Gospel, I stand with those who see this Gospel written shortly after 70 C.E., in the wake of the war of 66–70 C.E. between Rome and Palestine. Most scholars agree that the focus on suffering of the whole Gospel and more specifically on war in Mark 13, suggests that the narrative has been composed in connection with the war between Rome and Judaea of 66–70, culminating in the capture of the city of Jerusalem and destruction of its temple in July–August of the year 70.[4] The variation between major scholars on the time of writing of the Gospel of Mark ranges from times either during or after this war, that is from the late sixties to the early seventies. Evans and Robert Guelich agree with A. Y. Collins that the Gospel most likely took its final shape in the late sixties, during the war with Rome.[5] Even though he appeals to the same arguments as Collins about the impact on the war of Jewish zealots occupying the temple in 67–68 C.E., Marcus would extend the period in which the Gospel may have been written to the early seventies, as also would Frank Moloney.[6] The events of 70 C.E., especially the destruction of the Temple in Jerusalem, would be a very likely impetus to the Markan author to commit his narrative finally to writing, to put the war into perspective, to encourage the disciples of Jesus to remain faithful, knowing that they had not yet arrived at the end (Mark 13:7), and that they were still called to proclaim the gospel to all nations (Mark 13:10).

## Literary Terms and Dynamics

Since I am taking a literary approach, it is necessary to explain some terms and dynamics I see operating in this chapter, shaping its meaning. They include the location of Mark 13 in the larger literary structure of the Gospel of Mark, the temporal location of the author and the originally envisaged audience(s) of the whole Gospel relative to the events described in Mark 13 and some literary terms helpful for explaining the dynamics at work within the narrative.

---

4  Marcus, *Mark 1-8*, 37.
5  See Evans, *Mark 8:27—16:20*, lxii; Guelich, *Mark 1—8:26*, lxiii; Collins, *Mark,* 14.
6  See Collins, *Mark,* 14; Marcus, *Mark 8—16,* 30, 35; Moloney, *The Gospel of Mark,* 14–15.

## Literary Location of Mark 13 in the Gospel of Mark

For the literary structure of Mark 13 I will rely on that presented by Moloney, who sees Mark 13 in a larger sequence of chapters from Mark 11–13 in which Jesus predicts four endings, which are in process of happening in Mark 13. The four endings are 1) the End of the Temple and its Cult (Mark 11:1–25); 2) The End of Religious Leadership in Israel (Mark 11:27—12:44); 3) The End of Jerusalem (Mark 13:1–23); 4) The End of the World as We Know It (Mark 13:24–37).[7] Of these four endings, by the time of Mark 13 the first two have already been depicted in Mark 11—12. First, in his prophetic action in the Temple Jesus prevented the cult from being carried out even if only temporarily (Mark 11:15–17). Second, the debates between Jesus and the leadership of Israel in the Temple in Mark 11:27—12:44 resulted in no one from that leadership daring to ask Jesus any question (Mark 12:34) and thus bringing about the symbolic loss of the Jewish leadership's moral authority over the people. It is immediately following this event that Jesus comes out of the Temple and is next depicted sitting on the Mount of Olives (13:1–3) where he makes the speech in which he predicts the next two endings, those of Jerusalem (13:1–23) and of the world as we know it (13:24–37).

## Temporal Location of the Originally Envisaged Audience of the Gospel of Mark

One aspect of provenance that does need to be considered is the location in time of both the writer of the Gospel and his initially envisaged audience. If Mark was written either during or more likely after the war of 66–70 between Rome and Palestine, Jesus and the disciples within the Gospel are portrayed as living in the middle of the endings Mark depicts, after the symbolic ending of the Jewish temple cult and religious leadership but before the end of Jerusalem and the whole world. The writer of the Gospel and the initially-intended audience are most likely situated after the third predicted ending, that of Jerusalem, but obviously before the end of the world and the coming of the Son of Man. They look back on some events as having happened very recently

---

7   See Moloney, *The Gospel of Mark*, ix–x.

and anticipate others, at they know not what imminence. Thus, within the story world, for Jesus and his disciples, two endings have occurred and will be followed by two more major changes to their world, both of which Jesus predicts in Mark 13. For Mark and his contemporaneous audience, one of these two events that Jesus is depicted as predicting, namely the destruction of Jerusalem, has in fact occurred. This makes Jesus' final prediction, of the end of the world which is yet to occur, all the more convincing.

### *Audiences of Mark*

From the text of Mark 13 we can see that there are two categories of audience intended. First, after the opening conversation in which Jesus declares that the stones of Jerusalem will not be left standing, the narrator names the well-known first-chosen three disciples, Peter, James, and John as well as Andrew. These are the ones who were first to be called, who had already witnessed and were yet to witness further highly significant events in Jesus' life. The first three had been the only ones to see Jesus' raising of a dead young girl to life (5:22–24a;35–43) and his transfiguration on the mountain top (9:2–9). Even with the addition of Andrew, we sense that this audience will receive privately from Jesus a privileged teaching. As the narrative moves into the Passion narrative this sense of being a privileged audience is expressed in Jesus' selection of them to be with him in the garden where they prove to be incapable of staying awake with him as he prays (Mark 14:32–42).

The second audience to which Mark 13 speaks specifically and quite unusually is *any* audience of the Gospel of Mark itself, whether those of Mark's own time or any other audience in the two millennia since—a much longer history of reception than the Gospel writer could probably have imagined. This second and all subsequent audiences is addressed when Jesus, in the final verse of Mark 13, declares that what he says to the inner group of four disciples, he says to 'all' (13:37).

## Literary Features of the Gospel of Mark

I come now to the literary features and devices that operate in the whole Gospel narrative but with particular impact in Mark 13 as it leads into the Pasion Narrative. I will deal with Mark's use of prediction and its fulfilment and the allied use of words for time; the use of verbs of perception throughout the narrative and the use of what is called the 'fourth wall technique' in Mark 13:35. It is important to state that no one of these features alone could have the effect I claim for them; it is the cumulative effect of all these features that carries the responsive audience out of a world of observation alone and into the challenge to be a disciple of Jesus.

## *Prediction and fulfilment*

First then, prediction and its fulfilment is a well-known literary device that operates in the Gospel, especially in its second half. These examples range from simple predictions fulfilled immediately, such as a donkey being available for Jesus to ride into Jerusalem (11:2–6), to prediction fulfilled some time later, such as the scattering of disciples when the leader is attacked (14:27,50). More complex is the triple passion predictions of Mark 8:31; 9:31; and 10:32–34, which are depicted as fulfilled with regard to the suffering and death of Jesus, and as announced by an enigmatic young man in the empty tomb with regard to Jesus' resurrection (14:1—16:8). Just as complex are the predictions of the end of Jerusalem and the end of the world, neither of which is depicted in the narrative but the first of which I argue is known to the Gospel writer and the initial audience. Together, they constitute a device that propels the narrative forward as the reader seeks to know if the predictions are realised.

In Mark 13, a number of predictions make links with both the Passion Narrative but also beyond it, for both the four disciples within Mark 13 who hear Jesus speak and all other audiences, who hear the Gospel long after the first generation of believers has gone. The predictions Jesus makes in this chapter are of three kinds, progressing from simple to more complex. The first kind is of events to come that are not depicted as fulfilled in the Markan story but which I argue are known about by the writer of the Gospel and his contemporaneous audience. These occur in the first half of the chapter; they are about the end of Jerusalem (2); the distractions of false prophets and messiahs (5–6,21–22) and wars, violent social strife, famine, earthquakes, and upheaval following an 'abomination of desolation' (7–8,12–13,14–20). The second kind is a prediction that comes with advice to the disciples about how to act when they are subjected to persecution on account of the gospel (9–13). This prediction is made complex by the fact that it describes what in fact happens to Jesus in Mark 14—16 where he then models the advice he gives to his disciples. The third kind is of predictions that are not depicted as fulfilled in the Markan narrative but which are still anticipated. Both are of major importance in Mark: the prediction at vv.24–27 looks to the eschatological return of the Son of Man, the culmination of all of creation and salvation history; the second, of the unpredictable return of the master, told parabolically in vv.34–36, introduces a new language, that of the four watches of the night which becomes the time scheme of the Passion Narrative and all time beyond the resurrection. As the only hint Jesus gives his disciples about when things will happen, the last piece of advice he gives them before the passion narrative begins, this language is surely meant to be highly significant.

### *Times in the Gospel of Mark: Chronos and Kairos*

Predictions and fulfilment happen in the course of time. Most narratives, the Gospel of Mark among them, tell a narrative that moves through regular time that can be measured in earthly terms of hours, days, weeks, and years. I call this *chronos* time, from the Greek χρόνος which can refer to a specific time, or time with a sense of chronological accuracy.[8] It is in this time frame, which we tend to think of as normal, the way time flows, that most narratives construct their necessary sense of a beginning, a middle, and an end. Mark does use this word for time, twice, to refer to moments in everyday life (2:19; 9:21). By contrast, Mark uses another Greek word for time that conveys the sense of a time that is appropriate, ripe for a particular event or situation. This word, καιρός, is used five times in Mark (Mark 1:15; 10:30; 12:2; 11:13; 13:33); each is significant in Mark's theology but the last and the first carry a great deal of freight.[9] It is not until we have heard the final καιρός in 13:33 that we begin to see how meaningful the first καιρός in 1:15 has been and will continue to be.

---

8   See Liddell, *A Greek-English Lexicon*, for the definition of χρόνος as 'a definite time, a while, period, season'.
9   See Liddell, *A Greek-English Lexicon*, 859–860 for the definition of καιρός as 'the right point of time, the proper time or season of action, the exact or critical time'.

## Verbs of Perception in the Gospel of Mark

A second literary device to be noted is the way verbs are used, with a shift from past to future tense and from indicative mood narration of events to portrayal of imperative mood speech by Jesus in Mark 13. Many scholars note that while Mark uses the ordinary tenses of narration for most of the Gospel, in Mark 13 the verbs are used much more frequently in the future tense or the imperative mood. This creates the sense of the narrative having moved into a different space: outside the regular temporal position of the narrative as it unfolds, we are being told about how the present in which the Gospel writer and his contemporary audience live was foreseen by Jesus as the future for which he sought to prepare his first disciples.

Mark's pointed use of various verbs of perception—hearing, seeing, being awake, understanding, remembering, and knowing—all play an important role in Mark 13. In Mark the ordinary mode the narrator uses to refer to people perceiving what is going on around them is hearing, very often expressed in participial mode. Of the forty-one uses of ἀκούω between Mark 1:1—16:8, seven are in the imperative mood. The first four of these imperatives occur in the parable Chapter 4 (4:3,9,23,24), all enjoining those who have ears to hear Jesus' parables to understand them. Of the other three, the first (7:14) is also an injunction to a surrounding crowd to hear and understand Jesus' teaching. In the final two, divine authority is invoked: at 9:7, at the transfiguration, a voice from heaven commands Jesus' disciples to listen to him; at 12:29 Jesus cites Deuteronomy 6:4, which calls on Israel to hear and to orient themselves correctly by acknowledging God as God, from which all else flows. In a few verses, both seeing and hearing are brought together (4:12; 4:24) and in one verse only, Jesus challenges his disciples that they neither see nor hear nor remember despite having every opportunity to do so (8:18).

In marked contrast to the regular focus on hearing, in Mark 13 the sense perception appealed to changes from hearing to seeing. The disciples asking Jesus to observe the great stones and buildings of the Temple introduce sight, saying to Jesus, 'Look!' ἴδε (13:2). Jesus responds in like kind, beginning with the most common word for looking or seeing, βλέπω, but progressing through the chapter to words that mean 'be awake' or 'be alert', 'keep watch'. Βλέπω is used fourteen times in the Gospel, five times in Mark 13, four of which are imperatives (vv.5,9,23,33). After βλέπω has been heard four times, Mark uses synonymously with it the verb ἀγρυπνεῖτε (13:33) which carries the sense of being watchful through a sleepless night—which unlike first time readers, experienced readers know is what the disciples will fail to do in the coming night in the garden of Gethsemane.[10] Having turned seeing into being watchful, Mark concludes chapter 13 with three uses of the verb γρηγορέω, which conveys the sense of 'remaining awake because of the need to continue alert'.[11] This word will be repeated in Mark 14 where three times within four verses (vv.34,37,38) Jesus directs his inner core of three disciples to 'stay awake and alert'. Allied with these appeals to use the senses is the challenge to understand, even though there are some things that they do not know.[12] Close to the end of his speech, at 13:33 Jesus warns his disciples that they must 'look, be alert for [they] do not know when the *kairos* moment is'.[13] By every measure, Mark 13 shows Jesus directing his disciples within the story world and the hearers of the Gospel narrative to attune themselves to a heightened sense of vision with a strong sense that there is something that they will need to prepare to see.

One of the insights of performance criticism highlights what Mark is communicating by this focus on verbs expressing perception. First, Joanna Dewey notes that in the kind of narrative that Mark is, namely a written version of something that was originally delivered orally, the audience is assisted to remember the narrative by frequent repetition of materials that are introduced early and then are echoed through the

---

10 See Liddell, *A Greek-English Lexicon*, 16, for the definition of ἀγρυπνέω as 'to lie awake, to pass a sleepless night, to be watchful'.
11 See Louw and Nida (eds.), *Greek-English Lexicon* # 23.72 for this meaning of γρηγορέω.
12 The word συνίημι is used in chapters 4–8, when Jesus says that outsiders to the kingdom will not understand (4:12); the narrator tells us that the disciples did not understand about Jesus' multiplication of the loaves (6:52); when Jesus calls the crowd to him to understand the true reason for what makes a person unclean (7:14); when Jesus challenges the disciples who persist in not knowing and not understanding about the loaves (8:17 where Jesus asks all the perception words: perceive, understand, see, hear, remember; 8:21 when he asks do they not yet understand).
13 βλέπετε, ἀγρυπνεῖτε· οὐκ οἴδατε γὰρ πότε ὁ καιρός ἐστιν.

subsequent story.[14] As we have seen above, Mark introduces the language of hearing and seeing early in the narrative, focusing strongly on hearing. At one point he links hearing and seeing as a means of coming to understanding (4:12) and at another he treats them as interchangeable forms of perception, when he says at 4:24, βλέπετε τί ἀκούετε literally 'see what you hear'.

Second, in the middle phase of the Gospel, from Mark 7:31—10:52, Mark takes this focus on sense perception to a new level when he shows Jesus healing four people from disabilities of hearing or seeing.[15] Having shown Jesus talk about the concepts of hearing and seeing in a new way, Mark now depicts Jesus restoring people's capacity to see and hear. Mark exploits this sequence of stories ironically by showing that while Jesus can heal these men of their bodily inability to hear and see, he proves unable to lead his disciples to hear and see what he teaches them, especially the necessity of Jesus, the Son of Man and Messiah, suffering, dying, and rising from the dead. As Dewey writes, 'the four healings of 7:31—10:52 ring the changes on restoring hearing, speech and sight. They seem to punctuate—or frame—discipleship material'.[16] These treatments of hearing and seeing in the early and middle phases of the Gospel narrative prepare for the way perception is treated in Mark 13, as we will see in the final section of this paper.

### *The Fourth Wall Dramatic Technique in the Gospel of Mark*

Finally, Mark's single but striking use of what is called the 'fourth wall' technique in 13:37 must be taken into account. In narrative, the 'fourth wall' is a notional or invisible barrier between the world in which the narration takes place and the world of the audience. The idea is that the audience of a drama can see into this world but the characters of the narrative cannot see out. When, either from the drama stage or from behind the camera, a character does look away from the scene he or she is in, directly at the audience, the 'fourth wall' is broken. This creates

---

14  See Dewey, *Oral Ethos*, 76, for her citation of Eric Havelock's explanation that 'Oral narrative "operates on the acoustic principle of the echo"'.
15  These healings are the healing of a deaf mute (Mark 7:31–37); the restoration of sight of a blind man at Bethsaida (Mark 8:22–26); the exorcism of a deaf and mute boy (Mark 9:14–29) and the restoration of sight of Bartimaeus at Jericho (Mark 10:46–52).
16  Dewey, *Oral Ethos*, 72.

an intimacy, even a complicity, between that character and the audience. In this way, the audience is given the sense of being offered a privileged insight into the character and the story. This technique is known in both current-day and ancient dramatic narratives. Dewey comments that:

> We know from contemporary study that oral performers often make direct addresses to the live audiences. 'What I say to you, I say to all', serves to extend the teaching embedded in the event from the four disciples who are part of the episode, and to apply it to the listening audience.[17]

In his 'On the Sublime,' the first century C.E. writer Longinus explains, 'Change of person gives an equally powerful effect, and often makes the audience feel themselves set in the thick of the danger'.[18] He then cites examples from the *Iliad*, from Aratus' *Phaenomena*, and from Herodotus to illustrate how a sudden turn in the narrative from third person to second person address can throw the audience members themselves into the situation the narrative is depicting.

Thus, when Jesus says to his audience of four disciples within the narrative, 'what I say to you I say to all' (Mark 13:37), the Markan narrator has Jesus break the fourth wall and speak to all who will hear the Gospel. Mark has already addressed the 'reader' in Mark 13:14, but in 13:37 he speaks directly to the audience in the second person plural, ὑμῖν, 'you'. 'You' here has a double reference: it refers primarily to the audience of the entire extended discourse of Jesus, the four disciples within the narrative itself, named in 13:3. However, because of the further explication that Jesus speaks to 'all', 'you' also speaks to the audience of the narrative of all times who are 'outside' the story but are now in this way drawn into it. This audience, like the four disciples within the narrative, are in this way challenged to take up the responsibilities of seeing in a fully conscious way the things that are about to occur in the Passion Narrative which begins in the very next verse, at 14:1.

Of course, the Markan audience outside the Gospel narrative must

---

17 Dewey, *Oral Ethos*, 82.
18 Longinus, 'On the Sublime,' #26 (Halliwell, et al, p.247).

use their imaginations or must allow their imaginations to be activated and directed by Mark's story-telling techniques. If they are prepared to collaborate with the drama of the narrative, Mark offers this audience an encounter with Jesus that is distinctly their own, experienced as keenly as the encounter the original disciples had with Jesus in the flesh. The power of narrative to draw an audience into the vividly apprehended mental construction of a scenario, with all its key physical, emotional, and intellectual components alive in the audience's consciousness, makes the audience's encounter with that world a genuine encounter that can change the audience. It can make it possible for people who have never seen Jesus in the flesh to know him and commit to following him as disciples in a faith that is every bit as authentic as that of those who knew Jesus in his earthly life.

## Reading of Mark 13

On the basis of these details, I will now read through Mark 13 focusing on two concerns: first, how Mark 13 leads into the Passion Narrative and second, how, by connecting Mark 13 with the larger narrative, Mark attempts to ensure that the faith of generations of Christian believers other than those who knew Jesus in the flesh could be as grounded in reality as the faith of Peter, James, John, and Andrew.

In vv.1–2, the narrator moves Jesus and his disciples out of Jerusalem, the site of conflict between Jesus and the custodians of his own religious tradition, to a place opposite the city. Removed symbolically from the physical confines of the city and its Temple and from the time scheme of its violent agenda against him, Jesus has the space in which to speak the agenda of God, which he does in vv.5–37.

One of Jesus' disciples calls Jesus' attention to the solidity of great stones and buildings and when Jesus predicts the end of Jerusalem, asks a *chronos* time question. Responding to the request that he 'see' the stones of the temple Jesus warns his disciples to 'see to it' (βλέπω) that in a time to come after Jerusalem is destroyed, they are not led astray by the distraction of people coming in his name or by the continuing stresses of ordinary life. These stresses are not to be seen as the end of everything but merely the beginning of birthpangs (vv.5–8).

This word, 'birthpangs', so strongly associated with apocalyptic expectation, gives the first hint of my response to my second concern: that faith for all disciples, both those within the story and those in the audience of the Gospel, must go through some kind of birthpangs. A similar warning prediction about deceiving pseudo-messiahs is made in vv.14–23, concluding with βλέπω. While the prediction is made to the disciples within the story, its content relates to events not told in the story, which would be relevant to Mark and his initial audience. However, for all disciples it is important to hear Jesus' words not only of warning but also of consolation: 'I have told you everything' (v.23).

In between these two large sections, vv.9–13 presents material that has many layers of meaning. To the disciples who are with him on the Mount of Olives Jesus predicts that they will be handed over to councils, beaten in synagogues, and will stand before governors and kings because of Jesus, in witness (v.9). Jesus insists that the gospel must first be proclaimed to all nations (v.10). He advises the disciples who are with him how to respond, by leaving it to the Holy Spirit what to say when they are brought to trial and handed over (v.11). The plain meaning of these verses is that they relate to the life of the disciples after the destruction of Jerusalem, in the time beyond where the Gospel narrative will end, the time that relates to my second issue. However, experienced readers of the Gospel know that what Jesus predicts and advises here is what he himself does in the immediately following chapters of the narrative. Jesus models all the behaviour he advises here. Here is one clear instance of Mark 13 connecting with the Passion Narrative, my first concern.

Mark 13:14–23 makes a strong focus on *chronos* time events that were probably known to the originally envisaged audience of the Gospel. Because it is their experience it must be acknowledged and related to the events of the Gospel. The narrative portrays Jesus already anticipating this event, sympathising with those who will suffer through it, advising about the urgency of response. Jesus does not give *kairos* time responses to the disciples' initial *chronos* time question but he is shown predicting *chronos* events through which his followers must suffer. Jesus' disciples who proclaim his word will be held to account by authorities, vv.9–13; some people will have to flee from an unthinkable time of suffering, related to the establishment of a desolating sacrilege, whatever that may be (vv.14–23). There is no escape from the demands of *chronos* time: it is the world in which we live, it massively shapes our lives. It will provide a structure for telling the events of Jesus' last days and the announcement of his resurrection. But it is not the only time. Jesus warns about the challenges of *chronos* life, which he himself will model to the ultimate degree in the Passion Narrative. Thus, the audience sees Jesus in sympathy with the *chronos* time life experiences of his followers, either already experienced at the time of writing the Gospel or still potentially to occur. But the Markan evangelist also wants to provide a literary dynamism built out of the events of both Jesus' life and the life experiences of the early Christian community that will carry his audience from and via entry into the narrative of Jesus' life, to life beyond the moment of Jesus.

Mark 13:24–27 anticipates the Passion Narrative, although its primary meaning refers to something not depicted in the Markan narrative. Jesus predicts the undoing of creation in the failure of the great cosmic lights that will precede the coming of the Son of Man to gather his elect from the four winds (vv.24–27). This is taken up in the Passion Narrative in the last three hours of Jesus' dying, when '[at] noon, darkness came over the whole land until three in the afternoon' (Mark 15:3). However, the final coming of the Son of Man is not told in the narrative that ends at 16:8 and remains as something projected beyond those events. Similarly, advice given by Jesus about reading the signs of the imminent arrival of the Son of Man in the same way that one reads the changing signs of the seasons on a fig tree (vv.28–29) is not depicted in any literal sense in the narrative and looks for fulfilment beyond 16:8.

In 13:28–29, the focus of *chronos* on being able to calculate the empirical time when an event will happen is shifted from the temporal to the spatial by a slight change in terminology in the analogy Jesus creates around the term ἐγγύς. In v.28, the term is defined by the temporal reference to a season of the year, namely summer (ἐγγὺς τὸ θέρος ἐστίν). In the very next verse, v.29, in a sequence that begins in exactly the same way as v.28, the final words are slightly rearranged almost as a pun, to emphasise that the subject of the verb (to be) has moved from being a feature of the natural world, the coming near of summer, to the coming near of the Son of Man (ἐγγύς ἐστιν ἐπὶ θύραις). However, in this second clause, while the subject has now to be read from the verb alone, there is an added adverbial phrase, ἐπὶ θύραις, usually translated 'at the very gates'. This is a spatial metaphor, qualifying the meaning of ἐγγύς. This shifts the focus of the word from its *chronos* meaning, loosening the grip of that way of thinking about time. In rapid succession time has been treated as something experienced in the natural world, to something that has a spatial dimension with a hint of urgency, something powerful at the very entry point to a place.

Immediately after this in two verses that use the verb παρέρχομαι (to pass away, pass by) three times (vv.30–31), Jesus insists that his word about these things will last even through the dissolution of the whole natural world. Next, Jesus insists that no one knows the *chronos* information about the events he has described—not himself in the earthly *chronos* condition nor the angels in heaven, but only the Father. In the very next verse (v.33), Jesus uses both *chronos* (πότε, 'when') and *kairos* terms side by side, with *kairos* now the dominant term.

Following this verse Mark presents Jesus telling a new parable in which he introduces *chronos* terms which will become the basis for temporal structure of the Passion Narrative. They will be the scaffolding on which the appalling story is told so that it can progress from moment to moment. When Jesus introduces the language of the four watches of the night through which the disciples must 'keep awake', namely evening, midnight, cockcrow, and morning (v.35), he is leading his disciples of all times out of the *chronos* time concerns of Mark 13:4 into another whole dimension of time, the *kairos* moment that is appropriate for the action of God. Each of these *chronos* terms is resonant with meaning. One in particular, however, will enable the narrative and the receptive hearer to merge from *chronos* concerns into *kairos* reality. Πρωΐ, the fourth temporal term that Jesus' parable lists (Mark 13:35) names part of the diurnal round in which Jesus' suffering and death will be shown to occur (15:1) but it also names the moment of transition at 16:2 when faithful disciples can hear the resurrection of Jesus proclaimed. From this moment they can hear the instruction that they are to go to Galilee, to encounter Jesus and to hear again but as though for the first time that the *kairos* is fulfilled and that the reign of God is close and thus, seeing the world afresh, to trust Jesus as good news (Mark 1:14–15).

In the final section, 13:33–37, there is an intensification of the language of seeing to 'being alert' and 'keeping awake'. Jesus stresses that it is because 'they do not know when' either the time or the master will come, that his disciples must stay awake. These verses, 33–37, are complex in their layers of meaning. Mark 13:34–37 links very specifically into the Passion Narrative, providing a way of structuring the narration of this event. First, the intense word for keeping awake, γρηγορέω, will be directed to the same inner core of disciples in the garden of Gethsemane, repeated three times as the disciples fail to watch while Jesus prays (Mark 14:34,37,38). Second and very importantly, the language of the four watches of the night becomes the time scheme in which both the suffering, death, and burial of Jesus as well as the women's discovery of the empty tomb are narrated. While 'midnight' is never stated, it is logically understood as the narrative progresses through the other three times that are named, beginning at 'evening' when Jesus goes to celebrate Passover with the Twelve disciples (14:17) through the (mid)night of Jesus' garden agony, arrest and trial before the Sanhedrin (14:32–71), to Peter's betrayal before cockcrow (14:72). Jesus' trial is conducted before Pilate in the morning, followed by his condemnation to death, crucifixion and death before his burial in the evening (15:1–47). After an intervening period for the sabbath, the women come to the tomb in a new morning to do the processes of death only to be confronted with the proclamation that death has not held Jesus (16:2).

Thus, 13:34–37 links very specifically into the Passion Narrative, providing a way of structuring the narration of this event. However, apart from these links to the Passion narrative, the combination of the time scheme introduced in v.35 and Jesus' sudden address to 'all' means that this instruction from the Master relates not only to the disciples depicted in Mark 14—16, but also to those beyond 16:8 in the time of the writer of the Gospel and after that. This is because the accumulating impact of the features described in Mark 13 makes it both necessary and possible for the hearer of Mark 16:8 to be projected in their imagination into a situation in time and life beyond that verse.

First, the language of the four watches introduced at the very end of Mark 13 makes it possible to place the women's bewildering discovery of the empty tomb and confrontation with the resurrection proclamation on the morning of a new day, the first of the week when all possibility is open. Second, by addressing his final warning to 'all', Mark's Jesus means to speak to all beyond the narrative who would give him hearing. Third, the language of seeing, leading to keeping awake and linked to understanding, requires the sympathetic reader to persevere to a satisfactory resolution of the quandary of apparent, ultimate failure of the entire narrative's meaning, into which 16:8 plunges the hearer / reader. Fourth, when Jesus changes the time language in Mark from a *chronos* focus specifically to *kairos*, he directs the hearer to a very particular kind of destination, namely a point of spiritual awakening. This destination requires the disciples, as the young man in the tomb said, to return to Galilee. This may have reflected what some of the first or second generation disciples of Jesus literally did, during and after the war of 66–70 C.E.

But to go to Galilee has a symbolic meaning in Mark—it is to return to the beginning of the narrative, where Jesus began his mission and where he first called disciples to follow him. As he began in Galilee, the very first thing that Mark's Jesus declared was Πεπλήρωται ὁ καιρός (Mark 1:15). It is not mere *chronos* time that is completed; rather the time is ripe for the announcement of the reign of God that has come near: ἤγγικεν ἡ βασιλεία τοῦ θεοῦ (Mark 1:15). As close as Jesus announced the reign of God to be in the opening of the Gospel narrative, so close will the Son of Man be when he comes. Jesus' disciples will be able to see how close he is when they have learnt to read the signs of the kingdom and of God's actions, the way people ordinarily can read the evidence of the natural world around them (γινώσκετε ὅτι ἐγγύς ἐστιν ἐπὶ θύραις) (Mark 13:29).

To encounter the end of the Gospel of Mark is to be directed to return to the beginning, having persevered through the trauma of both the suffering and death of Jesus as well as the astonishing announcement of his resurrection. Mark institutes a circular process, whereby hearing the story of Jesus leads a disciple through a process in which the end takes one back immediately to the beginning, in a repeating cycle of increasing awaking to seeing, hearing, understanding, remembering, and coming finally to full alertness, full capacity to receive the kingdom of God, to be the kind of soil that is able to have God produce in it grain to 30, 60 and 100-fold yield (Mark 4:8).

Why is it that the ending sends the audience looking for a satisfactory answer? Not only does this ending's apparent failure to complete the story disappoint the hearer. It shakes up the audience quite literally, as a rough awakening does. Mark 16:2–7 provokes in the hearer the shocking hope that the death of Jesus was not in fact the last word—that there had been a disruption by heaven of this narrative of woeful death. But then in 16:8 the audience experiences the jolt of dropping from that astounding hope to the realisation that the women's fearful silence *is* the end of the story. As it tells us this fact, the story puts words of disturbance into the hearer's mind. The women are said to be trembling in a state of bewilderment, trance or ecstasy (τρόμος καὶ ἔκστασις, Mark 16:8). The audience that still remembers from Mark 13 that Jesus had declared not only that the 'the end is still to come' (v.7) but also that great suffering is 'but the beginning of the birthpangs' (v.8), can realise that it is in the process of being projected even violently in a birth from dull awareness, even sleep, into the full wakefulness of resurrection faith.

## Conclusion

How does this experience relate to the first audience of the Gospel of Mark and all those succeeding? It relates to these later audiences because the narrative provides a means of encounter with the full Jesus story for every disciple who was not with Jesus in the flesh.[19] This encounter is provided by way of the imaginative participation that every hearer or reader makes, unconsciously, as they follow a narrative. It may appear that Mark 13 is primarily concerned to show Jesus' foreknowledge and

---

19  It should be noted that the Gospel frequently shows that being with Jesus in the flesh, even for his hand-picked disciples, was no guarantee of successful understanding of Jesus, nor of faithful following of him.

already settled determination to face the suffering into which the narrative will plunge him immediately after Chapter 13, thereby showing that all that happens to Jesus lies within God's knowledge and acceptance. But Chapter 13 also offers the disciples within the story world the basis on which to endure their vision of Jesus in his suffering, death, and resurrection and to hope despite every appearance of the annihilation of Jesus Messiah, that there is a reality beyond. And further, Chapter 13, especially but not only because of the 13:37 rupture of the 'fourth wall' of narrative, when Jesus completes his speech insisting that he speaks not only to his audience within the story world of Chapter 13, but to 'all', means that he speaks directly to every audience of the Gospel, the one that Mark envisaged and those that he could not have imagined, such as ourselves.

Thus, not only those disciples who first walked with Jesus in Galilee and Jerusalem but all subsequent disciples can make the same journey imaginatively through the medium of the Markan narrative. In this narrative, Mark 13 plays a very significant role, showing that Jesus assures his followers that there is an eschaton in the vision of God: a goal towards which God brings God's whole creation when all will be resolved. In Mark 13 Jesus also assures his followers that suffering, and even violent death, lie in the path towards that goal but that even this lies somehow in the provident care of God. Jesus' warnings and advice in this chapter carry the narrative into the telling of the Passion Narrative, providing a structure that in itself says that this awful event occurs in a time that the Son of God declared beforehand, so that his disciples in the awful moment and all subsequent disciples could endure the narration of this terrible event. But in this chapter, the wise and insightful author of the 'second' Gospel, the one who deeply believes in the resurrection of Jesus, constructs the possibility for every sympathetic hearer of this story to pass over from interest in the narrative to awakening to resurrection faith lived in the time when we still await with hope the final coming of the Son of Man.

Michele A. Connolly
Catholic Institute of Sydney

## Bibliography

Collins, A. Y. — *Mark: A Commentary* (Hermeneia. A Critical and Historical Commentary on the Bible; Minneapolis, MN: Fortress, 2007).

Dewey, J. — *Oral Ethos of the Early Church: Speaking, Writing, and the Gospel of Mark* (Biblical Performance Criticism Series 8; Eugene, OR; Cascade, 2013).

Evans, C. A. — *Mark 8:27—16:20* (Word Biblical Commentary v. 34B; Nashville, TN: Thomas Nelson, 2001).

Guelich, R. A. — *Mark 1—8:26* (Word Biblical Commentary v. 34A; Waco, TX: Word Books, 1989).

Halliwell, S., W. Hamilton Fyfe, D. A. Russell, and D. Innes (eds.) — *Aristotle: Poetics, Longinus: On the Sublime, Demetrius. On Style* (Loeb Classical Library; Cambridge, MA: Harvard University Press, 1995).

Kelber, W. H. — *The Oral and the Written Gospel: The Hermeneutics of Speaking and Writing in the Synoptic Tradition, Mark, Paul, and Q* (Philadelphia, PA: Fortress, 1983).

Liddell, H. G. — *A Greek-English Lexicon* (Rev. and augmented throughout by Sir Henry Stuart Jones with the assistance of Roderick McKenzie and with the co-Operation of many scholars; Oxford: Clarendon, 1996).

Louw, J. P., and E. A. Nida, eds. — *Greek-English Lexicon of the New Testament: Based on Semantic Domains* (New York, NY: United Bible Societies, 1989).

Marcus, J. — *Mark 8—16: A New Translation with Introduction and Commentary* (The Anchor Yale Bible; v. 27A; New Haven, CN: Yale University Press, 2009).

Moloney, F. J. — *The Gospel of Mark: A Commentary* (Peabody, MA: Hendrickson, 2002).

Weissenrieder, A., and R. B. Coote. — *The Interface of Orality and Writing: Speaking, Seeing, Writing in the Shaping of New Genres* (Biblical Performance Criticism 11; Eugene, OR: Cascade, 2015).

CHAPTER 12

# The View from the Ditch: Reading the Good Samaritan Parable as Wisdom not Virtue

Denise Powell

## Abstract

The parable of the Good Samaritan is often understood as promoting altruistic behaviour towards our neighbour. As such, the message of the parable is: we should always be ready to act with selfless concern for the welfare of others, no matter who they are. In this chapter, I argue that the parable of the Good Samaritan can be read as a parable of pragmatic wisdom rather than one that primarily encourages virtue. Responding to a neighbour with compassion and mercy is a wise course of action that is ultimately in our best interests. This reading has much in common with other Lukan *Sondergut* parables that can also be read as wisdom parables. Placing the parable of the Good Samaritan alongside the real-world scenario of 'vaccine diplomacy' as an experiment in intertextuality both illustrates this reading of the parable and offers further insights into how the parable may be read as pragmatic wisdom.

## Introduction

The parable of the Good Samaritan has traditionally been understood as a story promoting selfless action towards our neighbour. Considering the parable through the lens of wisdom, however, suggests other interpretive possibilities, particularly when the parable is placed alongside an analogous contemporary situation in which helping a neighbour is in the best interests of the helper. This chapter argues that a valid reading of the parable of the Good Samaritan is one which provokes the audience to consider the pragmatic wisdom of generosity towards a neighbour.

The essay begins with a definition of wisdom as understood in Israel's Scriptures. This is followed by a brief discussion of four Lukan *Sondergut* parables from Luke 14—16, all of which promote action motivated by pragmatic wisdom. This discussion demonstrates that reading the Good Samaritan parable as a wisdom parable is, therefore, internally coherent. Next, the essay describes Mark Allan Powell's Tanzanian experience with the Good Samaritan parable in which the traditional Western understanding of the parable is inverted. Powell's experience provides the impetus for seeing 'intertextual' connections between the current global issue of 'vaccine diplomacy' and the Good Samaritan parable.

## Wisdom

Wisdom, as understood in Israel's Scriptures, is grounded in 'careful observation of life, especially the consequences of particular patterns of human behaviour'.[1] Wisdom literature explores how the world works rather than how the world *should* work. Wisdom is not necessarily virtue and, in fact, it can involve craftiness or cunning. It can encompass shrewd politics, pragmatism, even technical skill required to complete a difficult task.[2] Wisdom literature does not provide definitive instructions, but rather challenges its readers to reflect upon what is being said. After weighing up what is said against their own experience, readers are free to decide on an appropriate course of action for their specific

---

1  Lucas, *Exploring the Old Testament*, 80.
2  McLaughlin, *An Introduction to Israel's Wisdom*, 2–4.

circumstances. The goal of wisdom is not rigid adherence to a moral code, but mastery of life.³

## Four *Sondergut* Parables of Wisdom

Several parables in Luke 14—16 promote wisdom in the sense of calculated or shrewd action. In Luke 14:7–11, Jesus advises guests, 'When you are invited to a wedding feast, do not take the place of honour'. If a more important person arrives, Jesus warns, the first guest may find himself being moved to a seat of lesser importance, a disastrous outcome in an honour-shame culture. Instead, a guest should choose the least important place since, when the host notices, it may result in the guest being moved to a more important position. The motivation for choosing the least important seat is not altruism, but shrewd calculation; the way to the most important seat is by choosing the least important seat. Jesus is not dismissing notions of status but reinforcing them by promoting the advantage of a lowly position as the way to receive great honour.⁴ In the Kingdom of God, those who exalt themselves will be humbled, while the humble will be exalted (14:11).⁵

Jesus goes on to advise those hosting banquets,

> When you host a banquet, don't invite your friends or rich neighbours so you can be invited by them in return and get repaid. But when you host a banquet, invite the poor, the crippled, the lame and the blind. Then you will be blessed, *because* they cannot repay you, for you will be repaid at the resurrection of the righteous [emphasis added] (14:12–14).

The motivation for inviting the needy is not altruism but the benefit of repayment at the resurrection. The thought of Jesus suggesting to his followers that they act out of self-interest seems distasteful, and some scholars are intent on letting Jesus off the hook. Kistemaker,

---

3   McLaughlin, *An Introduction to Israel's Wisdom*, 5.
4   Levine and Witherington, *The Gospel of Luke*, 393. Carroll, *Luke: A Commentary*, 298–99.
5   The banquet motif in this passage resurfaces numerous times in the cluster of parables in Luke 14—16 finally culminating in the reversal of the plights of the rich man and Lazarus in Luke 16. In each case, the motif alludes to the eschatological banquet.

commenting on Luke 14:7–14 says Jesus 'teaches that our deeds should be performed without a thought of reciprocity'[6] even though an honest reading of the text implies the opposite.

Arguably, the same shrewdness can be seen in the decision of the younger son in the following chapter as he surveys his situation in the pig pen. Generations of readers have imagined the moment of the son 'coming to his senses' (15:17) as one of genuine remorse. An alternative reading is one in which the son has a moment of pragmatic wisdom and hatches a cunning plan to save himself.[7] This reading is supported by the first words of the son's interior monologue. It is not remorse for his past actions that is forefront in the son's mind but an unfavourable comparison of his desperate situation with that of his father's day labourers. This is typical of Luke's use of interior monologue which, in all other cases, reveals the morally ambiguous motivations of the character.[8]

Immediately following the parable of the prodigal son is the curious parable of the unjust manager (16:1–9) in which a prodigal manager is commended for acting *phronimōs*. Louw and Nida define *phronimōs* as an 'understanding resulting from insight and wisdom'.[9] In this case, the manager's wise action involved shrewdly weaselling his way into the good books of his master's clients to avoid a life of manual labour or begging on the streets. The punchline of the parable—make friends for yourselves by means of dishonest wealth so that when it is gone, they may welcome you into the eternal homes (16:9 NRSV)—serves as a proof text for the parable of the rich man and Lazarus (16:19–31). If the rich man had been wise enough to 'make friends' with Lazarus, he would have found himself welcomed into Lazarus' eternal home. Instead, the rich man's lack of wisdom in the way he used his wealth resulted in him being in a 'place of torment' (16:28).

The interpretation and implications of the parables discussed above are not the focus of this paper. Rather, the discussion highlights that

---

6   Kistemaker, *The Parables of Jesus*, 160.
7   Levine, *Short Stories*, 53. Levine suggests 'first-century listeners may have heard not contrition, but conniving'.
8   See Simon the Pharisee (7:39); the rich fool (12:17); the unjust manager (16:3); the unjust judge (18:4–5).
9   L&N 32.31.

each of the parables has characters who either acted, failed to act, or are urged to act with wisdom for their own self-interest.[10]

## Powell's Reader Response Experience

Considering the above parables as promoting shrewd wisdom rather than virtuous action may feel uncomfortable. But, as parable scholars affirm, the very nature of a parable is to provoke and disturb. Gooder says it best:

> I would say that the rule of thumb for interpreting parables – if you're tempted to go 'Oh that's nice' at the end of a parable, you've probably interpreted it wrong. What you should do at the end of a parable is feel *really* uncomfortable. If you're feeling *really* uncomfortable, then you may be somewhere in the ballpark of a good interpretation [emphasis reflects speaker's emphasis].[11]

Reader response criticism is well suited to unveiling alternative and sometimes more compelling, albeit disturbing, readings. In *Chasing the Eastern Star: Adventures in Reader Response Criticism*, American narrative critic Mark Allan Powell describes his experience with the parable of the Good Samaritan:

> I have heard, read, preached, and taught this tale for decades – mostly in mainline, middle-class Protestant churches. The details of interpretation and application have varied over time, but the general consensus has always been that 'the moral of the story' is that we ought to be willing to help anyone in need. Our commitment to relieving human suffering ought to transcend political, ethnic, and other sorts of rivalries: Who is my neighbour? Anyone who needs my help. ... So, I was a little surprised when I went to live in Tanzania and

---

10 For an intriguing and more detailed discussion on the place of wisdom in the parables of Luke 14–16, see Emmrich, *Heart of Luke*.
11 Gooder, 'Preaching Luke', 48:40. See also Levine, *Short Stories*, 3.

discovered that many people there understand the story differently. The 'moral of the story', these Tanzanians told me, is that people who have been beaten, robbed, and left for dead cannot afford the luxury of prejudice. They will (and should) accept help from whoever offers it. When grain is bought to a famished village, parents of starving children do not much care whether the Moslems, the Roman Catholics, or the Jehovah's Witnesses bring it. ...In short, the story was understood to answer the question 'Who is my neighbour?' not with 'Whoever needs my help' but with 'Whoever helps me'.[12]

This difference in interpretive perspective is, at least partially, a result of 'empathy choice'. Readers empathise with the character in the story with whom they most identify, perhaps because of their ethnicity, life experiences or social location. The Tanzanians had more experience in viewing life from the perspective of the injured man in the ditch than the mainline, middle-class American Protestants, who are more often in a position to give material help, and thus see the story from their position on the road.

Powell argues that the Tanzanian reading more closely aligns with the textual clues in the parable. As many have pointed out, there is a shift in perspective from the lawyer's initial question, 'Who is my neighbour?' to the question that Jesus asks at the end of the parable: 'Which of these three *became* a neighbour to the man?'.[13] Jesus suggests that the better question is not 'Is that man in the ditch my neighbour?' but 'Which of the men on the road is my neighbour?' The adaptation of the question suggests that Jesus wants the lawyer to view the situation from the ditch, to put himself in the shoes of the victim rather than those of the rescuer. From the victim's perspective, the theological musing of where neighbourly boundaries lie is of no concern. His overriding concern is to get out of the ditch, and he will gratefully accept help from anyone, even a Samaritan, a person he might not normally consider to be a neighbour.

---

12 Powell, *Chasing the Eastern Star*, 23. Levine testifies to a similar interpretation from a citizen of Sierra Leone. *Short Stories*, 73.
13 For example, Carroll, *Luke*, 246; Garland, *Luke*, 445; Forbes, *The God of Old*, 66–67.

## The Good Vaccine Supplier: An Exercise in Intertextuality

Powell's experience made such an impression on me that I have never been able to read the parable in the same way again. So, as I read various news articles in 2021 on the global vaccine rollout and the rise of vaccine diplomacy (which I define below), I could not help but see it as the parable of the Good Samaritan playing out before my eyes.

While there have been many complex challenges in the global vaccine rollout, one concern expressed by the World Health Organisation is the disparity of vaccine accessibility between wealthy and low-income countries. According to *Nature* journal, as of 30 July 2021, 'More than half of the population of high-income countries has received at least one dose of a COVID-19 vaccine, compared with about... 14% in lower-middle-income countries and 1% in low-income countries'.[14] As Arthur Caplan, director of the NYU Langone health system's medical ethics division reflected, 'There have been a few examples of sharing vaccines with a neighbor, but not many. We have failed, miserably, to distribute the supplies we have to those most in need'.

During the pandemic, Australia found itself in the role of neighbour in a real-world Samaritan scenario of its own. Consider this news article from ABC News on 2 August 2021:

> On two sides of Papua New Guinea's capital, there are duelling vaccine rollouts run by Australian and Chinese representatives taking place. In the face of a contagious new variant and widespread vaccine hesitancy, PNG is *taking help from any neighbour offering it*. [emphasis added] But vaccines have become a loaded political issue lately. On a Saturday morning in the car park of Papua New Guinea's biggest shopping centre, the country's first pop-up clinic has just opened. Music is playing, free shirts are being given away, and importantly, people are getting their jabs. While this Port Moresby clinic is being run by PNG's health authorities, Australian embassy staff are on site helping, and almost everyone is wearing face masks and shirts emblazoned with the 'AusPNG Partnership'

---

14  Maxmen, 'COVID boosters'.

logo. On the other side of the city, at Port Moresby's biggest hospital, another vaccine clinic has been set up. But this one is being run by a visiting Chinese medical team administering doses of the Sinopharm vaccine.

A little later in the article:

PNG's Health Minister, Jelta Wong, said the country did not 'take sides'. 'We are thankful to Australia for giving vaccines and we are thankful to China for giving vaccines', he said. 'Both countries help us in many ways, and *we will always be in debt to them* [emphasis added] for the times Papua New Guinea was in need and they came to our aid'.[15]

The news article gives PNG's 'view from the ditch' of the two neighbours who stopped to help: Australia and China. Papua New Guinea wisely accepted help from both neighbours in order to protect its own people.

But note the response of PNG to its two neighbours: 'we will always be in debt to them'. The analogous PNG situation suggests another element of the parable that is hiding in plain sight. Once we have viewed the parable from the perspective of the man in the ditch, our view from the road is inevitably altered. The Lukan parable is clear that the Samaritan acted altruistically, motivated by compassion. He neither expected nor demanded reciprocity. However, having viewed the story from the ditch, we now understand how indebted the injured man must feel towards the neighbour who showed mercy. And even more when the social milieu of the first-century Graeco-Roman world is taken into account.

As many scholars have shown, reciprocity (the giving and receiving of favours) was a key element in the Graeco-Roman culture.[16] DeSilva has demonstrated, from writers such as Aristotle, Cicero, Seneca, and the Jewish sage, Yeshua Ben Sira, the subtle tensions involved in reciprocity within patron-client relationships, that is, relationships between people of unequal social status.[17] Because resources and

---

15 Whiting, 'PNG caught in China-Australia power play'.
16 For example, DeSilva, *Honor*; Crook, 'Patronage'.
17 DeSilva, *Honor*, 95–119.

opportunities given by a wealthy and high-status patron could not be repaid in kind by the less wealthy lower status client, the client repaid the favour in public praise and loyal allegiance. This reciprocity was not seen as transactional but as relational. What matters is not the gift, but the relationship of mutual commitment expressed by the gift, and the reciprocal gratitude. Seneca described reciprocity as a 'dance of grace' in which a benefit given circles around to ultimately benefit the giver.[18] The patron must never give out of self-interest, with an expectation of reward, but the client is duty bound to respond with gratitude and allegiance. As deSilva, channelling Seneca, states: 'While the giver is to train his or her mind to give no thought to the return and never to think a gift lost, the recipient is never allowed to forget his or her obligation and the absolute necessity of making a return'.[19]

Consider the level of indebtedness that has been created in the parable's cultural setting. Jesus (via Luke) describes the long litany of favours given by the Samaritan to the injured man. Not only did the Samaritan stop while others passed by, he also bandaged the injured man's wounds, poured olive oil and wine on them, put the man on his own animal, brought him to an inn and took care of him. The Samaritan then paid the innkeeper to care for the injured man and promised to return to cover any additional expenses. In a culture where reciprocity is the only honourable response to favours, such a debt cannot be forgotten. Such overwhelming generosity will be repaid by an enduring allegiance to the Samaritan.[20]

This must raise an unsettling consideration for the lawyer who questioned Jesus. Having viewed the story from the perspective of the man in the ditch, the lawyer's perception has been altered even as he places himself back in the shoes of the passers-by on the road. The relational nature of reciprocity precludes crossed loyalties. A client may receive benefits from two patrons but only if they are not rivals to each other. Receiving benefits from patrons who were rivals or enemies would place the client in an untenable position; loyalty towards

---

18  DeSilva, *Honor*, 105–06.
19  DeSilva, *Honor*, 117.
20  Crook suggests the allegiance even crosses generational lines. Crook, 'Patronage', 45.

one would betray the other.²¹ How does the Jewish lawyer feel about the injured man owing a debt of allegiance and loyalty to a Samaritan? From the lawyer's perspective, the non-action of the priest and Levite now looks like folly, as well as a lack of compassion. If either had acted as a neighbour, the man in the ditch would not be indebted to a Samaritan.

PNG found itself indebted to two nations, China and Australia. This is a politically sensitive topic, and it is not the purpose of this article to discuss the political motivations of any nation. Nonetheless, the rival vaccine rollouts in PNG were dubbed by the media as 'vaccine diplomacy', the notion that countries making highly publicised donations of vaccines to low and low-middle income countries may be using such donations as political leverage.

Other news articles reported some consequences of vaccine diplomacy. The National Defense Industrial Association is a United States trade association of military manufacturers promoting defence and national security. A recent article in their magazine, *National Defense* is titled 'Vaccine Diplomacy in Latin America, Caribbean a PR Coup for China'.²² The article highlights the rising cases of COVID-19 in Latin America and addresses the perception that the United States did not adequately contribute to the supply of vaccines for Latin America. In contrast, the article says, China conducted clinical trials of its Sinovac and Sinopharm vaccines in various Latin American countries and subsequently supplied them with vaccine stocks. The article labelled these actions as 'vaccine diplomacy used to advance political and other strategic objectives'. It went on to note that Brazil and the Dominican Republic 'reversed prior commitments to exclude the Chinese vendor Huawei from their nations' 5G networks, after receiving Chinese commitments to deliver their vaccines'. The article concluded, 'It is in the strategic interest of the United States to help our neighbors more rapidly and effectively vaccinate their populations, while more aggressively pushing back against the Chinese narrative that China is generously rescuing the region'.

---

21  DeSilva, *Honor*, 116.
22  Ellis, 'Vaccine Diplomacy'.

A few weeks later, on 4 August 2021, Joe Biden held a press conference updating the United States' response to the COVID pandemic. Speaking about vaccines, Biden said,

> As of today, we have shipped over 110 million doses to 65 nations. According to the United Nations this is more than the donations of all 24 countries that have donated any vaccines to other countries, including China and Russia... These vaccine donations are free. We're not selling them. There are no demands, no conditions, no coercion attached. And there's no favouritism, no strings attached. We're doing this to save lives and end this pandemic. That's it. In fact, we're donating vaccines to countries we have real issues with.[23]

Without speculating on the motivations of any nation, these various press statements and news reports resonate with the Lukan parable of the Good Samaritan and its Graeco-Roman culture of reciprocity. Placing the parable of the Good Samaritan alongside media reports of the current global COVID vaccine rollout creates a dialogue between the two 'texts' that provoke new insights into both the parable and the impact of vaccine diplomacy.

In what ways then, does the rise of vaccine diplomacy inform our reading of the parable, and in what ways can the parable serve as a lens through which to view the global vaccine rollout? Is it valid to use the parable to promote a calculating and manipulative approach to helping our global neighbours? Do we give to less materially wealthy nations, in order to secure their political allegiance? No. This reading would be reading against the grain of the text. In contrast to the priest and the Levite, who saw the injured man and passed by, the Samaritan saw the man and *was moved with compassion*. The parable is clear that the Samaritan did not act from calculated self-interest. Jesus' instruction to the lawyer to 'Go and do likewise' encourages not manipulative behaviour designed to trap our neighbour into indebtedness towards us but merciful action motivated by compassion.

Nonetheless, the lawyer must surely find himself both unsettled by

---

23  Biden, 'President Biden Delivers Remarks', 13:28.

the reciprocity now owed to the Samaritan by the injured man and regretting the folly of the priest and Levite in missing the opportunity to participate in the reciprocal dance of grace. The rise of vaccine diplomacy highlights that acting with compassion towards our global neighbours is not only virtuous but is also a wise course of action.

Finally, in the honour-shame culture of the Graeco-Roman world, the lawyer must surely be shamed by the fact that a Samaritan benefactor has shown up the priest's and the Levite's lack of compassion towards a neighbour. Jesus' instruction to 'go and do likewise' is a challenge to the self-righteousness of the lawyer who, we are told, set out to prove himself righteous in asking Jesus 'who is my neighbour?' If vaccine diplomacy shames some nations, including our own, into being more generous neighbours then so be it. Perhaps the rise of vaccine diplomacy will prompt us to view life from the ditch, allowing us to stand in the shoes of our global neighbours who have less material wealth, and prompt political decisions that will benefit us both.

Denise Powell
Australian College of Ministries
Sydney College of Divinity

## Bibliography

Biden, J.     'President Biden Delivers Remarks on Progress Toward Fighting the COVID-19 Pandemic', Twitter, 4 Aug 2021, 32:44. https://twitter.com/i/broadcasts/1OdJrVzWoOYJX.

Carroll, J. T.     *Luke: A Commentary* (New Testament Library; Louisville, KY: Westminster John Knox, 2012).

Crook, Z. A.     'Patronage', in Z. A. Crook (ed.), *The Ancient Mediterranean Social World* (Grand Rapids, MI: Eerdmans, 2020), 45–63.

DeSilva, D.     *Honor, Patronage, Kinship & Purity* (Downers Grove, IL: IVP Academic, 2012).

Ellis, R. E.     'Vaccine Diplomacy in Latin America, Caribbean a PR Coup for China', *Nation Defense*, 12 July 2021. https://www.nationaldefensemagazine.org/articles/2021/7/12/vaccine-diplomacy-in-latin-america-caribbean-a-pr-coup-for-china.

Emmrich, M.     *At the Heart of Luke: Wisdom and Reversal of Fortune* (Eugene, OR: Pickwick, 2013).

Forbes, G.     *The God of Old: The Role of the Lukan Parables in the Purpose of Luke's Gospel* (Sheffield: Sheffield Academic Press, 2000).

Garland, D.     *Luke* (Grand Rapids, MI: Zondervan, 2012).

Gooder, P.     'Preaching Luke, Hope for Our Times (Part 1)', 2016 Clergy Conference Anglican Diocese of Toronto, filmed 30 May 2016. 53:52, https://www.youtube.com/watch?v=O4MG02deAgg.

Kistemaker, S.     *The Parables of Jesus* (Grand Rapids, MI: Baker Books, 1980; repr., 1994).

Levine, A.-J. and B. Witherington III.     *The Gospel of Luke* (NCBC; Cambridge: Cambridge University Press, 2018).

Levine, A.-J.     *Short Stories by Jesus: The Enigmatic Parables of a Controversial Rabbi* (New York, NY: HarperCollins, 2014).

Louw, J. P., and E. A. Nida     *Greek-English Lexicon of the New Testament: Based on Semantic Domains* (electronic edn of the 2nd edn; New York, NY: United Bible Societies, 1996).

Lucas, E. C.     *Exploring the Old Testament: A Guide to the Psalms & Wisdom Literature*, vol. 3 (Downers Grove, IL: InterVarsity Press, 2003).

Maxmen, A.     'COVID boosters for wealthy nations spark outrage', *Nature.com*, 19 August 2021. https://www.nature.com/articles/d41586-021-02109-1.

McLaughlin, J.     *An Introduction to Israel's Wisdom Traditions* (Grand Rapids, MI: Eerdmans, 2018).

Powell, M. A.     *Chasing the Eastern Star: Adventures in Reader Response Criticism* (Louisville, KY: Westminster John Knox, 2001).

Whiting, N.     'PNG caught in China-Australia power play as COVID-19 Delta variant infiltrates Pacific nation', *ABC News*, 2 August 2021. https://www.abc.net.au/news/2021-08-02/png-caught-between-australia-and-china-as-it-fights-delta/100329206.

CHAPTER 13

# From Petitionary Rhetoric to Eschatological Vindication: Comparing the Widow Aurelia Artemis from Theadelphia with Jesus' Persistent Widow (Luke 18:1–8)

James R. Harrison

## Abstract

The Lukan parable of the unjust judge (18:1–8), in which a widow persistently presents her petition for justice before an unresponsive judge, has not been examined against the backdrop of the papyrus petitions of antiquity. This chapter, after briefly touching on the 'widow' petitions in the papyri, will explore the rhetorical strategies of Aurelia Artemis of Theadelphia in her three petitions to the Roman governor of Egypt, comparing and contrasting their rhetoric and character presentation with that of Luke 18:1–8. In considering the respective audiences of Aurelia Artemis and the Lukan parable, we will be better placed to assess the parable's meaning in its original Palestinian context and to evaluate the integrity of its Lukan retelling three generations later.

At the outset, two brief prefatory remarks on the methodological problems facing the New Testament historians in such a task are apposite. First, in regards to the funerary inscriptions of women, very little about their honorands is revealed, widowed or otherwise.[1] As far as Luke 18:1–8, there are no relevant petitions from widows because the evidence of our epigraphic petitions is confined to imperial rescripts responding to petitions from private individuals, cities, and estates.[2] Second, in regards to the papyri, there is gratifyingly petitionary evidence from widows in Roman Egypt available for investigation. Unfortunately, very few of the petitions precede or are contemporary with the New Testament period, notwithstanding the large corpus of petitionary papyri we have.[3] Apart from a few exceptions (P. Lond. 7.176 [253 BC]; P. Oxy II 261 [55 AD], *infra*), our papyrus petitions relating to widows mostly belong to Late Antiquity. Furthermore, petitionary references to widows have their own stereotypical elements, often emphasising the motif of 'womanly weakness', which stands in sharp contrast to the portrait of the feisty widow in our Lukan parable. The social reality of such references is more likely rhetorical, 'seeking by such a *captatio benevolentiae* to urge the particular attention of a magistrate to the matters brought before him by a widow and her needs'.[4]

In sum, the documentary approach of our study allows us to draw rhetorical contrasts between different documents from different periods, each with different agendas, and each reflecting historical realities that are not readily accessible because of their rhetorical overlay.[5]

1  Mueller, *Strategies for Survival*, 79.
2  On petitions of private individuals and city-states to the imperial rulers, see Turpin, 'Imperial Subscriptions'; Hauken, *Petition and Response*; Hauken, 'Structures and Themes in Petitions to Roman Emperors'; Kallmes, *Petitions in the Epigraphic Record*.
3  Kotsifou ('A Glimpse into the World of Petitions', 318 n.1) writes regarding the spread of petitionary evidence spanning the Hellenistic, Roman and Late Antique periods: 'More than a thousand petitions survive from the entire papyrological millennium'.
4  Bagnall, 'Women's Petitions in Late Antique Egypt', 59.
5  In a Jewish context, the petition of Babatha against two guardians whom she brought to the notice of the governor of the province (P. Yadin 14–15, 27) might also be considered here. See Grubbs, *Women and the Law in the Roman Empire*, 250–52; cf. Cotton, 'The Guardianship of Jesus Son of Babatha'. Interestingly, there is no rabbinic parabolic counterpart to Luke 18:1–8 (cf. McArthur and Johnston, *They Also Taught in Parables*, 181–96). Is the parable's eschatology a distinctive which the rabbis eschewed? In the wider ancient Near Eastern context, see the Egyptian papyrus of the eloquent peasant: Simpson, *The Literature of Ancient Egypt*, 31–49. For discussion, see Shupak, 'A New Source for the Study of the Judiciary and the Law of Ancient Egypt'.

The historical risks are real but such an approach should allow us to see what is rhetorically distinctive about Jesus' parable in its original context against such a papyrological backdrop. However, we need to recognise that the parables, which were originally delivered by the historical Jesus in an early first-century Palestinian context, underwent retelling in the preaching of the first generation of believers and were subsequently placed in the literary contexts of the Gospels for differing audiences. Consequently, each parable that has come down to us in the Gospel tradition may or may not reflect the original historical and social context of Jesus' ministry, given the theological creativity and pastoral concerns of each of the evangelists. Nevertheless, the documentary approach enunciated above, despite its embedded rhetorical complexities, should allow us to grapple successfully with the Lukan parabolic tradition in this instance.

## 1. Luke 18:1–8 in Modern Scholarship

Traditionally, in the hands of interpreters like Bede and Bonaventure, Jesus' parable about prayer (Luke 18:1) is one of dissimilarity: the merciful and just God is totally dissimilar to the unmerciful and unjust judge. Calvin, however, presses the similarity of the petition of the widow and believers. In Calvin's view, it is seen in their waiting upon the judge and God for their desired result.[6] Modern scholarship has long since moved beyond this traditional rhetorical construct of what is happening in the parable. The new interpretative question posed is whether the parable was ever about prayer, as Luke's contextual frame posits (Luke 18:1). The parable (Luke 18:2–5), it has been argued, is dissonant with its interpretative framework (18:1,6–8).[7]

---

6  Wright, *The Voice of Jesus in Six Parables and Their Interpreters*, 68–69.
7  Spicq, 'La parabole de la veuve obstinée et du juge inerte'; Linnemann, *Parables of Jesus*, 119–24; Jeremias, *The Parables of Jesus*, 153–57; Derrett, 'Law in the New Testament'; Bailey, *Through Peasant Eyes*, 127–41; Freed, 'The Parable of the Judge and the Widow'; Donahue, *The Gospel in Parable*, 180–85; Brandon, *Hear Then the Parable*, 175–77; Blomberg, *Interpreting the Parables*, 271–74; Herzog, *Parables as Subversive Speech*, 215–32; Bovon, 'Apocalyptic Traditions in the Lukan Special Material'; Hultgren, *The Parables of Jesus*, 252–62; Curkpatrick, 'Dissonance in Luke 18:1-8'; Cotter, 'The Parable of the Feisty Widow and the Threatened Judge'; Schottroff, *The Parables of Jesus*, 190–94; Snodgrass, *Stories with Intent*, 449–62; Haacker, 'Lukas 18:7 als Anspeilung auf den *Deus absconditus*'.

Consequently, it has been proposed that the parable was originally about justice, a pervasive theme in Luke's Gospel (e.g. Luke 1:46–55; 4:18–19; 6:20–26; 16:19–31). The evangelist has shifted the character framework of the parable, thereby creating the dissonance. In effect Luke has created a second parable, with a different theological and pastoral intent, turning the judge into the major character of the parable, as opposed to the original parable about an audacious widow whose sole quest was legal justice. This new superimposed framework, it is argued, changes the parable into an allegory.[8]

Others who assert the unity of the parable (Luke 18:1–8) claim that the widow is superfluous to the real thrust of the parable. Here the judge's actions are considered the real *leitmotiv* of the parable: namely, the divine vindication of the elect because of their perseverance in prayer. In this construct 'from the lesser to the greater' proposals (*a minori ad maius*) come strongly to the fore: God is entirely dissimilar to the judge, not needing to be badgered or cajoled into action on behalf of the elect.[9]

Furthermore, the parable should be situated in its wider eschatological context. The eschatological vindication of the elect (Luke 18:8a) hearkens back to Jesus' teaching about the eschatological crisis immediately preceding in Luke 17:22–37, provoked by the question of the

---

8   This assumes that an allegorical approach to Jesus' parables is misconceived. Elements of allegory were present in the Old Testament (2 Sam 12:1–10) and rabbinic parables (McArthur and Johnston, *They Also Taught in Parables*, 181–96). It is churlish to demand that the historical Jesus, a first-century Jew, did not on occasion employ allegorical elements in his parables (e.g. Matt. 13:24–30,36–43; Mark 4:3–20). This position derives from Adolf Jülicher's contention (*Die Gleichnisreden Jesu*) that parable and allegory are to be sharply differentiated. See the decisive critique, using the rabbinic evidence, of Fiebig, *Altjüdische Gleichnisse und die Gleichnisse Jesu*; idem, *Die Gleichnisreden Jesu im Lichte der rabbinischen Gleichnisse des neutestamentlichen Zeitalters*. For further discussion, see Johnston, *Parabolic Interpretation Attributed to Tannaim*; Young, *Jesus and His Jewish Parables*; Westermann, *The Parables of Jesus*. For excellent overviews of the issue, see McArthur and Johnston, *They Also Taught in Parables*, 95–101; Blomberg, *Interpreting the Parables*, 29–69.

9   However, note the legitimate objection of Schottroff (*The Parables of Jesus*, 193) to this approach: '… the conclusion has very often been taken as a *minore ad maius*: If even an unjust judge does justice, how much more will God. But the judge is not a mini version of God; he is God's opposite'. Contra, Blomberg (*Interpreting the Parables*, 272) argues: 'Jesus' description of an unscrupulous authority figure does not prevent one from seeing the judge as in some sense standing for God. The logic is a fortiori (from the lesser to the greater); the only aspect of the judge's behaviour which makes him resemble God is his rewarding the woman's persistent pleas. God is not being likened to one who normally cares little for justice or who is afraid of getting worn out'.

Pharisees in 17:21–21. Is this scenario merely an instance of Lukan redaction of a parable about an audacious widow seeking justice (Luke 18:1–5), which has been contextually adjusted to the wider theological context of eschatology (Luke 17:22–37)? If this is the case, Luke is pastorally comforting and equipping a suffering Christian community, animated by intense apocalyptic expectations, for its future endurance.[10]

Alternatively, does the unified parable (Luke 18:1–8) represent the pastoral instruction of the historical Jesus on how the elect should prepare themselves for the crisis precipitated by the advent of the eschaton? Luke sets the contextual frame for the parable, but it accurately reflects the wider pastoral and teaching strategies of the historical Jesus regarding the eschaton. Otherwise, what was the frame of the original parable if it is disconnected from its Lukan eschatological framework (Luke 17:22–37; 18:8a)? We are left in the dark: the unframed parable (Luke 18:2–5) reflects Luke's concern for justice, but in what regard and with what import?[11]

Last, a few commentators on the parable interact minimally with the papyrological evidence.[12] Wendy Cotter ranges more widely in the ancient sources in discussing the portraits of the judge and widow, referring to three 'widow' papyri, specifically, P. Tebt. 2.237, 334; P. Oxy. 63.4393.[13] She considers Luke's parable to be a burlesque of the entire legal system, unveiling prophetically the power available to those who operate outside of the social codes in their quest for justice.

What light, then, do the petitionary papyri throw on the plight of the widow and how does this enable us to better understand this Lukan parable?

---

10 Linnemann, *Parables of Jesus*, 119–20.
11 Bernard B. Brandon (*Hear Then the Parable*, 177) concedes that 'the parable demands an interpretation ... but that the parable demands this particular interpretation is not obvious'. Instead, Brandon proposes that 'Jülicher's original argument that the interpretation results from the church under persecution seems more likely' (ibid.). Contra, see Snodgrass, *Stories with Intent*, 455–56.
12 Schottroff, *The Parables of Jesus*, 192 (P.Oxy. 8.1120); Snodgrass, *Stories with Intent*, 452 (P. Mich. 29; P. Tebt. 776). Additionally, see Schottroff, *Lydia's Impatient Sisters*, 101–18.
13 Cotter, 'The Parable of the Feisty Widow', passim.

## 2. The Figure of the Widow in the Petitionary Papyri: A Case Study of Artemis of Theadelphia

### 2.1 General Epigraphic Examples of the Vulnerability of Women Occasioning Petitions in Hellenistic and Roman Egypt

Before we explore the three papyrus petitions of Artemis of Theadelphia, a brief exploration of other pertinent papyri is worthwhile. In rare cases, we see the vindication of the widow at the hands of the judge, either in the present or the recent past (P. Berl. 1024; P. Freib. 11).[14] But, in the papyri below, it is not always clear whether the elderly female petitioner is actually a widow or not, because her marital status is not explicitly stated in the papyrus. In some cases, it can probably be inferred (e.g. P. Berl. 1024, *infra*). In one case, it is the exploited daughter of a deceased widow who is the focus (P. Oxy. 34.2713). Notwithstanding, the papyri below reveal the vulnerability of females presenting petitions before the legal system, including the early appearance of the 'weakness' *topos* in the papyri.

- **P. Lond. 7.176 (253 B.C.)**

In this petition, Haynchis, a female beer seller, complains that her daughter had been seduced and taken away from her by a married man with children. The loss of her daughter meant that the mother's business collapsed, leaving the mother in a desperate struggle to acquire the necessities of life.[15]

- **P. Oxy. 2.261 (A.D. 55)**

In a petition of the elderly Demetria, the woman was accompanied in court by her male guardian or legal representative (*kyrios*)[16]—possibly a relative in this instance—and was legally represented by her grandson in the proceedings. Significantly, the petitioner is described as 'not being able to be in attendance in court on account of womanly weakness'.[17] Here we see that a prominent stereotype of female and widow petitioners in particular had emerged by New Testament times.

---

14  I am indebted to Mueller, *Strategies for Survival* for several of the examples below.
15  See Mueller, *Strategies for Survival*, 106.
16  See Kotsifou, 'A Glimpse into the World of Petitions', 322.
17  Grubbs, *Women and the Law*, 52–53.

- **P. Oxy. 34.2713 (A.D. 297)**

This is not a widow's petition but rather the petition of the young daughter of a deceased widow to the Egyptian prefect. She asks that the rightful third of her inheritance, corruptly appropriated by her two brothers, be reinstated. Importantly for our purposes, she depicts herself as a woman 'easily despised on account of the weakness of our nature'.[18]

- **P. Oxy. 1.71 (A.D. 303)**

A wealthy widow of high status, whose full name is not known due to papyrus damage (Aurelia G [– – –]), had hired two men to manage her affairs because her two sons, being in the army, were absent. Exposed to these crooks who unscrupulously manipulated her accounts, she had experienced the theft of two oxen (or cows).[19]

- **P. Freib. 11 (Early 4th cent. A.D.) / Chrest. Mitt. 126 (= P. Amh. 141: 4th cent. A.D.)**

In a revealing early fourth century A.D. papyrus, a widow, Aurelia Thaesis, who had successfully recovered her property in a previous petition, nevertheless continued to experience harassment at the hands of fellow villagers who beat her tenants.[20] In another petition (Chrest. Mitt. 126 [= P. Amh. 141]: 4th cent. A.D.), Aurelia mentions how she had experienced violence at the hands of her brother and his wife, again highlighting the motif of the 'weak widow':

---

18  See Grubbs, *Women and the Law*, 53–54. For a petition from a 'weak widow', see P. Oxy. 8.1120. Bagnall (*Egypt in Late Antiquity*, 95) cites the complaint of a woman (P. Oxy. 12.1470: A.D. 336) whose small land plot, bought for her by her (now deceased) father, had been illegally retained by her brother's agent. She portrays the agent 'as despising my orphan condition'. Bagnall (*Egypt in Late Antiquity*, 95: CPR 7.15 [A.D. 336]) also cites a papyrus which reveals that tax collectors were often disposed to collect twice from a widow. In a Roman imperial context, the emperors Septimius and Caracalla respond to thirteen legal questions in petitions from Alexandria from March 14–16 A.D. 200, including one from a widowed mother whose children require a guardian (P. Col. 123). The number of petitions dealt with by the Roman rulers in such a short period from just one region in the empire is remarkable. See Herz, *Playing the Judge*, 68–69.
19  See Mueller, *Strategies for Survival*, 122.
20  See Mueller, *Strategies for Survival*, 124. See Byren, 'Visibility and Violence in Petitions from Roman Egypt'.

He attacked me along with his wife Ria. They knocked me on the ground with their fearsome blows and nearly killed me with their punches and kicks all over my body, and there are bruises appearing on my face. They knocked me half-dead, and what is more, they tore my clothes. Thus, not being able to keep silent about this, since I am a weak and widowed woman, I submit this petition to you telling you about such things and asking that I receive justice from you.[21]

- **P. Berl. 1024 (4th/5th cent. A.D.)**

In this transcript of a legal case, an old impoverished woman, Theodora, had been forced to give her daughter to a brothel keeper in order eke out an economic existence for herself and her daughter. However, upon the murder of her daughter by an enamoured Alexandrian magistrate, a councillor called Diodemus, the mother petitions the Egyptian prefect for compensation, because she was now bereft of any financial support. The prefect, pitying Theodora's plight, condemns Diodemus to death and awards her one tenth of the councillor's property.[22]

In sum, from the seven papyrus examples above, the exposure of women generally and widows more specifically to a wide range of abuses (physical, sexual, financial, familial, legal, and theft of property) is graphically highlighted. These force Egyptian women to seek legal address by means of a petition in the court, the appeal extending at times as high as the Prefect of Egypt himself. At first blush, the petitioners range from wealthy women of high social status to the those victimised by their families or crooks, the impoverished, and elderly. But, as we will see in our case-study below, many of these Late Antiquity widows come from wealthy and powerful families, having ready access to and familiarity with the processes of the law courts. Such women are not bereft of support, being routinely attended by a male guardian or legal representative. Of vital importance for our understanding of Luke 18:1–8 is the frequent rhetorical self-representation of women in courts as 'weak', a strategy designed to manipulate

---

21 Byren, 'Visibility and Violence', 189–90, translation Byren.
22 See Mueller, *Strategies for Survival*, 105–6.

the judge into issuing a positive verdict in their favour.[23] We turn now to an investigation of Aurelia Artemis from Theadelphia, a case-study that will provide further valuable papyrological evidence for our petitionary profile of widows and other vulnerable women in the Egyptian courts.

## 2.2 Artemis from Theadelphia: A Case Study in the Petitionary Weakness of Women

In A.D. 280 a widow called Aurelia Artemis from Theadelphia, a village situated in the oasis of Fayum, launched three petitions for justice before the Roman prefect of Egypt on behalf of her underage children (P. Sakaon 31, 36, 37). The letters of Aurelia belong to an archive of Sakaon, an Egyptian farmer in Thaedelphia, and their contents span the period from A.D. 310 to c. 342.[24] The narrative of events in each letter of Aurelia was dictated to a scribe who wrote the complaint down, shaping it rhetorically into the petition presented at the legal proceedings by Aurelia's representative. The rhetoric employed in P. Sakaon 36 especially, where Artemis complains about a local notable invading her home and stealing her property, is a masterpiece in rhetorical strategy and in the arousal of the emotion of pity before the prefect with a view to carrying the day legally. Aurelia depicts herself as 'weak' and 'helpless', defenceless, powerless, and desperate, begging the judicial system to take cognisance of her vulnerabilities. This extended insight into the petitionary habits of widows in the Sakaon papyri may throw contrasting light upon Jesus' own rhetoric in Luke 18:1–8, albeit in a first-century Judean context as opposed to late Roman Empire Egypt.

In P. Sakaon 36 (A.D. 280), Aurelia Artemis petitions the governor (*epistrategos*) regarding the illegal actions of Sryion, an influential

---

23 For another (restored) example of the same rhetoric, see SB 16.12692 col. 1 (17 May A.D. 339 AD, Karanis): 'Since a lawsuit has arisen between us and the heirs of Atisis concerning [property, of which they allege that they] belonged [to our father] Atisis, even though they have absolutely nothing to do with him, and since I myself am not able [because I am a weak woman, to represent myself] before the defensor, who at the instructions of his Highness the Prefect of Egypt [to whom we submitted a petition?] has been given us as a judge, therefore I appoint and authorize you and give you full power to conduct the proceedings against them ... in accordance with the rights which belong to us, as if I were present'.
24 See Parássoglou, *The Archive of Aurelius Sakaon*.

figure in the community, towards her and her children.²⁵ She does not speak in court, but is represented by her advocate Isodorus, not even having a relative (*kyrios*) to accompany her in court, as was the case in P. Oxy. 2.261. First, the honorifics applied to the Roman prefect are revealing and strategic for securing his good will at the outset. The 'care of the governor for all, especially for women and widows' is mentioned prominently at the beginning. The restitution of her property by the governor's 'benevolent decision', who is designated 'lord and benefactor of all', is affirmed at the end of the petition, along with the expectation that 'the excellent *epistrategos* will judge the matter according to what is most just'. While such eulogies of the prefect are *de rigueur* in petitionary rhetoric, there is no lack of confidence expressed in the Egyptian court system, the generosity of the ruling prefect, and the rightful application of Roman justice to such cases. As Chrysi Kotsifou observes, '… the petitioner appeals to the governor's pride, at the same time indirectly reminding him of the importance of reciprocity in the relations between subjects and authorities'.²⁶

Second, the charge against Syrion is articulated clearly: upon the death of Aurelia's husband, Syrion exploited 'his local power' by taking 'hold of our flocks', along with 'the grain of my deceased husband' without any 'receipt for the payments in kind that were due'. He had sent Aurelia away with 'threats' when she tried to regain her property. There is very strong emotional emphasis on the death-bed nature of Syrion's theft: '… wishing to snatch away the property of my infant children from my husband's very bed and with his body lying there'.

Third, Aurelia's vulnerability as a widow is especially highlighted. Not only is the death-bed rapidity of Syrion's actions underscored, but also the ensuing position of Aurelia's abject weakness and, correspondingly, the malicious intent of Syrion is stated forcefully: it was always Syrion's nature 'to despoil me, a widow with infant children'.²⁷ The telling addition of *infant* children, mentioned four times in the petition,²⁸ adds pathos.

---

25  See Grubbs, *Women and the Law*, 257–58.
26  Kotsifou, 'A Glimpse into the World of Petitions', 323.
27  See Grubbs, *Women and the Law*, 258–59.
28  Kotsifou, 'A Glimpse into the World of Petitions', 322.

We do not know whether Aurelia was ultimately able to recover her children's property, but subsequently in P. Sarakon 31 (A.D. 280/281) we hear the reiteration of her complaint that Syrion, 'greedily eyeing the animals left to them by their father', had seized sixty of them. However, as this new petition points out, Syrion, who was away on important state business, had ignored the court adjudication to restore the flocks (goats and sheep: cf. P. Sarakon 37) to the children, a decision which had previously been issued against him by the *strategos* and governor.

Finally, in P. Sarakon 37 (January/February A.D. 284),[29] we learn that there exists a financial dispute between Aurelia Artemis and the sister-in-law of Aurelia, Aurelia Annous. The nub of the problem was that Aurelia Artemis claimed that she had paid the inheritance taxes on behalf of her sister-in-law, a donation which the latter denied. Thus Aurelia Artemis is faced with a double payment of the inheritance taxes and, consequently, in her petition she emphasises her needy and underage children six times. She demands that she be paid back what she is owed from her sister-in-law. Once again, the rhetorical tone of the plea to the governor is obsequious in its approach, reflecting the delicate protocols of the reciprocity system between social unequals as favours are potentially conferred:

> Therefore, I flee to your feet, begging and pleading on behalf of my underage children, so that you might order the strategos of the nome, or whomever your Magnificence approves, to force Annous to fulfil and render the accounts for the land, since she has received her paternal inheritance. For thus, having received aid, we will be able to acknowledge the greatest thanks to you for everything.

However, such petitions of the kind enunciated by Aurelia Artemis have to be treated with a measure of scepticism regarding the legitimacy of their rhetorical self-representation. As Chrysi Kotsifou notes, and as has been observed above (e.g. P. Oxy 1.71, *supra*), many of these Late Antiquity widows came from well-to-do families who would have

---

29  See Grubbs, *Women and the Law*, 259–60.

been able to provide the widow a *kyrios* from the wider household to accompany them to court (e.g. P. Oxy 2.61, *supra*).[30] Thus their depiction of social isolation, illustrated by their non-appearance at court, was designed to evoke pity on the part of the governor. Genuine cases of systemic and recent impoverishment certainly do exist (e.g. P. Berl. 1024 (4th/5th cent. A.D.; P. Lond. 7.176, *supra*), but many of our petitioners belong to the propertied classes (P. Freib. 11; P. Oxy. 1.71, *supra*). Therefore, the exaggerated depiction of womanly weakness and vulnerability on the part of widows such as Aurelia Artemis represents a calculated rhetorical ploy to garner the sympathy of the governor before whom their petition would be heard, with a view to a successful outcome of their plea.[31]

How do the three petitions of Aurelia Artemis compare to Jesus' parable of the persistent widow and the unjust judge of Luke 18:1–8. What similarities and contrasts in rhetorical approach do we notice in each case? Who are the important characters in each rhetorical scenario? What do the different rhetorical strategies demonstrate about Jesus' original parable, the context of the first-century A.D. Lukan community, and the late antique community of Thaedelphia in the oasis of the Fayum?

## 3. Luke 18:1–8 in Ancient Petitionary and Rhetorical Context

At the outset, the methodological riskiness of what we are undertaking should be noted. A first-century Lukan rendering of a Palestinian parable of the historical Jesus, which narrates a widow's petitionary process before a judge, is being compared to a third-century scribal rendering of the petitions of Aurelia Artemis, a widow from Roman Egypt, who narrates before the governor injustices done to herself and her sons. This comparison of narratives and characters ranges across different genres of evidence, each belonging to different cultural contexts and chronological eras. Nevertheless, there is common narrative

---

30  Kotsifou, 'A Glimpse into the World of Petitions', 321.
31  Kotsifou, 'A Glimpse into the World of Petitions', 321.

petitionary context, with the arbiters of the petitions also accorded attention in each instance, and in the case of the petitionary papyri, exhibiting rhetorical elements and stereotypical *topoi* which span the first three centuries A.D. If the Lukan rendering of the parable of Jesus retains distinctive elements in the face of a dominant Graeco-Roman petitionary tradition, we must ask what light that throws on the modern problems of dissonance and unity aired at the beginning.

We begin with the distinctive differences. First, the stereotypical rhetorical presentation of the feminine weakness and vulnerability of Aurelia Artemis, designed to evoke the pity of the governor, has no connection with the portrait of the determined, relentlessly feisty, and persistent woman of Jesus' parable (Luke 18:1–5). A highly vulnerable widow, expecting and trusting in divine mercy as a helpless suppliant, could viably have been presented within the traditions of Second Temple Judaism, should Jesus and the redactor of his teaching, Luke, have so desired. But, instead, we are presented with a woman who through her own efforts actively pursues justice as opposed to passively awaiting its divine extension to her. This distinctive is no doubt an emphasis of the historical Jesus, who dispenses with the meek and subservient role assigned to women in the courts, being ushered in and out by their male *kyrios*, if at all. This widow, as rendered by Jesus, does not keep to her expected social role.[32]

Second, within Graeco-Roman petitionary culture, the arbiter of justice, the governor, is depicted as dispensing just outcomes, on occasion out of pity for the suppliant (P. Berl. 1024; cf. P. Freib. 11). Even where no such outcome is indicated or necessarily guaranteed, the reciprocity culture that regulates social relations between unequals ensures that extravagant rhetorical honours are given the governor in the expectation that he might be induced to allocate favour to the petitioner. There is no prior indication in Graeco-Roman petitionary

---

32  Cotter, 'The Parable of the Feisty Widow', 341.

culture of a negative outcome.³³ This is even the case in Jewish petitions where Babatha speaks of the governor in this manner: '... giving thanks for the most blessed times of the governorship of the governor Julius Julianus ...' (P. Yadin 15).

However, in the parable of Jesus no such expectation is given: the judge is characterised dishonourably as neither fearing God nor caring what people thought (Luke 18:2,4). There is no sense of the LXX and Second Temple Judaism expectations regarding the impartiality of God as a judge and his attentiveness to the supplications of the fatherless and the widow, the care of whom was to be extended to his covenantal people (Prov. 6:35; Sir 35:12–25; cf. Exod. 22:21–24; Deut. 10:18; 14:28–29; 16:19; 24:17; 27:19; Job 24:3; 31:16–18; Ps. 68:5; 94:6; 146:9; Isa. 1:23; 9:17; Jer. 7:6; 22:3; Mal. 3:5; Zech. 7:10).³⁴ Jesus moves in directions diametrically opposed to the Graeco-Roman petitionary tradition, including its later Jewish expression in the papyrus archive of Babatha. Even though the judge in Jesus' parable eventually relents, it is not because of pity or reciprocation of honour, as per the Graeco-Roman petitionary tradition, but rather it is due to his exhaustion in the face of the widow's relentless barrage. Quite possibly, as Wendy Cotter suggests, a fear of public ridicule, through a loss of face in not being able to dismiss this 'serial pest', may have been another trigger for him to resolve the issue by granting her justice.³⁵

What commonality is there between the Graeco-Roman petition-

---

33 Note the clear expectation of justice from the petitioner in his address to the judge, the Prefect of Egypt, in P. Ryl. Gr. 2.113 (A.D. 133, Letopolis): 'Since therefore the case requires the exercise of your hatred of wrongdoers, I expect you, my lord and just judge, to hear me against them ...'. Even in very difficult circumstances, there is the expectation on the part of the petitioner that the correct legal processes will be carried out against his opponents (P. Erasm. 1.1: 148–147 B.C., Arsinoites [Fayum]): 'Thus, they have forced me to flee to you. I ask that you send my petition to the chrēmatistai who judge private matters, whose eisagōgeus is Harmodius, so that they may receive it for trial, and summon Herakleides and Horion via Theodoros, epistatēs of the village, and command them not to strip me, so as to prevent them from initiating thefts, nor to force their way into my house, nor to take pledges in any manner .....'. This does not imply, however, that injustice is somehow always circumvented. See SB 20.14401: 19 October A.D. 147, Arsinoites [Fayum]): 'Accordingly having likewise committed groundless acts of outrage against me too, lord, via those under him, if we ever want to make an approach to the strategus about his violence, up until now he has been dragging the present matters before the office of the strategus and it is they who sit in council with the judge'. On the corruption of judges in the late Empire, see Harries, *Law and Empire*, 153–71.
34 Oakman, *Jesus, Debt, and the Lord's Prayer*, 83. See Thurston, *The Widows*, 9–19.
35 Cotter, 'The Parable of the Feisty Widow', 341–42.

ary culture and Jesus' parable? Although Aurelia Artemis operates within the sharply defined boundaries of Graeco-Roman petitionary culture, she nevertheless shows a dogged perseverance. She continues her petitions without any known response from the governor: she extended all the correct honour rituals, maintains a strategic personal absence from the court in order to display her marginalised status, and adopts the persona of a weak woman in order to evoke the governor's pity. In her Graeco-Roman context, therefore, Aurelia Artemis is just as persistent as Jesus' widow. What distinguishes the persistence of Jesus' widow from Aurelia Artemis is her relentless commitment to justice as part of God's moral order, trusting in God's commitment to vindicate the fatherless and widows over their persecutors. Her persistence, therefore, is an expression of her deep faith in YHWH, despite experiences of injustice to the contrary. Consequently, she becomes an exemplum for believers facing sufferings in the present age and, in the future, the time of distress accompanying the final throes of the eschaton. There is no reason to assume that either the judge or the widow is prioritised over the other in Luke 18:1–8. Both the governor and the widow are accorded significant attention in Graeco-Roman petitionary culture and the same dual emphasis is reflected in Luke 18:1–8. But, as we have seen, Jesus' portrait of the widow and judge exhibits distinctive hues when considered against the backdrop of Graeco-Roman petitions. Consequently, a heavy Lukan redaction of Jesus' parable—transferring its focus from justice to eschatology and its genre from parable to allegory—is not likely, given the considerable attention that the special Lukan tradition (L) devotes to parables of the historical Jesus.

Additionally, the Lukan placement of the parable in a wider eschatological context (Luke 17:22–37) makes perfect sense if the eschatological application in 18:6–8a was originally attached to the parable's narrative (18:2–5). The emphasis on crying out to God 'day and night' so that God might bring justice to his chosen ones (Luke 18:7) is clarified elsewhere by the parable of the friend at midnight (Luke 11:5–8). As Blomberg rightly notes, 'this little parable is a twin to the parable of the unjust judge'.[36] The widow's continuous plea for justice before

---

36 Blomberg, *Interpreting the Parables*, 275.

an indifferent judge finds its counterpart in the unabashed request of the man at the door at midnight: the friend's shameless audacity (Luke 11:8) becomes a further paradigm for persevering prayer (11:9–10).[37] The coherence of Jesus' teaching across these two parables indicates that the prayer for eschatological vindication in Luke 18:6–8a was inexorably tied from the very beginning of the parabolic tradition to the exemplum of the widow and her successful petition before the judge (18:2–5). Justice will prevail for the elect through their shamelessly bold prayers and their faithfulness to God until the eschaton. There is also the hint that the elect will proleptically experience occasions of gracious release before the final vindication ('Will he keep putting them off?': Luke 18:7b), as the widow of our parable experienced herself.

Finally, there are clear Lukan redactional elements to the parable, above all the contextualising frames of prayer (Luke 18:1) and faithfulness until the eschatological return of the Son of Man (18:8b).[38] We have seen that the increasing emphasis on womanly weakness in the petitions of Roman Egypt became a strategy in Late Antiquity to extract favours from the Roman governor by the wealthy propertied classes, as opposed to the genuinely marginalised. The scribal composers of the petitions for widows such as Aurelia Artemis knew well the rhetorical 'rules of the game' that they had to play if they were to have legal success in the governor's court. By contrast, third generation believers such as Luke (Luke 1:1–4) transmitted the parabolic tradition of the historical Jesus intact, respecting not only its deeply unconventional social attitudes but also highlighting the strong justice and eschatological focus of Jesus' teaching. In a world where earthly justice was the preserve of the propertied classes and the powerful elites, Luke strove to alert marginalised believers to the importance of prayer in waiting for the triumph of the just God and his Son at the eschaton in the face of the prevailing uncertainties of the present evil age.

---

37  Hengel and Schwemer, *Jesus and Judaism*, 482.
38  Hengel and Schwemer, *Jesus and Judaism*, 482 n.23.

## 4. Conclusion

The traditional interpretation of Luke 18:1–8—which espoused the dissimilarity between the merciful and just God and the unmerciful and unjust judge—has been challenged by modern scholarly approaches to the parable. Some have argued that the original parable of the historical Jesus depicted an audacious widow who had quested after legal justice (Luke 18:2–5). However the third-generation evangelist allegorised the parable, providing its current (dissonant) interpretative framework of persevering prayer (18:1,6–8). By contrast, those who argue for the unity of the parable propose that the judge, not the widow, is the real focus, being totally dissimilar in its depiction of God, who, as the incomparably just Judge, does not need to be prompted to vindicate eschatologically his elect. The parable's pastorally charged eschatology (Luke 18: 6–8a, esp. v.7; cf. 11:5–8) is consonant with Jesus' preceding teaching on eschatological crisis (Luke 17:22–37), a response prompted by the Pharisees' question on the issue (17:20–21).

We have suggested that an interpretative way forward in this scholarly impasse could be conducted more effectively by comparing Jesus' parable in verses 2–8a with the Graeco-Roman petitions of widows and other imperilled women, assessing what is common and distinctive in each instance against this well-known rhetorical genre of antiquity. The 'weakness' motif of the widow in the papyrus petitions aligned well with the vulnerability of widows depicted in the literature of Second Temple Judaism, but it stood in sharp contrast to the feisty widow of the historical Jesus' parable. The indifference of the judge to the widow's relentless requests in Jesus' parable was inconsistent with the (largely) positive portrait of judges in establishing justice in the papyrus petitions. Notwithstanding, the perseverance of Aurelia Artemis in continuously seeking justice in the face of adverse circumstances resonated with the widow's relentless wearing down of the judge with her petitions in the parable.

In conclusion, we are witnessing here distinctives of the historical Jesus in his handling of these widespread rhetorical traditions found in petitions—at least, as rendered by Luke—in the Graeco-Roman world and in Second Judaism Temple, as well as his endorsement of thematic commonplaces in the same traditions. The complexity of Jesus' radical departure from and, simultaneously, commitment to diverse petitionary traditions in his first-century context means that we cannot easily play off the parable's characters (i.e. 'widow' versus 'judge') against each other in our redactional reconstructions of the tradition—which unhelpfully compartmentalise the overall message in the process—as the parable moved from initial kerygma to inherited oral tradition to written manuscript. This means that allowance should be made in a unified parable for the relentless quest for earthly justice, eschatological vindication, and petitionary persistence for its advent in the teaching of the historical Jesus (Luke 8:2–8a). To be sure, Luke frames the parable with redactional markers (Luke 8:1,8b), but nonetheless he has demonstrated that he is a very careful listener to and faithful reproducer of the parabolic tradition of the historical Jesus.

James R. Harrison
Sydney College of Divinity

## Bibliography

| | |
|---|---|
| Bagnall, R. S. | *Egypt in Late Antiquity* (Princeton, NJ: Princeton University Press, 1996). |
| Bagnall, R. S. | 'Women's Petitions in Late Antique Egypt', in R. S. Bagnall, *Hellenistic and Roman Egypt: Sources and Approaches* (Aldershot: Ashgate, 2006), 53–60. |
| Bailey, K. E. | *Through Peasant Eyes: More Lucan Parables, Their Culture and Style* (Grand Rapids, MI: Eerdmans, 1980). |
| Blomberg, C. L. | *Interpreting the Parables* (London: Apollos, 1990). |
| Bovon, F. | 'Apocalyptic Traditions in the Lukan Special Material: Reading Luke 18:1–8', *Harvard Theological Review* 90.4 (1997), 383–91. |
| Brandon, B. B. | *Hear Then the Parable: A Commentary on the Parables of Jesus* (Minneapolis, MN: Fortress, 1989). |
| Byren, A. Z. | 'Visibility and Violence in Petitions from Roman Egypt', *Greek, Roman and Byzantine Studies* 48 (2008), 181–200. |
| Cotter, W. | 'The Parable of the Feisty Widow and the Threatened Judge (Luke 18:1–8)', *New Testament Studies* 51 (2005), 328–43. |
| Cotton, H. | 'The Guardianship of Jesus Son of Babatha: Roman and Local Law in the Province of Arabia', *The Journal of Roman Studies* 83 (1993), 94–108. |
| Curkpatrick, S. | 'Dissonance in Luke 18:1–8', *Journal of Biblical Literature* 121.1 (2002), 107–21. |
| Derrett, J. D. D. | 'Law in the New Testament: The Parable of the Unjust Judge', *New Testament Studies* 18 (1972), 178–91. |
| Donahue, J. R. | *The Gospel in Parable* (Philadelphia, PA: Fortress, 1988). |
| Fiebig, P. | *Altjüdische Gleichnisse und die Gleichnisse Jesu* (Tübingen: Mohr Siebeck, 1904). |
| Fiebig, P. | *Die Gleichnisreden Jesu im Lichte der rabbinischen Gleichnisse des neutestamentlichen Zeitalters* (Tübingen: Mohr Siebeck, 1912). |
| Freed, E. D. | 'The Parable of the Judge and the Widow', *New Testament Studies* 33 (1987), 38–60. |

| | |
|---|---|
| Grubbs, J. E. | *Women and the Law in the Roman Empire: A Sourcebook on Marriage, Divorce, and Widowhood* (New York, NY: Routledge, 2002). |
| Haacker, K. | 'Lukas 18:7 als Anspeilung auf den *Deus absconditus*', *Novum Testamentum* 53 (2011), 267–72. |
| Harries, J. | *Law and Empire in Late Antiquity* (Cambridge: Cambridge University Press, 1999). |
| Hauken, T. | *Petition and Response: An Epigraphic Study of Petitions to Roman Emperors 181–249* (Athens: The Norwegian Institute at Athens, 1998). |
| Hauken, T. | 'Structures and Themes in Petitions to Roman Emperors', in D. Feissel and J. Gascou (eds.), *La Petition a Byzance: Table Ronde, XXe Congress International des Etudes Byzantines, 19–25 auot 2001* (Paris: Association des amis du centre d'histoire et civilization de Byzance, 2004), 11–22. |
| Hengel, M., and A. M. Schwemer | *Jesus and Judaism* (translated by W. Coppins; Waco, TX: Baylor University Press/ Mohr Siebeck, 2019). |
| Herz, Z. | 'Playing the Judge: Law and Imperial Messaging in Severan Rome' (PhD diss., Columbia University, 2018). |
| Herzog, W. R. III | *Parables as Subversive Speech: Jesus as Pedagogue of the Oppressed* (Louisville, KY: Westminster/John Knox, 1994). |
| Hultgren, A. J. | *The Parables of Jesus: A Commentary* (Grand Rapids, MI: Eerdmans, 2000). |
| Jeremias, J. | *The Parables of Jesus* (rev. edn; London: SCM, 1972). |
| Johnston, R. N. | 'Parabolic Interpretation Attributed to Tannaim' (PhD diss., The Hartford Seminary Foundation, 1977). |
| Jülicher, A. | *Die Gleichnisreden Jesu* (2nd edn, 2 vols; Tübingen: Mohr Siebeck, 1899). |
| Kallmes, K. | 'Petitions in the Epigraphic Record: Development of the Legal Order Outside of the Imperial Hierarchy' (Masters diss. in Greek, University of North Carolina, 2017). |
| Kotsifou, C. | 'A Glimpse into the World of Petitions: The Case of Aurelia Artemis and Her Orphaned Children', in A. Chaniotis (ed.), *Unveiling the Emotions: Sources and Methods for the Study of the Emotions in the Greek World* (Stuttgart: Franz Steiner Verlag, 2012), 317–27. |

Linnemann, E.     *Parables of Jesus: Introduction and Exposition* (London: SPCK, 1966).

McArthur, H. K., and R. M. Johnston     *They Also Taught in Parables: Rabbinic Parables from the First Centuries of the Christian Era* (Grand Rapids, MI: Academie, 1990).

Mueller, I.     'Strategies for Survival: Widows in the Context of Their Social Relationships' (PhD diss., University of Chicago, 2004).

Oakman, D. E.     *Jesus, Debt, and the Lord's Prayer: First-Century Debt and Jesus' Intentions* (Eugene, OR: Cascade, 2014).

Parássoglou, G. M., ed.     *The Archive of Aurelius Sakaon: Papers of an Egyptian Farmer in the Last Century of Theadelphia* ( Papyrologische Texte und Abhandlungen 23; Bonn: Habelt, 1978).

Schottroff, L.     *Lydia's Impatient Sisters: A Feminist Social History of Early Christianity* (Louisville, KY: Westminster John Knox Press, 1995).

Schottroff, L.     *The Parables of Jesus* (Minneapolis, MN: Fortress, 2006).

Shupak, N.     'A New Source for the Study of the Judiciary and the Law of Ancient Egypt: "The Tale of the Eloquent Peasant"', *Journal of Near Eastern Studies* 51.1 (1992), 1–18.

Snodgrass, K. R.     *Stories with Intent: A Comprehensive Guide to the Parables of Jesus* (Grand Rapids, MI: Eerdmans, 2008).

Spicq, C.     'La parabole de la veuve obstinée et du juge inerte, aux décisions impromptues (Lc. XVIII, 1-8)', *Revue Biblique* 68 (1961), 68–90.

Thurston, B. B.     *The Widows: A Woman's Ministry in the Early Church* (Minneapolis, MN: Fortress, 1989).

Turpin, W.     'Imperial Subscriptions and the Administration of Justice', *The Journal of Roman Studies* 81 (1999), 101–18.

Young, B. H.     *Jesus and His Jewish Parables: Rediscovering the Roots of Jesus' Teaching* (New York, NY: Paulist, 1989).

Westermann, C.     *The Parables* of Jesus in the Light of the Old Testament (Minneapolis, MN: Fortress, 1990).

Wright, S. I.     'The Voice of Jesus in Six Parables and Their Interpreters' (PhD thesis, Durham University, 1997).

CHAPTER 14

# Realised Eschatology in the Gospel and Letters of John: John's Focus and Purpose and why it still Matters to All Christians

Debra Snoddy

## Abstract

First popularised by C. H. Dodd (1884–1973) in 1935, realised eschatology can be defined as the theory that the eschatological passages in the New Testament refer not to a future apocalypse, but to an era which was inaugurated by Christ's presence and ministry on earth. In the Gospel of John we find a unique tension between Jesus' coming as the light and the difference this makes for the Johannine community's understanding of past, present, and future. Eternal life is a current reality but so is human death, it is a time of insight, but there are those who still remain in their blindness. Thus we find a dissonance in search of resolution which means moving forward until the dissonance resolves into harmony. But how does this happen in the Johannine Gospel? To what purpose? And does it still matter to Christians today? This essay will seek to trace several instances from the Johannine Corpus to show how and to what purpose the eschatological dissonance is resolved into a unique Johannine harmony. Further, it will show that not only was it relevant to the community of faith then, but how much more so it is of relevance to communities of faith now.

## Introduction

Those with even a brief acquaintance with the Gospel of John will know that for the author of the Fourth Gospel, Christology, eschatology, and soteriology often overlap, and it can be hard, at times, to differentiate between them. Johannine Christology cannot be collapsed into eschatology as to do so would skew faith perilously, and obscure the accents and nuances needed between them—Christology is bigger; perhaps one might say that Christology is the cause and eschatology the effect, but this too may be a violation of the sacred texts and their chameleon possibilities. Indeed, harmony and balance are as important in exegesis as they are in life. Mindful of this need for distinction, I will present one of many valid interpretations of John's polyvalent eschatology. One thing that is clear is that, from the very beginning of the Gospel, John presents his account from a resurrection faith perspective.[1] This has an impact on his eschatology as this paper will demonstrate. With Aune, I argue that 'the distinctive eschatological emphases of the Fourth Gospel are the expression of the traditional beliefs of the Johannine community and not the individualistic *Tendenz* of a creative theologian'.[2] The author writing for the community of believers is using forms of eschatology that they already know and understand. What is this eschatological form? And how is one to understand it?

---

1   This perspective is that Jesus lived, died and was resurrected by God to live eternally. One day Jesus will return to earth in the 'second coming' or Parousia to inaugurate a new reign for the faithful. Jesus' victory over death also conquered death for all the faithful. So Brown and Moloney, *Interpreting the Gospel and Letters of John*, 113. It is the last element, the conquering of death that proves to be pivotal for Johannine eschatology.
2   Aune, *Cultic Setting*, 64.

## Defining 'Eschatology'

The theological problems posed by the term 'eschatology' are numerous and complex,[3] not least because the semantics of the word have become problematic and muddled. Marshall notes that the term 'eschatology' has been used nine different ways.[4] Theologians discussing eschatology were using the same word, but mean different things.[5] Here the article by Charles Horne proves useful: he favours the view that eschatology is the controlling thematic of theology and examines the main proponents of eschatology and their stances *vis-à-vis* this branch of theology.[6] The diagram below is a visual aid to the discourse that follows it.

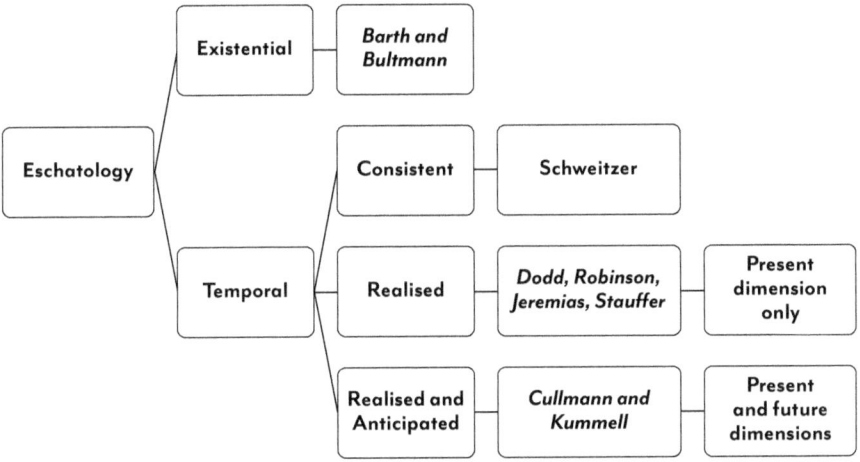

Rudolf Bultmann may be viewed as the proponent of the existential view of eschatology. In an attempt to make the message of the New Testament relevant to the modern age, 'as an exegete he is already

---

3   Allison, 'Eschatology', 209.
4   Marshall, 'Slippery words In Eschatology', 264–269.
5   Brower, '"Let the Reader understand"', 119, states that, 'Eschatology is a notoriously slippery word for which a bewildering variety of definitions confronts us'. See Rowland, 'Eschatology', and Sauter, *What dare we hope?*, 3 ff. for a thorough analysis and discussion of the problematic nature of the use and interpretation of the word 'eschatology'. Thomas, 'A Holy God', esp. 55, for example, interprets eschatology as the study of ultimate things, ultimate realities.
6   Horne, 'Eschatology', 53–63.

reinterpreting eschatology existentially in divesting it of its temporality'.[7] Karl Barth and Paul Tillich who also follow a more existential eschatology see that the 'universal relevance of eschatology was gained by a radical redefinition in which the horizon of the future disappeared into the eternal depths of the present moment'.[8] Neither Barth nor Bultmann gives a horizontal line of history that moves outward and forward. 'Theology was eschatological in terms of the vertical dialectic between eternity and time, above and below, but at the prize of the horizon of the future'.[9]

Of those espousing a more temporal view of eschatology, Albert Schweitzer advocates for a consistent eschatology or an exclusive futuristic eschatology—it may be considered 'the consistent interpretation of Jesus' eschatology as an expression of an imminent end' which, according to Schweitzer, proved to be an illusion.[10] The second temporal view is realised eschatology—an eschatology of the present, whose representatives number C. H. Dodd, J. A. T. Robinson, Joachim Jeremias, and Ethelbert Stauffer. This view holds that Jesus did not speak of an eschatological event in the distant future but of events in the impending history of Israel.[11]

Oscar Cullmann and W. G. Kummel assert that a realised and anticipated eschatology, with both a present and futuristic component, is the basic feature characterising Jesus' proclamation of the Kingdom of God. Cullmann asserts that the tension between the 'already' and 'not yet' is key to understanding NT salvation history.[12] Two 'days' as it were, the first at a midpoint in history where Jesus' Kingdom of God breaks the power of evil and the second the Parousia when these powers will be finally destroyed and the Kingdom fill the earth. Rudolf Schnackenburg and A. M. Hunter are among others representing a variant of this view, and use the formula, *promise, fulfilment,* and *consummation* wherein the *promise* made in the OT finds *fulfilment* in the

---

7   Horne, 'Eschatology', 59, quotation from Cullmann, *Salvation in History*, 41.
8   Horne, 'Eschatology', 59, quotation from Braaten, *The Future of God*, 22 ff.
9   Horne, 'Eschatology', 59, quotation from Braaten, *The Future of God*, 22 ff.
10  Horne, 'Eschatology', 59, quotation from Braaten, *The Future of God*, 19 ff.
11  Horne, 'Eschatology', 61.
12  Cullmann, *Salvation in History*, 166 ff.

NT when the kingdom irrupts into history with Jesus[13] and will reach *consummation* either in history (in the future) or at the end of history. This very brief survey of the scholarly positions regarding eschatology resolves something of the muddle many neophyte scholars experience on this topic. But what of the community of John? What is their eschatological view? How have scholars understood the eschatological frame of the Fourth Gospel?

## Trying to Gain Clarity for the Johannine Form of Eschatology

C. H. Dodd (1884–1973) in 1935 defined 'realised eschatology' as the theory that the eschatological passages in the New Testament refer not to a future apocalypse, but to an era which was inaugurated by Christ's presence and ministry on earth. Dodd based the development of his eschatology on Jesus' proclamation, as Dodd asserts:

> Something has happened, which has not happened before, and which means that the sovereign power of God has come into effective operation. It is <u>not</u> a matter of having God for your King in the sense that you obey His commandments: it is a matter of being confronted with the power of God at work in the world. In other words, the 'eschatological' kingdom of God is proclaimed as a present fact, which [humans] must recognize, whether by their actions they accept or reject it.[14]

Dodd's assertion would have one believe that there is only one possible form of eschatology, a present, realised form and Dodd held to this view firmly for much of his career. He expressed this view succinctly saying that, 'all that the church hoped for in the second coming of Christ is already given in its present experience of Christ through the Spirit'.[15]

---

13  Matthew 12:28 with Jesus' own assertion that the Kingdom has come.
14  Dodd, *The Parables of the Kingdom*, 29.
15  Dodd, *Apostolic Preaching*, 174. However, note the following comment by Keener, *The Gospel of John*, 1:320: 'Although C.H. Dodd emphasized realized eschatology, scholars point out that in his final publication he did allow that early Christian eschatology included a futurist element—ambiguously as he may have kept that concession'.

However, this is not the case. Rather, the academy has usually interpreted eschatology in at least three ways as David Aune has shown.[16] First, a minority of scholars emphasise the futuristic dimension, the 'end-times' eschatology as it were, wherein the realised dimension retains no independent significance because it is subject to the futuristic or apocalyptic elements. Second, those who assess realised eschatology as characteristic of Johannine theology and assert that apocalyptic eschatology has no place in the Gospel, a position not dissimilar to that of Dodd.[17] This form of a 'present tense' eschatology focuses exclusively on how salvation can be experienced now.[18] Union with God can be experienced at the moment one accepts Jesus as the Christ and the Son of God, and further, that one also believes that God's new covenant is put in place through Jesus. In this way then, a reign of God can be experienced in our time.

The third, the majority view, is accepted by those who affirm that both realised and futuristic aspects in eschatology are genuinely Johannine because 'they can and do exist together'.[19] My own position is a slightly more nuanced version of this third position. With Jürgen Moltmann, I assert that, 'from first to last ... Christianity is eschatology, is hope, forward looking and forward moving, and therefore also revolutionizing and transforming the present ... the key in which everything in it is set, the glow that suffuses everything here in the dawn of an expected new day'.[20] In a world increasingly experiencing unprecedented levels of hopelessness among all levels of society from all socio-economic backgrounds, this hope needs to be articulated and experienced. I do not, however, share his view that the future defines the present—this would be to make eschatology one-sided, for as Horne rightly points out, 'the theology of Hope comes very close to identifying God with the future'.[21] That said, hope is an integral part

---

16 For categories see Aune, *The Cultic Setting of Realized Eschatology*, 49–54. Major names include Schweitzer, C. H. Dodd, Rudolf Bultmann; Glasson, Robinson, to name a few.
17 Apocalyptic eschatology is viewed exclusively in terms of redactional intrusions or impractical survivals.
18 Brown and Moloney, *Interpreting the Gospel and Letter of John*, 114.
19 Brown and Moloney, *Interpreting the Gospel and Letters of John*, 114.
20 Moltmann, *Theology of Hope*,16.
21 Horne, 'Eschatology', 54.

of what it means to be a Christian (1 Pet. 3:15).²² It is possibly better to say that there is a merging of horizons, wherein the worlds of the past Christological event and present Christian context help to create God's future for what happened at the Christ-event. The past is not 'definitively past', but past as 'continuing into the present and moving forward to the future'. The *context* of the past (which is itself ongoing) then, facilitates one's understanding of the *content* of the present, enabling Christians to live into the *call* here and now to generate the ongoingness of the history of salvation which has not yet been consummated. The eschatological hope for the future makes the labour of the present worthwhile, spurring Christians into dynamic action for the establishment of the eternal kingdom, the gap between what is and what will be demands action from the communities of faith.

There is both a present and a future dimension to John's realised eschatology, but more than that, I assert that within the futuristic dimension there are both transitional eschatological and final eschatological elements. This means that the future dimension is split in two, the first stage being a provisional, intermediate, or in-between phase and the second part the ultimate or terminal stage. I leave open the question of whether realised eschatology involves an event in the process of being accomplished, or whether it is an act or a process. My own position is that it is both an act and a process, where the present and the future fulfilment of the promise of salvation are resolved in the current experience (act) and the imminent hope (process) of the believer. What this means is that John's concept of eschatology is not dependent of conventional notions of time.

> John's sense of time – his eschatology – is shaped by his recognition that in the coming of Jesus the light has made a decisive difference between the past and present. But John also knows that the present is the scene of conflicting claims. True life is a current reality, yet so is death; some people can now see; yet others have become blind. These truths grate against each other like a dissonant sound pressing for resolution. The

---

22 The Letter reads at this part as follows, ' ... but in your hearts sanctify Christ as Lord. Always be ready to make your defence to anyone who demands from you an account of the hope that is in you'.

Gospel assumes that there is no going back, as if Jesus never came. There can only be going forward to the point where the dissonance resolves into harmony.[23]

What Craig Koester is saying here is that Jesus' coming has changed how we understand an eschatology that has multiple tensions within it. The seeming dissonance between the competing truth claims of the present can only be resolved by moving forward. There can be no going back—only the inexorable forward motion to the ultimate fulfilment of John's eschatology.

## The Johannine Eschatological Focus: Present and Future Dimensions

**The present dimension** of Johannine eschatology must be understood as both already accomplished and not yet consummated, the 'now' and the 'not yet' of Johannine soteriology. How is this so? Some examples from the Gospel of John will illustrate my point. Eternal life[24] in the Fourth Gospel is presented as a present reality and possession in the following verses:

- John 3:15 ἵνα πᾶς ὁ πιστεύων ἐν αὐτῷ **ἔχῃ**[25] ζωὴν αἰώνιον (so that all believing in him **may have** life eternal);
- John 3:36a ὁ πιστεύων εἰς τὸν υἱὸν **ἔχει**[26] ζωὴν αἰώνιον ...(the [one] believing in the son **has** life eternal);
- John 5:24b ... ὅτι ὁ τὸν λόγον μου ἀκούων καὶ πιστεύων τῷ πέμψαντί με **ἔχει** ζωὴν αἰώνιον ... (that the [one] the word of me hearing, and believing the [One] who sent me, **has** life eternal);
- John 6:47 ... ὁ πιστεύων **ἔχει** ζωὴν αἰώνιον (the [one] believing **has** life eternal).

---

23 Koester, *The Word of Life*, 176.
24 See also 3:15,36; 5:24,40; 6:40,47,53,68; 10:10; 1 John 3:13,15; 5:12,13,16. The references in text are given as examples only.
25 From the Greek verb ἔχω meaning 'to have or hold'. Here it is in the 3rd sing. pres. subj. act.
26 From the Greek verb ἔχω meaning 'to have or hold'. Here it is in the 3rd sing. pres. indic. act. as are the forms of the same verb in 5:24b and 6:47.

Van Hartingsveld interprets eternal life in the Fourth Gospel 'as an eschatological gift of salvation which is only "promised" and appropriated in a preliminary way "by faith"'.[27] However, again using Aune in support, I favour the view that the very grammatical usage of the key phrase ἔχειν ζωὴν αἰώνιον 'to have/ possess eternal life' reflects that 'the possession of "eternal life" from the Johannine perspective is decisively and emphatically a factor in the present experience of the believer'.[28] There is a direct relationship between believing and the immediate possession of eternal life since the semantic relationship may be understood as subordinate, logical, and a means leading to a result.[29]

Considering John's eschatology as both already accomplished and not yet consummated also has a consequence for the Johannine understanding of sin. Unlike the Pauline Epistles where repentance for **sins (pl.)** is an emphasis, for the fourth Gospel **sin (sing.)** is unbelief in Jesus and consequently a rejection of him and his claims (*cf.* esp. 8:21–24 and 15:21–24). The primary purpose of the Gospel is to strengthen belief in Jesus as the Christ and the Son of God (20:30–31) and this is reflected in the narrative plot of the Gospel where belief is centred on the recognition (or not) of Jesus' true identity.[30] Jesus is seen as the source of salvation: in the Prologue he is designated the 'true light' (1:9); he refers to himself as the One who provides living water (4:10); the 'bread of life' (6:35,48); the 'light of the world' (8:12; 9:5; 12:46); the Good Shepherd (10:11,14); the 'resurrection and the life' (11:25); the 'way the truth and the life' (14:6) and the 'true vine' (15:1,5). The signs of the Gospel serve as pointers

---

27 Aune, *Cultic Setting*, 106, who is quoting van Hartingsveld's interpretation. This author has been unable to source van Hartingsveld's article to verify. See also Mburu, 'Realized Eschatology', esp. 6.
28 Aune, *Cultic Setting*, 106.
29 'Linguists have noted the importance of understanding the function of a word within the larger linguistic unit, the sentence. The syntagmatic relation refers to linear relationship of a word with surrounding terms in the speech-act. The paradigmatic relations are the vertical or associative relationship of a word with other words that could replace it, such as synonyms. Paradigmatic relations are useful in helping one determine the parameters for the use of a word. This is particularly significant for technical and semi-technical terms. These linear and vertical interrelationships, which form aspects of the linguistic context, must be taken into account in determining how any word is used. Further, the grammatical, syntagmatic, and semantic relationships indicate that eternal life is obtained as a present possession.' Mburu, 'Realized Eshatology', 11.
30 Culpepper, *Anatomy of the Fourth Gospel*, 85–88.

beyond themselves to the One performing them proving his messiahship and authenticating his claims to be uniquely related to God. The audience of the Gospel is thus brought to the point of decision, for or against Jesus as the Christ of God. A decision for Jesus leads to life, here and now (3:15,36; 5:24; 6:47) as a realised act through one's belief.

Indeed the emphasis on realised eschatology in the Gospel of John is sometimes so strong that it can almost overshadow its futuristic dimensions. This does not mean that the latter can be ignored, it simply means that, 'it was far more important for John to stress realized eschatology in a Gospel addressed to conflict with Jewish authorities who denied, not future hope, but the inauguration of that hope in Jesus'.[31] In John 5:28–29 the phrase ἔρχεται ὥρα (the time / hour is coming) clearly refers to the future event of bodily resurrection, despite some critics' comments to the contrary.[32]

The Greek text reads, $^{28}$μὴ θαυμάζετε τοῦτο, ὅτι ἔρχεται ὥρα ἐν ᾗ πάντες οἱ ἐν τοῖς μνημείοις ἀκούσουσιν τῆς φωνῆς αὐτοῦ $^{29}$καὶ ἐκπορεύσονται οἱ τὰ ἀγαθὰ ποιήσαντες εἰς ἀνάστασιν ζωῆς, οἱ δὲ τὰ φαῦλα πράξαντες εἰς ἀνάστασιν κρίσεως. ($^{28}$Do not be astonished at this; for the hour is coming when all who are in their graves will hear his voice $^{29}$and will come out—those who have done good, to the resurrection of life, and those who have done evil, to the resurrection of condemnation.) We identify 5:28 as a future transitional eschatological verse and 5:29 as a future final eschatological verse because hearing

---

31 Keener, *John*, 1:323. For instance, future bodily resurrection and eternal life in 5:21,28–29; 6:39,40,44,54 (see also 4:14,36; 5:29; 6:27; 12:25; 1 John 2:18,25), future judgement in 12:48, and perhaps even a reference to the Parousia in 14:3.
32 Some critics have suggested that this text is a later interpolation as it seems not to reflect reflect authentic Johannine teaching on eschatology or that they consist of a combination of two unassimilated eschatologies, one spiritual and the other realistic. However, Ladd regards that, '[l]ife is to be experienced in two stages: life in the present in the spiritual realm and life in the future in the resurrection of the body'. Ladd, *A Theology of the New Testament*, 341. Dodd favours the view that Lazarus' resurrection illustrates that eternal life in Christ is confined to the present and should therefore not be anticipated in the future. Dodd, *Apostolic Preaching*, 170. But the text of 11:25–26 shows that Jesus has life in himself that can by appropriated by those who believe in him and this life is more than physical, bodily life so a spiritual resurrection life is a reality. Further, those who show authentic faith 'now' have this spiritual life 'now' and will continue to live on *after* physical, bodily death, in a clear reference to future resurrection life. See further, 5:21; 6:39,40,50. Cf. 4:14,36; 5:29; 6:27; 12:25; 1 John 2:18,25.

Jesus' voice transitions one to the final, definitive resurrection life or the final, definitive resurrection judgement. So while believers in Jesus as the Christ of God may hold eternal life here and now (as we have shown above) its final definitive form will only take shape at the transitional phase of 'hearing his voice'.

Another instance of his futuristic eschatology is found in the 'resurrection and life' statement Jesus makes to Martha in 11:25–26, which reads, ²⁵εἶπεν αὐτῇ ὁ Ἰησοῦς· Ἐγώ εἰμι ἡ ἀνάστασις καὶ ἡ ζωή· ὁ πιστεύων εἰς ἐμὲ κἂν ἀποθάνῃ ζήσεται, ²⁶καὶ πᾶς ὁ ζῶν καὶ πιστεύων εἰς ἐμὲ οὐ μὴ ἀποθάνῃ εἰς τὸν αἰῶνα· πιστεύεις τοῦτο; (²⁵Jesus said to her, 'I am the resurrection and the life. Those who believe in me, even though they die, will live, ²⁶and everyone who lives and believes in me will never die. Do you believe this?') The text demonstrates two things: 1) only those who believe in Jesus can appropriate the life that he himself has—this life is not mere physical life, as the Gospel continually demonstrates, therefore, present spiritual life is a current reality for believers; 2) Even after physical death, believers will continue to live on, which is a clear reference to future final resurrection. Again we see that the Gospel of John exhibits both present and future eschatological hopes side by side, wherein spiritual life 'now' through belief in Jesus will lead to final resurrection life in the future. One explains the other! Jesus' irruption into human history has impacts for John's present reality, and because he writes from both a pre- and post-resurrection point of view his writing naturally reflects both the present and future dimensions of eschatology.

## The Purpose of Johannine Eschatology: A Case Study from 1 John

While the Gospel of John may underrepresent the future elements of Johannine eschatology, because of the author's concern to stress a realised eschatology to address the ongoing conflict with Jewish authorities, in 1 John, conversely, the Elder addresses secessionists whose eschatology is wholly realised, and so his focus is more on the future hopes for believers who remain true to the faith. The ethical import 'now' of future eschatological hopes can be seen in 1 John. The tension is most clearly illustrated in 1 John 3:2 where present, future (transitional) and future (final) eschatology are clearly in evidence.³³

> **1 John 3:2** ἀγαπητοί, <u>νῦν</u>³⁴ τέκνα θεοῦ ἐσμεν, καὶ <u>οὔπω</u>³⁵ ἐφανερώθη τί ἐσόμεθα. οἴδαμεν ὅτι <u>ἐὰν</u>³⁶ φανερωθῇ ὅμοιοι αὐτῷ ἐσόμεθα, ὅτι ὀψόμεθα αὐτὸν καθώς ἐστιν.
>
> *(Beloved (pl.) **<u>now</u>** we are children of God, and what we will be has been revealed **<u>not yet</u>**. We know that **<u>when</u>** he appears like he we will be, for we will see him as he is).*

As 1 John 3:2 shows, the 'now' and 'not yet' aspects are unmistakeable as the temporal markers indicate. They exist side by side with each enabling and, indeed, explaining the other. The present eschatological act is progressively transformational while its future fulfilment may be seen in terms of the transitional and final events of the eschaton. By using 1 John 3:2 as a model we can determine how the elements of 1 John 2:18,28; 3:2,3; and 4:17 show a not dissimilar pattern.

| Text | Present Eschatology | Future Eschatology (Transitional) | Future Eschatology (Final) |
|---|---|---|---|
| 1 John 3:2 | ἀγαπητοί, <u>νῦν</u> τέκνα θεοῦ ἐσμεν, | καὶ <u>οὔπω</u> ἐφανερώθη τί ἐσόμεθα. | οἴδαμεν ὅτι <u>ἐὰν</u> φανερωθῇ ὅμοιοι αὐτῷ ἐσόμεθα, ὅτι ὀψόμεθα αὐτὸν καθώς ἐστιν. |
| | Beloved (pl.) **<u>now</u>** we are children of God | and what we will be has been revealed **<u>not yet</u>** | We know that **<u>when</u>** he appears like he we will be, for we will see him as he is. |

---

33 Here we acknowledge our debt to R. A. Culpepper and his distinction between historical and eschatological forms of external prolepsis in the Fourth Gospel: Culpepper, *Anatomy of the Fourth Gospel*, 64. He goes on to explain that external prolepses are of two basic types: 'historical prolepses, those which refer to events which will occur among the disciples and later believers, and eschatological prolepses, those which refer to "the last day", the end of time'. He concludes that, '[w]ith John's emphasis on "realized eschatology" it is not surprising that its historical prolepses outnumber its eschatological prolepses'.

34 A primary particle of present time νῦν meaning 'now'. Referring to this Stählin says that, 'Already in this νῦν of the Fourth Gospel ... there is an awareness of being in transition, of being almost completely absorbed into the realization that in the Now of Christ the end, the consummation is present'. See Stählin, 'νῦν', 1106–1123.

35 Negative adverb used as a temporal particle οὔπω meaning 'not yet'.

36 Conditional particle or conjunction ἐάν, here used with a temporal sense meaning 'when'.

| Text | Present Eschatology | Future Eschatology (Transitional) | Future Eschatology (Final) |
|---|---|---|---|
| 1 John 2:18 | Παιδία, <u>ἐσχάτη ὥρα</u>[37] <u>ἐστίν</u>, καὶ καθὼς ἠκούσατε ὅτι <u>ἀντίχριστος</u> ἔρχεται, καὶ νῦν <u>ἀντίχριστοι</u> πολλοὶ γεγόνασιν· ὅθεν γινώσκομεν ὅτι ἐσχάτη ὥρα ἐστίν.<br><br>Children, it **is the last hour**! As you have heard that **antichrist** is coming, so **now** many **antichrists** have come. | | |
| 1 John 2:28 | Καὶ <u>νῦν</u>, τεκνία, μένετε ἐν αὐτῷ<br><br><br><br><br><br><br>And **now**, little children, abide in him | ἵνα <u>ἐὰν</u> φανερωθῇ σχῶμεν παρρησίαν καὶ μὴ αἰσχυνθῶμεν ἀπ' αὐτοῦ ἐν τῇ <u>παρουσίᾳ αὐτοῦ</u>[38]<br><br>so that **when** he is revealed we may have confidence and not be put to shame before him at **his coming**. | |
| 1 John 3:3 | καὶ πᾶς ὁ <u>ἔχων</u> τὴν ἐλπίδα ταύτην ἐπ' αὐτῷ <u>ἁγνίζει</u> ἑαυτὸν καθὼς ἐκεῖνος <u>ἁγνός ἐστιν</u>.<br><br>(And all who **have** [lit. having] this hope in him **purify themselves**, just as **he is pure**) | | |

---

37 The only occurrence of this phrase in the NT.
38 The imminence of the Parousia by the Elder is also found in other early Christian literature. Cf. 1 Cor. 7:29ff; 16:22; Rom. 13:11; Phil. 4:5; 1 Thess. 5:1ff; 2 Thess. 2:2f; Heb. 10:25,37; James 5:8; 2 Pet. 3:9; 1 Clem. 23.2; Did. 10.6; Barn. 4.1ff; 21.3,6; cf. also Mark 13:6. We note that in these texts no specific use of the noun 'antichrist' occurs; cf. Schnackenburg, *The Johannine Epistles*, 133 n.6.

| Text | Present Eschatology | Future Eschatology (Transitional) | Future Eschatology (Final) |
|---|---|---|---|
| 1 John 4:17 | ὅτι καθὼς ἐκεῖνός ἐστιν καὶ ἡμεῖς ἐσμεν ἐν τῷ κόσμῳ τούτῳ.<br><br>because as he is, so are we in this world. | | ἐν τούτῳ τετελείωται ἡ ἀγάπη μεθ' ἡμῶν, ἵνα <u>παρρησίαν ἔχωμεν</u> ἐν <u>τῇ ἡμέρᾳ τῆς κρίσεως</u>,<br><br>...<br><br>Love has been perfected among us in this: that <u>we may have boldness on the day of judgement</u>, ... |

The 'last hour' in 1 John 2:18 sees the Elder describe his present time period as an eschatological moment, the last hour in salvation history. Danker[39] confirms this when he defines ὥρα in this context as 'a point of time as an occasion for an event, time'. Therefore, Schnackenburg[40] rightly states that the 'last hour' does not mean the entire period since the coming of Christ, or since his resurrection. The Elder wants only to say that his own time ['now'] has an eschatological importance and his warning that the 'antichrists have come' is used with this in mind. For the Elder, the coming of the antichrist marks the event of the 'last hour'.[41]

The word ἀντίχριστος is used both in its singular and plural forms—the singular form probably relates to the leader of the group of schismatics (the plural form), though no leader is named. This leader is also designated by the Elder as both 'Deceiver' and 'Liar' and his followers are characterised in a similar manner.[42] The noun, ἀντίχριστος does not appear in the Jewish inter-testamental literature, the Midrashim, nor the Talmud. It seems to come from the apocalyptic tradition where it may have been used to symbolise the rise of evil at the end-times and may have become a title used for the schism that centred on differing

---

39 Danker, *Greek English Lexicon*, 1103.
40 Schnackenburg, *Johannine Epistles*, 133. Neither is it a phase nor a particular period within time as it draws to its close. This reference also does not imply a precise chronological scheme for the Elder's eschatological understanding. Also see Van der Merwe, 'ὥρα a possible theological setting', 253–285, esp. 253ff. for the Fourth Evangelist's use of ὥρα as a possible theological setting for the understanding of Johannine eschatology.
41 Painter, *1, 2, and 3 John*, 203.
42 Painter, *1, 2, and 3 John*, 203.

views of Christ. The Elder appears to be familiar with the term from the Johannine tradition and this explains his repeated use of it.[43] He seems to have reshaped the tradition in view of the circumstances of the community schism at that time.[44] 2 John 7 clearly shows that the tradition was used by the Elder to refer to a specific historical situation. This, by deduction, means that a mythological figure has been historicised as the community's own self-understanding is played out in the immediate context of the end-time apocalypse. The arrival of the antichrists means that the community recognised that the 'end-time' has arrived, an end-time that the Elder describes as the Parousia. Thus, it is unsurprising that in 1 John 2:28 we have a reference to the future coming of Jesus as the Christ (παρουσία αὐτοῦ).[45] The Parousia here is the liminal stage between the present eschatological event and the final end-time, and so, in this sense, it can be identified as future transitional eschatology.[46] This also shows how 2:28; 3:2–3; and 4:17 relate to each other as the following comparison shows.

| 2:28 Καὶ νῦν, τεκνία, μένετε ἐν αὐτῷ, ἵνα ἐὰν φανερωθῇ <u>σχῶμεν παρρησίαν</u> καὶ μὴ αἰσχυνθῶμεν ἀπ' αὐτοῦ ἐν <u>τῇ παρουσίᾳ αὐτοῦ</u>. | 3:2 ἀγαπητοί, νῦν τέκνα θεοῦ ἐσμεν, καὶ οὔπω ἐφανερώθη τί ἐσόμεθα. οἴδαμεν ὅτι ἐὰν <u>φανερωθῇ</u> ὅμοιοι αὐτῷ ἐσόμεθα, ὅτι ὀψόμεθα αὐτὸν καθὼς ἐστιν. | 3:3 καὶ πᾶς ὁ ἔχων τὴν ἐλπίδα ταύτην ἐπ' αὐτῷ ἁγνίζει ἑαυτὸν <u>καθὼς ἐκεῖνος ἁγνός ἐστιν.</u> | 4:17 ἐν τούτῳ τετελείωται ἡ ἀγάπη μεθ' ἡμῶν, ἵνα <u>παρρησίαν ἔχωμεν</u> ἐν τῇ <u>ἡμέρᾳ τῆς κρίσεως,</u> ὅτι καθὼς ἐκεῖνός ἐστιν καὶ ἡμεῖς ἐσμεν ἐν τῷ κόσμῳ τούτῳ. |
|---|---|---|---|
| (And now, little children, abide in him, **so that when he is revealed** we may have confidence and not be put to shame before him at **his coming**.) | (Beloved, we are God's children now; what we will be has not yet been revealed. What we do know is this: **when he is revealed**, we will be like him, for we will see him as he is.) | (And all who have this hope in him purify themselves, just as he is pure.) | (Love has been perfected among us in this: that we may have boldness on **the day of judgement,** because as he is, so are we in this world.) |

---

43  Strecker, *The Johannine Letters*, 62; Painter, *1, 2, and 3 John*, 202.
44  Painter, *1, 2, and 3 John*, 204; Schnackenburg, *Johannine Epistles*, 134.
45  Schnackenburg, *Johannine Epistles*, 133, holds that it is believed by the Elder to be imminent.
46  Cf. Dunn, *The Theology of Paul the Apostle*, 295.

The parallel phrases σχῶμεν παρρησίαν (2:28) and παρρησίαν ἔχωμεν (4:17) are both references to Jesus' future coming. Further, both 2:28 and 4:17 also refer to the confidence that believers have for this event which is described as τῇ παρουσίᾳ αὐτοῦ (his coming, 2:28) and τῇ ἡμέρᾳ τῆς κρίσεως (the day of judgement, 4:17). Therefore, Jesus' revelation[47] mentioned in 2:28 and 3:2 is depicted as both Parousia (the event) and the day of judgement (the purpose of the event).[48] The use of the verb for revelation cannot be an accident here, since the Elder has already mentioned the other revelation of Jesus, namely, his incarnation (1:2; cf. 3:5,8). The two events, incarnation and Parousia, converge and the tensile unity of present and future eschatology is clearly seen linked by the use of φανερόω (to make visible, make clear). In this way then, the Elder makes three ethical exhortations that believers must accomplish 'now' (present eschatology) so that they conform to be just as he is (καθὼς ἐκεῖνος ἐστιν, 3:3). These are

1. μένω ἐν αὐτῷ—to remain in him (2:28).

2. ἁγνίζω ἑαυτὸν καθὼς ἐκεῖνος ἁγνός ἐστιν—to purify oneself just as he is pure (3:3).

3. τελειόω[49] ἡ ἀγάπη μεθ' ἡμῶν... ὅτι καθὼς ἐκεῖνός ἐστιν καὶ ἡμεῖς ἐσμεν ἐν τῷ κόσμῳ τούτῳ—to perfect love among us... because as he is, so are we in this world (4:17).

Each exhortation is linked to Jesus, and conforming to him **now** will be the measuring stick used in the **future**, in the day of judgement (ἐν τῇ ἡμέρᾳ τῆς κρίσεως). For this to happen both the individual child of God and the collective community in this present eschatological time must be aware that they are in a time of transition by being absorbed into the 'now' of Christ, the end-times, which means that the consummation has also, paradoxically, begun. But what do the ethical nuances of 2:28; 3:3; and 4:17 mean for the lived reality of the individual and

---

47 From the Greek verb φανερόω meaning 'to make visible, make clear'. In 2:8 the verb is in the 3rd sing. aor. subj. pass. and in 3:2 it is in the 3rd sing. aor. ind. pass.
48 Painter, *1, 2, and 3 John*, 214, points out that both φανερόω and παρουσία refer to the eschatological future coming, that is implied by the earlier declaration that ἐσχάτη ὥρα ἐστίν (2:18).
49 The Greek verb meaning 'to bring to an end, to complete, perfect'.

the collective? How is a believer to perfect love, or remain in him or make oneself pure? The answer to this question leads into the vexed territory of Johannine ethics. If being a Christians is motivated by one's understanding of God and God's world around us, what can a Johannine ethic offer to one's motivation as a Christian?

## Is There a Johannine Ethic?

Wayne A. Meeks asserts that 'the Fourth Gospel meets none of our expectations about the way ethics should be constructed',[50] while others deny that ethics exist in the Johannine corpus.[51]

> Apart from the love that imitates Jesus' love for his own, John's Gospel is practically amoral. We look in vain for the equivalents of Jesus' teaching on divorce, oaths and vows, almsgiving, prayer, fasting, or the multitude of other specific moral directives strewn across the pages of Matthew's Gospel. Everything comes down to imitating Jesus' love for his disciples; what concrete and specific actions should flow from this love are largely left unspoken.[52]

It is clear that the Johannine corpus lacks the explicit ethics of Paul, Matthew, or even Luke;[53] however that does not mean that an ethical perspective is not part of the fabric of the texts of John. Christopher W. Skinner is surely correct in maintaining that the ethics of the Johannine literature are broad, inclusive, and valuable for the construction of Christian ethics. So, by extension, to this present eschatological time, when believers must be aware that they are in a time of transition being absorbed into the 'now' of Christ, the end-times, and to the ultimate consummation of the future final event. '[T]he narrated text reveals an underlying value system and ethical reflection *sui generis*, which

---

50   Meeks, 'The Ethics of the Fourth Evangelist', 320.
51   So Houlden: 'Even when [John] speaks of the command to love and of doing what Jesus commands, John's real concern is not primarily ethical at all. His concern is with the new condition of life conferred on the believers through Christ'. See *Ethics and the New Testament*, 47–48.
52   Meier, 'Love in Q and John', 47–48.
53   See for Paul Gal. 5:16–26; 1 Cor. 13:1–13 for example; for Matthew 5:1—7:29; for Luke 6:17–49.

can retrospectively be classified as "ethics" or better as "implicit ethics".[54] So, rather than being devoid of any ethical material the Gospel, particularly, requires a more detailed engagement across the narrative so as to offer new insights into the implicit notion of Johannine ethics. Kobus Kok favours a 'missional-incarnational ethos' using Jesus' interaction with the Samaritan woman in John 4, positing that the story is connected to the wider notion of mission in the narrative.[55] Jey Kanagaraj sees the Decalogue as the roots to John's ethics demonstrating how each of the commandments is implicitly embedded in the narrative of the Fourth Gospel.[56] Richard Burridge articulates his views of Johannine ethics as 'imitating Jesus' since our understanding of the Gospel genre as broadly following the category of Graeco-Roman *bioi*, which, of their nature, are concerned to demonstrate the virtues of a given individual.[57] The advantage of Burridge's approach is that it stops one reading the NT texts as ethical treatises, and so, as Burridge argues, John's Jesus is a model of imitable behaviour since he calls people to follow God and be part of an inclusive community. Using a narrative exegetical approach, the work of Jörg Frey looks at the love language of John, which he sees as universal rather than sectarian. Reading the Gospel in its entirety he endeavours to establish a semantic network of John's love language, and so John's ethical perspective emerges in an organic fashion.[58] My own approach owes much to the work of both Frey and Francis J. Moloney, in that I follow Frey's assertions of the need for a reading of the Gospel to understand the semantic network of John's love language and Moloney's sustained narrative exegesis of the text of John in its final form in concert with the historical discussions about the Johannine community. Such nuanced practices show that for the two thousand years of its continual preaching, the Gospel asks 'readers and hearers to "remember Jesus" and put their lives where their words are'.[59] In other words, one's belief in Jesus must shape one's

---

54  van der Watt and Zimmerman, *Rethinking the Ethics of John*, x.
55  Kok, 'As the Father Has Sent Me', 168–96.
56  Kanagaraj, 'Implied Ethics', 33–60.
57  Burridge, 'Imitating Jesus', 281–90.
58  Frey, 'Love-Relations', 171–198, see esp. 198.
59  Moloney, *Love in the Gospel of* John, 210. A not dissimilar position, arrived at via a slightly different hermeneutic, is held by C. W. Skinner, 'Virtue in the New Testament', 313–315.

life as a Christian—and it really is that simple! The living out of this, of course, is not. The Fourth Gospel has a positive, though limited ethical contribution to make to the lives of Christians—it 'does say *something* about an understanding of Christian love, even though it must not be claimed that it says *everything*'.[60] As such it is clear then that belief in Jesus as the Christ and Son of God brings life (20:31). But as Frey and Moloney make clear, this belief is predicated on the Johannine command to love (15:12,17). The Gospel of John is a witness to the presence of the eschatological event in the in-breaking of Jesus into human history. The Fourth Gospel shows us 'the Lamb of God... who takes away the **sin** [sing.] of the world' (John 1:29). John teaches that with this Lamb the fate of humankind is at once unveiled and disclosed, that eschatology is revealed and fulfilled. The tension between the 'already' and 'not yet' dimensions of Johannine eschatology is paradoxical for two reasons. 1) Jesus' irruption into human history means that his work of salvation has a temporal impact on present existence. 2) John is writing from both the standpoint of the time of Jesus as well as the post-resurrection understanding of the significance of the Christ event, and so his eschatology naturally reflects both dimensions.[61] The conquering of death by Jesus leads the believer to eternal dwelling in union with the Father and the Son as Christ, which is the essence of eschatology and its intersection with soteriology. As Dodd has said, Christ is realised eschatology.

## Why John's Unique Eschatology Still Matters

The ethical import of John's implicit ethic of love finds fulfilment in contemporary Christian communities. Christians are duty bound by the belief in Christ to build a biblical concept of the future that is consistent with God's kingdom. This means that as God reigns in the lives of Christians 'now', Christians themselves ought to be working forward to the eternal kingdom of God in (or at the end of) history. So the reign of God that is 'already' at least partially fulfilled (transitional

---

60 Moloney, *Love in the Gospel of John*, 214 (emphasis from Moloney's text).
61 Barrett, *The Gospel According to St. John*, 68.

future eschatology) compels our ethics though the kingdom is 'not yet' mediated through Jesus by the Spirit acting into history (future final eschatology). This means then that Christians are to move to responsible action on behalf of others and creation itself in the present to make real the ultimate dawning of God's own kingdom. Christians celebrate our faith now in appreciation of the past and in anticipation of the future. It is only in this way that believers can demonstrate that they are

1. Remaining in him (1 John 2:28)
2. Purifying themselves (1 John 3:3)
3 Perfecting love among each other (1 John 4:17).

So, this essay has raised a further consideration for me: Can one speak of the eschatology of becoming? Of creating a future now that Christians live into?

Debra Snoddy
Catholic Institute of Sydney

## Bibliography

Allison, D. C., Jr. — 'Eschatology', in I. H. Marshall (ed.) *Dictionary of Jesus and the Gospels* (Leicester: Intervarsity Press, 1992), 495-501.

Aune, D. E. — *The Cultic Setting of Realized Eschatology in Early Christianity* (Testamental Supplement 28; Leiden: Brill, 1972).

Barrett, C. K. — *The Gospel According to St. John: An Introduction with Commentary and Notes on the Greek Text* (Philadelphia, PA: Westminster, 1978).

Braaten, C. — *The Future of God the Revolutionary Dynamics of Hope* (New York, NY: Harper and Row, 1969).

Brower, K. E. — '"Let the Reader understand": Temple and Eschatology in Mark Hope', in K. E. Brower and M. W. Elliot (eds.), *The Reader must Understand. Eschatology in Bible and Theology* (Cambridge: Apollos, 1997), 119-144.

Brown, S. and F. J. Moloney — *Interpreting the Gospel and Letters of John: an Introduction* (Grand Rapids, MI: Eerdmans, 2017).

Burridge, R. A. — 'Imitating Jesus: An Inclusive Approach to the Ethics of the Historical Jesus and John's Gospel', in P. N. Anderson, F. Just, and T. Thatcher (eds.), *John, Jesus, and History, vol. 2, Aspects of Historicity in the Fourth Gospel* (Atlanta, GA: SBL, 2009), 281–90.

Cullmann, O. — *Salvation in History* (New York, NY: Harper and Row, 1967).

Culpepper, R. A. — *Anatomy of the Fourth Gospel: A Study in Literary Design* (Philadelphia, PA: Fortress, 1987).

Danker, F. W. (ed.) — *Greek English Lexicon of the New Testament and other Early Christian Literature* (3rd edn BDAG; Chicago, IL: University of Chicago Press, 2000).

Dodd, C. H. — *Apostolic Preaching* (New York, NY: Harper & Row, 1964).

Dodd, C. H. — *The Parables of the Kingdom* (Digswell Place: James Nisbet and Company, Ltd, 1961 [1935]).

Dunn, J. D. G. — *The Theology of Paul the Apostle* (London: T & T Clark, 2003).

Frey, J. — 'Love-Relations in the Fourth Gospel: Establishing a Semantic Network', in G. Van Belle, M. Labahn, and P. Maritz

| | |
|---|---|
| | (eds.), *Repetitions and Variations in the Fourth Gospel: Style, Text, Interpretation* (BETL 223; Leuven: Peeters, 2009), 171–198. |
| Horne, C. M. | 'Eschatology—The Controlling Thematic In Theology', *JETS* 13.1 (1970), 53–63. |
| Houlden, J. L. | *Ethics and the New Testament* (Harmondsworth: Penguin, 1973). |
| Kanagaraj, J. J. | 'The Implied Ethics of the Fourth Gospel: A Reinterpretation of the Decalogue', *TynBul* 52 (2001), 33–60. |
| Keener, C. | *The Gospel of John: A Commentary* (2 vols; Grand Rapids, MI: Baker Academic, 2012). |
| Koester, C. R. | *The Word of Life: A Theology of John's Gospel* (Grand Rapids, MI: Eerdmans, 2008). |
| Kok, K. | 'As the Father Has Sent Me, I Send You: Towards a Missional-Incarnational Ethos in John 4', in R. Zimmerman, J. G. van der Watt, and S. Luther (eds.), *Moral Language in the New Testament: The Interrelatedness of Language and Ethics in Early Christian Writings* (WUNT 296; Tübingen: Mohr Siebeck 2010), 168-193. |
| Ladd, G. E. | *A Theology of the New Testament* (Grand Rapids, MI: Eerdmans, 1974). |
| Marshall, I. H. | 'Slippery Words In Eschatology', *ExpT* 89 (1978), 264–269. |
| Mburu, E. | 'Realized Eschatology in the Soteriology of John's Gospel', *Testamentum Imperium* 3 (2011), 1–36. |
| Meeks, W. A. | 'The Ethics of the Fourth Evangelist', in R. A. Culpepper and C. C. Black (eds.), *Exploring the Gospel of John: In Honor of D. Moody Smith* (Louisville, KY: Westminster John Knox, 1996), 317-326. |
| Meier, J. P. | 'Love in Q and John: Love of Enemies, Love of One Another', *Mid-Stream* 40 (2001), 42-50. |
| Moloney, F. J. | *Love in the Gospel of John: An Exegetical, Theological, and Literary Study* (Grand Rapids: Baker Academic, 2013). |
| Moltmann, J. | *Theology of Hope* (New York, NY: Harper and Row, 1965). |
| Painter, J. | *1, 2, and 3 John* (Sacra Pagina series; Collegeville, PA: Liturgical, 2002). |

Rowland, C.     'Eschatology', in A. E. McGrath (ed.), *The Blackwell Encyclopedia of Modern Christian Thought* (Oxford: Blackwell Publishing, 1993), 161–164.

Sauter, G.     *What dare we hope? Reconsidering Eschatology* (Harrisburg, PA: Trinity Press International, 1999).

Schnackenburg, R.     *The Johannine Epistles* (New York, NY: Crossroad, 1992).

Skinner, C. W. and K. R. Iverson (eds.)     'Virtue in the New Testament: The Legacies of Paul and John in Comparative Perspective', in *Unity and Diversity in the Gospels and Paul: Essays in Honor of Frank J. Matera* (ECL 7; Atlanta, GA: SBL, 2012), 301-324.

Stählin, G.     'νῦν', *TDNT* 4:1106–1123.

Strecker, G.     *The Johannine Letters (A Commentary on 1, 2, and 3 John)* (Minneapolis, MN: Fortress, 1996).

Thomas, G. J.     'A Holy God among A Holy People in a Holy Place: The Enduring Eschatological Hope', in K. E. Brower and M. W. Elliot (eds.), *The Reader must Understand. Eschatology in Bible and Theology* (Cambridge: Apollos, 1997), 53–72.

Van der Merwe, D. G.     'ὥρα a possible theological setting for understanding Johannine eschatology', *Acta Patristica Et Byzantina* 13 (2002), 253–285.

van der Watt, J. G. and R. Zimmerman (eds.)     *Rethinking the Ethics of John: 'Implicit Ethics' in the Johannine Writings* (WUNT 291; Tübingen: Mohr Siebeck, 2012).

CHAPTER 15

# In the Last Days: Alteration, Eschatology, and the Spirit

John D. Griffiths

## Abstract

This chapter explores the impact that the editorial addition of 'in the last days' into the quotation of Joel 3:1–5 has on the meaning of the Lukan Peter's Pentecost sermon, and more broadly, the Pentecost narrative. It outlines how various authors see this editorial addition as both identificatory and descriptive, noting in particular that the addition of 'in the last days' is a direct quote from Isaiah 2:2, which describes the inauguration of the eschatological temple of God. This implies that the Pentecost narrative is likewise a temple inauguration. The essay concludes by exploring the temple imagery in Acts 2, noting how the addition of 'in the last days' fits into the broader Pentecost narrative.

While the Lukan Peter makes six changes from the LXX version of Joel 3:1–5 in his Pentecost sermon in Acts 2:17–21, his first change, replacing μετὰ ταῦτα with ἐν ταῖς ἐσχάταις ἡμέραις, potentially makes the most impact.[1] While it is clear that this editorial move is significant,

---

1  For a detailed analysis of these six editorial changes, see Menzies, *Empowered for Witness*, 178–86.

coming at the start of the Lukan Peter's speech to explain the coming of the Spirit at Pentecost, there is a variety of views as to what it indicates. This essay outlines the identificatory and descriptive power that the addition of ἐν ταῖς ἐσχάταις ἡμέραις brings to the Lukan Peter's quotation from Joel, and for Luke's overall portrayal of the Pentecost event.

However, before exploring the effect of this editorial move, a text-critical issue must be first addressed. Some manuscripts do not have the editorial alteration ἐν ταῖς ἐσχάταις ἡμέραις in Acts 2:17, following instead the LXX's version μετὰ ταῦτα.[2] Some regard μετὰ ταῦτα as original, such as Ernst Haenchen, who argues for the reading by stating, 'In Lucan theology the last days do not begin as soon as the Spirit has been outpoured',[3] despite the suitability of ἐν ταῖς ἐσχάταις ἡμέραις for the context of either Peter's speech or the Acts narrative being well-recognised, both before and after his time of writing.[4] Moreover, text-critical arguments favour the view that, finding the phrase already inserted in the text, an Alexandrian corrector re-conformed the quotation to the prevailing version of the Septuagint.[5] Therefore, since the external manuscript evidence favours the ἐν ταῖς ἐσχάταις ἡμέραις reading, and ἐν ταῖς ἐσχάταις ἡμέραις is compatible with Luke's eschatology, this reading will be assumed in the rest of this study.

## 1. 'In the Last Days' as Identificatory

One of the most common views of the editorial addition of ἐν ταῖς ἐσχάταις ἡμέραις is that Luke uses it to indicate the eschatological nature or level of this period in history. That is, it is identificatory, since it identifies the Pentecost event as occurring ἐν ταῖς ἐσχάταις ἡμέραις. There are three different ways that scholars see the addition of ἐν ταῖς ἐσχάταις ἡμέραις as identificatory.

First, some scholars argue that Luke is identifying the outpouring

---

2   The Sepuagint's μετὰ ταῦτα is found in B 076 cop^sa Cyril of Jerusalem, while ἐν ταῖς ἐσχάταις ἡμέραις occurs in ℵ A D E I P S 462 vg syr Irenaeus Hilary Macarius Chrysostom Augustine.
3   Haenchen, *The Acts of the Apostles*, 179.
4   For before, see, for example, Ropes, *Text*, 16–17; for recent scholars who argue that Luke considers that the eschatological age began before Pentecost, see note 10.
5   Haenchen, *The Acts of the Apostles*, 179.

of the Spirit at Pentecost as the start of the new eschatological age.⁶ Following Hans Conzelmann's three-epoch schema, these scholars see the changing of the epochs as occurring through the work of the Spirit. That is, the Spirit is given to Jesus at his baptism (Luke 3:22) to initiate the epoch of the Messiah, and likewise, the Spirit is given to the disciples at Pentecost (Acts 2:4) to initiate the epoch of the Church.⁷ For example, Darrell L. Bock states of the Lukan Peter's insertion of ἐν ταῖς ἐσχάταις ἡμέραις that 'what Peter is really saying here is that the coming of the Spirit is the beginning of "those [eschatological] days"'.⁸ Pentecost is seen as the changing of the epochs or the start of the eschatological age, which Luke indicates by the insertion of ἐν ταῖς ἐσχάταις ἡμέραις.

However, there are some variations of this position, especially since Conzelmann's three-epoch schema has increasingly been questioned by Lukan scholars.⁹ Recently, Kylie Crabbe has argued that the key event that initiates the last days is most likely the resurrection of Jesus, since in the speeches in Acts, it is the resurrection that forms the pivotal content of the witness of the apostles.¹⁰ As Crabbe concludes,

> Jesus' resurrection plays a central role in signalling the position of the historical present in Luke's schema of history. In his resurrection, Jesus is confirmed as the Messiah and divinely appointed judge, roles associated with the end of history. At the same time, the decisive action of God in raising him confirms the entry into a new and ultimate period of history.¹¹

Since it is the resurrection that inaugurates the present epoch, Luke does not use this editorial addition of ἐν ταῖς ἐσχάταις ἡμέραις to indicate the change into the eschatological age at Pentecost.

---

6   Dunn, *Baptism in the Holy Spirit*, 46–47; Bruce, *The Acts of the Apostles*, 61; Mainville, *The Spirit in Luke-Acts*, 44; Shepherd, *The Narrative Function of the Holy Spirit as a Character in Luke-Acts*, 164; Barrett, *Acts* 1–14, 136; Fitzmyer, *The Acts of the Apostles*, 252; Bock, *Acts*, 112.
7   For example, see Dunn, *Baptism in the Holy Spirit*, 46–47.
8   Bock, *Acts*, 112.
9   For example, Menzies, *Empowered for Witness*, 304–7.
10  Crabbe, *Luke-Acts and the End of History*, 304–7. Along a similar vein, Shelton, *Mighty in Word and Deed*, 166, states, 'The ascension also played a key role in bringing in the eschaton'. Menzies has argued that the last days began with the infancy narratives in Luke 1–2, see Menzies, *Empowered for Witness*, 180.
11  Crabbe, *Luke-Acts and the End of History*, 307.

Others, while not connecting the addition of ἐν ταῖς ἐσχάταις ἡμέραις to Hans Conzelmann's three-epoch understanding of Luke's salvation history, still see the Lukan Peter as heightening the eschatological nature of Pentecost with this editorial addition.[12] That is, Pentecost does not represent the beginning of the last days, but a key moment in the ongoing period of the last days. For example, Eckhard J. Schnabel notes that 'Peter clarifies that what follows in Joel's prophecy relates to the last days of God's history of salvation, which is now identified as the new age ushered by Jesus'.[13] According to these scholars, the Lukan Peter, by adding this phrase, heightens the eschatological nature of the events of Joel 3:1–5, and by extension, the whole of the Pentecost narrative.

However, again there are limitations to this position. First, the content of Joel 3:1–5 is already clearly eschatological in nature.[14] The universal outpouring of the Spirit is accompanied with cosmic wonders, which draws upon 'the day of the Lord' imagery used throughout the OT, while the 'day of the Lord' is also explicitly mentioned in Joel 3:4. That is, the quotation from Joel 3:1–5 describes common events that happen in the last days. Second, the intertextuality of the second half of Joel 2 likewise describes events commonly attributed to the eschatological future. After Yhwh relents in Joel 2:18, Joel foresees peace and creational prosperity, where Israel will no longer be ashamed but rather will know Yhwh. Since the use of Joel 3:1–5 and, even more broadly, the events of Pentecost are highly eschatological, it is unlikely that this editorial move 'heightens' the eschatological nature of the Pentecost narrative.

While seeing the editorial addition of ἐν ταῖς ἐσχάταις ἡμέραις as identificatory, one final group of scholars sees this addition as underlying or clarifying the eschatological nature of Pentecost.[15] For example,

---

12 Johnson, *The Acts of the Apostles*, 49; Witherington, *The Acts of the Apostles*, 142; Hur, *A Dynamic Reading of the Holy Spirit in Luke-Acts*, 228; Schnabel, *Acts*, 135–36. Similarly, Turner and Wenk both see this alteration as identifying the Spirit at Pentecost as 'the eschatological promise', see Turner, *Power from on High*, 270; Wenk, *Community-Forming Power*, 252.
13 Schnabel, *Acts*, 136.
14 Menzies, *Empowered for Witness*, 180–81.
15 For the language of 'underlying', see Keener, *Acts*, 876; Crabbe, *Luke-Acts and the End of History*, 307. See also, Menzies, *Empowered for Witness*, 180–81.

Crabbe notes that 'perhaps in order to be completely clear, Luke adds the time reference "in the last days" to the LXX quotation'.[16] Similarly, Robert P. Menzies has argued that the addition of ἐν ταῖς ἐσχάταις ἡμέραις is drawn from the close parallel with ἐν ταῖς ἡμέραις ἐκείναις in Acts 2:18 (quoted from Joel 3:2).[17] While it is possible that Luke is underscoring the eschatological significance of Pentecost, to a certain degree this would make the editorial addition somewhat redundant.

## 2. 'In the Last Days' as Descriptive

Another way to approach the use of ἐν ταῖς ἐσχάταις ἡμέραις is that it is descriptive. That is, rather than identifying the eschatological period, ἐν ταῖς ἐσχάταις ἡμέραις is used to describe an eschatological event. For example, Joshua Noble, drawing upon a non-Jewish context, explores how a Roman listener would have understood ἐν ταῖς ἐσχάταις ἡμέραις.[18] From a Roman imperial background, this mention of the last days could have evoked the contemporary belief in the return of the Golden Age.[19] The Golden Age myth was a retelling of the primitive beginnings of humanity before human civilisation, with each successive age (after the primitive beginning) being characterised by a metal of lesser quality; the silver age, the bronze age, and so on. In the Golden Age there was peace, harmony, and abundance of fertile land. This myth was politicised with the rise of Augustus, when it was believed that the primitive Golden Age had returned, with additional characteristics of this returned Golden Age including common property and political peace.[20] Therefore, it is possible that a Gentile listening to Acts would discern an allusion to the return of the Golden Age in the coming of the Spirit and this may be further supported with the following description

---

16  Crabbe, *Luke-Acts and the End of History*, 307.
17  Menzies, *Empowered for Witness*, 181. While this suggestion is interesting, it does minimise the significant difference in meaning between ἐσχάταις and ἐκείναις, and the argument that ἐν ταῖς ἐσχάταις ἡμέραις is a direct quotation from Isaiah 2:2, as argued below.
18  Noble, *Common Property*, 87–89.
19  Noble, *Common Property*, 87–89.
20  For an overview of the Golden Age myth in the Graeco-Roman literature, see Noble, *Common Property*, 15–84. See also Craig Evans' contributions to this volume.

of the sharing of possessions at the end of Acts 2.[21]

While a Gentile listener may associate ἐν ταῖς ἐσχάταις ἡμέραις with the Golden Age, for a Jewish listener of Acts 2, this editorial move could have been identified as a direct quotation from the LXX's version of Isaiah 2:2.[22] Indeed, the LXX's version of Isaiah 2:2 has the exact same phrase as is used in Acts 2:17a (ἐν ταῖς ἐσχάταις ἡμέραις), while Micah 4:1 uses the similar phrase (ἐπ᾽ ἐσχάτων τῶν ἡμερῶν), with the main differences being the use of the genitive plural in Micah 4:1 compared to the dative plural in Isaiah 2:2, the preposition ἐπί in Micah 4:1 compared with ἐν in Isaiah 2:2, and the position of the article. That is, the Lukan Peter seems to have inserted a short citation of Isaiah 2:2 into his larger quotation from Joel 3:1–5.

This technique of using two texts from the LXX together has been explored extensively in intertextuality studies.[23] For example, C. M. Blumhofer notes that 'a brief textual citation or allusion, when juxtaposed to another text, can serve as the generative force for determining the meaning of the passage as a whole'.[24] Although brief, short textual citations within a larger quotation can produce a significant (even dominant) generative force of meaning that the author seeks to convey, as Bruce N. Fisk notes (of the use of Psalm 107:32 in Ps.-Philo, *LAB* 11:8), 'the biblical allusion *functions as exegesis*'.[25] Therefore, not only does the Lukan Peter insert Isaiah 2:2 into the quotation from Joel 3:1–5, but where Isaiah 2:2 resonates with Joel 3:1–5, Isaiah 2:2 will have the generative force for determining meaning.

Blumhofer argues that Isaiah 2:2 resonates with Joel 3:1–5 on the topic of the fate of the nations.[26] Joel's understanding of the scope of

---

21 Noble, *Common Property*, 114–46.
22 Beale, 'The Descent of the Eschatological Temple: Part 1', 94; Blumhofer, 'Luke's Alteration of Joel 3.1–5 in Acts 2.17–21', 504–5; Lidbeck, *Resurrection and* Spirit, 104, 154, 170. Others note that ἐν ταῖς ἐσχάταις ἡμέραις is a direct quotation from Isaiah 2:2, but do not explore how this affects the Lukan Peter's quotation of Joel 3:1. For example, see Bruce, *The Acts of the Apostles*, 61; Bock, *Acts*, 112; Kuecker, *The Spirit and the Other*, 120.
23 Hays, *Echoes of Scripture in the Letters of Paul*; Fisk, *Do You Not Remember*; Hays, *Echoes of Scripture in the Gospels*.
24 Blumhofer, 'Luke's Alteration of Joel 3.1–5 in Acts 2.17–21', 505. See also, Fisk, *Do You Not Remember*, 13–53.
25 Fisk, *Do You Not Remember*, 21; on the same phenomenon, cf. pp.24, 63, 305, 319.
26 Blumhofer, 'Luke's Alteration of Joel 3.1–5 in Acts 2.17–21', 505.

salvation is quite restricted, as Joel 3:1–5 precedes the judgement of the nations in Joel 4, and there is no indication that salvation is offered to the nations. In contrast to the restricted salvation in Joel, Isaiah 2 envisions all the nations coming to Jerusalem to hear the word of the Lord (Isa. 2:3). Moreover, while Joel 4:10 envisions the nations beating ploughshares into swords and pruning hooks into spears in their coming war with Yʜᴡʜ, Isaiah 2:4 envisions the opposite, as the nations, after hearing the word of the Lord, beat swords into ploughshares and spears into pruning hooks.[27] Therefore, by inserting Isaiah 2:2 into the quotation from Joel 3:1, Luke seeks to override the restrictive salvation envisioned by Joel 4 with the broader salvation of the nations envisioned in Isaiah 2.

## 3. Establishing the Temple of the Lord 'in the Last Days'

Beyond addressing the restrictive salvation implied in the intertextuality of Joel 3:1–5, inserting Isaiah 2:2 into this quotation also describes a specific type of eschatological event that precedes the word of the Lord going to the nations, that is, a temple inauguration.[28] Isaiah 2:2 (and Mic. 4:1) describes an eschatological future, which involves the house of the Lord being established on the mountain of the Lord, which is a description of the Jerusalem temple. The specific phrase that Luke utilises at the beginning of Peter's sermon, ἐν ταῖς ἐσχάταις ἡμέραις, when used in the LXX, envisions the eschatological temple of God being established in Jerusalem.

This allusion to the inauguration of the eschatological temple implied in the insertion of Isaiah 2:2 fits well into the overall depiction of the Pentecost narrative (Acts 2:1–41) as a temple inauguration.[29] While earlier Lukan scholarship focused on the parallels between the Pentecost theophany and the Sinai theophany (Exod. 19:16–19; Deut. 4:36), more recently, scholars draw connections between Pentecost

---

27  Blumhofer, 'Luke's Alteration of Joel 3.1–5 in Acts 2.17–21', 504–5.
28  Beale, 'The Descent of the Eschatological Temple: Part 1', 93–94.
29  For the recent discussions on the Temple-Pentecost connection, see Beale, 'The Descent of the Eschatological Temple: Part 1', 73–102; Beale, 'The Descent of the Eschatological Temple: Part 2', 63–90; Lidbeck, *Resurrection and Spirit*, 188–99.

and the Temple inaugurations (1 Kgs 8:10–11; 2 Chr. 7:1–3).³⁰

There are numerous connections that can be made between the temple inaugurations and the Pentecost theophany. The description of wind from heaven that ἐπλήρωσεν ὅλον τὸν οἶκον (filled the whole house) used in Acts 2:2 deeply resonates with the temple inaugurations, as the glory of Yhwh ἔπλησεν τὸν οἶκον (1 Kgs 8:10; 2 Chr. 7:1).³¹ Moreover, similar phrases are used in the LXX's prophetic literature for Yhwh residing in the heavenly temple (Hag. 2:7; Ezek. 10:4, 43:5, 44:5; see also 2 Chr. 5:13–14; Isa. 6:1).³² The language of a wind from heaven filling the house has clear parallels with the glory of Yhwh filling the Jerusalem temple or Yhwh's heavenly temple.

This language of a wind from heaven filling the house can be further connected to temple inaugurations through considering the geographical location of the Pentecost events. While Acts 1:13 describes the believers gathering in the τὸ ὑπερῷον (upper room), the events of Acts 2:1–4 occur in τὸν οἶκον (the house), which has led some to argue the Pentecost theophany occurred in the temple, that is the house of God.³³ This is supported by the observation that Acts 2:5–11 describes the crowds, which at the feast of Pentecost would have been gathered at the temple (e.g. Exod. 23:16–17,19; Num. 28:26–31), hearing the Spirit-empowered praise.³⁴ Moreover, the temple, and not a residential house, has the capacity for large crowds to hear Peter's message and the facilities to baptise 3,000 people in one day (Acts 2:41).³⁵ It is therefore likely that the entire Pentecost narrative is geographically located in the temple, giving further support to discerning

---

30 For the Sinai-Pentecost discussion, see Dunn, *Baptism in the Holy Spirit*, 48–49; Johnson, *The Acts of the Apostles*, 46; Fitzmyer, *The Acts of the Apostles*, 234; Witherington, *The Acts of the Apostles*, 131; Turner, *Power from on High*, 289; Wenk, *Community-Forming Power*, 246–51; Schnabel, *Acts*, 113. However, the limitations of this position have been persuasively argued by Menzies, *Empowered for Witness*, 198; Gunkel, Hirsch-Luipold, and Levison, 'Plutarch and Pentecost', 68.
31 Beale, 'The Descent of the Eschatological Temple: Part 2', 64–65; Lidbeck, *Resurrection and Spirit*, 194–95.
32 Beale, 'The Descent of the Eschatological Temple: Part 2', 64–65. Also, both the temple inauguration and the Pentecost theophany result in praise (2 Chr. 7:3; Acts 2:4), and use the imagery of fire (2 Chr. 7:1; Acts 2:3).
33 Beale, 'The Descent of the Eschatological Temple: Part 2', 65; McKinney, 'The Location of Pentecost', 80–85.
34 Beale, 'The Descent of the Eschatological Temple: Part 2', 65.
35 Beale, 'The Descent of the Eschatological Temple: Part 2', 65.

a temple inauguration motif being present in Luke's depiction of Pentecost.

Finally, there are connections between the atypical phrase γλῶσσαι ὡσεὶ πυρός (tongues as of fire) used in Acts 2:3 and Jewish temples. The phrase γλῶσσαι ὡσεὶ πυρός is only found in Jewish literature in Isa. 30:27; 1 En. 14:8–15, 71:5; 1Q29; 4Q376, with each of these passages being set in the context of the temple.[36] Isaiah 30:27–29 depicts Yhwh returning to the temple, protecting the temple and the people of Zion with a 'tongue like a consuming fire' (Isa. 30:27).[37] *1 Enoch* 14:8–15 and 71:5 describe Enoch ascending into heaven and seeing Yhwh's heavenly temple being built on tongues of fire (*1 En.* 14:9,10,15; 71:5).[38] Finally, the Qumran community's *Three Tongues of Fire* (1Q29; 4Q376) describes the high priest coming out of a theophanic cloud that surrounds the temple and using tongues of fire to discern a prophetic word.[39] These texts therefore link the language of tongues of fire with the temple, further strengthening the validity of seeing the temple inauguration motif in Acts 2.

From the imagery used in Acts 2:1–4, Luke seems to be describing the descent of the revelatory presence of God in the coming of the Spirit, with the believers in Jesus being the eschatological temple of God. That is, the Spirit comes upon the early believers in Jesus as the glory of God had come upon the temple in the temple inauguration scenes in the Hebrew Bible. This understanding of the early Jesus community as being the new temple of God would then be similar to Paul's understanding of the church as the temple of God (1 Cor. 3:16–17; 6:1) and to the Qumran community's understanding of their community as the temple of God's Spirit (1QS 3:6–9).

Recently, some scholars have questioned this conclusion, for they

---

36 Menzies, 'Pre-Lucan Occurrences', 27–60; Beale, 'The Descent of the Eschatological Temple: Part 1', 84–91.
37 Menzies, 'Pre-Lucan Occurrences', 33–34; Beale, 'The Descent of the Eschatological Temple: Part 1', 84–86.
38 Menzies, 'Pre-Lucan Occurrences', 34–44; Beale, 'The Descent of the Eschatological Temple: Part 1', 87–89.
39 Menzies, 'Pre-Lucan Occurrences', 44–55; Beale, 'The Descent of the Eschatological Temple: Part 1', 89–91; Lidbeck, *Resurrection and Spirit*, 195–96.

see the temple replaced only by Jesus.[40] Steve Smith has recently rejected the position that the early believers in Jesus in some way replace the temple, stating: 'Jesus is the locus of God's salvific action, and has taken this function from the temple [... therefore it] is wrong to understand the descent of the Spirit at Pentecost as the replacement of the temple; it is Jesus'.[41] Smith bases this position on the earlier work of Steve Walton, who similarly argued that Jesus takes up the salvific functions of the Jerusalem temple.[42] However, Walton notes that the Jerusalem temple's salvific function is only one of four functions that the Jerusalem temple had, alongside the temple being the symbolic centre of Israel, a microcosm of the heavenly world, and a place of the immanent-transcendent presence.[43] Moreover, Walton notes that the Spirit in Acts fulfils the temple's role of the immanent presence of God, and so, Jesus does not wholly replace all of the temple's functions.[44] While Jesus does fulfil most of the temple's functions, Smith has reduced the temple's function to its salvific role, overlooking that the Spirit in Acts could also fulfil some of the temple's functions.

In this context, it is indeed probable that the Lukan Peter, at the start of his Pentecost sermon, which functions as both an apologetic for the actions of the Spirit-filled believers and an explanation of the Pentecost theophany, would draw upon Isaiah 2:2 to help explain the coming of the Spirit. This reading resonates with recent studies on Acts 2, which draw the connection between the temple inaugurations and the Pentecost narrative.

## 4. Conclusion

To summarise, the Lukan Peter's insertion of ἐν ταῖς ἐσχάταις ἡμέραις into his quotation of Joel 3:1–5 is both identificatory and descriptive. This alteration identifies Pentecost as a key moment in the already

---

40 Smith, *The Fate of the Jerusalem Temple in Luke-Acts*, 187.
41 Smith, *The Fate of the Jerusalem Temple in Luke-Acts*, 187.
42 Smith, *The Fate of the Jerusalem Temple in Luke-Acts*, 187; Walton, 'A Tale of Two Perspectives', 144–46.
43 Walton, 'A Tale of Two Perspectives', 144–45.
44 Walton, 'A Tale of Two Perspectives', 146.

inaugurated eschatological age, but it also has a broader descriptive purpose. It is likely that a Jewish hearer of this editorial alteration would have recognised it as a direct quotation of Isaiah 2:2, which describes the inauguration of the eschatological temple of the Lord. In this way, this editorial alteration contributes to the overarching portrayal of the outpouring of the Spirit of God on the early believers as the revelatory presence of God filling the new eschatological temple of God.

Rev. Dr. John D. Griffiths
Alphacrucis University College

## Bibliography

Barrett, C. K. *Acts 1–14* (London: T&T Clark, 1994).

Beale, G. K. 'The Descent of the Eschatological Temple in the Form of the Spirit at Pentecost: Part 1: The Clearest Evidence', *TynBul* 56 (2005), 73–102.

Beale, G. K. 'The Descent of the Eschatological Temple in the Form of the Spirit at Pentecost: Part 2: Corroborating Evidence', *TynBul* 56 (2005), 63–90.

Blumhofer, C. M. 'Luke's Alteration of Joel 3.1–5 in Acts 2.17–21', *NTS* 62 (2016), 499–516.

Bock, D. L. *Acts* (BECNT; Grand Rapids, MI: Baker Academic, 2007).

Bruce, F. F. *The Acts of the Apostles* (NICNT; Grand Rapids, MI: Eerdmans, 1988).

Crabbe, K. *Luke-Acts and the End of History* (BZNW, 238; Berlin: de Gruyter, 2019).

Dunn, J. D. G. *Baptism in the Holy Spirit: A Re-Examination of the New Testament Teaching on the Gift of the Spirit in Relation to Pentecostalism Today* (London: SCM Press, 1970).

Fisk, B. N. *Do You Not Remember? Scripture, Story and Exegesis in the Rewritten Bible of Pseudo-Philo* (JSPSup, 37; Sheffield: Sheffield Academic, 2001).

Fitzmyer, J. A. *The Acts of the Apostles* (The Anchor Yale Bible; New Haven, CT: Yale University Press, 1998).

Gunkel, H., R. Hirsch-Luipold, and J. R. Levison 'Plutarch and Pentecost: An Exploration in Interdisciplinary Collaboration', in J. Frey and J. R. Levison (eds.), *The Holy Spirit, Inspiration, and the Cultures of Antiquity: Multidisciplinary Perspectives* (Ekstasis, 5; Berlin: de Gruyter, 2017), 63–94.

Haenchen, E. *The Acts of the Apostles: A Commentary* (Philadelphia, PA: Westminster, ET: 1971 [German: $^{14}$1965]).

Hays, R. B. *Echoes of Scripture in the Gospels* (Waco, TX: Baylor University Press, 2016).

Hays, R. B. *Echoes of Scripture in the Letters of Paul* (New Haven, CT: Yale University Press, 1989).

| | |
|---|---|
| Hur, J. | *A Dynamic Reading of the Holy Spirit in Luke-Acts* (London: T&T Clark, 2004). |
| Johnson, L. T. | *The Acts of the Apostles* (Sacra Pagina; Collegeville, MN: The Liturgical Press, 1992). |
| Keener, C. S. | *Acts: An Exegetical Commentary: Introduction and 1:1–2:47* (Grand Rapids, MI: Baker Academic, 2012). |
| Kuecker, A. | *The Spirit and the Other: Social Identity, Ethnicity and Intergroup Reconciliation in Luke-Acts* (LNTS, 444; London: Bloomsbury, 2011). |
| Lidbeck, B. W. | *Resurrection and Spirit: From the Pentateuch to Luke-Acts* (Eugene, OR: Wipf & Stock, 2020). |
| Mainville, O. | *The Spirit in Luke-Acts* (Woodstock: The Foundation for Pentecostal Scholarship, 1991). |
| McKinney, C. | 'The Location of Pentecost and Geographical Implications in Acts 2', in B. J. Beitzel (ed.), *Lexham Geographic Commentary on Acts through Revelation* (Bellingham, WA: Lexham, 2019), 77–93. |
| Menzies, G. | 'Pre-Lucan Occurrences of the Phrase "Tongue(s) of Fire"', *Pneuma* 22 (2000), 27–60. |
| Menzies, R. P. | *Empowered for Witness: The Spirit in Luke-Acts* (JPTSS; London: T&T Clark, 1994). |
| Noble, J. | *Common Property, the Golden Age, and Empire in Acts 2:42–47 and 4:32–35* (LNTS, 636; London: T&T Clark, 2021). |
| Ropes, J.H. | *The Beginnings of Christianity. Part I: The Acts of the Apostles. Vol. III: The Text of Acts* (London: Macmillan, 1926). |
| Schnabel, E. J. | *Acts* (ZECNT; Grand Rapids, MI: Zondervan, 2012). |
| Shelton, J. B. | *Mighty in Word and Deed* (Eugene, OR: Wipf & Stock, 1991). |
| Shepherd Jr., W. H. | *The Narrative Function of the Holy Spirit as a Character in Luke-Acts* (SBLDS, 147; Atlanta, GA: Scholars, 1994). |
| Smith, S. | *The Fate of the Jerusalem Temple in Luke-Acts: An Intertextual Approach to Jesus' Laments Over Jerusalem and Stephen's Speech* (LNTS, 553; London: T&T Clark, 2017). |

| | |
|---|---|
| Turner, M. | *Power from on High* (JPTSS, 9; Eugene, OR: Wipf & Stock, 2000). |
| Walton, S. | 'A Tale of Two Perspectives? The Place of the Temple in Acts', in T. D. Alexander, and S. J. Gathercole (eds.), *Heaven on Earth* (Carlisle: Paternoster, 2004), 135–49. |
| Wenk, M. | *Community-Forming Power* (JPTSS, 19; London: T&T Clark, 2004). |
| Witherington, B. III | *The Acts of the Apostles* (Grand Rapids, MI: Eerdmans, 1998). |

CHAPTER 16

# "In the last days …" (Acts 2:17): Eschatology, Cultural Diversity, and the Challenge of Inclusivity in Acts

Francis Innocent Otobo

## Abstract

In the eschaton, argued Peter in Acts 2:17–21, God's salvific activities will transcend Israel (homogeneous culture) to include everyone (cultural heterogeneity). In the unfolding of Acts, Luke highlights the fulfilment of this eschatological expectation in the communities of the early followers of Jesus. While Luke presents cultural diversity as a fulfilment of eschatological hope, Luke also depicts a situation of real-life challenges of inclusivity in the communities (Acts 6:1–7; 11:1–18; 13:44–45; 15:1–35), a situation occasioned by the emerging cultural heterogeneity experienced in the communities. Why would Luke bring up these challenging accounts in a narrative about the expansion of the church from Jerusalem to the ends of the earth?

## Introduction

The reading of Acts in this essay is as a narrative that was produced by its own circumstances and addresses its own readership, within a context of a mixed group of people from diverse cultural backgrounds.[1]

From the infancy narrative in the Gospel to the end of Acts, Luke constantly draws the reader's attention to God's saving plan extending beyond Israel to include non-Jews (for instance, Luke 2:29–32; Acts 28:28). This particular emphasis is further strengthened in the narrative about the outpouring of the Spirit upon Gentiles in Acts (cf. 10:44—11:18), which plays a major role in the legitimation of mission among non-Jews.[2] It is therefore pertinent that in Luke's work, the first exhortation of the followers of Jesus should address this important aspect of the narrative namely, the Spirit poured out on 'all flesh'. This opens up the invitation, inclusive of everyone, to experience salvation (Acts 2:21).

This essay explores the suggestion that originating from a broad homogeneous cultural context (among Judaeans in Jerusalem), the mission of the church, begun at Pentecost, expanded to include other cultures (cultural heterogeneity), amidst culture-oriented challenges. Luke's Pentecost rhetoric through the mouthpiece of Peter summarises what Luke argues in the rest of Acts: that though the early communities of the Jesus group experienced culture-oriented controversies and challenges (Acts 6:1–7; 11:1–18; 15:1–5), they convoked assemblies to discuss and resolve such matters amicably (cf. Acts 6:2–6; 11:18; 15:6).[3] The result each time is the expansion of the church and further inclusion of a wider variety of cultural groups (Acts 6:7; 15:3–4; 19:1–10). Acts thus recognises culturally diverse backgrounds in the communities, while drawing attention to the common denominator—the Holy Spirit in operation across cultural boundaries.[4]

This essay explores (1), cultural diversity in the communities as an

---

1 Cf. Moloney, 'God So Loved the World', 195. Acts will be read, not in isolation, but alongside its companion volume—the Gospel of Luke, both volumes hereafter referred to as Luke-Acts.
2 This is the subject-matter of my PhD dissertation, 'Overcoming Resistance: The Holy Spirit as Legitimator of Mission in Luke-Acts', presented to the University of Divinity, 2019.
3 Keener, *Acts*, 2, 1249.
4 Franklin, *Christ the Lord,* 11–12.

eschatological expectation in Luke-Acts, and (2), Luke's portrayal of the challenges of inclusivity emanating from the fulfilment of this hope.

## Luke-Acts and Eschatological Discourse

Lukan scholars generally agree that Luke-Acts is rich in eschatological discourse.[5] The nature of this discourse in the Lukan corpus, however, is variously debated. For instance, Conzelmann argues that the delay of the Parousia ignited some level of anxiety in the community of believers, a problem which Luke sets out to explain.[6] For Conzelmann, therefore, eschatology in Luke-Acts is delayed eschatology, and that this orchestrated the entirety of Luke's work—Luke arguing for eschatology as part of God's saving plan.[7] Mattill, on the other hand, citing the text of Acts 17:31 ('he has fixed a day on which he will judge the world in righteousness by a man whom he has appointed'), suggests that eschatology in Luke-Acts is imminent. Mattill argues that Luke probably had hopes of bringing about the day of the Lord ahead of time.[8] Midway between Conzelmann and Mattill are Wilson and Ellis who viewed eschatology in Luke-Acts as both imminent and delayed.[9]

Jesus, during his ministry in the Gospel, makes a series of eschatological predictions that find fulfilment in the reading of Acts. For instance, in response to the remarks of some of his followers regarding the beauty of the temple stones, Jesus says: 'As for these things that you see, the days will come when not one stone will be left upon another; all will be thrown down', (Luke 21:16).[10] In verses 7–28, Jesus refers to events that will materialise in 'the days' to come. Of significance is the

---

5   Rather than being an exposition of the eschatology of Luke-Acts, this section is a brief reading of some eschatological texts in Luke-Acts, in order to pave the way for our concern—cultural diversity in the community as an eschatological hope in Luke-Acts, and the challenges posed by the fulfilment of this hope. For a detailed reading of eschatology in Luke-Acts, see Ward, 'Eschatology in Luke-Acts', 147–156; Wilson, 'Lukan Eschatology', 330–347; Ellis, *Eschatology in Luke*; Mattill, *Luke and the Last Things*; Gaventa, 'The Eschatology of Luke-Acts', 27–42.
6   Conzelmann, *Theology of St Luke*, 95–136.
7   Conzelmann, *Theology of St Luke*, 103, 131–132.
8   Mattill, *Luke and the Last Things*, 233.
9   See Ellis, *Eschatology in Luke*, 11–20; Wilson, 'Lukan Eschatology', 336–347.
10  The eschatological theme of the text becomes clearer when read against Acts 2:19–21. See Ward, 'Eschatology in Luke-Acts', 155.

statement in verse 20: 'When you see Jerusalem surrounded by armies, then know that its desolation has come near'.[11] This in a way signals the fulfilment of the prediction in verse 6. The reader in Luke's time would know that this part of the eschatological prediction has taken place.[12] Equally, reading through Acts, the reader can find fulfilment of other eschatological predictions of Jesus, for instance: earthquake (16:26), famine (11:28), signs and wonders (4:30; 8:13), imprisonments (4:3), trials before rulers of the synagogues (4:5), kings (4:26), and governors (18:12). Peter and the rest of the followers of Jesus bear witness to Jesus through the power of the Spirit (2:32; 3:15; cf. 2:1–4; 4:8). The disciples are persecuted (8:1b; 12:3–5), and Stephen (7:54—8:1a) and James (12:1–5) are killed. In Luke's narrative, these things are bound to happen in 'the days' to come, but the end (τέλος) will not follow immediately (Luke 21:9). However, to Luke's contemporary reading Luke-Acts, these things have happened, suggesting that they are already in 'the days' to come that Jesus predicted. In this narrative and others, Luke draws attention to those predictions which had already been fulfilled.[13]

Further, Acts 1—2 is replete with eschatological references. Jesus promises the disciples that they will be baptised with the Holy Spirit not many days from now (vv. 4–5). This baptism, Luke emphasises, is distinguished from that of John both in the synoptic tradition (Matt. 3:13-17; Mark 1:7-8; Luke 3:21-22) and elsewhere in Acts (11:16; 18:24—19:7). In the narrative sequence, immediately following this promise, the disciples enquired of Jesus whether it is time to restore the Kingdom to Israel (v.6). Jesus' response suggests that the disciples asked the wrong question (v.7).[14] For Jesus, the emphasis is not to be placed on the Parousia but on the present—witnessing to the exaltation of Jesus in the power of the Spirit (v.8).[15] This point is emphasised with the word ἀλλά (but) placed at the beginning of the sentence.

---

11 This is an important factor in determining the date of Luke-Acts. Most scholars believe that Luke-Acts was written during the war that led to the destruction of the Jerusalem temple, probably just before or after the destruction. See Bock, *Luke 9:51—24:53*, 1675.
12 Ward, 'Eschatology in Luke-Acts', 156.
13 Gaventa, 'The Eschatology of Luke-Acts', 27.
14 Conzelmann, *Theology of St Luke*, 121.
15 Franklin, 'Ascension and Eschatology', 191.

With these words, Jesus then ascends, the disciples are promised that he will return in the same way that they see him go, and they return to Jerusalem awaiting the fulfilment of the promises (1:12–26). Acts 1:6–8 thus is a composite of an inquiry, a rejection of the inquiry, and three promises—(1) Spirit empowerment; (2) world-wide mission; and (3) the return of Jesus.[16] The rest of the narrative of Acts tells the reader about the fulfilment of the first two promises—the outpouring of the Spirit (2:1–4; 8:17; 10:44; 19:6), and mission from Jerusalem towards the ends of the earth (8:4–39; 9:15; 10:1–48; 28:28). While the third promise—the return of the Lord—still awaits fulfilment, the fulfilment of the first two in Acts provides the trustworthy guarantee for the third.[17]

## Pentecost and Eschatological Expectations

As stated in the text of Acts 1:8, the universal mission to the ends to the earth will become possible after the pouring forth of the Spirit. At Pentecost those present are Jews (2:5) and proselytes (2:10b), drawing together two themes woven together: the reconstitution of Israel and the incorporation of the nations.[18] This is reminiscent of Isaiah 2:2 which refers to 'all the nations' gathering to the mountain of the house of Lord 'in the days to come'. Read against this background, Acts 2:5–11 could thus be seen as fulfilling this text from Isaiah.

Peter's address to 'all the house of Israel' (2:36) following the outpouring of the Spirit calls on Israel to recognise and respond to this reconstitution (2:14,22,36). As it is, the disciples' question about the restoration of the kingdom (1:6) is a response to the promise of the Spirit in the preceding verse (cf. 1:5). It is therefore the case that an eschatological promise prompts an eschatological question.[19] For, as Franklin asserts,

> the restoration of Israel also issues in the wider, universal significance by which she becomes the light to the nations

---

16 Gaventa, 'Eschatology of Luke-Acts Revisited', 36.
17 Franklin, *Christ the Lord*, 40–41; Wilson, 'The Ascension: A Critique', 280.
18 Franklin, 'Ascension and Eschatology', 196.
19 Francis, 'Eschatology and History', 52.

(2.17ff, 39). Both the reconstitution of Israel and the incorporation of the nations are, in the Old Testament, accompaniments of the final saving act of God in Jerusalem and it is as this that Luke portrays the Pentecost scene.[20]

Thus, 'Pentecost, whilst witnessing to the Exaltation of Jesus, is also the foreshadowing of the universal mission which is to be under the eschatological power of the Spirit'.[21] The Spirit-inspired witnessing narrated in Acts is the one aspect of Luke's writing to which he explicitly applies the terms ἐσχάταις ἡμέραις (last days).[22] Luke's accounts of the outpouring of the Spirit in Acts and the consequent and subsequent witnessing inspired by the Spirit, therefore, are to be properly understood as expressions of the eschatological character of the life expected (and lived out) in the community of believers before the day of the Lord comes (cf. for instance, Luke 24:45–49; Acts 1:4–5,6–8; 2:33,38–39; 4:31; 5:32; 8:14–17; 9:17; 10:44–46; 11:16; 19:6; 26:6).[23] Luke is alluding to this new beginning (Luke 24:49; Acts 1:5).

## 'In the Last Days' (Acts 2:17)

In his Pentecost sermon, Peter states: 'In the last days it will be, God declares, that I will pour out my Spirit upon all flesh' (2:17), 'then everyone who calls on the name of the Lord shall be saved' (v.21). Luke, in Peter's opening statement, has changed Joel's 'afterwards' to 'in the last days'. Although individually the words 'last' and 'day/s' are not peculiar to Luke-Acts in the New Testament,[24] the phrase 'in the last days' only occurs here in the Gospels and Acts (Acts 2:17). The closest phrase in the Gospels appears in John 7:37 which uses the singular form, ἐν δὲ τῇ ἐσχάτῃ ἡμέρᾳ (now in the last day). Here, John writes of a chronological 'last day' of a festival in which Jesus is present. This is

---

20 Franklin, 'Ascension and Eschatology', 196.
21 Franklin, 'Ascension and Eschatology', 196.
22 Francis, 'Eschatology and History', 51–52.
23 Francis, 'Eschatology and History', 52.
24 For instance: Last (Matt. 12:45; Mark 9:35; Luke 11:26; John 6:39; Acts 2:17; Phil 4:10); day (Matt 6:11; Mark 1:21; John 1:29; Rom. 2:5; 1 Cor. 1:8); days (Matt. 2:1; Mark 1:9; Luke 1:5; John 2:12; Acts 1:3; Gal. 1:18; Rev. 2:13).

the same sense in which the term 'last' is employed in the other usages in the Gospels and in Acts.[25] Herein lies the importance of this particular usage in Acts 2, which records the first testimony of the church post-Pentecost. As Keener indicates, Luke has changed Joel's text not ignorantly, but deliberately.[26]

Luke employs the phrase in an eschatological sense by implying that what he is about to state had been declared by God in the past but that the fulfilment of what God had declared belonged not in the era of the declaration but in a future time.[27] In Luke's estimation, that future time is fulfilled in the hearing of his listeners (cf. Luke 4:21).[28] Hence, before citing the words from Joel, Luke states: καὶ ἔσται ἐν ταῖς ἐσχάταις ἡμέραις, λέγει ὁ θεός ('and it will be in the last days, God declares'; Acts 2:17a). The phrase ἐν ταῖς ἐσχάταις ἡμέραις emphasises the eschatological nature of the Pentecost event which Luke is going to use to expound his message to the church. What Peter's interpretation suggests is that the gift of the Spirit is, in itself, a sign of the last days. This resonates with Baker's argument that, 'Changing "after this" to "in the last days" ties the Pentecost "pouring out" of the Spirit to a particular stage of salvation history—in fact, the final one'.[29] Similarly, Marshall avows that the pouring out of the Spirit at Pentecost is a public announcement that 'God's final act of salvation has begun to take place'.[30] However, since the narrative has previously included instances of Spirit reception, even moreso than the gift, it is the scope of recipients which speaks of the event as belonging to the last days. Hence, Peter's reference to the outpouring of the Spirit 'upon all flesh', and preceding this citation with 'in the last days' emphatically suggests the eschatological nature of the event, fulfilling Joel's prophecy. This is strengthened by the emphasis later in verse 39, 'for the promise is for you, for your children, and for all who are far away, everyone whom the Lord our God calls to him'. The citation is

---

25  See for instance, Matt. 19:30; Mark 12:6; Luke 12:59; John 8:9.
26  Keener, *Acts*, 1.874–875.
27  For the eschatological sense of the phrase in other NT texts, see, for instance, 2 Tim. 3:1; Heb. 1:2; Jas 5:3; 2 Pet. 3:3.
28  Keener, *Acts*, 1.877.
29  Baker, 'Theological Program', 55.
30  Marshall, *The Acts of the Apostles*, 73.

thus programmatic for, and fulfilled in, the subsequent narrative.[31] As Gaventa argues, 'someone who read only this much of Acts would be struck by its fervor for the last days'.[32]

Commenting on Acts 2:17–21, Daniel Baker asserts that, 'Luke gives us numerous narrative signposts to tell us that the words in Acts 2:17–21 are important and even *how* they are important'.[33] Baker mentions five areas of importance as follows: (1) the historical moment of Peter's proclamation—the ascension and enthronement of the Christ and the subsequent pouring out of the Spirit; (2) the proclamation in a speech form, and especially a speech of the import of Peter's;[34] (3) the length of the citation from a minor prophet in comparison to citations from major prophets;[35] (4) the citation emphasising major Lukan themes across both volumes of Luke's work; and (5) the parallels between Luke 4:18–19 and Acts 2:17–21.[36]

Unpacking Baker's fourth item, two points needed to be made which are particularly emphasised in the citation of Joel, and which encapsulate Peter's entire speech, namely: (1) that in these recent events (of Pentecost), the *eschaton* has come upon his hearers;[37] and (2) that in this time, God's salvific acts have no ethnic preference, and so will transcend Israel (a single cultural group) to include everyone who calls on the name of the Lord (v.21). With this, Luke highlights cross-cultural mission as part of the eschatological hope.

The particular concern of this essay is essentially not the pouring out of the Spirit, but the scope of the recipients of this divine gift—all flesh—and what this implies for the eschatological communities

---

31  Salter, *Power of Pentecost*, 98.
32  Gaventa, 'Eschatology of Luke-Acts', 34.
33  Baker, 'Theological Program', 52.
34  As Baker indicates, speeches provide authorial commentary on the narrative. Cf. Peter's speeches (2:14–40; 3:12–26; 10:34–43); Stephen (Acts 7:2–53); Paul (13:1; 16:41; 17:22–31; 20:18–35; 22:1–21; 24:10–21; 26:2–23; 28:25–28).
35  The full 95-word excerpt from Joel can be compared, for instance, with the great Isaiah prophecies so prominent in Luke-Acts: the 43-word citation from Isa. 40:3–5 in Luke 3:4–6; the 26-word Isa. 61:1–2a/58:6 quoted in Luke 4:18–19, the 39-word quotation of Isa. 53:7–8 in Acts 8:32–33, and the 54-word quotation of Isa. 6:9–10 in Acts 28:26–27.
36  Baker, 'Theological Program', 52–53.
37  Baker, 'Theological Program', 55, though later states that Peter's citation of Joel 2:28 in Acts 2:17 suggests that his hearers are in the last days, by omitting this from his list, Baker does not give it the importance that it deserves in the narrative.

of the followers of Jesus. Following Acts 2:19–20 which addresses the 'Day of the Lord' (cf. Luke 21:25–27), the offer of salvation in verse 21 is to 'everyone'. Though Salter sees the fulfilment of Joel particularly in 'the presence of prophecy, dreams and visions, and signs and wonders',[38] what follows explores the fulfilment of the prophetic text in the pouring out of the Spirit upon 'all flesh' and the availability of salvation to 'everyone' who calls on the name of the Lord. This is more significant because this fulfilment is taking place 'in the last days', according to God's declaration (v.17). The present tense λέγει ὁ θεός (God says/declares) supports the argument that the declaration of God in the past (Joel 2:28) concerning an outpouring of the Spirit 'in the last days' (Acts 2:17) is relevant and valid in the present moment, that is, what was declared is taking place now. By implication, the effect of the divine initiative which applies to two universal categories (all flesh, and everyone), and which forms an inclusio in the citation, becomes an eschatological expectation which the community looks forward to. As Luke clearly indicates, the experience of the Holy Spirit in the upper room 'immediately flowed out of the Upper Room and began to accomplish its ultimate purpose by drawing the various cultures symbolically represented in Jerusalem for the Feast'.[39] Thus for Luke, Pentecost sets in motion the geographic expansion of the gospel 'to the ends of the earth' (Acts 1:8; cf. 2:39), and also emphasises a barrier-breaking inclusivity (Acts 2:39). The Holy Spirit poured out by Jesus serves as God's eschatological agent extending the divine invitation of hospitality to Israel and the nations.[40]

This is further substantiated by Peter's assertion in v.39: 'For the promise is for you, for your children, and for all who are far away, everyone whom the Lord our God calls to him'. Peter reiterates that what happened to the one hundred and twenty in the upper room (Acts 2:1–4) is available to 'all flesh' (πᾶσαν σάρκα, v. 17).[41] This is why Gaventa's argument that Francis is 'forcing a consistency which

---

38  Salter, *Power of Pentecost*, 98.
39  Sala, 'Pentecostal Culture', 108.
40  Mittelstadt, 'Theology of Hospitality', 135.
41  Baker, 'Theological Program', 57.

the text does not support' needs to be reviewed.⁴² Gaventa states: 'While Francis is right to insist on the eschatological character of the Pentecost event, that does not necessarily mean that every manifestation of the Spirit in Acts is eschatological. Indeed, only by importing 2:17 into other texts could one conclude that the Spirit is an eschatological gift (cf. 8:14-24; 10:44-48, 19:1-7)'.⁴³ Contrary to Gaventa's argument, it is plausible to submit that by replacing Joel's 'afterwards' with 'in the last days' and suggesting that the outpouring of the Spirit fulfills Joel's text, Luke indicates that the Pentecost event is eschatological. Following on from this, if the pouring out of the Spirit upon 'all flesh' is eschatological because of the 'in the last days' of verse 17, then the subsequent instances of the outpouring of the Spirit upon 'all flesh' (from then on) in the narrative are also eschatological, since they all belong in 'the last days' which start at Pentecost as indicated by 2:17. Peter's statement in Acts 11:15 that, 'The Holy Spirit fell on them just as on us at the beginning (ἐν ἀρχῆι)' drives home the point. His reference to 'just as on us at the beginning' (ἐν ἀρχῇ) emphasises that the outpouring of the Spirit in Acts 10:44, referred to in 11:15, is also part of the expected activities of the 'the last days' of Acts 2:17. This means that this is equally a fulfilment of Joel 2:28-32 as was the first outpouring in Acts 2:1-4. To state it more clearly, Peter addresses fellow Israelites (Acts 2:14,22,29 and 36), and affirms the universality of the divine gifts also 'for all who are far away' (v.39). This point is particularly significant, for from this beginning the emphasis on universality sets the tone for cross-cultural mission and the inclusion of non-Jews in the community of believers.

The question then may be asked: Why has the Lukan Peter read this text this way, replacing Joel's 'afterwards' with 'in the last days'? This essay proposes that the rendering of this prophetic text (from Joel) in Acts strengthens Luke's assertion that cross-cultural mission and, therefore, its consequence, cultural diversity in the communities, both fulfill God's eschatological plan for the church (cf. Acts 10:34-35). This assertion becomes necessary as Luke sets out to encourage

---

42  Gaventa, 'Eschatology of Luke-Acts', 38.
43  Gaventa, 'Eschatology of Luke-Acts', 38.

community members to embrace cultural diversity which, as will be shown below, presented some challenges in the communities.

## Cultural Diversity in Luke-Acts

The sociologist Peter Berger argues that culture is the product of human externalisation. By externalisation Berger means the 'ongoing outpouring of human being into the world, both in the physical and mental activity of men'.[44] Dimitri Sala observes that this happens as human beings extend themselves into the world by creating for themselves products and activities, material and non-material.[45] The outcome of this extension is therefore the emergence of material things like food, clothing, building style, farming implements; and non-material things like language, greetings, and other behavioural patterns—in other words, the development of a people's way of life. On the basis of this human culture is developed, varying from place to place depending on the group of humans making it.[46]

While culture is a human construct, eventually culture begins to shape up and build human beings within particular cultural settings, such that the human person becomes a product of that culture.[47] Consequently, culture which constitutes the totality of human products, once produced, cannot so easily be altered even by its adherents.[48] Nevertheless, culture is ultimately unstable because it is a human construct, and human lives do change.[49] It is the conflict between the craving for cultural stability on the one hand and the altered cultural experiences on the other hand among the early followers of Jesus that resulted in the challenges of inclusivity as narrated in the Acts of the Apostles.

From the above, being the 'way of life' of a group, or groups, of people, culture can be classified in various ways, for instance, by ethnicity,

---

44 Berger, *Social Reality*, 14.
45 Sala, 'Pentecostal Culture', 105.
46 Sala, 'Pentecostal Culture', 105.
47 Berger, *Social Reality*, 14.
48 Berger, *Social Reality*, 16.
49 Sala, 'Pentecostal Culture', 105.

sex, age, religion, politics, or even class.⁵⁰ This suggests that within a broad cultural setting, there can be varied cultural groups. What this means, for instance, is that, people who identify with the same ethnic group (for instance, Hebrews and Hellenists—Jews) have a lot in common. Within the same ethnic setting, people of the same political interest or age bracket or religious group can have a way of doing or seeing things differently from others.⁵¹ To identify with a particular cultural group already entails the recognition of other groups of people who see and do things differently from the way those within that chosen group. Thus, as Yntema noted, 'the things we wear and use and the ways in which we speak, behave and think are often linked to the different identities we assume under various circumstances [ ... ], these identities are not exclusively *ethnic* in nature but may often be *cultural* identities'.⁵² They are cultural in the sense that the extension of the human person in activities and production has resulted in the construction or creation of particular behavioural patterns that are different from other groups. Cultural diversity thus recognises the existence of a variety of cultural groups even within a society or an institution. Most of the time, this explains the way an individual collaborates with others, and also how particular social groups accept or dissociate from others.

Luke highlights this in several texts in Luke-Acts. For instance, Luke refers to a group known as 'tax collectors' who are identified as sinners by the 'crowd', and indicates that association with these tax collectors is abhorred (Luke 19:1–7; cf. 5:27–32). The followers of Jesus identified as Christians (Acts 11:26) were held in high esteem by 'the people' (Acts 5:13). Luke 4:16–30; Acts 13:44–45; and 14:1–7,19–20 also refer to different cultural groups. As Kuecker indicates, 'our sense of identity—who we understand ourselves to be—is intimately connected to the manner in which we live and interact in all our relationships. In a reciprocal manner, the relationships that we cultivate

---

50   Ethnic identities are usually assumed by groups of people that believed they had a common origin or shared a common past. Yntema, 'Material Culture', 145.
51   Within the same Jewish ethnicity, for instance, there are those who identify as Pharisees, others as Sadducees, and yet there are the Essenes, the Zealots, the followers of Jesus, and so on. Although belonging to the same broad ethnic background, each of these groups have different cultural identities.
52   Yntema, 'Material Culture', 146.

are inseparable from our sense of identity'.⁵³ Following from this, it is reasonable to say that to identify with a group referred to as Jews, Gentiles, or Christians is to belong to a particular cultural identity group. In the ancient Mediterranean world, the group-identity was so significant for the social identity of an individual, that clear boundary lines existed between the in-group and out-groups. Thus, for one to belong to a particular group like the Jews, implied that one had inclusive and exclusive social boundaries.⁵⁴ We see this demonstrated in Acts 11:1–3 when Peter (a Jewish Christian leader) is reprimanded for going to the 'uncircumcised' and eating with them. This is consistent with Kuecker's further argument that cultural groups can be incubators of positive identity based upon communal solidarity (cf. Acts 2:44–45; 4:23–24,32), or they can be breeding grounds for intergroup conflict (cf. Acts 4:1–31; 6:1,8–15; 8:1–3 and so on).⁵⁵ As can be observed in the instances mentioned above (Luke 4:16–30; Acts 13:44–45; and 14:1–7,19–20), a group which identifies as Jews reacts negatively when that which is considered as their heritage is given to 'others' who are of a different cultural background.

The reader of Acts already knows from the Gospel that the message of Jesus will extend to people across cultural boundaries (Luke 2:32; 24:47), although this will not be without its challenges (cf. Luke 4:28–29). This expectation finds fulfillment in Acts, which tells the story of how the followers of Jesus' post-resurrection program for the church take up mission from Jerusalem to the ends of the earth (Acts 1:8; cf. Acts 28:28—'Let it be known to you then that this salvation of God has been sent to the Gentiles; they will listen'). This indicates the proclamation of salvation across cultural settings. This cultural boundary-breaking soteriological proclamation also resonates with Peter's Pentecost sermon—that in the eschaton the mission of the followers of Jesus will open up to everyone who calls on the name of the Lord (2:21; cf. v.39). This suggests that in Luke's mind and narrative, cross-cultural mission is part of the eschatological activities of the believers in Jesus. While in the unfolding of Acts Luke shows that the

---

53 Kuecker, *The Spirit and the 'Other'*, 24.
54 Kok, 'Social Identity', 1–9.
55 Kuecker, *The Spirit and the 'Other'*, 27.

eschatological expectation/hope of cultural heterogeneity in the community of Christ-believers is being fulfilled, Luke also signals consequences for the community.

As Luke highlighted at several points in the narrative, between Jerusalem and the ends of the earth, different culturally diverse identity groups make their way into the communities of the followers of Jesus: the Aramaic-speaking Jews (Acts 2:41; cf. vv.14,22,29,36,37); the Greek-speaking Jews (6:1); the Samaritans (8:14); and other cultural groups that are broadly classified as Gentiles (for instance, 8:26–40; 10:47–48; 15:3–4; 16:34; 19:5). Also, other groups who are recognised as making their way into the body of believers in Jesus are the priests (6:7), former sorcerers/magicians (8:13; 19:17–20), and others of the Pharisees' sect (15:5). This is Luke's recognition of different cultural backgrounds among the early believers in Jesus.

While it is interesting to note Luke's announcement of the emergence of cultural heterogeneity in the community of the followers of Jesus, it is also pertinent to observe Luke's introduction of occasions of internal conflicts within the communities at such times when the communities experience cultural diversity, which was not the case when the community was culturally homogeneous.[56] The cause of conflict on each occasion, as highlighted by Luke, is related to the another culture sub-group—the Greek-speaking Jews, the Gentiles, the uncircumcised —, whose very presence provokes the challenges to inclusivity that erupted within the community of believers in Jesus.

Let us now take a cursory look at some of the challenges as presented in Acts.

## Challenges of Inclusivity in the Communities

There is inclusion when everyone in a particular cultural setting feels equally welcomed, valued, appreciated, and respected. This is the case when everyone can have equal access to opportunities and resources, and be able to contribute to the improvement of their society. A

---

56 That is, in the earlier stage when the community was culturally a predominantly Aramaic-speaking Jewish group.

challenge to inclusivity arises when some in a given community or society are denied the right of being fully included in the fabric of community life. This is so when some are treated as 'other' in the community. In other words, those who suffer the bite of the 'challenge of inclusivity' do not enjoy the full privilege of bona fide citizens.

This situation is reflected in the early Christian communities as narrated in the text of Acts. Kok's summary of the situation is apt:

> As more and more non-Judeans or Hellenists joined the movement, and the exclusive Judean boundary markers came under pressure, so did the internal plurality and tension within the Christ-movement increase. Subsequently, we find in Peter evidence of the internal struggle in which he found himself, which was symptomatic of the Christ-following movement as a whole.[57]

Bock presents it this way: 'The need to resolve the issue became more intense as Gentiles began to come in and the community's character became clearer. The new community was no longer going to be a purely Jewish institution, but it did not sense a calling to abandon its connection to Judaism'.[58]

Let us now focus briefly on some representative texts in Acts which highlights the community's growth and the consequent challenges to inclusivity.

## Acts 2:44; 4:32

In this first summary account of the community life and growth, Luke states that 'all who believed were together and had all things in common' (Acts 2:44). Similarly, in 4:32, Luke confirms this state of affairs by stating that: 'Now the whole group of those who believed were of one heart and soul, and no one claimed private ownership of any possession, but everything they owned was held in common'. The whole group of believers here would refer to the initial group of Christ

---

57 Kok, 'Social Identity', 6.
58 Bock, *Acts*, 37.

followers which began in Jerusalem among Jews who were all Hebrew/ Aramaic speaking. As can be observed from Luke's presentation of the community to the reader, at this point in time all the members of the community had all things in common, and no one complained of being in want because 'no one claimed private ownership of any possessions'. This appears to be a perfect community of believers. Luke, however, quickly alerts the reader to the fact that this perfect situation did not last. With the admission of believers from other cultural backgrounds came several internal challenges.

## Acts 6:1-7

The focus here is verse 1—'Now during those days, when the disciples were increasing in number, the Hellenists complained against the Hebrews because their widows were being neglected in the daily distribution of food'. A few things are worth noting: (1) Since it refers to a period, the phrase, 'during those days', suggests that what Luke is about to mention has been happening for quite some time. This is different from the reference to a particular day as in Acts 2:1 (τὴν ἡμέραν—the day). This reported case is not a one-off issue, rather it indicates a persisting state of affairs, as indicated by the imperfect tense παρεθεωροῦντο ('were being neglected').[59] The particular time-scale, however, is not indicated.[60] (2) The misdemeanour in the community that Luke points out is an issue of one group within the community being unfair to another. By identifying Hellenists (Greek-speaking Jews) in distinction to Hebrews (Aramaic-speaking Jews),[61] Luke introduces the presence of another culture sub-group, for 'anyone who functions in a single or predominant language is almost certainly a product of the culture which that language embodies'.[62] With this introduction, Luke mentions the emergence of unfairness in the community of believers—unequal treatment against the emerging new cultural

---

59 Dunn, *The Acts of the Apostles*, 82.
60 Dunn, *The Acts of the Apostles*, 81.
61 Witherington classifies them as two distinct cultural groups. See Witherington, *The Acts of the Apostles*, 249.
62 Dunn, *The Acts of the Apostles*, 81.

sub-group. (3) This incessant and recurring misbehaviour leads to the grumbling of the Hellenists against the Hebrews. Though some scholars suggest that the neglect of the Hellenists' widows was created by a 'growth problem', this is not clear in the passage.[63] One might then ask, if the unfair treatment is caused by a growth problem, why would it be one particular cultural group that suffers this unfair treatment? Luke is clear on 'what is', not on 'what caused it'. However, taking Acts 2:44 and 4:32 (cf. also 5:12) into consideration, the narrative of Acts 6:1–7 suggests that these Hellenists in the community began to suffer the bite of discriminatory exclusion on account of cultural diversity.[64]

## Acts 10–11

The beginning of the last phase of the mission program—witness to the ends of the earth—posits more dramatic episodes with regards to cultural heterogeneity and the challenge of inclusivity in the communities. At the start of the Cornelius story (Acts 10), Peter's vision and his reaction reflects the initial tension in the community on account of cultural differences. When Peter is commanded to 'Get up, Peter; kill and eat' (10:13), Peter responded: 'By no means, Lord; for I have never eaten anything that is profane or unclean' (10:14; cf. v.28). The command to Peter, Peter's response, and the reaction of the voice—'What God has made clean, you must not call profane'—all point to how traditional Jews viewed the non-Jews at the time. That Luke pointed out how the entire dialogue between Peter and the voice happened three times (10:16), indicates how strongly this feeling among Jews would have been. Even when these non-Jews became believers in Christ, they were still considered unclean and not worthy of fellowship. This is further substantiated in Luke's narrative when in 10:46, after Cornelius and household have received the Holy Spirit, Peter had to ask: 'Can

---

[63] Witherington, *The Acts of the Apostles*, 249; Johnson, *The Acts of the Apostles*, 105; Bock, *Acts*, 257.
[64] It is worth taking into consideration Stenschke's suggestion that 'one can only speculate whether other issues were contested as well; '"When they heard this"', 73. See also Keener, *Acts*, 2.1253–1260, for other possible issues. This essay has focused on the case of cultural difference as the primary issue.

anyone withhold the water for baptising these people who have received the Holy Spirit just as we have?' Peter's question suggests that some in the community would have questioned the baptism of these new believers of non-Jewish origin. As the narrative unfolds, in 11:1–3 Luke indicates that in the community some are called circumcised, and others are referred to as uncircumcised. Peter is reprimanded for associating with the uncircumcised. While Johnson insists that 'the leaders of the church in Jerusalem and the ordinary believers had no problem with the conversion and baptism of Cornelius',[65] the text is not so clear about this at this point of the narrative. What is clear is that, this narrative in Acts 10—11, when placed against the first summary account of the community in 2:44, 4:32, and 5:12, and side-by-side the response of the Jerusalem church at receiving the news of conversion in Samaria (8:14), one is left to ask why it is now unfit for some 'believers' to be in the company of others or why the question had to be raised before the baptism of some. It then comes to light that there was an issue with including Gentiles as Gentiles into the people of God.[66] Thus, while Luke is interested in the conversion of these Gentiles, he is much more interested in the conversion of Peter's and the Jerusalem church's perspectives.[67]

## 13:44–45

While the incident recorded here is technically not within the Christian community, it does portray the reaction of some Jews at seeing so many non-Jews coming into what they consider to be their religious space. This is not the case when these same Jews are in the company of other non-Jews who are ethnically regarded as Gentiles, but culturally Judaisers (for becoming devout converts to Judaism). As Luke mentions, 'when the meeting of the synagogue broke up, many Jews and devout converts to Judaism followed Paul and Barnabas, who spoke to them and urged them to continue in the grace of God' (v.43).

---

65  Johnson, *The Acts of the Apostles*, 197.
66  Stenschke, "'When they heard this'", 75.
67  Keener, *Acts*, 2.1817.

Seen from a broad perspective, these Jews and these converts to Judaism now share a particular cultural trait (they are all Judaisers) though they are ethnically of different origin. But, the next sabbath when other non-Jews who have not converted to Judaism (therefore do not belong in the cultural family of Judaism) come up to hear the message of Paul and Barnabas, the Jews were filled with rage (v.45).[68] As Keener suggested, the devout converts to Judaism (who underwent circumcision as well—for males) may also not have been pleased by this new 'lower' standard for other Gentiles.[69] Kilgallen puts it more forcefully, that the move beyond god-fearers to include all Gentiles in the claim that every person who believes in the Lord will be justified was what caused the opposition to the word.[70] Again, this signifies a challenge to inclusivity on cultural grounds.

## 15:1–5

This text gives us the background to the Council at Jerusalem (15:6–29). From the narrative so far, it is clear that now there are many Jewish believers (2:37–42; cf. 6:1; 10:45; 11:2), as well as Gentile believers (10:48; 11:1; 14:1,27). Many Jewish believers now acknowledge the redemptive mission extended to the non-Jews (11:18). What is at stake now is not the admission of Gentiles, but the conditions for such admission.[71] As Luke noted, some of the Jewish followers of Jesus who came to Antioch expressed the sentiment that Gentiles are excluded from salvation unless they become like Jews, by being circumcised according to the custom of Moses (15:1). As if that was not enough, others of the Pharisaic sect insisted that Gentile believers must be 'ordered to keep the law of Moses' (v.5). Of course, this did not go down well with Paul and Barnabas who refuted this teaching and opinion. Antioch is the centre of the Gentile mission, and should circumcision

---

68 This recalls Stenschke's assertion that, had the Jews with whom Peter shared table-fellowship (cf. 11:1–18) become proper law-abiding Jewish proselytes, the problem would not have arisen. Stenschke, "'When they heard this'", 75.
69 Keener, *Acts*, 2.2095.
70 Kilgallen, 'Hostility to Paul', 1–15.
71 Conzelmann, *Acts,* 115; Stenschke, "'When they heard this'", 77.

be now proclaimed as necessary, then the Antioch Gentile mission in general and Paul's mission program in the Diaspora in particular are in question.[72] Though these Judaeans do not have the authority of the Jerusalem church, the fact that some in the community of believers held this view against fellow believers in Christ and were bold enough to speak up about it suggests conflict within the community. This is pointed out in verse 2 which refers to 'no small dissension and debate' between Paul and Barnabas and these Judaeans. The matter could not be resolved in the debate that ensued, so it is referred to the apostles and elders in Jerusalem for resolution (15:2). The bottom line is that these Judaean believers are of the conviction that all non-Judaeans believers could not be included in the community of Christ believers unless they (the non-Judaeans) become like Judaeans by being circumcised and continuing to keep the law of Moses. This is a concrete case of the challenge to inclusivity on cultural grounds.

In all these instances, Luke makes a point—that with the expansion of the church beyond the Aramaic-speaking Jewish cultural group to include people from different cultural backgrounds (though this fulfilled eschatological hope), the challenge to inclusivity was a consequence all the way. However, on each occasion these Christ-believers sought to overcome the challenge, looking to the Holy Spirit working cross-culturally in the communities (cf. 11:4–18; 15:8).[73]

## Conclusion

Luke, through Peter's Pentecost sermon, especially in his employment of universal terms, 'all flesh', and 'everyone', indicated that cultural diversity prevailed in the eschatological communities of Christ-believers. Luke equally, in several instances, showed that this situation (cultural diversity in the communities) carried with it challenges to inclusivity. This resonates with the fact that sometimes sub-cultures within a broad cultural setting can become quite exclusive. So to return to our question

---

72  Keener, *Acts*, 3.2210.
73  Stenschke has adequately attended to the resolution of each challenge in his recent article, "'When they heard this'", 69–89.

at the beginning, Why would Luke bring up these challenging accounts in a narrative about the expansion of the church from Jerusalem to the ends of the earth? As an answer to this question, it seems reasonable to suggest that, wanting to resolve issues of inclusion confronting his contemporaries, Luke draws on his knowledge of the OT (Septuagint) to appeal to the communities in their experiences of cultural diversity and the consequent challenges to inclusivity. The starting point of the Pentecost speech, with its emphasis on 'all flesh' and 'everyone', taken from Joel 2:28–32, provided the foundational argument for the admission of individuals from culturally diverse groups into the Christian communities. Luke in this narrative appeals to the early Christian communities (and all believers through every age) to be intentionally, positively, and proactively receptive of, and engaging with, cultural diversity in the communities. This, as Luke shows, fulfils God's eschatological plans. The question would still need to be asked: What constitutes cultural diversity in the experiences of the church today? And how does this pose challenges to inclusivity in Christian communities?

Francis Innocent Otobo,
Yarra Theological Union,
University of Divinity, Melbourne

## Bibliography

| | |
|---|---|
| Baker, D. J. | 'The Complete Theological Program of Acts 2:17–21 in Luke-Acts', *Pneuma* 42.1 (2020), 50–67. |
| Berger, P. L. | *The Social Reality of Religion* (Middlesex, England: Penguin Books, 1967). |
| Bock, D. L. | *Acts* (Grand Rapids, MI: Baker Academic, 2007). |
| Bock, D. L. | *Luke 9:51—24:53* (Grand Rapids, MI: Baker Academic, 1996). |
| Conzelmann, H. | *The Theology of St Luke* (trans. G. Buswell; New York, NY: Harper and Row, 1961). |
| Dunn, J. D. G. | *The Acts of the Apostles* (Peterborough: Epworth, 1996). |
| Ellis, E. E. | *Eschatology in Luke* (Philadelphia, PA: Fortress, 1972). |
| Franklin, E. | 'The Ascension and Eschatology in Luke-Acts', *Scottish Journal of Theology* 23.2 (1970), 191–200. |
| Franklin, E. | *Christ the Lord: A Study in the Purpose and Theology of Luke-Acts* (Philadelphia, PA: Westminster, 1975). |
| Francis, F. O. | 'Eschatology and History in Luke-Acts', *Journal of the American Academy of Religion* 37.1 (1969), 49–63. |
| Gaventa, B. R. | 'The Eschatology of Luke-Acts Revisited', *Encounter* 43.1 (1982), 27–42. |
| Johnson, L. T. | *The Acts of the Apostles* (Collegeville, MN: The Liturgical Press, 1992). |
| Keener, C. S. | *Acts: An Exegetical Commentary vol. 1* (Grand Rapids, MI: Baker Academic, 2012). |
| Keener, C. S. | *Acts: An Exegetical Commentary vol. 2* (Grand Rapids, MI: Baker Academic, 2013). |
| Keener, C. S. | *Acts: An Exegetical Commentary vol. 3* (Grand Rapids, MI: Baker Academic, 2014). |
| Kilgallen, J. J. | 'Hostility to Paul in Pisidian Antioch (Acts 13:45)—Why?', *Biblica* 84 (2003), 1–15. |
| Kok, J. | 'Social Identity Complexity Theory as Heuristic Tool in New Testament Studies', *HTS Theological Studies* 70.1 (2014). Art. #2708, 9 pages. http://dx.doi.org/10.4102/hts.v70i1.2708. |

| | |
|---|---|
| Marshall, I. H. | *The Acts of the Apostles: An Introduction and Commentary* (Grand Rapids, MI: Eerdmans, 1980). |
| Mattill, A. J. | *Luke and the Last Things: A Perspective for the Understanding of Lukan Thought* (Dillsboro, NC: Western North Carolina Press, 1979). |
| Martin W. M. | 'Eat, Drink, and be Merry: A Theology of Hospitality in Luke-Acts', *Word and World* 34.2 (2014), 131–141. |
| Moloney, F. | 'God So Loved the World: The Jesus of John's Gospel', *ACR* 178 (1998), 195–200. |
| Sala, D. | 'Pentecostal Culture, or Pentecost of Culture?: Transformation, Paradigm, Power, Unity', *Spiritus* 6.1 (2021), 103–122. |
| Salter, M. C. | *The Power of Pentecost: An Examination of Acts 2:17–21* (Eugene, OR: Wipf and Stock, 2011). |
| Stenschke, S. | '"When they heard this, they were silenced" (Acts 11:18): Some Inner-Christian Conflicts and their resolution in Acts 6—15:35', *JGAR* 4 (2020), 69–89. |
| Ward, R. B. | 'Eschatology in Luke-Acts', *Restoration Quarterly* 5.3 (1961), 147–156. |
| Wilson, S. G. | 'Lukan Eschatology', *NTS* 16.4 (1970), 330–347. |
| Wilson, S. G. | 'The Ascension: A Critique and an Interpretation', *Zeitschrift für die Neutestamentliche Wissenschaft* 59 (1968), 269–280. |
| Witherington, B. III | *The Acts of the Apostles: A Socio-Rhetorial Commentary* (Grand Rapids, MI: Eerdmans, 1998). |
| Yntema, D. | 'Material Culture and Plural Identity', in T. Derks et al. (eds.), *Ethnic Constructs in Antiquity: The Role of Power and Tradition* (Amsterdam: Amsterdam University Press, 2009), 145–166. |

CHAPTER 17

# Contrary to Popular Tradition, Saul/Paul was not Converted to Christianity on the Road to Damascus

Charles Bruce Riding

## Abstract

A 'Damascus Road Experience' denotes a spectacular conversion from one religion or belief system to a diametrically opposed one. It is based on the tradition that the arch-enemy of Christianity, Saul of Tarsus, was so converted to Christianity, becoming Paul, Christian missionary and 'Apostle to the Gentiles'. This essay will argue that Ananias' words to him in Damascus three days later prove that he was still an unbeliever before their conversation.

The point at issue is not some ivory-tower abstract hair-splitting. Luke, despite his limited space, relates Paul's conversion three times in detail—more verses are given to it than to Pentecost, the conversion of Cornelius, and the Jerusalem council, all events of the greatest importance.

When and where Paul was converted has implications for other important topics such as *Baptismal Regeneration* and whether the *Baptism with the Holy Spirit is a Second Blessing* or not.

## 1. Introduction

Everybody knows that Saul of Tarsus was dramatically converted to Christianity on the road to Damascus, don't they? Can anyone seriously even think of questioning such a firmly held traditional interpretation? Yet this essay mounts exactly that challenge and claims to justify it by showing that what the Scriptures teach is that Paul was converted to Christianity in Damascus in response to the challenge of Ananias (Acts 22:16), not on the road to Damascus three days earlier.

The point at issue is not some medieval ivory-tower hair-splitting. F. F. Bruce recognises that:

> Luke realized the importance of Paul's conversion in the history of salvation, for, despite his limited space, he relates it in some detail three times, once in the third person (chapter 9), and twice as narrated by Paul himself (chapters 22 and 26).[1]

So too does Gerstner, who observes:

> The sheer space devoted to Paul's conversion indicates its tremendous importance. For example, more verses are given to it than to Pentecost, the conversion of Cornelius, and the Jerusalem council, all events of the first magnitude; indeed more than to any other subject in Acts.[2]

## 2. Analysis of Paul's Conversion in Acts

The three passages describing Paul's conversion are not word-for-word repetitions.[3] Moreover, none of the three accounts contains all the data—each one has selected from the totality of the material, thus representing a contextualisation of Paul's message to the audiences he addressed, and also by Luke to his reading audience.

A synopsis of the three accounts of Paul's conversion is given in the following table.

---

1 Bruce, 'Acts', 983. NKJV is used throughout, unless indicated otherwise.
2 Gerstner, 'Acts', 200.
3 Winn, *Acts of the Apostles*, 118.

| Event | Acts 9 | Acts 22 | Acts 26 |
|---|---|---|---|
| Saul goes to Damascus to arrest Christians | 1–3a | 4–5 | 9–12 |
| Bright flashes of light and a voice | 3b–7 | 6–10 | 13–18 |
| 'Why are you persecuting Me?' | 5b | — | 14b |
| 'It is hard kicking against the goads/pricks'. | 5c | — | 14c |
| 'Who are you, Lord κύριε (kurie)?' | 5a | 8a | 15a |
| 'I am Jesus' | 5b | 8b | 15b |
| Saul goes into Damascus, blind, and fasts for three days | 8–9 | 11 | — |
| Ananias's vision and questioning God's instructions to him | 10–16 | — | — |
| Ananias's words; Saul receives his sight back, is baptised, and eats | 17–18 | 12–16 | — |
| Ananias challenges Saul's procrastination τι μελλεις (ti melleis) | — | 16 | — |
| Paul in Damascus, now preaching Christ | 19–22 | — | 19–20 |

## 3. The Current Understanding

At present, we find that virtually every commentator either says explicitly or implies that Saul of Tarsus was converted to Christianity to become Paul, the apostle to the Gentiles, on the road nearing Damascus. During the Reformation, for example, Calvin (1555) says it was on the road to Damascus that: 'Paul had put his stiff neck under the yoke of Christ, he is now governed by His hand'.[4] This understanding has been echoed at least since then by commentators of all theological persuasions and all denominational allegiances, giving rise to our expression 'a Damascus Road Experience' for describing a dramatic conversion. Matthew Henry (1705) talks of: 'The convincing, converting work of Christ [...] and the resignation of [Paul's] will to the will of Christ' on the road to Damascus.[5] Robertson (1915) says that on

---

4 Calvin, *Commentary upon the Acts of the Apostles,* 1080.
5 Henry, *Matthew Henry's Commentary,* 1679–1680.

the road to Damascus Paul 'saw Jesus and surrendered to Him [...] His surrender to Jesus was instantaneous and complete'.[6]

Macgregor and Ferris (1956) say: 'On the way [to Damascus] occurred the event which changed him suddenly from the fiercest enemy of the faith to its foremost apostle'.[7] They add that Ananias was the 'interpreter' of this event to Paul.[8] Purdy (1962) refers to Paul's 'conversion experience on the Damascus Road' (9:3; 22:6; 26:12), noting that Paul himself never uses the word 'conversion'.[9] Bruce (1970), commenting on Acts 9, relates it was 'on his journey to Damascus, that Saul was confronted by the vision of the risen Christ which wrought such a revolution in his life, and made him thenceforward the most zealous champion of the faith he had hitherto sought to destroy'.[10] Similarly, his comments on Acts 22 refer to 'his conversion near Damascus'.[11] To describe what happened on the road to Damascus, Ellis (1974) says that 'Paul's encounter with the risen Christ [was] a miraculous act, which transformed Christ's enemy into His apostle'.[12] Blaiklock (1975) states that on the road:

> Paul's whole mind and conduct were based on the certainty that the imposter [Jesus] was dead. If that were not so, the whole foundation crumbled beneath his feet. Then, in the mid-course of his mad career, he saw Jesus, so clearly, so unmistakably, that he could not disbelieve. He saw, he heard, he knew; and there was no alternative [but] to surrender.[13]

Betz (1992) says:

> While Paul was approaching Damascus he suddenly experienced a vision of Christ. This experience had dramatic consequences, changing his entire life, self-understanding,

---

6  Robertson, 'Paul, the Apostle', 2279.
7  Macgregor and Ferris, *Acts*, 119.
8  Macgregor and Ferris, *Acts*, 122–125.
9  Purdy, *Paul the Apostle*, 684.
10  Bruce, 'Acts', 983.
11  Bruce, 'Acts', 1003.
12  Ellis, *Paul*, 943.
13  Blaiklock, *The Acts of the Apostles*, 87–90.

theological views and goals [...] It turned him from a persecutor to a propagator of Christianity.[14]

Longenecker (2007) on Acts 22 says: 'As in Acts 9, here both Paul and Luke describe Paul's conversion to Jesus as God's Messiah'.[15] On 22:16, he comments that Ananias' exhortation 'is reminiscent of Peter's invitation at Pentecost in 2:38'.[16] He does not make the connection that Peter's exhortation was to the still unconverted crowd in the temple at Jerusalem. Even Wikipedia (2019) says Paul's 'conversion [...] took place on the road to Damascus'.[17]

## 4. Alleged Discrepancies

Commentators have discovered minor variations between the three accounts of Paul's conversion (Acts 9; 22; 26). If someone is hostile to the Bible, or if they are looking for disagreements, then these variations are magnified into inconsistencies and/or contradictions. Most commentators tend to simply treat any variations as merely reiterations of Chapter 9 in Chapters 22 and 26. Bruce says:

> The differences between his narration here [Acts 9] and to the Jerusalem mob in ch.22 are mainly differences of emphasis; on each occasion he emphasised those aspects of the story which were likely to interest his audience at the time.[18]

This becomes crystal clear when we examine these contextualisations in detail.

Longenecker, for example, recognises three variations of details.[19] Firstly, who heard the voice? Was it Paul only (Acts 22:9, and perhaps implied in 26:14), or was it all of his companions as well (Acts 9:7)? He resolves this quandary by proposing Paul heard and understood the

---

14 Betz, *Paul*, 187.
15 Longenecker, *Acts*, 1044.
16 Longenecker, *Acts*, 1045.
17 <https://en.wikipedia.org/wiki/Paul_the_Apostle#Conversion> [accessed 14 December 2021].
18 Bruce, 'Acts', 1006.
19 Longenecker, *The Ministry and Message of Paul*, 32–36.

words, whereas his companions only heard the sound. Something similar happened in John 12:27–33. There, Jesus heard God's declaration (John 12:28), while others heard only thunder (John 12:29).

Secondly, Longenecker identifies that 'goads/pricks' (Acts 26:14) were more relevant for the Gentile King Agrippa, being a common Greek proverb, but not so applicable for the Jerusalem crowd of Jews, where 'delay' or 'waiting' would be more appropriate (Acts 22:16).[20] Both phrases contain the idea of resistance or holding out. Were Ananias a Greek, he might have used the *Goads* proverb too, not Saul's delaying. Incidentally, God used *goads/pricks* with Saul (Acts 9:5), who would have known about it from being raised in Tarsus, a predominantly Gentile city.

Thirdly, when exactly did Paul receive his commission as a missionary, particularly as a missionary to Gentiles? Was it from Jesus on the road (Acts 26:16–18), from Ananias in Damascus (Acts 22:14–15; and implied in Acts 9:15–16, since chapter 9 only records God telling Ananias of Paul's future mission, not Ananias' relaying it to Paul), or by both of them? Longenecker correctly deduces that Acts 26 was abbreviated for King Agrippa, making this difference an instance of contextualisation, not contradiction.[21] Therefore the most logical solution is 'from both Jesus and Ananias', since the accounts have been abridged for the particular audiences by omitting less relevant details as discussed above. Similarly, Paul omits mention of the reception of the Spirit (9:17), which was not necessary in the context of addressing Agrippa, Festus, and Bernice (26:2–23).[22]

Like Bruce, I am convinced that the three accounts are not contradictory but complementary, each contextualising the message to the different audiences addressed.[23]

---

20 Longenecker, *The Ministry and Message of Paul*, 32.
21 Longenecker, *The Ministry and Message of Paul*, 33.
22 Marshall, *Acts*, 357.
23 Bruce, *The Acts of the Apostles*, 196.

## 5. The Traditional Position

The following six arguments have been advanced in support of the traditional view that Paul was converted on the road to Damascus. First, Paul is told that persecuting members of Jesus' Church is persecuting Jesus Christ himself, and so, realising this, he converts to Christianity. However, this is the first time he heard Jesus' name in his vision/audition. It leads to his question, 'Who are you, Lord?' (Acts 9:5a; 22:8a; 26:15a), not to instant recognition, acceptance of the identity of the speaker as Jesus, and faith in him.

Secondly, Saul calls the voice κύριε *(kurie)*. This term is used in three ways in the New Testament. It could denote Jesus, recognising his divinity (in 2 Cor. 13:10; Gal. 5:10, for example), meaning Paul had converted to him already, acknowledged him and accepted him as Lord. Or it could mean the Septuagint translation of the OT name for God, traditionally *the* LORD, *Jehovah,* or YHWH (Heb. 1:10; 7:21), or in full *I Am/Will Be Who I Am/Will Be'* (Exod. 3:14). This would also mean that Paul was converted at this point, since he would have accepted Jesus' claim to be God (John 5:18 for example).

Finally, it could simply mean 'sir', the common polite form of address (Matt. 13:27; 21:30, for example). Bruce takes it in this third sense, commenting on Paul's word of address: 'κύριε "sir" "my lord"; a title of respect, as Saul did not yet know who was speaking to him'.[24] Barnett and Jensen remind us: 'Note that Cornelius called an *angel* "Lord" and obeyed him (Acts 10:1–8)'.[25] I agree that Bruce's interpretation of *kurie* as 'sir' is possible, but I prefer the second option—the LORD, Jehovah, or YHWH. I would maintain that Saul recognised that he was receiving a theophany from the God of the Old Testament. It was when the speaker identified himself as Jesus a moment later that Paul's mind was thrown into complete turmoil and utter confusion.

Thirdly, Ananias addressed him as 'Brother Saul' (Acts 9:17; 22:13), which, Macgregor and Ferris argued, should be taken in the sense of a brother Christian, and therefore Paul was converted already.[26]

---

24 Bruce, *The Acts of the Apostles*, 198.
25 Barnett and Jensen, *The Quest for Power*, 33.
26 Macgregor and Ferris, *Acts*, 124.

However, it may be that Ananias simply called him a brother Jew, whether a Christian or not. As Barnett and Jensen point out, in Acts 2:29,37, the crowd at the temple call the apostles 'brothers', and Peter calls them 'brothers' before they are converted (see also Acts 13:26).[27]

Fourthly, Paul obeyed the voice, which turned out to be that of Jesus, and so he was an obedient Christian then. I do not think that Paul's obedience is significant enough to argue for his conversion. After all, what else could he do? He was blind, in a distant foreign land, had just received an unexpected 'mind-blowing' experience that had shaken his world comprehensively and that had totally demolished his current world-view. When he finally sorted it out and converted to Christ, it had been turned completely upside-down. But at that stage, he was still in turmoil, a confused unbeliever, not yet a Christian.

Marshall observes that Paul 'fasted *for three days*, no doubt still overcome by shock and probably by penitence as the enormity of his action increasingly dawned upon him'.[28] Admittedly, most fasting in the Bible is connected to penitence, which, if so in Paul's case, would mean he was converted already. However, if his fasting was connected to searching or seeking (like David's in 2 Samuel 12:23; and Jehoshaphat's in 2 Chronicles 20:3; cf. Ezra 8:21–23; Neh. 1:4; Acts 13:2–3; 14:23) then that would be consistent with his not yet being converted. Jesus' fasting just before His temptations would also fall into this category, since in Jesus' case it was definitely not done in penitence (Matt. 4:2; Luke 4:2).

Sixthly, Blaiklock recognises:

> Few conversions take place 'out of the blue' [...] The moment of a conversion may seem quite sudden and unexpected, but experience shows that such a fundamental and abrupt occurrence always has a long period of unconscious 'incubation'.[29]

He goes on to describe the 'incubation' that Paul had already received, particularly from hearing Stephen's sermon and witnessing his

---

27 Barnett and Jensen, *The Quest for Power*, 33.
28 Marshall, *Acts*, 170.
29 Blaiklock, *Acts*, 87–90.

martyrdom (Acts 8). Winn says that Paul felt guilty over Stephen's martyrdom and was thinking inwardly in turmoil: 'It was the turning point of his life [...] the time of [his] conversion'.[30] Stott too acknowledges Saul had been prepared for this moment, but hitherto was still resisting, or 'kicking against the goads' (Acts 9:5; 26:14).[31] I am effectively arguing that Paul was still 'kicking against the goads', and that therefore he still needed more 'incubation', even after this spectacular theophany.

All six lines of reasoning could mean that Paul was converted then on the Damascus road or they could mean he was not. The point is none of these arguments proves *conclusively* that Paul had been converted to Christianity on the road to Damascus. All could equally be taken the opposite way, as I am propounding. I am not disputing that Paul's conversion, indeed anyone's conversion, was an act of the Holy Spirit, nor am I seeking to totally psychologise it, as some have done. Whatever was happening in Paul's psyche, there is no question that it was the work of the Triune God. An almighty God could certainly have given Paul faith on the road to Damascus. My question is: 'Did he?' To answer it we should seek: 'What has God revealed?'

Having shown that there are no inconsistencies between the three accounts of Paul's conversion, two different major problems ensue. If Paul was converted on the Damascus road, then he follows the traditional Pentecostal/Charismatic schema of the Baptism of the Holy Spirit (Acts 9:17 before Ananias in Damascus) being a separate, subsequent experience to conversion (Acts 9:3–6 on the road three days earlier). If this is the case, the *Baptism with the Holy Spirit* is definitely a *Second Blessing*.

Secondly, if Paul was converted on the Damascus road, then baptismal regeneration would be taught here. Paul's faith would not have been enough for salvation—he still needed water baptism to wash away his sins (Acts 22:16). This would mean the water used in baptism actually does something—it is not just a sign and seal of what has already happened in a believer's life.

---

30  Winn, *Acts of the Apostles*, 67.
31  Stott, *The Message of Acts*, 171.

## 6. Investigation Into These Three Problems

The first problem is one of accurate exegesis—does the Bible teach Saul was converted on the road to Damascus or not? The chief difficulty with the traditional view of Paul being converted then arises from Ananias' words to Saul in Acts 22:16. In this verse, Paul himself relates part of what Ananias said to him in the house of Judas on Straight Street in Damascus, three days after his experience on the road: 'Now, why are you waiting? Arise and be baptized, and wash away your sins, calling on the name of the Lord' (Acts 22:16). Is this the sort of thing you would say to a Christian or to a non-Christian? One might challenge an unbaptised Christian to cease delaying and stop putting off receiving water baptism. However, a Christian cannot be challenged to either 'call on Jesus' name' or to 'wash away their sins'. They have already done both—that is what made them a Christian in the first place. Therefore, Ananias is addressing Saul as a non-Christian.

Virtually all commentators see no problem here. Macgregor and Ferris make no specific comment at all on 22:16.[32] Three commentators do recognise something is not quite right, and a fourth hints at this problem. Marshall says: 'Ananias's somewhat reproachful question *why do you wait?* is slightly odd'.[33] His solution is:

> The Greek phrase may simply mean *'What are you going to do?'* Paul is to get up, i.e. act straightaway, and submit to baptism. As in 2:38 (cf. 2:21) baptism is the expression of faith in Jesus by appealing to *His Name*, and it symbolises the forgiveness of sins—in this case, the sin of persecution is especially in mind.[34]

Regarding baptismal regeneration, Bruce comments on Ananias' challenge to Saul (Acts 22:16):

> The imperatives are in the middle voice: 'get yourself baptized and get your sins washed away' [...] His baptism was the 'out-

---

32 Macgregor and Ferris, *Acts*, 117–125, 290–293, 325–328.
33 Marshall, *Acts*, 357.
34 Marshall, *Acts*, 357.

ward and visible sign' of his inward and spiritual cleansing, achieved by 'calling on His Name' (Acts 22:16e).[35]

He then refers to Paul's developed teaching on baptism in Romans 6:3 and following. As a result, he does not see any problem. Calvin too, assuming Paul was converted on the road into Damascus, launches into a quite lengthy discussion denying baptismal regeneration, a pressing problem in his day.[36] This means Calvin saw the problem: baptismal regeneration is logically implied here, and he then took lengthy steps to deny and refute it.

Regarding the baptism of the Holy Spirit being at a different time to conversion, Green proffers:

> It would be very precarious to found a doctrine of two-stage initiation on the three day delay in Paul's conversion experience. As we have seen from his own writings, he was clearly a one-stage man, for whom justification and sonship were symbolised and sealed in baptism and the reception of the Spirit.[37]

His solution is: 'Luke, too, sees the whole three day experience as one'.[38] I am not convinced that the problem is solved by this line of reasoning.

These three problems cannot be written off so easily. They need more extensive explanations, more detailed exegesis of the texts of Acts, and more theological reflection on the issues.

Only Barnes, Barnett, and Jensen specifically deny that Paul was converted to Christianity on the Damascus Road. Barnett and Jensen conclude that Paul's 'experience was quite normal, as set out in Acts 2:38'.[39] There Peter tells the Jerusalem crowd on the first Day of Pentecost that faith in Jesus, repentance, being baptised in the Holy Spirit, and Christian water baptism all go together: 'Repent, and let every one of you be baptized in the name of Jesus Christ for the

---

35 Bruce, *The Acts of the Apostles*, 403.
36 Calvin, *Commentary upon the Acts of the Apostles*, 1281–1282.
37 Green, *I Believe in the Holy Spirit*, 134.
38 Green, *I Believe in the Holy Spirit*, 134.
39 <http://www.biblecharts.org/apostlepaulcharts/3%20-%20Pauls%20Conversion.pdf> [accessed 14 December 2021]; Barnett and Jensen, *The Quest for Power: Neo-Pentecostalism & the New Testament*, 34.

remission of sins; and you shall receive the gift of the Holy Spirit. For the promise is to you and to your children, and to all who are afar off, as many as the Lord our God will call' (Acts 2:38–39)'. Incidentally, Peter, like Ananias, discerned that many in the crowd were wavering, delaying, or procrastinating, and so he added further exhortations like, 'Be saved from this perverse generation!' (Acts 2:40). In response, about 3,000 heeded Peter's urging on that day, just like Paul did later in response to Ananias' exhortation (Acts 2:41; 9:18b). So too, Barnes concludes from his analysis that Saul was not saved on the road to Damascus. He was still in his sins when Ananias came to him. Ananias then told him what he 'must' do (Acts 22:16); whereupon 'Saul obeyed the gospel in the same manner we are to obey the gospel today'.[40]

## 7. A Proposed Solution

I propose that in Damascus, Ananias addressed Saul as a non-Christian because at that point in time he was still a non-Christian. He had not converted to Jesus Christ on the road outside Damascus. His mind was still in turmoil. He was questioning, rethinking all his beliefs, remembering all the Bible passages he knew, and how they related to the promised Messiah. He was recalling the preaching of Christians like Stephen that Jesus of Nazareth was that Messiah, now seated at God the Father's right hand in heaven (Acts 7:50). He was earnestly searching for answers, with fasting being the sign of his earnestness. However, he was still delaying, still putting off a commitment to Jesus of Nazareth being the Christ, the Messiah.

In Acts 22:16, Ananias asks, nay more—he challenges Saul:

> 'Why tarriest thou?' (AV),
> 'Why do you delay?' (NRSV and NASB),
> 'Why do you wait?' (ESV),
> 'Why are you waiting?' (NKJV), and
> 'What are you waiting for?' (NIV).

---

[40] <http://www.biblecharts.org/apostlepaulcharts/3%20-%20Pauls%20Conversion.pdf>

These expressions all translate the Greek words τί (*ti*) 'why', and μέλλεις (*melleis*) second person, singular, present tense, active voice, indicative mood of the verb μέλλω (*mello*), about which Strong's dictionary says:[41]

> μέλλω **mello** ; a strengthened form of μέλω melo (through the idea of expectation); to intend, i.e. be about to be, do, or suffer something (of persons or things, especially events; in the sense of purpose, duty, necessity, probability, possibility, or hesitation): about, after that, be (almost), (that which is, things, + which was for) to come, intend, was to (be), mean, mind, be at the point, (be) ready, + return, shall (begin), (which, that) should (after, afterwards, hereafter) tarry, which was for, will, would, be yet.

This would mean that Paul 'was about to' or 'intended' to call on Jesus' name. He 'probably' would but was 'hesitating'. He 'meant to', 'was at the point of', 'was ready to', 'would afterwards', or 'would hereafter' believe in Jesus, but at that stage he had not yet done it—he was still an unbeliever when Ananias said it to him in Damascus, three days after his experience on the road.

From God's words to him, Ananias expected that Paul, God's 'chosen vessel' (Acts 9:15), had already believed in Jesus. However, after delivering God's message to him, Ananias discerned that Saul's tardiness was procrastination—he had not yet called on Jesus' name, and so had not had his sin washed away. However, at Ananias' challenge or mild rebuke, Saul stopped holding out. The delay was over. He finally believed in Jesus Christ, accepted him as his Lord and Saviour, called on his name, and got his sins washed away. His blindness was cured. He was 'baptised in the Holy Spirit', or 'received the Holy Spirit', or was 'filled with the Holy Spirit' for the first time. It would then be a daily reality for him, as he later wrote to other Christians (Eph. 5:18 uses the present tense, meaning 'keep on being filled with the Spirit'). Fee says that Christians should expect further experiences of the Holy

---

41 μέλλω in Strong, *Hebrew and Chaldee Dictionary of the Old Testament*.

Spirit after conversion.[42] Acts 4:31 relates one such instance of 'further experiences'. It should be an ongoing reality, being filled with the Spirit daily. As a result, Paul was baptised. Strictly speaking, according to the Greek tense, he 'gets himself baptised', as Bruce translates.[43] This strikes a good balance, in that while baptism is something we do, the focus is not on what we do, but on Jesus Christ who gives us the reality behind the sign of baptism.

## 8. Corollaries of This Resolution

If Paul was converted in Damascus, when, at Ananias's challenge, he called on Jesus' name, got his sins washed away, and got himself baptised, then it clearly follows that there is no baptismal regeneration taught here. We are regenerated or born again at conversion, not at our water baptism. Baptism with water is a sign of past and present realities—it does not 'do anything' in and of itself. Paul is one more instance of this general principle.

Similarly, Paul's baptism with Holy Spirit happened at his conversion in Damascus before Ananias. Fee, 'a Pentecostal scholar [...] one of our truly master exegetes [...] one of the finest Biblical expositors', says that,

> At issue is the relationship between baptism in water and the experience of the Spirit. In Acts 19:1–7, the coming of the Spirit happens in conjunction with baptism [and the conversion of these disciples of John the Baptist to Jesus], whereas in Acts 10, baptism is in response to the prior coming of the Spirit.[44]

He concludes: '1 Cor. 2:1–5 seems conclusive that Paul understood the Spirit as being received at conversion, in the hearing of the Gospel by faith, not later at baptism'.[45] This is my understanding as well. In this,

---

42  Fee, *Paul, the Sprit, and the People of God*, 201, 202.
43  Bruce, *The Acts of the Apostles*, 403.
44  Fee, *Paul, the Sprit, and the People of God*, back cover, 193–194.
45  Fee, *Paul, the Sprit, and the People of God*, 200.

Fee is in disagreement with the majority of Pentecostals/Charismatics who say Paul was converted on the road to Damascus and baptised with the Holy Spirit three days later in Damascus. Instead, baptism in the Holy Spirit is part of the 'package deal' of accepting Jesus Christ's salvation, along with justification, adoption, and being born again.

The fact that Paul was not converted immediately when he received the vision of the risen Christ and heard him speaking adds an extra dimension to Jesus' words: 'If they do not hear Moses and the prophets, neither will they be persuaded though one rise from the dead' (Luke 16:31). Saul of Tarsus had thus far rejected the teaching of Moses and the prophets that showed Jesus of Nazareth was the Christ, just like the other Pharisees to whom Jesus said: 'You search the Scriptures, for in them you think you have eternal life; and these are they which testify of me' (John 5:39). Consequently, Saul was not initially persuaded when the risen Jesus appeared to him in his vision. It exposes the lie in statements like: 'If Jesus appeared to me then I would convert to him' and 'Lord, show us the Father, and it is sufficient for us' (John 14:8). This reminds us that faith is a gift from God to people who would never believe in him without it (Eph. 2:8–9), even if they saw Jesus Christ risen from the grave (Luke 16:30). People are dead in sin and remain dead in sin unless God the Holy Spirit gives them new life that enables them to believe in Jesus Christ and be saved. Paul was probably the most renowned application of these words of Jesus.

Penultimately, this exercise also demonstrates how our message needs to be contextualised to our audiences, evaluating what will pique the interest of our hearers most.[46] We do not need to preach everything in a text every time we use it. Instead, we should select what points in the text (traditionally three) our congregation needs to hear at that time, sometimes denoted 'exegeting your congregation,' as well as exegeting the Word of Scripture. We see Paul doing this throughout his lifetime, whether as recorded in the book of Acts or in his letters. In the case of using his conversion as a sermon illustration, with the mob at Jerusalem Paul relates his delaying, implying they were also 'delaying' in converting to Jesus Christ. His 'kicking against the

---

46 Bruce, 'Acts', 1006.

goads' seems to have helped his message resonate with Agrippa's kicking against goads, as the latter's reaction, 'You almost persuade me to become a Christian' (Acts 26:28) would indicate. Therefore, we need to do likewise.

Finally, in our witnessing to non-Christians, we might need to allow for and perhaps gently rebuke them for their delaying or procrastinating by sharing how we ourselves used to put off our decision to believe in Jesus Christ.

## 9. How Could We Have Missed It ?

The analysis above leads naturally to one more question: 'How could we have missed this teaching of the Bible for so long?' I suggest it is because the key verse, Acts 22:16, is not in the first occurrence of Paul's conversion in Acts. From the synopsis above, it is the only detail omitted from Acts 9. With such a fuller narration in Acts 9, it is easy to get the idea when we encounter Paul's conversion again in Acts 22 and 26, 'I've heard *all* this before', and skim over it without paying much attention to it. Macgegor and Ferris, for example, devote nine pages in their commentary on 9:1–19, but only four pages to 22:3–23, and another four to 26:9–23, with no specific comment on 22:16.[47] Similarly, in studying the Old Testament, how much attention do we give to the books of Samuel and Kings compared to our reading and study of Chronicles?

I suggest this is how the place of Paul's conversion has gone so long unchallenged. The account in Acts 9 does sound like Saul was converted immediately on the road to Damascus. This quickly became a tradition, handed on unquestioned, unexamined, and unchecked from one generation of exegetes to the next. It was blithely assumed by all that this is what the Bible says. It stands as a warning to us to diligently study all the Scriptures and not skim over parts we think we know already.

Finally, such a re-examination will show how serious we are about the Bible and about getting its teaching right. Protestants aver loud and clear that our traditions are not inerrant. We affirm that only the Scriptures are infallible, and every teaching we make is subject to

---

47 Macgregor and Ferris, *Acts*, 117–125, 290–293, 325–328.

# CONTRARY TO POPULAR TRADITION

revision if shown to be wrong. John Knox's statement in the preface to the First Scotch Confession says this admirably (in its original Scotch or Scottish dialect):[48]

> Gif onie man will note in this our confession onie Artickle or sentence repugnand to God's halie word, that it wald pleis him of his gentleness and for Christian charities sake to admonish us of the same in writing; and we will upon our honours and fidelities, be God's grace do promise unto him satisfaction fra the mouth of God, that is fra his haly scriptures, or else reformation of that quhilk he sal prove to be amisse.

Both the world and the Church will take the Bible more seriously if we demonstrate how serious we are about it being God's inspired word.

## 10. Summary

The sequence of events surrounding Paul's conversion should be:

1. God had been preparing Paul for his conversion and mission, 'incubating' him through means such as having him hear Stephen preach to the Sanhedrin. Even so, he still needed more 'incubation'.
2. Paul appeared to have some doubts about Judaism that he tried to suppress with increased zeal in persecuting these 'renegade' Christians, which turned out to be 'kicking against the goads'. He even followed some of the Christian refugees to Damascus to arrest them and return them to Jerusalem.
3. About noon, while nearing Damascus, Paul experienced a vision and an audition. He rightly deduced that the light and voice was that of God, Jehovah, the great I AM addressing him. However, when he was asked by this voice, 'Why are you persecuting me?' he was thrown into mental turmoil. He asked a confirmatory question: 'Who are you, Lord?' The answer 'Jesus' rocked him to the core.
4. Paul was not converted then, although he should have been. For that matter, he should have been converted much earlier, and

---

48  Knox et al., *The First Scotch Confession of Faith*, 438.

not 'kicked against the goads' by holding out at all. He was still procrastinating.
5. He was led into Damascus, blind and confused, and tried to sort things out, fasting as a sign of his earnestness.
6. In response to God's command, Ananias hesitatingly came and delivered God's message to him. There Ananias discerned and challenged his delay.
7. Paul finally submitted to the Gospel, repented of his sins, believed in Jesus Christ, was baptised in the Holy Spirit, had his blindness cured, and was baptised with water.
8. He started preaching that Jesus Christ is the Messiah, as it had been revealed to him, beginning in Damascus.

From this, two implications follow. The Bible does not teach baptismal regeneration since Paul's experience conforms to the norm of water baptism being only a sign and seal of our faith in Christ. Nor is the baptism with the Holy Spirit a second blessing, but is part of the 'package deal' of Jesus' comprehensive salvation that we receive by faith in him. There are probably other consequences as well.

I suggest that the exact circumstances of Paul's conversion were missed because they are not spelled out fully in the first narration of it in Acts 9, but in Acts 22. Exegetes tend to skim over repeated material, thinking there is nothing new in it, but that it merely reiterates what was said already in earlier account/s.

Finally, Christians would be taken more seriously if they admitted their error and showed how serious they are about believing the Bible to be God's word and how important it is to get its interpretation accurate.

Charles Bruce Riding
Presbyterian Church of Australia, retired minister
Australian College of Theology, alumnus

## Bibliography

Barnett, P. W., and P. F. Jensen — *The Quest for Power: Neo-Pentecostalism & the New Testament* (Sydney: ANZEA, 1973).

Betz, H. D. — 'Paul', in D. N. Freedman (ed.), *Anchor Bible Dictionary* (6 vols; New York, NY: Doubleday, 1992), vol. 5, 187–201.

Blaiklock, E. M. — *The Acts of the Apostles: An Historical Commentary* (Tyndale New Testament Commentaries, edited by R. V. G. Tasker; Grand Rapids, MI: Eerdmans, 1975).

Bruce, F. F. — *The Acts of the Apostles* (London: Tyndale, 1970).

Bruce, F. F. — 'Acts' in D. Guthrie and J. A. Motyer (eds.), *The New Bible Commentary Revised* (London: IVP, 1973), 968–1011.

Calvin, J. — *Commentary upon the Acts of the Apostles* (Calvin's Commentaries; Wilmington, DE: AP&A, 1555).

Ellis, E E. — 'Paul', in J. D. Douglas (ed.), *The New Bible Dictionary* (London: IVP, 1974), 643–955.

Fee, G. D. — *Paul, the Sprit, and the People of God* (Peabody, MA: Hendrickson, 1996).

Gerstner, J. H. — 'Acts', in C. F. H. Henry (ed.), *The Biblical Expositor: The Living Theme of the Great Book* (3 vols; London: Pickering & Inglis, 1900), vol. 3, 183–226.

Green, M. — *I Believe in the Holy Spirit* (I Believe Series, ed. M. Green; London: Hodder & Stoughton, 1975).

Henry, M. — *Matthew Henry's Commentary on the Whole Bible: Complete and Unabridged* (Peabody, MA: Hendrickson, 2008 [1705]).

Knox, J. et al. — 'The First Scotch Confession of Faith A.D. 1560: The Confession of the Faith and Doctrine Belevit and Professit be the Protestantis of Scotland', in P. Schaff (ed.), *Creeds of Christendom* (3 vols; Grand Rapids, MI: Baker, 1979), vol. 3, 437–85.

Longenecker, R. N. — *The Ministry and Message of Paul* (Contemporary Evangelical Perspectives; Grand Rapids, MI: Zondervan, 1971).

Longenecker, R. N. — 'Acts' in T. Longman III and D. E. Garland (eds), *The Expositor's Bible Commentary, Revised Edition* (13 vols; Grand Rapids: Zondervan, 2007), vol. 10, 663–1102.

| | |
|---|---|
| Macgregor, G. H. C., and T. P. Ferris | 'Acts', in G. A. Buttrick (ed.), *The Interpreter's Bible* (12 vols; New York, NY: Abingdon, 1956), vol. 9, 1–352. |
| Marshall, I. H. | *Acts* (Tyndale New Testament Commentaries, ed. R. V. G. Tasker; Leicester: IVP, 1998). |
| Purdy, A C. | 'Paul the Apostle', in G. A. Buttrick (ed.), *The Interpreter's Dictionary of the Bible* (4 vols; New York, NY: Abingdon, 1962), vol. 3, 681–704. |
| Robertson, J. A. | 'Paul, the Apostle', in J. Orr (ed.), *International Standard Bible Encyclopedia* (5 vols; Chicago, IL: Howard-Severance Co, 1937), vol. 4, 2264–88. |
| Stott, J. R. W. | *The Message of Acts* (The Bible Speaks Today, ed. J. A. Motyer and J. R. W. Stott; Leicester: IVP, 1991). |
| Strong, J. | *Hebrew and Chaldee Dictionary of the Old Testament* (<http://www.bf.org/bfetexts.htm>: Bible Foundation eText Library, 2016). |
| Winn, A. C. | *Acts of the Apostles* (The Layman's Bible Commentary, 20; ed. B. H Kelly; 25 vols; Atlanta, GA: John Knox, 1960). |

www.ingramcontent.com/pod-product-compliance
Lightning Source LLC
Chambersburg PA
CBHW041303110526
44590CB00028B/4232